Making Art With Generative AI Tools

Shalin Hai-Jew
Hutchinson Community College, USA

IGI Global
PUBLISHER of TIMELY KNOWLEDGE

A volume in the Advances in Media, Entertainment, and the Arts (AMEA) Book Series

Published in the United States of America by
IGI Global
Information Science Reference (an imprint of IGI Global)
701 E. Chocolate Avenue
Hershey PA, USA 17033
Tel: 717-533-8845
Fax: 717-533-8661
E-mail: cust@igi-global.com
Web site: http://www.igi-global.com

Library of Congress Cataloging-in-Publication Data

CIP PENDING

Making Art With Generative AI Tools
Shalin Hai-Jew
2024 Information Science Reference

ISBN: 9798369319505 (h/c)
ISBN: 9798369349946 (s/c)
eISBN: 9798369319512

This book is published in the IGI Global book series Advances in Media, Entertainment, and the Arts (AMEA) (ISSN: 2475-6814; eISSN: 2475-6830)

British Cataloguing in Publication Data
A Cataloguing in Publication record for this book is available from the British Library.

For electronic access to this publication, please contact: eresources@igi-global.com.

Advances in Media, Entertainment, and the Arts (AMEA) Book Series

Giuseppe Amoruso
Politecnico di Milano, Italy

ISSN:2475-6814
EISSN:2475-6830

Mission

Throughout time, technical and artistic cultures have integrated creative expression and innovation into industrial and craft processes. Art, entertainment and the media have provided means for societal self-expression and for economic and technical growth through creative processes.

The **Advances in Media, Entertainment, and the Arts (AMEA)** book series aims to explore current academic research in the field of artistic and design methodologies, applied arts, music, film, television, and news industries, as well as popular culture. Encompassing titles which focus on the latest research surrounding different design areas, services and strategies for communication and social innovation, cultural heritage, digital and print media, journalism, data visualization, gaming, design representation, television and film, as well as both the fine applied and performing arts, the AMEA book series is ideally suited for researchers, students, cultural theorists, and media professionals.

Coverage

- Cultural Heritage
- Fine Arts
- Computer aided design and 3D Modelling
- Fabrication and prototyping
- Print Media
- Gaming
- Cross-Media Studies
- Blogging & Journalism
- Digital Heritage
- Design Tools

IGI Global is currently accepting manuscripts for publication within this series. To submit a proposal for a volume in this series, please contact our Acquisition Editors at Acquisitions@igi-global.com or visit: http://www.igi-global.com/publish/.

The Advances in Media, Entertainment, and the Arts (AMEA) Book Series (ISSN 2475-6814) is published by IGI Global, 701 E. Chocolate Avenue, Hershey, PA 17033-1240, USA, www.igi-global.com. This series is composed of titles available for purchase individually; each title is edited to be contextually exclusive from any other title within the series. For pricing and ordering information please visit http://www.igi-global.com/book-series/advances-media-entertainment-arts/102257. Postmaster: Send all address changes to above address.

Titles in this Series

For a list of additional titles in this series, please visit: www.igi-global.com/book-series/advances-media-entertainment-arts/102257

Exploring the Impact of OTT Media on Global Societies
Nithin Kalorth (Mahindra University, India)
Information Science Reference • copyright 2024 • 332pp • H/C (ISBN: 9798369335260) • US $295.00 (our price)

Advancements in Socialized and Digital Media Communications
Gülbuğ Erol (Iğdır University, Turkey) and Michael Kuyucu (Alanya University, Turkey)
Information Science Reference • copyright 2024 • 364pp • H/C (ISBN: 9798369308554) • US $230.00 (our price)

Using Traditional Design Methods to Enhance AI-Driven Decision Making
Tien V. T. Nguyen (Industrial University of Ho Chi Minh City, Vietnam) and Nhut T. M. Vo (National Kaohsiung University of Science and Technology, Taiwan)
Information Science Reference • copyright 2024 • 503pp • H/C (ISBN: 9798369306390) • US $245.00 (our price)

News Media and Hate Speech Promotion in Mediterranean Countries
Elias Said Hung (Universidad Internacional de la Rioja, Spain) and Julio Montero Diaz (Universidad Internacional de la Rioja, Spain)
Information Science Reference • copyright 2023 • 364pp • H/C (ISBN: 9781668484272) • US $215.00 (our price)

Examinations and Analysis of Sequels and Serials in the Film Industry
Emre Ahmet Seçmen (Beykoz University, Turkey)
Information Science Reference • copyright 2023 • 389pp • H/C (ISBN: 9781668478646) • US $215.00 (our price)

Using Innovative Literacies to Develop Leadership and Agency Inspiring Transformation and Hope
Limor Pinhasi-Vittorio (Lehman College, CUNY, USA) and Elite Ben-Yosef (The BYEZ Foundation, USA)
Information Science Reference • copyright 2023 • 287pp • H/C (ISBN: 9781668456149) • US $215.00 (our price)

Music and Engagement in the Asian Political Space
Uche Titus Onyebadi (Texas Christian University, USA) and Delaware Arif (University of South Alabama, USA)
Information Science Reference • copyright 2023 • 254pp • H/C (ISBN: 9781799858171) • US $215.00 (our price)

IGI Global
PUBLISHER of TIMELY KNOWLEDGE

701 East Chocolate Avenue, Hershey, PA 17033, USA
Tel: 717-533-8845 x100 • Fax: 717-533-8661
E-Mail: cust@igi-global.com • www.igi-global.com

Table of Contents

Detailed Table of Contents

Today, advancements in artificial intelligence (AI) and its applications have resulted in its widespread use in creative industries. The goal of this study is to investigate the relationship between artificial intelligence and creativity through the perspective of Generative AI (GenAI) utilized in these industries. To perform this investigation, the study first introduces the concepts of creativity and its key components, along with GenAI and AI creativity. The study's analysis is founded on 14 key components of creativity identified in the previous literature. In the analysis section, the study examines whether these key components are present in today's GenAI tools, drawing on current debates about AI and AI-based applications. Additionally, the capabilities, limitations, and challenges of GenAI are investigated for each key component. In the discussion section, the study makes projections about potential problems that may be encountered when using GenAI and discusses possible redefinitions of key components in the future.

Text-to-image (TTI) synthesis models represent a creative approach in the realm of artificial intelligence, specifically designed to transform textual input into visually realistic images. The essence of TTI generation lies in its ability to harness the power of language and convert it seamlessly into visually compelling content, showcasing creative image synthesis. Initially using GANs and transformers, text-to-image generation evolved with diffusion models introducing noise. Integration with large models, TTI models now produce results near-real images. Breakthroughs like ControlNet and 3D object synthesis redefine possibilities. Editing text or images adds versatile dimensions, showcasing generative technologies'

Preface

The uses of art-making generative AI (A-GAI) tools has popularized with prize-winning visuals co-generated between humans and technologies. There has been a broad range of mainstream articles. People have debated their rights when copyrighted works have been harnessed for some of the A-GAI training sets. There may be concerns that artists' signatures—arrived at over a lifetime of toil and visioning and skill-building—may be boiled down reductively to only a set of visual affectations enabled through neural networks (Hai-Jew, 2022). For many, the generative AI may be seen as diminishing human creativity. In this particular slice-in-time, it may seem more advisable to be more subtle and less direct about admitting usage of A-GAI tools.

Or another way to look at it is that A-GAI has opened up new vistas for human expression and exploration and experimentation. Out from these collaborations may emerge a new generation of art and art-making and art appreciation. In some ways, this new art can be highly emulative of prior works; in other ways, it outputs something else altogether, including works that evoke both the analog and the digital. These works may read as pan-global more than something emergent from a culture and a life and a social community. Some may suggest that art by A-GAI is more about human curation, but even that may mean people throwing conversations among themselves and building towards new futures that are co-determined by people. These works may democratize common artfulness. They may enable common folk to see differently and to look again. These works may de-center the so-called anthropo-normative works and enable movement in new evolutionary directions (even as the A-GAI were trained on human artworks).

They may enable an enrichment of visuals on social media. They may share their own respective dreamworlds with others and learn how others would depict their own imaginations visually.

Machine-created works may still evoke emotions in people. And at some level, the A-GAI and its outputs will speak to and change humanity, in the present, and perhaps in a retrospective in the future (when the A-GAI visuals may be viewed as a collective psychogram of this present moment).

Making Art With Generative AI Tools is a collection of works by researchers about various approaches to art-making generative AIs.

AN INITIAL BRAINSTORM

The call for proposals included the following:

Inside large language models (LLMs) powering generative AI for art-making

...for video-making
...for visual storytelling
...for animations
...for augmented reality

Case studies in the usage of generative AIs (GAIs) for still visuals
Case studies in the usage of generative AIs (GAIs) for motion visuals
Edge cases related to art-making generative AIs
Getting started with (web-facing) art-making generative AIs
Creating visuals with art-making generative AIs for storytelling
Creating visuals with art-making generative AIs for teaching
Creating visuals with art-making generative AIs for learning
Creating visuals with art-making generative AIs for decoration
Representations using art-making generative AIs (reality, art, imagination, innovation, design, and others)
Illustrating via art-making generative AIs
Exemplification via art-making generative AIs
Exploring symbology using art-making generative AIs
Visual punning using art-making generative AIs
Humor using art-making generative AIs
Comics using art-making generative AIs
Book illustration using art-making generative AIs
Cultural exploration using art-making generative AIs
Applying alt-texting and other textual descriptors to engage transparently with sharing works designed with art-making generative AIs
The design of text prompts for art-making generative AIs
The design of seeding images to prompt art-making generative AIs
Using multimodal text and image prompts for generative AIs
Online communities around art-making generative AIs
Making a living in commercial space with co-created visuals from art-making generative AIs
Art-making generative engines and programs and tools
Online art styles from art-making generative AIs
Learning about common art with art-making generative AI (compositing, modifiers, language, experimentation, and others)
Promoting broad creativity with art-making generative AIs
Dividing the work between the human and the machine (with art-making generative AIs)
Ensuring originality with pre-production and post-production of still visuals, videos, and animations
The human-machine nexus with art-making generative AIs
Social communities online around art-making generative AIs (such as on the platforms)
Avoiding stereotypical visuals in art-making generative AIs
Avoiding social toxicity in art-making generative AIs
Enabling subtle visual effects using art-making generative AIs
Creating articulate visual messaging using art-making generative AIs
Authorship and crediting around works with art-making generative AIs

Intellectual property and art-making generative AIs
Legal considerations regarding the use of art-making generative AIs
Using art-making generative AIs for idea creation
Using art-making generative AIs for reference visuals
Augmenting work with art-making generative AIs
Research into art-making generative AIs
Manual detection for works created by generative AIs? Computational detection? Accuracy? Confidence?
Persuasiveness of works of generative AI (at various levels from pixel to global)?

The call for chapters shows the potential ranges of ideas, and this list is a non-comprehensive one. Many other ideas would work as well.

An Extended Table of Contents

As to the text itself, an extended Table of Contents (TOC) follows below. The book is organized into four sections.

Section 1: Artmaking Generative AI Tools
Section 2: Applied Artmaking With A-GAI
Section 3: Research Potential With Synthetic AI-Generated Imagery
Section 4: Human-Computer Collaboration and Intellectual Property

SECTION 1: ARTMAKING GENERATIVE AI TOOLS

Revisiting the Key Components of Creativity through Generative AI

Today, advancements in artificial intelligence and its applications have resulted in its widespread use in creative industries. The goal of this study is to investigate the relationship between artificial intelligence and creativity through the perspective of Generative AI (GenAI) utilized in these industries. To perform this investigation, the study first introduces the concepts of creativity and its key components, along with GenAI and AI creativity. The study's analysis is founded on 14 key components of creativity identified in the previous literature. In the analysis section, the study examines whether these key components are present in today's GenAI tools, drawing on current debates about AI and AI-based applications. Additionally, the capabilities, limitations, and challenges of GenAI are investigated for each key component. In the discussion section, the study makes projections about potential problems that may be encountered when using GenAI and discusses possible redefinitions of key components in the future.

Generative AI for Text to Image: A Comprehensive Survey

Text-to-image (TTI) synthesis models represent a creative approach in the realm of artificial intelligence, specifically designed to transform textual input into visually realistic images. The essence of TTI generation lies in its ability to harness the power of language and convert it seamlessly into visually compelling content, showcasing creative image synthesis. Initially using GANs and Transformers, text-to-image generation evolved with diffusion models introducing noise. Integration with large models, TTI models now produce results near-real images. Breakthroughs like ControlNet and 3D object synthesis redefine possibilities. Editing text or images adds versatile dimensions, showcasing generative technologies' transformative capabilities. Our survey explores scaling TTI models, focusing on various descriptions and ControlNet's role. We categorize literature, offer nuanced comparisons, and discuss applications. Looking ahead, we foresee TTI's potential for productivity enhancements, especially in the Metaverse era, and expansion into intricate tasks like video and 3D generation.

Generative AI and Generative Pre-Trained Transformer Applications: Challenges and Opportunities

Generative AI, such as Generative Pre-trained Transformer (GPT), has seen rapid advancements in recent years, offering a wide range of applications, but it also presents several challenges and opportunities. GPT can automate content generation for various industries, including journalism, marketing, and entertainment, reducing the need for manual content creation. Generative AI can personalize content and recommendations in e-commerce, streaming services, and more, enhancing user experiences. Generative AI, such as GPT, offers immense potential across various sectors but requires careful management to address bias, ethics, and quality control challenges. As technology evolves, finding the right balance between control and creativity will be crucial for maximizing its benefits while minimizing risks. Based on the above, we will systematically review the bibliometric literature on how Generative AI and Generative Pre-trained Transformer applications challenge opportunities using the Scopus database by analysing 49 academic and/or scientific documents.

SECTION 2: APPLIED ARTMAKING WITH A-GAI

The Human-Machine Nexus with Art-Making Generative AIs

The chapter delves into the dynamic interplay between human creativity and artificial intelligence, exploring the transformative landscape of art creation facilitated by generative AI tools. As the realms of technology and artistic expression converge, this chapter navigates the intricate relationship between human artists and machine-generated algorithms. It scrutinizes how generative AI tools serve not as replacements for human ingenuity but as collaborators, augmenting the creative process and challenging conventional notions of authorship in the realm of art. Through a comprehensive examination of case studies and examples, the chapter illustrates the symbiotic fusion of human intuition, emotion, and conceptualization with the computational capabilities of AI, shedding light on the profound implications for the future of artistic endeavors.

Children's Book Visualizations From an Artmaking Generative AI

How would a well-known artmaking generative AI (A-GAI) go about illustrating children's books? This chapter uses multiple prompting approaches to elicit children's book illustrations for known stories and more original plots to identify some early visual patterns from Deep Dream Generator. The research explores a variety of questions around the quality of the output images in conveying visual meaning in the children's book space (albeit using fictional prompts). This exploratory work provides some early and preliminary insights into this space, including in how to set up a light experiment using an A-GAI.

Exploratory Visual Digital Character and Visual Digital Scene Design Using Artmaking Generative AI: Enhancing Story Problems and Other Pedagogical Narratives

Static visual illustrations with characters and scenes play an important role in story problems and other pedagogical narratives. Such visuals may better engage learners, connect learners with the learning sequence, set the emotional tone, evoke settings, emphasize critical moments, and support the teaching and learning in other ways. With the popularization of artmaking generative AI, a practical question is how well this tool can make visual characters based on character design prompts for both animate and inanimate characters? What about the computerized drawing of scenes in which such characters may be placed, alone or in relation to each other? How difficult is it to prompt the generative AI to create consistent characters from different angles and perspectives? To create consistent scenes and backgrounds? This work explores how practically usable the AI-generated visuals are for the making of characters and scenes, with some light pre-production and post-production, as needed.

Synthesis of Art and Technology: Digital Expression in Jewelry Design

This chapter delved into the intricate intersection of artificial intelligence and the realm of jewelry art, exploring how AI catalyzes the emergence of novel forms of artistic expression within the traditional domain of jewelry art while simultaneously extending its influence to other branches of art. Moreover, it elucidated the myriad opportunities AI presents for artists, ushering in a new era of creativity and innovation. In addition to examining the symbiotic relationship between art and technology, this chapter delves into synthesizing these two seemingly disparate realms. By amalgamating the evolution of artistic expression in jewelry design with the avant-garde perspectives offered by artificial intelligence, a fertile ground for experimentation and exploration is unveiled.

SECTION 3: RESEARCH POTENTIAL WITH SYNTHETIC AI-GENERATED IMAGERY

Conducting Legitimate Research Using Various Synthetic Imagery From Artmaking Generative AIs: An Exploration

For researchers, in-world phenomena offer many opportunities to learn in systematic ways (through various types of observation, research, and analysis). One phenomenon that can bear higher levels of insight involves artmaking generative AIs, not only in terms of how the systems work and are designed, but in terms of their output images. This work asserts that AI-generated imagery may be informative of the underlying training imageset, human culture, design, and symbolism on one level but beyond this, offer insights about in-world phenomena. This work suggests that as artmaking generative AIs advance (and some of the more sophisticated ones now), the output imagery and imagesets may be interpreted more deeply for insights about not synthetic versions of the world but of the world itself. Precise proposals are included in this work. Both manual and computational analytics methods are proposed. And there is a proposed approach for validating / invalidating the perceived insights from the imagery.

Remote Virtual Sanctuary: Exploring an Online Social Network on an Artmaking Generative AI Platform Post COVID-19

Y2023 was an original year, with global humanity emerging from a deadly pandemic (COVID-19), facing the advent of artmaking generative AIs, and surviving in a time of geopolitical turmoil, economic and financial pressures, and social strife. What role does an online social network (built up around an artmaking generative AI platform) play for people in this present moment? How does the remote virtual community enable participants to seek various fulfillments? The web-facing Deep Dream Generator tool and platform has proven itself to be a powerful social space for many with rich immersions and remote social interactions. This work is a practice-led case study.

Generative AI Methodology for Assisted Art Within the Historical-Cultural Identity of Southern Brazil

Generative Artificial Intelligence is an emerging technology that has impacted society recently and with productivity gains in the coming years. This technology learns from existing data to generate high-quality content such as text, images, music, speech, videos, and code. As part of the creative industries, collaboration between generative algorithms and human creativity brings challenges due to producing content and artistic images in response to natural language requests. Thus, this chapter establishes a methodology based on text-to-image Generative Artificial Intelligence for producing assisted art in contextualized cultural content to generate unique and diverse images of the historical-cultural identity of southern Brazil. The steps of the methodology that can portray elements of Brazil's biome, cultural, and historical events are dataset assembling, model training and fine-tuning, and content enhancement and post-processing. In addition, the methodology allows an immersed experience with people being transported in period clothing and within a historical or cultural setting.

SECTION 4: HUMAN-COMPUTER COLLABORATION AND INTELLECTUAL PROPERTY

Artistic Expressions, Generative AI, and Legal Tapestry: Exploring the Dynamics of Copyright Laws in the Confluence of AI and Artistic Creation

This study delves into the transformative impact of generative artificial intelligence (AI) on creative production, exploring the collaborative efforts of artists and cutting-edge technology. The convergence of human ingenuity and AI in artistic expression expands creative boundaries but introduces complex intellectual property (IP) challenges. Examining beyond visual art, the study reveals the intricate engagement between humans and advanced algorithms, offering a unique perspective on the creative process. The intersection of AI and creativity raises critical copyright concerns, challenging traditional concepts of authorship and infringement. Addressing the global scope of AI-generated art, the study advocates for a unified framework to navigate legal complexities and ensure ethical considerations in the evolving landscape of creative technology.

Artificial Intelligence in Architecture: Innovations, Challenges, and Ethical Considerations

The advent of artificial intelligence (AI) has significantly impacted many disciplines, including architecture. AI started redefining design boundaries and possibilities by opening up new realms of creativity. Within this scope, this chapter investigates the integration of AI in architectural design by exploring the potential of these advanced technologies. Moreover, ethical considerations regarding the role of AI in architectural design, which is an area of increasing importance and complexity, will also be investigated. The chapter will also engage with concerns about the potential loss of human touch in the design process, a critical aspect considering the intrinsic value of personal creativity and intuition in architecture. By addressing these concerns and presenting a detailed view, the chapter aims to foster a comprehensive understanding of AI's role in architecture, proposing an informed approach to integrate AI tools in the architectural design process.

Ethical Dilemmas in the Integration of AI in Common Digital Art and Digital Crafting: An Artistic View on Morality

The integration of artificial intelligence (AI) into common digital art and digital crafting has ushered in a new era of creative possibilities, but it has also brought forth a myriad of ethical dilemmas that require careful consideration. This chapter explores the ethical complexities and challenges arising from AI perspectives in the realm of digital art and crafting, shedding light on the nuanced interplay between technology, creativity, and ethical values. At the heart of the discussion lies the concept of ethical dilemmas, which emerge at the intersection of AI and digital creativity. These dilemmas encompass a range of issues, including bias in AI algorithms, ownership and authorship disputes, environmental impact, exploitative uses of AI-generated content, fairness, sustainability, intellectual property rights, creative rights, and responsible practices.

Machine-to-Machine Play

On a lark, the editor asked a generative AI (the former BardAI) what topics to ask a generative AI to draw.

The response reads as follows:
A nebula in the night sky
A waterfall cascading down a mountainside
A field of flowers in bloom
A flock of birds flying overhead
A cityscape at night
A forest at sunrise
A desert sunset
A snow-capped mountain range
A coral reef teeming with life
A glacier calving into the ocean

A volcano erupting
A thunderstorm rolling in
A rainbow after a storm
A snowflake under a microscope
A crystal formation
A DNA molecule
A neuron firing
A heart beating
A lung breathing
A muscle contracting
A cell dividing
A molecule of water
A molecule of oxygen
A molecule of carbon dioxide
A molecule of nitrogen
A molecule of helium
A molecule of hydrogen

Indeed, the generative AI may autogenerate topics and create *ad infinitem.* It is important to realize the importance of the human nexus. It is important to slow the computation down and enable people to direct the work.

It is easy enough to be superficial about A-GAI tools. It is easy enough to be blasé about the multimodal creations that can be created with a whisper and a visual clue. It helps to have opportunities to immerse in the technologies, to try different ones, and to test limits. The present is ever-pressing and demanding of attention and potent in its potential effects.

Making Art With Generative AI Tools captures rich ideas about the potentials of art-making generative AIs to seed the future of human and machine endeavors…and to coax value from very expensive large language models (LLMs) and perhaps some less expensive models. This is a very early moment in the process, but time slips by quickly, and is lost irreparably.

Thanks!

I am deeply grateful to the contributors to this research text. Also, IGI Global is professional and supportive in all things. Thank you.

Shalin Hai-Jew
Hutchinson Community College, USA
March 2024

REFERENCES

Hai-Jew, S. (2022). *Common Visual Art in a Social Digital Age*. Nova Science Publishers. doi:10.52305/BKOT1869

Section 1
Artmaking Generative AI Tools

Chapter 1
Revisiting the Key Components of Creativity Through Generative AI

Orkan Zeynel Güzelci
https://orcid.org/0000-0002-5771-4069
Istanbul Technical University, Turkey

Ilker Karadag
https://orcid.org/0000-0001-7534-2839
Manisa Celal Bayar University, Turkey

ABSTRACT

Today, advancements in artificial intelligence (AI) and its applications have resulted in its widespread use in creative industries. The goal of this study is to investigate the relationship between artificial intelligence and creativity through the perspective of Generative AI (GenAI) utilized in these industries. To perform this investigation, the study first introduces the concepts of creativity and its key components, along with GenAI and AI creativity. The study's analysis is founded on 14 key components of creativity identified in the previous literature. In the analysis section, the study examines whether these key components are present in today's GenAI tools, drawing on current debates about AI and AI-based applications. Additionally, the capabilities, limitations, and challenges of GenAI are investigated for each key component. In the discussion section, the study makes projections about potential problems that may be encountered when using GenAI and discusses possible redefinitions of key components in the future.

INTRODUCTION

The debates on the relationship between artificial intelligence (AI) and creativity are not new. Alan Turing's study "Computing Machinery and Intelligence" (2009) raised important questions about the possibly creative capacities of machine intelligence. Margaret Boden's 1977 book *Artificial Intelligence and Natural Man* established frameworks for understanding creativity and its potential connections with

DOI: 10.4018/979-8-3693-1950-5.ch001

AI. In their book *The Cognitive Computer: on Language, Learning, and Artificial Intelligence*, Roger Schank and Peter G. Childers (1984) discuss the promise of artificial intelligence in terms of language and learning, as well as how it is possible to program a computer so that it not only understands but also generates natural language. Although this assumption was not directly relevant to AI creativity, Roger Schank's ideas at that time served as a foundation for understanding AI creativity. In a seminal 1982 paper titled "Why People Think Computers Can't," Marvin Minsky noted that creativity is not only about novelty but also about learning from experience.

Prior to the emergence of artificial intelligence, creativity research was concerned with humans (Esling & Devis, 2020; Wu et al., 2021). It was first difficult to relate computer notions with creativity (Boden, 2004). Today, as artificial intelligence and its applications advance, this relationship has evolved in a variety of ways within the creative industries. The creative industries include but are not limited to design, architecture, music, video games, fashion, advertising, and media (DCMS, 1998; Flew, 2002). Discussing AI creativity in connection to the definition of human creativity generates new concerns and challenges. At this point, rather than making a comparison, it is necessary to reconsider the concept of creativity for AI.

This study aims to offer an overview by exploring the capabilities, limitations, and challenges of various AI-assisted technologies in the context of creativity. In this sense, the chapter focuses on attempts to define creativity through its key components and then investigates whether these characteristics are present in today's Generative AI (GenAI). The significance of these attempts stems from the fact that debates on AI creativity are approached from various perspectives. While some researchers highlight the positive aspects of AI in fostering creativity, others adopt a more conservative stance regarding AI's role in creative processes. Rather than attempting to define creativity, Jordanous (2012) identifies its key components after conducting a comprehensive interdisciplinary review that integrates multiple academic perspectives. These key components are expected to provide a foundational basis for the analysis conducted in this study, offering a structured approach to understanding GenAI's potential and limitations in creative contexts.

RELATED CONCEPTS

Creativity and Its Key Components

There is no universally accepted definition of creativity, and its meaning varies depending on the field of application. A shift in perspective can highlight different aspects of creativity (Jordanous, 2012; Jordanous & Keller, 2016). The definitions of creativity provided by dictionaries capture the essence of generating new, useful, and original ideas or products. According to two of the main dictionaries, creativity is characterized by the ability to create, emphasizing the creative power or faculty and the ability to produce something unique and previously unknown (Oxford English Dictionary, 2023; Cambridge Dictionary, 2024). The dictionary definitions of 'creative' support this notion, with terms like 'inventive,' 'imaginative,' and 'productive' (Collins English Dictionary, 2024).

Creativity is considered an interactive process that concludes in the creation of something original as a part of different domains, recognized as useful by a community (Amabile, 1996; Boden, 2004; Csikszentmihalyi, 1997; Stein, 1963). This notion is expanded by Sternberg and Lubart (1999), who define creativity as the ability to produce work that is original, unexpected, and acceptable while following the limits of certain tasks. Boden (2004) and Hennessey and Amabile (2010) further describe creativity as the capacity to generate ideas or artifacts that are new, surprising, and valuable. Plucker et al. (2004), along with Rhodes (1961), highlight the dynamic nature of creativity, defining it as the outcome of the interaction between an individual's abilities. As noted by Glück et al. (2002), there is a dynamic interplay between individual characteristics, environmental factors, and the creative process itself. This perspective is supported by Amabile (1983) who aligns with the notion that creativity involves not only the generation of new ideas but also their practical application and the context of their development. Such a view recognizes the complex nature of creativity and the importance of a wide range of perspectives, including those outlined by other scholars (Guilford, 1950; Runco & Jaeger, 2012; Sternberg & Lubart, 1999). Briefly, previous studies highlight that creativity is not an isolated event but deeply integrated into both mental activity and social context.

Anna Jordanous (2012) highlights the challenge of defining creativity due to its varied interpretations across dictionaries, disciplines, and individual perspectives. Emphasizing creativity as a dynamic, context-dependent phenomenon rather than a static skill, Jordanous identifies 14 key components essential to creativity. These components are as follows:

1. *Active Involvement and Persistence* describes being actively involved in the creative process, responding to it while intentionally influencing it, as well as having a willingness to carry it through to the end, even in the face of challenges.
2. *Dealing with Uncertainty* involves managing incomplete, missing, inconsistent, conflicting, ambiguous, and/or unreliable data.
3. *Domain Competence* refers to the skill and capacity to develop, produce, validate, and promote new ideas in a domain while having a sufficient understanding of the field to identify gaps, needs, or problems.
4. *General Intellectual Ability* refers to general intelligence and particularly good mental capacity.
5. *Generation of Results* refers to the process of creating something—tangible or intangible—that did not previously exist while working toward a specific end target, goal, or result.
6. *Independence and Freedom* refers to the ability to work autonomously, having control over decisions and actions, and being free to do it without being constrained by preconceived notions, rules, or biases.
7. *Intention and Emotional Involvement* refers to personal and emotional engagement, immersion, self-expression, and participation in the creative process.
8. *Originality* refers to creating a new product or performing something in a novel way; discovering new connections and relationships between previously unrelated concepts that produce results that are unanticipated, unexpected, unusual, and surprising.
9. *Progression and Development* refers to advancement and evolution during a process that may or may not be linear. Although the goal may be ambiguously described, the entire process should indicate some progress in a specific task.
10. *Social Interaction and Communication* refers to the persuasive and positive promotion of work to others, as well as mutual impact, feedback, sharing, and collaboration between society and individuals.
11. *Spontaneity/Subconscious Processing* refers to not having to be in control of the entire process and being able to react fast and spontaneously when necessary, without spending too much time

considering the possibilities. It also means thoughts that may influence the process subconsciously but are inaccessible to cognitive evaluation, or that may attract less attention than others.

12. *Thinking and Evaluation* refers to intentionally examining numerous possibilities to recognize potential value in each and find the best option, utilizing reasoning and skilled judgment, as well as choosing the final option among various possibilities without allowing the process to become stuck due to uncertainty.
13. *Value* refers to providing a helpful contribution that is valued by others and recognized as an achievement and influential advancement; it is viewed as unique, rather than something that any individual might produce.
14. *Variety, Divergence, and Experimentation* refers to generating various ideas to compare and choose from, as well as the ability to be open to various viewpoints and experiment with alternative options without bias. (Jordanous, 2012; Jordanous & Keller, 2016).

AI Creativity

The concept of AI creativity is often aligned with computational (Jordanous, 2012) or machine (Frich et al., 2018; Mazzone & Elgammal, 2019) creativity. Colton and Wiggins (2012) define computational creativity as the philosophy, science, and engineering of computers that exhibit creative behaviors when completing certain tasks. On the other hand, machine creativity refers to the creativity performed by machines, and it challenges conventional assumptions by claiming that machines can carry out intelligent and creative acts that were previously assumed to be only possible among humans (Still & d'Inverno, 2019).

In the literature, the concept of AI creativity is often interpreted as conditions in which any content is simply generated. In other words, the mere existence of a created output is considered artificial intelligence creativity. Since creativity is based on mental activities such as composing ideas, remembering, thinking, and self-criticism, Boden (1998) associates creativity with human intelligence, viewing it as a challenge to artificial intelligence. Franceschelli and Musolesi (2021) address the distinction between simple generation and creativity through AI by referring to Boden's (1998; 2004) three criteria (new, surprising, and valuable) that are essential to be recognized as creativity.

For two decades, collaborative creativity has been prioritized over individual creativity in human-computer interaction studies (Amershi et al., 2019; Frich et al., 2018). However, the expectation for individual creativity from artificial intelligence has significantly increased today. To discuss the creative behavior of a computer, Graeme Ritchie (2001) identified multiple features that should be associated with a possibly creative program. Twenty years after Ritchie's work, Franceschelli and Musolesi (2021) conducted an extensive review of several methods developed for assessing computational creativity and AI creativity.

Instead of offering a traditional definition, Wu et al. (2021) described AI creativity as a strategy where humans and AI collaborate to utilize each other's strengths, complementing each other to generate more alternatives and increase productivity. Mazzone and Elgammal (2019) shift the focus from mere human-machine interaction to supporting the partnership between human and machine creativity, seeing this collaboration as a way to boost the creative capabilities of both sides. Rafner et al.'s (2023) work furthers this viewpoint by highlighting that AI creativity goes beyond the machines' ability to produce novel outputs; it also involves deeper exploration into the synergies between human and machine intelligence in creative activities.

Generative AI

Generative Artificial Intelligence (GenAI) refers to a subset of AI technologies capable of generating synthetic outputs. According to Boden (1998), AI technologies can be used to generate new outputs by combining well-known or familiar ideas. This argument correlates with the working principles of GenAI that analyze the data of previous examples, detect the patterns, and learn the structures of the data to generate outputs that mimic existing ones or are entirely new. GenAI technologies include various models that learn from large datasets to generate outputs like text, images, audio, and videos (Jovanović & Campbell, 2022). Notably, GenAI models such as Generative Adversarial Networks (GAN), Generative Pre-trained Transformers (GPT), Generative Diffusion Model (GDM), and Geometric DL (GDL) are recognized for their ability to produce human-like and realistic results. Generative AI finds applications across diverse domains, including education, art, design, architecture, entertainment, and medicine (Chan & Hu, 2023; Gozalo-Brizuela & Garrido-Merchán, 2023; Jovanović & Campbell, 2022; Murugesan & Cherukuri, 2023; Vaswani et al., 2017). Although GenAI was initially a concept addressed only in the research field, today it has become a part of daily life for users who have no expertise in computer-related fields (Vinchon et al., 2023).

Some of the most common types of GenAI include applications such as text-to-text (e.g., ChatGPT, Bard) (OpenAI, 2022a; Google, 2023), text-to-image (e.g., DALL-E, Midjourney) (OpenAI, 2022b), image-to-image (e.g., Pix2Pix, CycleGAN) (Isola et al., 2017; Zhu et al., 2017), and image-to-text (e.g., VizWiz, COCO-Text) (Bigham et al., 2010; Veit et al., 2016) generators. Although these are the primary categories, GenAI's application is not limited to these. In their study, Gozalo-Brizuela and Garrido-Merchán (2023) provided a structured taxonomy of more than 350 GenAI applications.

In addition to creating new outcomes, GenAI applications can be used to summarize, analyze, organize, manipulate, and evaluate existing productions (Chan & Hu, 2023; Gozalo-Brizuela & Garrido-Merchán, 2023; Mizumoto & Eguchi, 2023). They can also help researchers comprehend concepts from unfamiliar domains and design new experiments (Murugesan & Cherukuri, 2023). With its wide range of applications across multiple disciplines and the challenges it faces, the field of GenAI is rapidly expanding.

ANALYSIS OF KEY COMPONENTS IN GENERATIVE AI

This section discusses the key components of creativity presented by Anna Jordanous in 2012, through current debates on AI and AI-based applications.

Active Involvement and Persistence

There is a consensus on the involvement of AI in the creative processes (Magni et al., 2023), however, the key component discussed here is *Active Involvement*. GenAI is not actively involved in creative processes similar to humans. On the other hand, GenAI actively takes place in the creative process, primarily in a supportive and collaborative role (Vinchon et al., 2023). In terms of creativity, GenAI cannot generate a human-like spark or vision. However, when used alongside human imagination as a collaborative tool, GenAI can enhance the creative process (Eapen et al., 2023; Mazzone & Elgammal, 2019). These arguments highlight the idea of AI's *Active Involvement* being distinct from human creative processes, while still playing a significant and supportive role.

The term creativity involves the key component of *Persistence*, which requires the tenacity to continue despite challenges. While lacking human-level persistence in creative processes, GenAI can maintain goal-oriented tasks under user guidance. In this context, how the model is trained over time and the tendencies it is taught become significantly important. Based on the persistence pathway that is necessary for creativity, GenAI demonstrates its strength in systematically exploring specific concepts or problems in depth (Nijstad et al., 2010). This characteristic allows GenAI to refine ideas or optimize outputs by iterative processing.

Dealing With Uncertainty

The ability of AI-based systems to process and make decisions on ambiguous, imprecise, and incomplete data presents a significant challenge in their functionality and reliability (Sachan et al., 2021). In this context, Eshraghian (2020) highlights the necessity for AI systems to operate effectively in uncertain situations. The work by Salehi and Burgueño (2018) shows that AI has certain abilities in solving complex problems and dealing with uncertainties.

A review of current studies reveals that GenAI supports tasks involving uncertainty, such as code generation (Vasconcelos et al., 2023), and can automatically complete sentences or paragraphs (Shi et al., 2022). This capability of GenAI is attributed to the maturity of coding and natural language models. However, when confronted with an ambiguous and open-ended problem, GenAI may offer multiple responses, and then the human can become responsible for navigating the uncertainty by selecting the most appropriate answer or output. Engaging AI with contradictory topics can encourage it to find unexpected solutions. This can lead to more creative and innovative perspectives (Rafner et al., 2023).

Domain Competence

Human beings can make connections and identify differences between two domains without having extensive knowledge about these domains, but even though it is trained with large datasets, this is quite challenging for GenAI. George et al. (2019) discuss the potential and challenges of GenAI in adapting to new domains. In their work, Kim et al. (2017) have developed a GAN model that aims to recognize data across different domains and understand their relationships. While reviewing the applications of GenAI models across different domains, Simon et al. (2022) discuss how understanding across domains can be formed by training the AI models from different datasets. In brief, despite being trained with large datasets, there are no claims that GenAI can become an expert in a domain, and human still plays a role as a domain expert. However, the main strength of GenAI is to gather data in different formats from various sources, learn from the collected data, and gain the understanding to relate these domains (Gozalo-Brizuela & Garrido-Merchán, 2023).

General Intellectual Ability

GenAI successfully mimics intelligence within the domains they are trained in, but they lack the broader understanding and reasoning characteristic of general intelligence. While some GenAI systems exhibit advanced capabilities in particular fields, such as language processing in GPT models or visual recognition in DALL-E (Amershi et al., 2019; Murugesan & Cherukuri, 2023; Raneri et al., 2023), these are instances of narrow or specialized intelligence, not human intellect.

Generation of Results

Anantrasirichai and Bull (2022) critically examine the success and limitations of GenAI in generating results. While they observed GenAI as having modest creative capabilities, Na and Kim (2021) argue that GenAI should be viewed as more than a tool for achieving simple results in design. In today's conditions, although GenAI is capable of creating anticipated or unanticipated outcomes, its reliance on existing data and lack of intentional design limit its ability to diverge from established knowledge and create truly unprecedented work (Tigre Moura, 2023).

Independence and Freedom

Das and Varshney (2022) focus on the question of how GenAI models can achieve a certain level of independence and freedom during processing. They define independence as AI working autonomously and producing new products without being stuck with pre-existing solutions and biases. GenAI can work independently to some extent, yet, their actions are ultimately guided by their algorithm and the data on which they were trained. They operate within predefined parameters and lack true autonomy or freedom in the human sense. In this context, Das and Varshney (2022) discuss how models such as GAN and GPT can exceed their training materials to produce creative and independent solutions. On the other hand, Generative AI can exhibit bias (Jovanović & Campbell, 2022; Murugesan & Cherukuri, 2023). Bias in AI often arises from the data used to train the model, reflecting previous biases present in that data. The bias can also be a result of the choices made during the development of the GenAI.

Intention and Emotional Involvement

In creative processes, Gen AI models can be programmed to analyze users' emotional states and respond appropriately, thereby facilitating intention and emotional involvement in artificial intelligence. In this context, Chen et al. (2019) developed a system that integrates human brain waves and emotion data with AI algorithms. However, it should be noted that the AI does not experience a real emotional experience as a result of this integration. In the system developed by Chen et al (2019), AI produces outputs or makes decisions according to the emotional state of the human. In brief, different GenAI models can process data and produce results by simulating or imitating human intention, but cannot reveal a human-like interaction or emotional involvement. The reason for this is that the outputs obtained are in any case the consequence of actions such as programming and processing.

Originality

Generative AI can develop outputs that are statistically unlikely to have existed before by establishing connections and recombining parts from huge databases. These outputs could be novel combinations of existing concepts, resulting in new insights and unexpected outcomes. Beyond these constraints, GenAI can explore ideas, perhaps leading to truly original ideas (Dekel, 2023). The work of Guzik et al. (2023) also supports this argument. In their study, Guzik et al. (2023) evaluated ChatGPT's performance from an originality point of view by using the Torrance Tests of Creative Thinking (TTCT). The results showed that ChatGPT was in the top one percent for originality score. Based on this result, Guzik et al. (2023) underlined the potential of AI systems to enhance human creativity meaningfully.

Progression and Development

GenAI can be trained using human feedback to improve its creative outputs over time. This iterative process allows it to gain a better understanding of human preferences and aesthetic sensibilities, resulting in more refined and complex works. As McCormack and d'Inverno (2014) stated, machine learning techniques enable computers to behave differently through optimization or interaction. In this sense, Köbis and Mossink (2021) emphasized the adaptive and learnable characteristics of AI algorithms.

Social Interaction and Communication

Another perspective that needs to be addressed and is currently being studied is how users establish a social relationship with GenAI in creative processes (Ashktorab et al., 2020). GenAI frequently neglects the underlying understanding of social cues, emotions, and cultural differences that are essential for successful social interaction. Communication provided by GenAI is often one-way, with the AI delivering its products for humans. This lacks the back-and-forth exchange and shared understanding that characterizes real social interaction (Hohenstein et al., 2023).

Spontaneity/Subconscious Processing

GenAI appears to gain from spontaneity or subconsciousness in processes with the number of unexpected outputs it produces, however, these concepts conflict with the algorithmic nature of AI (Megahed et al., 2023). On the other hand, GenAI lacks the deep context awareness and experience that humans have. Similarly, Caulfield (1995) theoretically explored the concept of the computer's subconscious and concluded that the computer can only perform human-like creative activities by following rules or algorithms. As a result, GenAI's creativity is linked to algorithmic processes rather than true subconsciousness and spontaneity.

Thinking and Evaluation

GenAI may investigate various solutions, learn from feedback, and even improve its strategies based on performance. The study of Wan and Kaneko (2017) explores the use of GenAI in learning game strategies. They stated that GenAI can conduct high-quality training for the model if sufficient data is obtained from top-quality players. On the contrary, they have developed a model that aims to make AI more competitive in the game in cases where data is insufficient. In another current study, Fu et al. (2023) introduce a framework namely GPTScore to score generated text. Yet it is essential to mention that, these skills are obtained from training data and programmed algorithms, rather than from conscious thinking and evaluation.

Value

GenAI can generate valuable outputs in various fields, like designing, composing music, or crafting engaging educational content. AI-generated design, art, and music can evoke emotions and resonate with audiences. These subjective values play a crucial role in human perception of what is valuable. Aesthetic values are also difficult to define with words, and for a computer, it is even more challenging since computer models need clear definitions (Boden, 2004). Tigre Moura et al. (2023) view the value of AI-generated products as a complex concept, influenced by both the method of creation and the intrinsic nature of the product itself. This leads to an important discussion on the attribution of value: specifically, whether the value of a useful AI model should be regarded as a reflection of the programmer's creative capability.

Variety, Divergence, and Experimentation

Diversity and experimentation are the main features expected from Generative AI tools. GenAI applications must be experimental in nature to go beyond classical computational or algorithmic approaches. The autonomous systems can compete with humans due to their experimental nature (Slonim et al., 2021). In this sense, Cropley (2020) emphasizes the need for a type of AI that experiments with different approaches. Generative AI may surely create a wide range of ideas and experiment with different approaches. However, GenAI models are ultimately constrained by the data on which they are trained and this may limit the variety and diversity of their outputs.

DISCUSSION

This chapter investigates the relationship of AI and creativity, with a focus on Generative AI in creative industries. The goal expressed in the introduction section questions whether the key components of creativity exist in today's GenAI applications. The aim here is not to directly declare the success or failure of artificial intelligence in meeting specific criteria but rather to offer a roadmap for further research into AI creativity. Upon examining the key components in this context, it is observed that there is no consensus on some, others are intertwined, some are subject to debate, and there is even a need to redefine the components.

For instance, *Active Involvement and Persistence* and *Dealing with Uncertainty* both require a level of dedication that is critical to the creative process. *Active Involvement* highlights the importance of actively participating in the creative process and having the tenacity to carry it through despite challenges. *Dealing with Uncertainty*, on the other hand, emphasizes the ability to manage ambiguous or incomplete information. Further analysis of other key components such as *Domain Competence*, *General Intellectual Ability*, and *Generation of Results* shows that these elements are also intertwined. *Independence and Freedom* allow for autonomy in the creative process, *Intention and Emotional Involvement* ensure a deep personal connection to the work, and *Originality* emphasizes the production of novel and unique outcomes. Lastly, *Progression and Development* and *Social Interaction and Communication* highlight the iterative nature of creativity and the importance of communication and feedback. These key components that work together portray the multidimensional character of creativity. The interplay between these components emphasizes the complexity of the creative process, illustrating that creativity is not just about having original ideas, but also about the ability to develop, improve, and successfully express these ideas within a domain.

GenAI carries potential in creative processes while also bringing along many challenges. Positively, GenAI exhibits proficiency in handling large volumes of data, thereby enabling the generation of diverse ideas and solutions. Its ability to recognize and replicate complex patterns and trends facilitates the creation of innovative designs and concepts. Furthermore, GenAI's strength lies in its capability to execute tasks efficiently, significantly reducing the time required for certain creative processes. These attributes are particularly beneficial in fields requiring the generation of numerous ideas or solutions, where GenAI can serve as a valuable tool for expanding the creative horizon.

However, the contributions of GenAI to creativity are not without limitations. One of the primary drawbacks is its lack of emotional intelligence and the inability to experience or understand human emotions. Additionally, GenAI's reliance on existing data may lead to a lack of originality, as it tends to generate outputs based on patterns it has learned, potentially stifling true innovation. The absence of subconscious processing or spontaneity further restricts its participation in the depth of the creative process. Moreover, while GenAI can perform in-depth evaluation in specific areas, it falls short in critical thinking and evaluating the creative process as adeptly as humans. These insights emphasize the importance of synergizing human creativity with GenAI capabilities to maximize the potential of creative endeavors. On the contrary, being dependent too much on generative AI technology may hinder abilities like creativity, critical thinking, and problem-solving (Iskender, 2023).

The processes driven by GenAI have shown that individuals are not simply using computers but interacting with them. This interaction, along with the ability to control and even customize the computer, has made it possible for the end-users to enhance their computer literacy. It is also crucial to mention that the design of GenAI technologies should consider disabled individuals, ensuring accessibility and inclusiveness. Today, users benefit from GenAI environments to acquire information for daily life practices, career advancement, and personal development. Moreover, efforts are being made to integrate AI applications into educational programs.

While the creativity of AI is debated, a transparent and deep understanding of the inner working principles of GenAI models is still lacking (Jovanović & Campbell, 2022). Besides the lack of clarity on how GenAI produces its outputs, it also cannot assess whether its generated outputs or responses are valid. According to Jordanous (2012), it is difficult to measure the creativity of machines because there is no consensus on computer creativity where even human creativity has many ambiguous definitions. The content produced by GenAI can be dangerous, misleading, inconsistent, and biased. This issue often stems from the dataset the model was trained on. For instance, the use of GenAI can lead to disinformation, plagiarism, the use of inappropriate references, and not considering copyright rules. Moreover, GenAI tools can be used to create and conduct messages and conversations for cybercrime and fraud purposes. All these issues can lead to ethical and legal problems (Harrer, 2023; Kumar, 2023; Lubowitz, 2023; Murugesan & Cherukuri, 2023). When faced with these issues, intervention, and prevention through review and assessment are necessary, requiring human judgment, intuition, expertise, and perspective. This production and evaluation cycle can be seen as supporting a human-AI partnership aimed at achieving more effective results. Even if humans are to evaluate the productions, specialized legal frameworks and regulations for the copyright, originality, and ownership of GenAI-produced products should be established at international norms. In terms of social and economic values, GenAI can lead to situations such as potential job displacement, impact on income inequality, and the need for upskilling of the workforce.

GenAI tools, still in their early phases, have several constraints, but the constant improvements highlight the dynamic character of their advancement. These improvements not only indicate a rise in sophistication and the introduction of new capabilities, but they also indicate the possibility of overcoming current limitations. The redefinition of existing key components may encourage further investigation of the realms of creativity, triggering a reconsideration of the boundaries between technology and human intelligence.

REFERENCES

Amabile, T. M. (1983). The social psychology of creativity: A componential conceptualization. *Journal of Personality and Social Psychology, 45*(2), 357–376. doi:10.1037/0022-3514.45.2.357

Amabile, T. M. (1996). *Creativity in context: Update to the social psychology of creativity*. Westview Press.

Amershi, S., Weld, D., Vorvoreanu, M., Fourney, A., Nushi, B., Collisson, P., . . . Horvitz, E. (2019). Guidelines for human-AI interaction. In *Proceedings of the 2019 CHI Conference on Human Factors in Computing Systems* (pp. 1-13). Available at: https://www.microsoft.com/en-us/research/uploads/prod/2019/01/Guidelines-for-Human-AI-Interaction-camera-ready.pdf

Anantrasirichai, N., & Bull, D. (2022). Artificial intelligence in the creative industries: A review. *Artificial Intelligence Review, 55*(1), 589–656. doi:10.1007/s10462-021-10039-7

Ashktorab, Z., Liao, Q., Dugan, C., Johnson, J., Pan, Q., Zhang, W., Kumaravel, S., & Campbell, M. (2020). Human-AI Collaboration in a Cooperative Game Setting. *Proceedings of the ACM on Human-Computer Interaction, 4*(CSCW2), 1–20. doi:10.1145/3415167

Bigham, J. P., Jayant, C., Ji, H., Little, G., Miller, A., Miller, R. C., ... White, B. (2010). VizWiz: nearly real-time answers to visual questions. *UIST '10: Proceedings of the 23nd annual ACM symposium on User interface software and technology*, 333-342. 10.1145/1866029.1866080

Boden, M. A. (1977). *Artificial Intelligence and Natural Man*. Harvester Press.

Boden, M. A. (1998). Creativity and artificial intelligence. *Artificial Intelligence, 103*(1-2), 347–356. doi:10.1016/S0004-3702(98)00055-1

Boden, M. A. (2004). *The Creative Mind: Myths and Mechanisms*. Routledge. doi:10.4324/9780203508527

Cambridge Dictionary. (2024). *Creativity*. Available at: https://dictionary.cambridge.org/dictionary/english/creativity

Caulfield, H. J. (1995). The computer subconscious. *Kybernetes, 24*(4), 46–52. doi:10.1108/03684929510089349

Chan, C. K. Y., & Hu, W. (2023). Students' voices on generative AI: Perceptions, benefits, and challenges in higher education. *International Journal of Educational Technology in Higher Education, 20*(43), 1–18. doi:10.1186/s41239-023-00411-8

Chen, M., Jiang, Y., Cao, Y., & Zomaya, A. (2019). CreativeBioMan: A Brain- and Body-Wearable, Computing-Based, Creative Gaming System. *IEEE Systems, Man, and Cybernetics Magazine, 6*(1), 14–22. doi:10.1109/MSMC.2019.2929312

Collins English Dictionary. (2024). *Creativity*. Available at: https://www.collinsdictionary.com/dictionary/english/creative

Colton, S., & Wiggins, G. A. (2012). Computational creativity: The final frontier? *Proceedings of 20th European Conference on Artificial Intelligence*, 21-26. 10.3233/978-1-61499-098-7-21

Cropley, A. (2020). Creativity-focused Technology Education in the Age of Industry 4.0. *Creativity Research Journal, 32*(2), 184–191. doi:10.1080/10400419.2020.1751546

Csikszentmihalyi, M. (1997). *Creativity: Flow and the Psychology of Discovery and Invention*. Harper Perennial.

Das, P., & Varshney, L. R. (2022). Explaining Artificial Intelligence Generation and Creativity: Human interpretability for novel ideas and artifacts. *IEEE Signal Processing Magazine*, *39*(4), 85–95. doi:10.1109/MSP.2022.3141365

DCMS. (1998). *Mapping the Creative Industries*. Available at: http://www.culture.gov.uk/creative/creative_industries.html

Dekel, R. (2023). *A.I. And Human Originality and Creativity Will humanity run out of original, innovative ideas?* Available at: https://www.inc.com/inc-masters/ai-and-human-originality-and-creativity.html

Eapen, T. T., Finkenstadt, D. J., Folk, J., & Venkataswamy, L. (2023). How generative AI can augment human creativity. *Harvard Business Review*. Available at: https://hbr.org/2023/07/how-generative-ai-can-augment-human-creativity

Eshraghian, J. (2020). Human ownership of artificial creativity. *Nature Machine Intelligence*, *2*(3), 157–160. doi:10.1038/s42256-020-0161-x

Esling, P., & Devis, N. (2020). Creativity in the era of artificial intelligence. *arXiv:2008.05959*. https://doi.org//arXiv.2008.05959 doi:10.48550

Flew, T. (2002). Beyond ad hocery: defining creative industries. *Cultural Sites, Cultural Theory, Cultural Policy, The Second International Conference on Cultural Policy Research*. Available at: http:// eprints.qut.edu.au/archive/00000256

Franceschelli, G., & Musolesi, M. (2021). Creativity and machine learning. *Survey (London, England)*. Advance online publication. arXiv2104.02726. doi:10.48550/arXiv.2104.02726

Frich, J., Mose Biskjaer, M., & Dalsgaard, P. (2018). Twenty years of creativity research in human-computer interaction: Current state and future directions. *Proceedings of the 2018 Designing Interactive Systems Conference*, 1235-1257. 10.1145/3196709.3196732

Fu, J., Ng, S., Jiang, Z., & Liu, P. (2023). GPTScore: Evaluate as You Desire. *arXiv:2302.04166*. https://doi.org//arXiv.2302.04166 doi:10.48550

George, G. V. S., Arun, A. R. G., & Geetha, S. (2019). Generating Cross Domain Models using Generative Adversarial Networks. *International Journal of Innovative Technology and Exploring Engineering*, *8*(9), 1303–1306. doi:10.35940/ijitee.I8013.078919

Glück, J., Ernst, R., & Unger, F. (2002). How creatives define creativity: Definitions reflect different types of creativity. *Creativity Research Journal*, *14*(1), 55–67. doi:10.1207/S15326934CRJ1401_5

Google. (2023). *Bard*. Available at: https://beta.google.com/bard

Gozalo-Brizuela, R., & Garrido-Merchán, E. C. (2023). A survey of Generative AI Applications. *arXiv:2306.02781*. https://doi.org//arXiv.2306.02781 doi:10.48550

Guilford, J. P. (1950). Creativity. *The American Psychologist*, *5*(9), 444–454. doi:10.1037/h0063487 PMID:14771441

Guzik, E. E., Byrge, C., & Gilde, C. (2023). The originality of machines: AI takes the Torrance Test. *Journal of Creativity*, *33*(3), 100065. doi:10.1016/j.yjoc.2023.100065

Harrer, S. (2023). Attention is not all you need: The complicated case of ethically using large language models in healthcare and medicine. *EBioMedicine*, *90*, 104512. doi:10.1016/j.ebiom.2023.104512 PMID:36924620

Hennessey, B. A., & Amabile, T. M. (2010). Creativity. *Annual Review of Psychology*, *61*(1), 569–598. doi:10.1146/annurev.psych.093008.100416 PMID:19575609

Hohenstein, J., Kizilcec, R. F., DiFranzo, D., Aghajari, Z., Mieczkowski, H., Levy, K., Naaman, M., Hancock, J., & Jung, M. F. (2023). Artificial intelligence in communication impacts language and social relationships. *Scientific Reports*, *13*(1), 5487. doi:10.1038/s41598-023-30938-9 PMID:37015964

Iskender, A. (2023). Holy or unholy? Interview with open AI's ChatGPT. *European Journal of Tourism Research*, *34*(3414), 1–11. doi:10.54055/ejtr.v34i.3169

Isola, P., Zhu, J. Y., Zhou, T., & Efros, A. A. (2017). Image-to-image translation with conditional adversarial networks. *Proceedings of the Thirtieth IEEE Conference on Computer Vision and Pattern Recognition (CVPR 2017)*, 1125-1134. 10.48550/arXiv.1611.07004

Jordanous, A. (2012). A Standardised Procedure for Evaluating Creative Systems: Computational Creativity Evaluation Based on What it is to be Creative. *Cognitive Computation*, *4*(3), 246–279. doi:10.1007/s12559-012-9156-1

Jordanous, A., & Keller, B. (2016). Modelling creativity: Identifying key components through a corpus-based approach. *PLoS One*, *11*(10), e0162959. doi:10.1371/journal.pone.0162959 PMID:27706185

Jovanović, M., & Campbell, M. (2022). Generative artificial intelligence: Trends and prospects. *Computer*, *55*(10), 107–112. doi:10.1109/MC.2022.3192720

Kim, T., Cha, M., Kim, H., Lee, J. K., & Kim, J. (2017). Learning to discover cross-domain relations with generative adversarial networks. *Proceedings of the International Conference on Machine Learning (ICML) 2017*, 1857-1865. 10.48550/arXiv.1703.05192

Köbis, N., & Mossink, L. D. (2021). Artificial intelligence versus Maya Angelou: Experimental evidence that people cannot differentiate AI-generated from human-written poetry. *Computers in Human Behavior*, *114*, 106553. doi:10.1016/j.chb.2020.106553

Kumar, A. H. (2023). Analysis of ChatGPT tool to assess the potential of its utility for academic writing in biomedical domain. *Biology, Engineering, Medicine and Science Reports*, *9*(1), 24–30. doi:10.5530/bems.9.1.5

Lubowitz, J. H. (2023). ChatGPT, an artificial intelligence chatbot, is impacting medical literature. *Arthroscopy*, *39*(5), 1121–1122. doi:10.1016/j.arthro.2023.01.015 PMID:36797148

Magni, F., Park, J., & Chao, M. M. (2023). Humans as Creativity Gatekeepers: Are We Biased Against AI Creativity? *Journal of Business and Psychology*, 1–14. doi:10.1007/s10869-023-09910-x

Mazzone, M., & Elgammal, A. (2019). Art, Creativity, and the Potential of Artificial Intelligence. *Arts*, *8*(1), 26. doi:10.3390/arts8010026

McCormack, J., & d'Inverno, M. (2014). On the future of computers and creativity. *AISB 2014 Symposium on Computational Creativity*. Available at: https://doc.gold.ac.uk/aisb50/AISB50-S04/AISB50-S4-McCormack-paper.pdf

Megahed, F., Chen, Y., Ferris, J., Knoth, S., & Jones-Farmer, L. (2023). How Generative AI models such as ChatGPT can be (Mis)Used in SPC Practice, Education, and Research? An Exploratory Study. *ArXiv: abs/2302.10916*. https://doi.org//arXiv.2302.10916 doi:10.48550

Minsky, M. (1982). Why People Think Computers Can't. *AI Magazine*, *3*(4), 3–15. doi:10.1609/aimag.v3i4.376

Mizumoto, A., & Eguchi, M. (2023). Exploring the potential of using an AI language model for automated essay scoring. *Research Methods in Applied Linguistics*, *2*(2), 100050. doi:10.1016/j.rmal.2023.100050

Murugesan, S., & Cherukuri, A. K. (2023). The Rise of Generative Artificial Intelligence and Its Impact on Education: The Promises and Perils. *Computer*, *56*(5), 116–121. doi:10.1109/MC.2023.3253292

Na, H., & Kim, W. (2021). A Study on The Practical Use of Generative Design in the Product Design Process. *Archives of Design Research*, *34*(1), 85–99. doi:10.15187/adr.2021.02.34.1.85

Nijstad, B. A., De Dreu, C. K., Rietzschel, E. F., & Baas, M. (2010). The dual pathway to creativity model: Creative ideation as a function of flexibility and persistence. *European Review of Social Psychology*, *21*(1), 34–77. doi:10.1080/10463281003765323

OpenAI (2022a). *ChatGPT*. Available at: https://beta.openai.com/docs/models/gpt

OpenAI (2022b). *DALL-E*. Available at: https://openai.com/dall-e/

Oxford English Dictionary. (2023). *Creativity*. Available at: https://www.oed.com/search/dictionary/?scope=Entries&q=creativity

Plucker, J. A., Beghetto, R. A., & Dow, G. T. (2004). Why isn't creativity more important to educational psychologists? Potentials, pitfalls, and future directions in creativity research. *Educational Psychologist*, *39*(2), 83–96. doi:10.1207/s15326985ep3902_1

Rafner, J., Beaty, R. E., Kaufman, J. C., Lubart, T., & Sherson, J. (2023). Creativity in the age of generative AI. *Nature Human Behaviour*, *7*(11), 1836–1838. doi:10.1038/s41562-023-01751-1 PMID:37985916

Raneri, S., Lecron, F., Hermans, J., & Fouss, F. (2023). Predictions through Lean startup? Harnessing AI-based predictions under uncertainty. *International Journal of Entrepreneurial Behaviour & Research*, *29*(4), 886–912. doi:10.1108/IJEBR-07-2021-0566

Rhodes, M. (1961). An analysis of creativity. *Phi Delta Kappan*, *42*(7), 305–310.

Ritchie, G. (2001). Assessing creativity. *Proceedings of AISB Symposium on AI and Creativity in Art and Science*. Available at: https://citeseerx.ist.psu.edu/document?repid=rep1&type=pdf&doi=bc6d0d0a04de633978fa924b097c50eb1d6db467

Runco, M. A., & Jaeger, G. J. (2012). The standard definition of creativity. *Creativity Research Journal, 24*(1), 92–96. doi:10.1080/10400419.2012.650092

Sachan, S., Almaghrabi, F., Yang, J. B., & Xu, D. L. (2021). Evidential reasoning for preprocessing uncertain categorical data for trustworthy decisions: An application on healthcare and finance. *Expert Systems with Applications, 185*, 115597. doi:10.1016/j.eswa.2021.115597

Salehi, H., & Burgueño, R. (2018). Emerging artificial intelligence methods in structural engineering. *Engineering Structures, 171*, 170–189. doi:10.1016/j.engstruct.2018.05.084

Schank, R. C., & Childers, P. (1984). *The Cognitive Computer: on Language, Learning, and Artificial Intelligence*. Addison-Wesley.

Shi, S., Zhao, E., Tang, D., Wang, Y., Li, P., Bi, W., Jiang, H., Huang, G., Cui, L., Huang, X., Zhou, C., Dai, Y., & Ma, D. (2022). Effidit: Your AI Writing Assistant. *arXiv:2208.01815v2*. https://doi.org//arXiv.2208.01815 doi:10.48550

Simon, C., Faraki, M., Tsai, Y. H., Yu, X., Schulter, S., Suh, Y., ... Chandraker, M. (2022). On generalizing beyond domains in cross-domain continual learning. In *Proceedings of the IEEE/CVF Conference on Computer Vision and Pattern Recognition* (pp. 9265-9274). 10.1109/CVPR52688.2022.00905

Slonim, N., Bilu, Y., Alzate, C., Bar-Haim, R., Bogin, B., Bonin, F., Choshen, L., Cohen-Karlik, E., Dankin, L., Edelstein, L., Ein-Dor, L., Friedman-Melamed, R., Gavron, A., Gera, A., Gleize, M., Gretz, S., Gutfreund, D., Halfon, A., Hershcovich, D., ... Aharonov, R. (2021). An autonomous debating system. *Nature, 591*(7850), 379–384. doi:10.1038/s41586-021-03215-w PMID:33731946

Stein, M. I. (1963). A transactional approach to creativity. In C. W. Taylor & F. Barron (Eds.), *Scientific Creativity: Its Recognition and Development* (pp. 217–227). John Wiles & Sons.

Sternberg, R. J., & Lubart, T. I. (1999). The concept of creativity: Prospects and paradigms. In R. J. Sternberg (Ed.), *Handbook of creativity* (pp. 3–15). Cambridge University Press.

Still, A., & d'Inverno, M. (2019). Can machines be artists? A Deweyan response in theory and practice. *Arts, 8*(1), 36. doi:10.3390/arts8010036

Tigre Moura, F. (2023). Artificial intelligence, creativity, and intentionality: The need for a paradigm shift. *The Journal of Creative Behavior, 57*(3), 336–338. doi:10.1002/jocb.585

Tigre Moura, F., Castrucci, C., & Hindley, C. (2023). Artificial intelligence creates art? An experimental investigation of value and creativity perceptions. *The Journal of Creative Behavior, 57*(4), 534–549. doi:10.1002/jocb.600

Turing, A. M. (2009). Computing Machinery and Intelligence. In R. Epstein, G. Roberts, & G. Beber (Eds.), *Parsing the Turing Test*. Springer., doi:10.1007/978-1-4020-6710-5_3

Vasconcelos, H., Bansal, G., Fourney, A., Liao, Q., & Vaughan, J. (2023). Generation Probabilities Are Not Enough: Exploring the Effectiveness of Uncertainty Highlighting in AI-Powered Code Completions. *ArXiv:abs/2302.07248*. https://doi.org//arXiv.2302.07248 doi:10.48550

Vaswani, A., Shazeer, N., Parmar, N., Uszkoreit, J., Jones, L., Gomez, A. N., ... Polosukhin, I. (2017). Attention is all you need. *Proceedings of 31st Conference on Neural Information Processing Systems (NIPS 2017)*, 1-11. 10.48550/arXiv.1706.03762

Veit, A., Alldrin, N., Chechik, G., Krasin, I., Gupta, A., & Belongie, S. (2016). COCO-Text: Dataset and benchmark for text detection and recognition in natural images. *Proceedings of the IEEE Conference on Computer Vision and Pattern Recognition*, 1200-1209. 10.48550/arXiv.1601.07140

Vinchon, F., Lubart, T., Bartolotta, S., Gironnay, V., Botella, M., Bourgeois-Bougrine, S., Burkhardt, J.-M., Bonnardel, N., Corazza, G. E., Glăveanu, V., Hanchett Hanson, M., Ivcevic, Z., Karwowski, M., Kaufman, J. C., Okada, T., Reiter-Palmon, R., & Gaggioli, A. (2023). Artificial Intelligence & Creativity: A manifesto for collaboration. *The Journal of Creative Behavior*, *57*(4), 472–484. Advance online publication. doi:10.1002/jocb.597

Wan, S., & Kaneko, T. (2017). Imitation Learning for Playing Shogi Based on Generative Adversarial Networks. *Proceedings of 2017 Conference on Technologies and Applications of Artificial Intelligence (TAAI)*, 92-95. 10.1109/TAAI.2017.17

Wu, Z., Ji, D., Yu, K., Zeng, X., Wu, D., & Shidujaman, M. (2021). AI creativity and the human-AI co-creation model. In Human-Computer Interaction. Theory, Methods and Tools: Thematic Area, HCI 2021 (pp. 171-190). Springer International Publishing. doi:10.1007/978-3-030-78462-1_13

Zhu, J. Y., Park, T., Isola, P., & Efros, A. A. (2017). Unpaired image-to-image translation using cycle-consistent adversarial networks. *Proceedings - IEEE International Conference on Computer Vision*, *2017*, 2223–2232. doi:10.1109/ICCV.2017.244

Chapter 2
Generative AI for Text to Image: A Comprehensive Survey

Shrishti Shah
Indian Institute of Information Technology, Nagpur, India

Shubhasri Tadepalli
Indian Institute of Information Technology, Nagpur, India

Lalitha Tanmai Vaddiparthi
Indian Institute of Information Technology, Nagpur, India

Nishat Afshan Ansari
Indian Institute of Information Technology, Nagpur, India

Ankit A. Bhurane
https://orcid.org/0000-0001-8181-7685
Visvesvaraya National Institute of Technology, Nagpur, India

ABSTRACT

Text-to-image (TTI) synthesis models represent a creative approach in the realm of artificial intelligence, specifically designed to transform textual input into visually realistic images. The essence of TTI generation lies in its ability to harness the power of language and convert it seamlessly into visually compelling content, showcasing creative image synthesis. Initially using GANs and transformers, text-to-image generation evolved with diffusion models introducing noise. Integration with large models, TTI models now produce results near-real images. Breakthroughs like ControlNet and 3D object synthesis redefine possibilities. Editing text or images adds versatile dimensions, showcasing generative technologies' transformative capabilities. The survey explores scaling TTI models, focusing on various descriptions and ControlNet's role. The authors categorize literature, offer nuanced comparisons, and discuss applications. Looking ahead, they foresee TTI's potential for productivity enhancements, especially in the Metaverse era, and expansion into intricate tasks like video and 3D generation.

DOI: 10.4018/979-8-3693-1950-5.ch002

INTRODUCTION

In the dynamic landscape of generative intelligence, the strides made in text-to-image synthesis are nothing short of extraordinary. Motivated by the remarkable progress in this domain, we embark on a journey to craft a survey that serves as a beginner-friendly guide to the evolution of Text-to-Image (TTI) models. This exploration unveils a universal narrative, connecting the past, present, and future of adversarial networks, with a special emphasis on the pioneering roles of generative adversarial networks (GANs) (Goodfellow, Pouget-Abadie, Mirza, Xu, Warde-Farley, Ozair, Courville, & Bengio, 2014) and diffusion models.

Our survey functions as an intellectual map, guiding readers through the intricate web of progress. From the foundational breakthroughs of StackGAN (Zhang et al., 2016) and DRAW (Gregor, Danihelka, Graves, Rezende, & Wierstra, 2015) to the revolutionary realms of DALL-E (Ramesh, Pavlov, Goh, Gray, Voss, Radford, Chen, & Sutskever, 2021) and Diffusion Models (Yang et al., 2022), each section unravels a pivotal moment in the transformative story of generative AI. The spotlight falls on the game-changing Denoising Diffusion Probabilistic Models (DDPM) and its influence on text-to-image synthesis, reshaping pixel and latent spaces through frameworks like GLIDE (Nichol, Dhariwal, Ramesh, Shyam, Mishkin, McGrew, Sutskever, & Chen, 2021), IMAGEN (Saharia et al., 2022), Stable Diffusion (Yang et al., 2022), and DALL-E 2 (Marcus et al., 2022).

Our journey began with the development of a transformative website, where generative AI breathed life into sketches based on text prompts, sparking our deep dive into the complexities of TTI models. This hands-on experience led to the birth of our comprehensive review. Here we used a hybrid generative AI model, ControlNet (Zhang, Rao, & Agrawala, 2023), combined with Stable Diffusion. This dynamic duo empowers the conversion of sketches and text prompts into cohesive and expressive images. This neural network architecture, adapting to large-scale text-to-image propagation patterns, wields previously learned algorithms to create a robust encoder. The versatility of ControlNet in accepting diverse inputs—from scribbles to edge maps, pose key points, and more—signifies its potential for widespread use in text-to-image linking.

Beyond image generation, our exploration extends to applications in 3D object synthesis, video generation, and image editing, promising limitless possibilities in the realm of creative AI. As we peer into the future, the survey delves into the limitations and potential improvements of Text-to-Image models, anticipating the emergence of AI-generated content and its impact on the metaverse. The chapter concludes with a comprehensive evaluation, inviting readers to join us on an exciting odyssey where each page unveils a new facet of generative AI, setting the stage for the metaverse era and beyond. Generative AI tools used in practice have also been described while concluding the chapter. In the rapidly evolving generative intelligence, the exponential growth is nothing short of astounding. Our aim is to provide a straightforward, beginner-friendly overview of the entire timeline across the TTI model evolution, through a variety of powerful models that are paving the way for advances in artificial intelligence.

1.1 Generative AI

Generative AI is a trending branch of artificial intelligence technology that can produce various types of content, including text, imagery, audio, and synthetic data. The current excitement around generative AI has been driven by the simplicity of new user interfaces for creating high-quality text, graphics, and videos making it easily adaptable .

Figure 1. Timeline of the text to image models

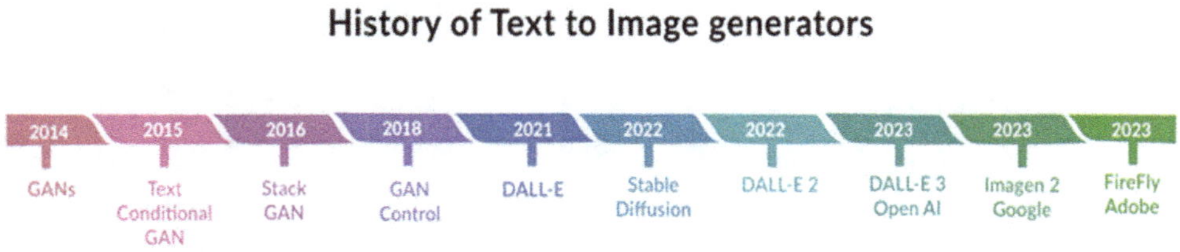

Generative AI was introduced in the 1960s in chatbots. But it was not until 2014, with the introduction of GAN, an algorithm that generative AI could create convincingly authentic images, videos, and audio of real people.

Generative AI has fostered collaboration between artificial intelligence and human artists. Many creators now use AI as a tool to augment their artistic processes, resulting in hybrid artworks that showcase the synergy between machine ingenuity and human creativity. In essence, generative AI's impact on creativity and art is profound, ushering in an era where technology and artistic expression converge seamlessly. Generative AI, particularly through advancements like GANs, has significantly excelled in the domain of text-to-image generation. Noteworthy for its creativity, it has achieved remarkable feats without direct applications. The ability to translate textual prompts into visually compelling images showcases the technology's inherent artistic capability (Bie et al., 2023).

HOW DOES GENERATIVE AI WORK IN TTI

Generative AI starts with a prompt that could be in the form of a text, an image, a design, a video or any input that the AI system can process. Specific AI algorithms then return new content in response to the given prompt and type. Content can include essays, solutions to problems, or realistic fakes created from pictures or audio of a person.

A timeline of Text-to-image generation models is shown in Figure 1 (AI, n.d.). Text-to-image generation involves models that process text input to produce high-fidelity images. This capability originated with GANs (Karras et al., 2018) and later evolved with 3 autoregressive Transformers. Diffusion models, characterized by introducing noises in repeated steps, have become a key player in image synthesis within TTI. These models aim to generate images based on text, requiring realistic and semantically accurate results. The challenge lies in handling high-dimensional image data distribution to produce visually convincing and contextually aligned images. Various frameworks and improvements have been proposed in the literature to enhance the realism, diversity, and semantic alignment of generated images. Evaluations of various generative models emphasize their distinctions in terms of visual authenticity, diversity, and alignment with textual descriptions. While being trained on input images, each model produces unique and distinct images, illustrating variations across different models

Their success has propelled TTI to the forefront of machine learning research. In the age of large models, scaling up model size and integrating with large language models have significantly enhanced TTI performance, generating results almost indistinguishable from real-world images (Caporusso, 2023).

Figure 2. Timeline of TTI model development

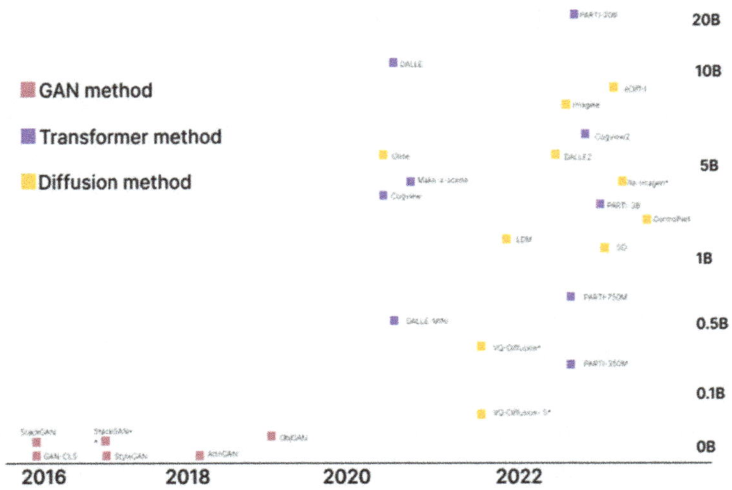

Figure 2 (Bie et al., 2023) expands on the timeline of TTI model development from Figure 1, providing a broader perspective with a richer array of models. This extended view, encompassing a variety of models, further emphasizes the growth and diversification within the field.

2.1 Few GAN Models in TTI

TTI stands out in machine learning by adeptly using diverse GAN models. This strategic integration empowers TTI to push the limits of large-scale models, achieving impressive results. The seamless synergy between TTI and GANs solidifies their leadership in the dynamic landscape of machine learning, generating outcomes that closely mimic real-world images.

2.1.1 Vanilla GAN

Vanilla GAN (Goodfellow, Pouget-Abadie, Mirza, Xu, Warde-Farley, Ozair, Courville, & Bengio, 2014) (see figure 3) is a term often used to refer to the original and basic form of a GAN. There are two kinds of models in the context of Supervised Learning, Generative and Discriminative Models.

The goal of Vanilla GAN is to generate new images through learning from the original image data. The model primarily consists of two parts, i.e. a generator that produces an image from noise z and a discriminator. which tries to distinguish between z and the true image x.

Generator - The generator's primary task is to create synthetic data that resembles real data. It takes random noise as input and generates data samples. The generator is typically implemented as a neural network that maps random noise vectors to data samples.

Discriminator - The discriminator's role is to distinguish between real data and fake data generated by the generator. It also takes the form of a neural network, but instead of generating data, it takes data samples as input and outputs a probability score indicating whether the input data is real or fake.

Figure 3. Basic architecture of GANs

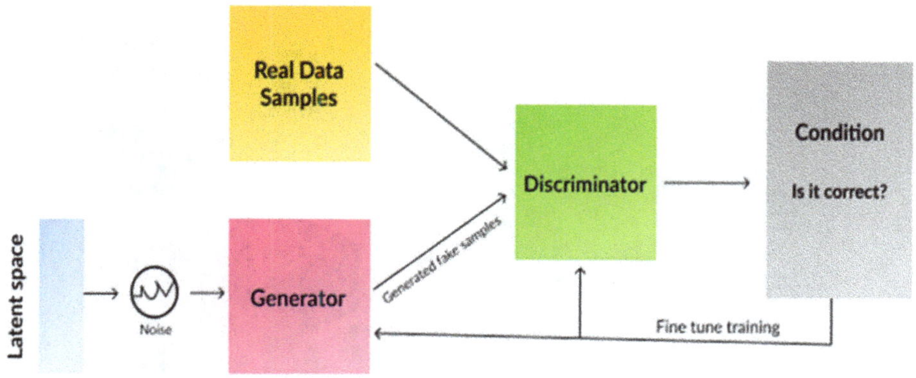

Non TTI models using GANs - Explore non-Text-to-Image (Elasri et al., 2022) applications of GANs, shedding light on the early understanding and utilization of these models. Noteworthy instances include models like StyleGAN (Karras et al., 2018), dedicated to crafting realistic images with customizable visual styles.

Another standout is CycleGAN (Zhu et al., 2017), specializing in unpaired image-to-image translation, allowing transformations between diverse domains without paired training examples. These models exemplify how GAN technology was initially harnessed for various creative applications, showcasing adaptability beyond text-centric tasks.

Cycle GAN - The Cycle Generative Adversarial Network, or CycleGAN (Zhu et al., 2017) is a type of generative adversarial network used for image-to-image translation tasks. The main idea behind CycleGAN is to learn a mapping between two different domains without requiring paired training data. CycleGAN is a methodology to train a deep convolutional neural network for image-to-image translation tasks. CycleGAN's notable strength is that it can produce remarkable results without the need for a paired dataset. It even works well for texture and color changes.

2.1.2 Style GAN

StyleGAN (Karras et al., 2018) is an extension of the GAN framework, developed by researchers at NVIDIA, particularly Tero Karras, Samuli Laine, and Timo Aila. It was introduced in 2018. It achieves this by introducing a 'style' component, which allows the model to separate the high-level features (content) and the low-level features (style) of an image. It uses an alternative generator architecture for generative adversarial networks, borrowing from style transfer literature; in particular, the use of adaptive instance normalization. One of the notable advantages of StyleGAN is its ability to generate highly realistic diverse images, making it a valuable tool for visual design. However, pose challenges for some applications due to its reliance on large-scale training data and computational resources.

2.1.3 StackGAN

StackGAN (Zhang et al., 2016) (see figure 4), which stands for 'Stacked Generative Adversarial Networks', is a generative model architecture designed for text-to-image synthesis. It is specifically developed

Figure 4. Architecture of StackGAN

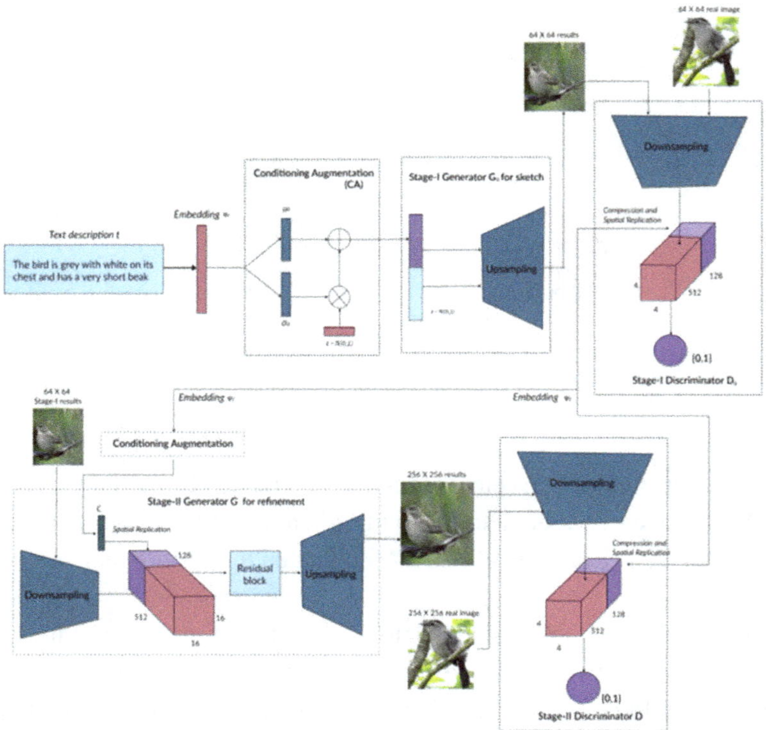

to generate high-resolution images from textual descriptions. To generate high-resolution images with photo-realistic details. It decomposes the text-to-image generative process into two stages:

Stage-I GAN: It sketches the primitive shape and fundamental colors of the object conditioned on the given text description, and draws the background layout from a random noise vector, yielding a low-resolution image.

Stage-II GAN: It addresses defects in the low-resolution image from Stage-I and completes the details of the object by reading the text description again, producing a high resolution photo-realistic image.

2.1.3.1 Practical Applications of StackGAN

- Generating high-resolution images automatically for entertainment purposes or educational purposes.
- Creating comics: With the use of a StackGAN, the process of creating comics can be reduced to days and assist in the creative process.

2.1.4 DRAW

DRAW (Gregor, Danihelka, Graves, Rezende, & Wierstra, 2015) (see figure 5), which stands for 'Deep Recurrent Attentive Writer', is a generative model designed for creating images from scratch based on a given textual description. A simplified explanation of how DRAW works is given below:

Figure 5. Architecture of DRAW

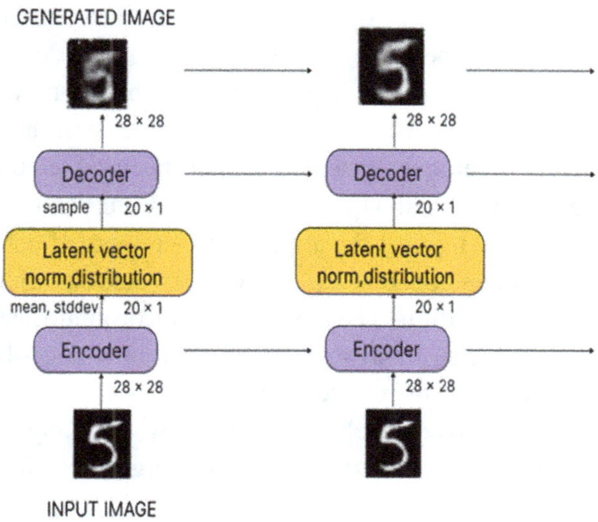

Encoder-Decoder Architecture- DRAW utilizes an encoder-decoder architecture, which is common in sequence-to-sequence models. The encoder processes the input data (in this case, textual descriptions) and produces a fixed-size representation, which is then fed into the decoder.

Recurrent Neural Network (RNN)- The core of DRAW involves the use of a recurrent neural network (RNN). RNNs are designed to handle sequential data, making them suitable for tasks involving sequences, such as generating images step by step.

Attention Mechanism- DRAW incorporates an attention mechanism, allowing the model to focus on different parts of the image as it generates it. This attention mechanism helps the model decide where to draw next.

Step-by-Step Generation- Instead of generating the entire image in one pass, DRAW generates the image step by step. At each step, the model decides where to place the next part of the image. This sequential generation process allows the model to refine its output over time.

Latent Variable- DRAW introduces a latent variable that serves as a sort of 'canvas' where the model can store information about what it has generated so far. This latent variable helps the model keep track of the drawing process.

Loss Function- The training of DRAW involves minimizing a loss function that measures the difference between the generated image and the target image. This loss function encourages the model to produce images that match the given textual descriptions.

DRAW has been influential in the development of generative models, and its architecture has inspired subsequent models that aim to improve the generation of images from textual descriptions, such as AlignDRAW (Mansimov, Parisotto, Ba, & Salakhutdinov, 2015) and StackGAN (Zhang et al., 2016). Each of these models introduces additional enhancements to address specific challenges in the image generation process.

2.1.5 AlignDRAW

Here is a general way to interpret the term 'AlignDRAW' (Mansimov, Parisotto, Ba, & Salakhutdinov, 2015) based on common themes in generative models:

Alignment Mechanism- The term 'Align' suggests that the model may have a particular focus on aligning the generated content with the textual descriptions. This could involve refining the attention mechanisms to better match the generated elements with the specified features in the text.

Improved Drawing Process- Similar to DRAW, AlignDRAW might involve a step-by-step drawing process, but with enhancements to improve the alignment of generated details with the given textual descriptions. This could lead to more coherent and contextually relevant image generation.

Latent Variables and Representation- The model might incorporate latent variables or representations to better capture the underlying structure and semantics of the images being generated, helping in aligning the generated content with the textual descriptions.

Loss Functions- Like other generative models, AlignDRAW would likely involve optimization through a loss function, encouraging the model to generate images that align well with the provided textual input.

2.2 Evolution Summary of GAN-Based Approach for Text to Image Synthesis

Before GANs, Mansimov et al. (2015) employed a recurrent neural network to create images from text captions. This approach focused on creating the image in multiple steps, akin to DRAW by Gregor (2015). Reed et al. (2016) later enhanced image generation by transitioning to a generative adversarial network rather than a recurrent variational auto-encoder (Zhang, Xu, Li, Zhang, Wang, Huang, & Metaxas, 2017). Progress was made over the next few years using various methods, which even led to modifying the generative model architecture. The work resulted in appreciable improvements in visual quality in comparison to the start. However, severe defects such as incorrect item placement, object deformation, or an unnatural blending of foreground and background elements still occur in some examples (Ramesh, Pavlov, Goh, Gray, Voss, Radford, Chen, & Sutskever, 2021). Constructing image pixels from text human written descriptions is an intricating undertake. To tackle this challenge, it is crucial to grasp the process of learning text feature representations that encapsulate visual details and leverage these features to create images with sufficient realism to deceive human observers. Image generation using GANs (Goodfellow, Pouget-Abadie, Mirza, Xu, Warde-Farley, Ozair, Courville, & Bengio, 2014) (see figure 3). The GANs consist of a generator and a discriminator that play the minimax game. This minimax game helps them by challenging each other and, thus, training them to be able to generate better images. At first, the samples are not good and are rejected with confidence by the discriminator, the generator trains itself to be better over time. The generator aims to produce realistic images from textual descriptions, adapting over time through training. The discriminator distinguishes between real and generated data, contributing to the model's refinement.

Several models, including DRAW (Mansimov, Parisotto, Ba, & Salakhutdinov, 2015) (see figure 5), AlignDRAW (Mansimov, Parisotto, Ba, & Salakhutdinov, 2015), and StackGAN (Zhang et al., 2016), StackGAN2 (Zhang, Xu, Li, Zhang, Wang, Huang, & Metaxas, 2017), have been proposed to address the complexity of creating images from textual descriptions. AlignDRAW (Mansimov, Parisotto, Ba, & Salakhutdinov, 2015) utilizes a soft attention method, while StackGAN (Zhang et al., 2016) introduces stacked generators to break down the task into manageable subproblems. Stage-I GAN creates a low-resolution image by first sketching the basic shape and colors of the item based on the text description provided and then laying out the backdrop using a random noise vector.

The CLIP-guided Generative Latent Space Search (CLIP-GLaSS) (Radford et al., 2021) framework combines CLIP (Radford et al., 2021) with a generative network to produce high-quality images matching target captions.Experimental results using StyleGAN2 (Zhang, Xu, Li, Zhang, Wang, Huang, & Metaxas, 2017) and generator GPT2 (GPT-2,) indicate promising potential, prompting a call for further comparative research in the burgeoning field of text-to-image synthesis.

The evolution of text-to-image generation has seen advancements through various models, notably GANs (Goodfellow, Pouget-Abadie, Mirza, Xu, Warde-Farley, Ozair, Courville, & Bengio, 2014) and autoregressive transformers. Diffusion models, introduced for image synthesis, have become crucial in this domain. Despite improvements in visual quality since earlier approaches, challenges like object deformation persist.

2.3 Large Model With Autoregressive Model

Transitioning into the discussion of large models with autoregressive components, DALL-E emerges as a recent standout. DALL-E leverages a discrete variational autoencoder (dVAE) for efficient image compression and employs byte pair encoding (BPE) to handle text, integrating these components into a decoder-only autoregressive Transformer.

2.3.1 DALL-E

DALLE (Ramesh, Pavlov, Goh, Gray, Voss, Radford, Chen, & Sutskever, 2021) is one of the latest text-to-image models that achieves impressive results with large models and datasets. The first stage involves training a discrete variational autoencoder (dVAE) that maps an image into 32 × 32 tokens where each grid has 8192 possible values. This is able to compress the 256 × 256 image data into a much smaller dimension with only slight information loss. In the next stage, text is encoded with byte pair encoding (BPE) to tokens of size 256, and concatenated with image tokens. The new tokens are then fed into a decoder-only autoregressive Transformer to compute text-image joint distribution. This Transformer consists of 64 self-attention layers with a casual mask for text attention and either row, column or convolution mask for spatial image attention.

2.4 Diffusion Models

Diffusion models are a cutting-edge category of generative models, they have become prominent for generating high-resolution images. While DALL-E and diffusion models operate within the broader domain of generative models, they represent distinct approaches to the task of text-to-image synthesis.

Diffusion models (Yang et al., 2022) (see figure 6), a cutting-edge category of generative models, have gained prominence for producing high-resolution images. Sohl-Dickstein et al. (2015) introduced the denoising diffusion technique, leveraging iterative forward and reverse diffusion processes inspired by non-equilibrium statistical physics.

In diffusion models, each time step corresponds to a level of noise, and the signal-to-noise ratio evolves as the model iteratively samples from the data distribution. The diffusion process creates a Markov chain

Figure 6. Architecture of stable diffusion

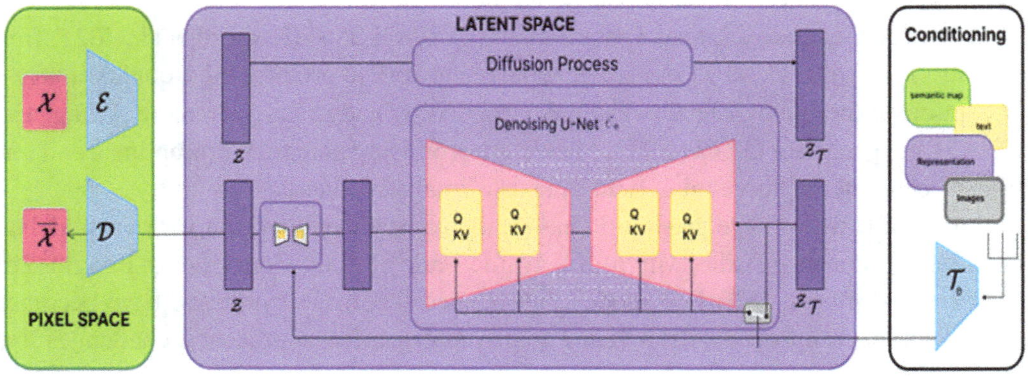

of latent variables, gradually adding Gaussian noise (Verma et al., 2023) to a sample from the data distribution. The posterior distribution is well-defined if the noise magnitude at each step is sufficiently large.

Diffusion models demonstrate favorable inductive biases for image data, achieving notable results through a weighted variational bound. Ho et al. (2020) proposed a connection between diffusion models and denoising score matching, leading to a reduced, weighted variational bound objective. Denoising Diffusion Probabilistic Models (DDPM) and Denoising Diffusion Implicit Models (DDIM) present attractive choices for generative modeling, providing log-likelihoods, high-quality samples, and efficient sampling.

Guided Language to Image Diffusion for Generation and Editing (GLIDE) (Nichol, Dhariwal, Ramesh, Shyam, Mishkin, McGrew, Sutskever, & Chen, 2021), introduced by Nichol et al., utilizes classifier-free guidance to generate realistic images based on text prompts. GLIDE outperforms classifier-free guidance in prompt matching and achieves competitive FID on MS-COCO (Lin et al., 2014) without explicit training on the dataset. Various recent papers, including those from OpenAI, Nvidia, and Google, have further improved diffusion models, with open-source tools like GLIDE (Nichol, Dhariwal, Ramesh, Shyam, Mishkin, McGrew, Sutskever, & Chen, 2021), DALLE-2 (Marcus et al., 2022), and Imagen (Saharia et al., 2022) showcasing the versatility of diffusion-based designs.

2.4.1 Background on Diffusion Model

The purpose of the DM study is to preserve the interaction of information with noise, that is, the diffusion process, for the design. Introduced in 2020 as a significant undertaking, the Denoising Diffusion Probabilistic Model (DDPM) (Ho, Jain, & Abbeel, 2020) has since ignited a rapidly growing interest within the generative models community. This overview aims to present a comprehensive introduction to DDPM, encompassing pertinent advancements preceding its development and elucidating the workings of unconditional DDPM through the lens of image synthesis using a concrete example.

Diffusion Probabilistic Models (DPM) - DPM (Sohl-Dickstein, Weiss, Maheswaranathan, & Ganguli, 2015) defines a forward (inference) process that converts a complex data distribution into a simpler one. The model then learns the mapping by reversing this diffusion process. Experimental results on multiple datasets show the effectiveness of DPM when estimating complex data distribution. DPM can be viewed as the foundation of DDPM (Ho, Jain, & Abbeel, 2020), while DDPM (Ho, Jain, & Abbeel, 2020) optimizes DPM with improved implementations.

Score-based Generative model(SGM) - SGM (Song & Ermon, 2019) introduced to perturb the data with random Gaussian noise of various magnitudes. With the gradient of log probability density as a score function, SGM generates the samples toward decreasing noise levels and trains the model by estimating the score functions for noisy data distribution.

How Does DDPM Work for Image Synthesis?

DDPM (Ho, Jain, & Abbeel, 2020) operates for image synthesis by functioning as a parameterized Markov chain, specifically designed to generate images through a series of finite transitions during the inference process. In the training phase, DDPM learns the transition kernels by perturbing natural images with noise in a reversed direction. This involves the addition of noise to the data at each step, and the optimization target is set to estimate and refine the parameters associated with this noise. In essence, DDPM leverages a parameterized Markov chain and a reverse transition process during training to effectively generate images by incorporating noise in a controlled manner.

SGM shares a similar optimization objective with DDPM during training, which is also discussed in Ho et al. (2020) that the DDPM under a certain parameterization is equivalent to SGM during training.

2.5 Types of Text-to-Image Diffusion Models

In this section, we present new text-to-image functions based on the diffusion model and classify them according to the pre-diffusion position (pixel position or latent position). The first group of methods directly produces high-dimensional pixel-level images, such as GLIDE (Nichol, Dhariwal, Ramesh, Shyam, Mishkin, McGrew, Sutskever, & Chen, 2021) and Imagen (Saharia et al., 2022). Alternatively, another set of methods compresses the image into a low-resolution image before training the diffusion model. Methods representing this latent space include constant variance (Yang et al., 2022), VQ diffusion, and DALL-E 2 (Marcus et al., 2022).

2.5.1 Frameworks in Pixel Space

GLIDE - Essentially, text to image is text conditional image synthesis. Therefore, it is intuitive to replace text in the DM category with text so that the design is text-based. Directional diffusion improves the accuracy of models in DM cases, and diffusion-free transitions help resolve free forms. Inspired by this, GLIDE (Nichol, Dhariwal, Ramesh, Shyam, Mishkin, McGrew, Sutskever, & Chen, 2021) adopts unclassified expressions in TTI by replacing the initial category names with text. GLIDE also learned the CLIP (Radford et al., 2021) grid, but for real-time image models and similar sentences, the grid was not well classified by human observers. The encoder, a key element in its framework, is configured as a 24-bit and 2048 wide (approximately 1.2B buffer) converter. Experimental results show that GLIDE outperforms DALL-E (Ramesh, Pavlov, Goh, Gray, Voss, Radford, Chen, & Sutskever, 2021) in FID and human evaluation.

IMAGEN - Imagen (Saharia et al., 2022) uses random instructions to generate images based on GLIDE. The main difference between GLIDE and Imagen is their choice of encoder. More specifically, GLIDE trains a text encoder with a pre-differentiated set of image data, while Imagen uses a large number of pre-learned and frozen text encoders. Freezing the weight of the pre-trained encoder facilitates offline text embedding, thus reducing the unnecessary burden of pre-learning the text-to-image distribution online. Additionally, text encoders can be prespecified in display devices (e.g., CLIP) or text-only (e.g., BERT, GPT, and T5). Text-only corpora are much larger than image text files and expose large language structures to rich and detailed text. For example, the read-only memory used in BERT is approximately 20 GB, and the read-only memory used in T5 is approximately 800 GB. Using different T5-based encoders, we show that the size of the word pattern improves image accuracy and image-text alignment more than the size of the propagation pattern in Imagen.

2.5.2 Frameworks in Latent Space

Stable diffusion - A representative framework that trains the diffusion models on latent space is Stable Diffusion (Yang et al., 2022), which is a scaled-up version of Latent Diffusion Model (LDM) (Rauniyar et al., 2023). In the footsteps of DALL-E, which utilizes a VQ-VAE to acquire a visual codebook, Stable Diffusion takes a step further by employing VQ-GAN for the initial stage's latent representation. Significantly, VQ-GAN enhances the capabilities of VQ-VAE by incorporating an adversarial objective, thereby amplifying the naturalness of the generated images. With the pretrained VAE, stable diffusion reverses a forward diffusion process that perturbs latent space with noise. Stable diffusion also introduces cross-attention as general-purpose conditioning for various condition signals like text.Experimental results demonstrate the superior performance of variable modeling in latent space compared to pixel space, revealing advantages in reducing complexity and preserving details. A related study on VQ diffusion was conducted using the mask-post-conversion technique. Similar to the observations in the pixel space method, the use of non-discrete aspects proves a significant improvement in the text-to-image propagation model in latent space.

Stable Diffusion is a latent text-to-image diffusion model capable of generating photo-realistic images given any text input. Stable Diffusion is a text-to-image model created by a collaboration between engineers and researchers from CompVis, Stability AI, and LAION.

The Variational Autoencoder (VAE) neural network has two parts: (i) an encoder and (ii) a decoder. The encoder compresses an image to a lower dimensional representation in the latent space. The decoder restores the image from the latent space.

The latent space of the Stable Diffusion model is 4x64x64, 48 times smaller than the image pixel space. All the forward and reverse diffusions we talked about are actually done in the latent space. So

Figure 7. Architecture of Dall-E2

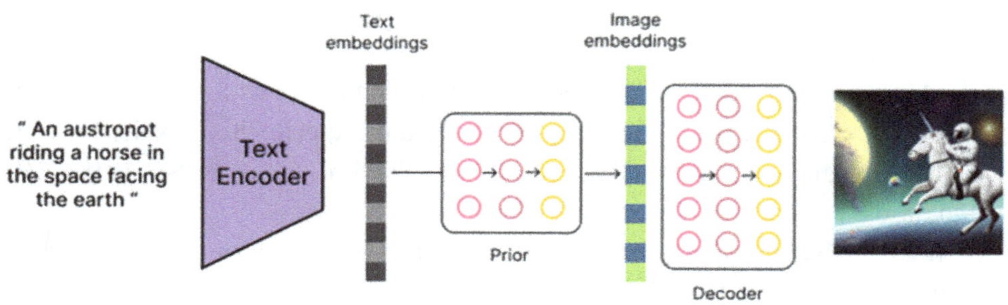

during training, instead of generating a noisy image, it generates a random tensor in latent space (latent noise). Instead of corrupting an image with noise, it corrupts the representation of the image in latent space with the latent noise.

Dall-E2 (Text-conditional Image generation): a multimodal latent space (Marcus et al., 2022)- DALL-E 2(see figure 7) is a state-of-the-art AI-powered image-generating platform created by OpenAI. It is the advanced and improved successor of DALL-E (Ramesh, Pavlov, Goh, Gray, Voss, Radford, Chen, & Sutskever, 2021). It can produce incredibly realistic and detailed pictures based on textual descriptions by utilizing deep learning techniques.

Uses of Dall-E2

- Can create original realistic images and art from text description. it can combine concepts, attributes and styles.
- Generating image variations.
- Language guided image manipulations
- Generating image interpolations.
- Can make realistic edits to existing images from a natural language caption. It can add and remove elements while taking shadows, reflections and textures into account.

Architecture of Dall-E2 - In this study, a fusion of two methodologies is employed to address the challenge of text-conditional image generation. Initially, a diffusion decoder is trained to reverse the image encoding process implemented by the CLIP model. The inversion process performed by our decoder is non-deterministic, enabling the generation of multiple images associated with a specific image embedding.

CLIP Training Process- In this phase, the model undergoes training to create a joint representation space for both text and images. This means that CLIP learns to associate text descriptions with corresponding images, essentially understanding the relationships between them.

Text-to-Image Generation Stage

Text Input- The process of generating images from text captions begins by providing a text caption as input.

CLIP Text Embedding- The input text caption is converted into a CLIP text embedding. This embedding captures the meaning and style of the text description. Importantly, the CLIP model, which is pretrained and has learned this shared representation space, is used to perform this conversion.

Prior Model (Autoregressive or Diffusion)- The CLIP text embedding is then fed into a prior model. This prior model can either be autoregressive or diffusion-based. The prior's role is to generate an image embedding based on the CLIP text embedding. This image embedding is a numerical representation that encodes the information needed to create an image that aligns with the text's content and style.

Image Embedding- The prior successfully produces the image embedding, which represents the desired image content and style guided by the input text.

Diffusion Decoder- The image embedding is used to condition a diffusion decoder. The diffusion decoder is responsible for taking this embedding and transforming it into the final image. The decoder generates pixel-level details and overall image structure based on the information contained in the image embedding.

Figure 8. On the COCO benchmark, Imagen currently achieved the best (lowest) zero-shot FID score of 7.27, outperforming DALL·E 2 with a 10.39 FID score

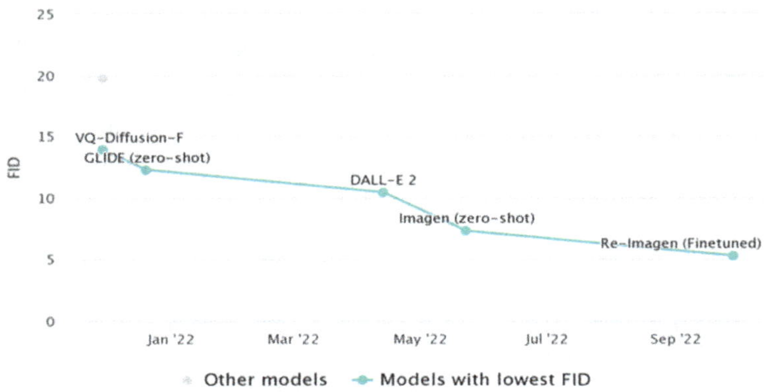

2.6 Evolution Summary of Diffusion Models in the Context of Text-to-Image Synthesis

An overview of diffusion models in the context of text-to-image synthesis, highlighting their significance in generating high-resolution images. Initially developed by Sohl-Dickstein et al (2015), diffusion models simulate a random walk, gradually removing structure from a data distribution and then recovering it, offering adaptability and manageability.

In diffusion models, sampling involves reversing a slow noise process, where each time step corresponds to different noise levels. Sohl-Dickstein et al. (2015) proposed probabilistic models that reverse a multi-step noise process to fit a data distribution. Ho et al. (2020) introduced a connection between diffusion models and denoising score matching, resulting in a reduced variational bound objective. The models create a Markov chain of latent variables, gradually adding Gaussian noise to the data distribution sample (Nichol, Dhariwal, Ramesh, Shyam, Mishkin, McGrew, Sutskever, & Chen, 2021).

The important thing is that this model gives good results in terms of log similarity, quality and model speed. The Denoising Diffusion Probability Model (DDPM) and the Denoising Diffusion Implicit Model (DDIM) have been shown to be good choices for modeling; DDIM can produce the best model.

Guide to Distribution Images (GLIDE) (Nichol, Dhariwal, Ramesh, Shyam, Mishkin, McGrew, Sutskever, & Chen, 2021) is a different type of propagation model for creating and manipulating, that has non-discrete expression, can extend to a variety of formats, and can create images with shadows, reflections, and real images. different textures. GLIDE outperforms distribution-free guidance of match marks and achieves the match FID of MS-COCO (Lin et al., 2014) without specifying data. The paper concludes by touching on the latest developments(see figure 8) in modeling offered by OpenAI, Nvidia and Google, and citing open source tools such as GLIDE, DALLE-2 (Marcus et al., 2022) and Imagen (Saharia et al., 2022) as examples of different models.

Figure 9. ControlNet allows users to add conditions like Canny edges (top), human pose (bottom), etc., to control the image generation of large pretrained diffusion models. The default results use the prompt 'a high-quality, detailed, and professional image'. Users can optionally give prompts like 'an astronaut on the moon'.

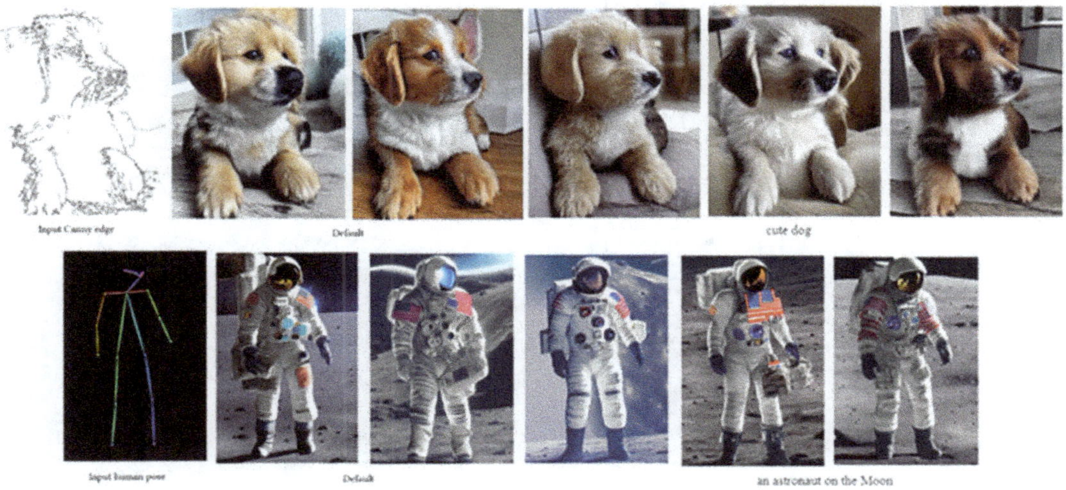

2.7 ControlNet

ControlNet (Zhang, Rao, & Agrawala, 2023) innovatively stabilizes diffusion models by introducing learned conditions, enhancing control in text-to-image synthesis. The incorporation of controlled conditions allows fine-tuning, addressing specific challenges and advancing customization. This adaptive mechanism contributes significantly to generative AI, promising tailored image synthesis. ControlNet stands out, offering researchers refined tools for high-quality image synthesis from textual inputs.

Many of us have experienced flashes of visual inspiration that we wish to capture in a unique image. With the advent of text-to-image diffusion models (Midjourney, 2023; Open, 2023; Rombach et al., 2022), we can now create visually stunning images by typing in a text prompt.

ControlNet (see figure 9) is a neural network that controls a pre-trained image Diffusion model (e.g. Stable Diffusion). Its function is to allow input of a conditioning image, which can then be used to manipulate the image generation.

The original model and trainable copy are connected via 'zero convolution' layers that eliminate harmful noise during training. Researchers verify that ControlNet can effectively control Stable Diffusion with single or multiple conditions, with or without prompts. On diverse conditioning datasets, the ControlNet structure demonstrates versatility, indicating its potential applicability to a wider range of conditions and its facilitation of relevant applications.

2.7.1 What Does Control Net Do?

The combination of ControlNet and Stable Diffusion enables Stable Diffusion to take in a condition input that guides the image generation process, resulting in enhanced performance of Stable Diffusion.

Figure 10. Architecture of ControlNet

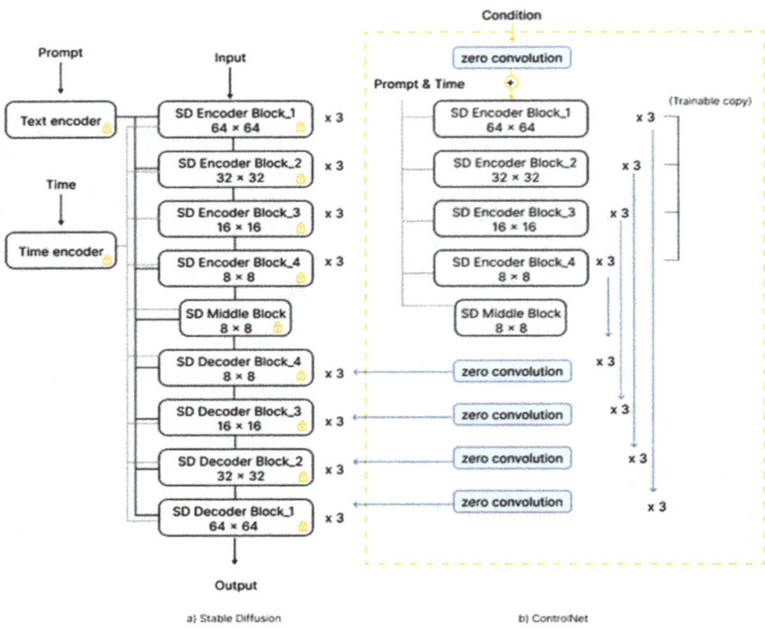

It can accept scribbles, edge maps, pose key points, depth maps, segmentation maps, normal maps, etc., as the condition input to guide the content of the generated image.

ControlNet is a neural network structure to control diffusion models by adding extra conditions. It copies the weights of neural network blocks into a 'locked' copy and a 'trainable' copy. The 'trainable' one learns your condition. The locked one preserves your model. ControlNet locks the production ready large diffusion models, and reuses their deep and robust encoding layers pretrained with billions of images as a strong backbone to learn a diverse set of conditional controls.

2.7.2 Architecture of ControlNet

Training with a small dataset of image pairs will not destroy the production-ready diffusion models. The zero convolution is 1×1 convolution with both weight and bias initialized as zeros. The neural architecture is connected with zero convolutions' that progressively grow the parameters from zero and ensure that no harmful noise could affect the finetuning.

Additionally, there are other notable models, such as PTIT (Wang, Zhang, Zhang et al, 2022), Sketch-Guided Diffusion (Voynov et al., 2022), and Taming Transformers (Esser et al., 2021), which further contribute to the overall landscape of image generation.

EVALUATION METRICS AND COMPARISON OF EXISTING METHODS

Evaluating the performance of text-to-image models (Bie et al., 2023) (see Table 1)is challenging due to the complexity of defining good images, encompassing visual realism, and diversity. Beyond realism, semantic alignment between generated images and text descriptions is crucial. Evaluation metrics such as Inception Score (IS) and Fréchet Inception Distance (FID) have been utilized for model comparison. The study emphasizes the importance of access to fair automatic evaluation criteria for comprehensive assessment and improvement measurement in text-to-image synthesis.

Inception Score (Barratt & Sharma, 2018) - The Inception Score is an algorithm designed for assessing the effectiveness of image generative models. This metric demonstrates a strong correlation with human evaluations regarding the realism of generated images. The underlying mechanism involves utilizing an Inception v3 network, which has been pre-trained on the extensive ImageNet dataset. In essence, the Inception Score contributes a nuanced and data-driven approach to evaluating the performance of image generative models, bridging the gap between computational assessments and human subjective judgments.

$$IS(G) = \exp(E_{x\sim}p_g\, D_{KL}(p(y|x) \,||\, p(y)) \text{ (i)}$$

In Eqn (i), $x_{\sim}p_g$ indicates that x is an image sampled from p_g, $D_{KL}(p||q)$ is the KL-divergence between the distributions p and q, p(y|x) is the conditional class distribution, $E_{x\sim}p_g$ denotes the expectation (average) over samples *x* drawn from the distribution $p_{g.}$ The exponential function in the Eqn (i) is introduced for ease of comparison, and for simplicity, we will consider ln(IS(G)) without loss of generality.

$$p(y) = \int_x p(y|x)p_g(x) \text{ (ii)}$$

Eqn (ii) denotes the marginal class distribution.

For effective text-to-image synthesis, generated images must exhibit clarity, avoiding blurriness. The Inception Network should express high confidence in a single object's presence (low p(y|x)).

Diversity across ImageNet classes is vital, reflected by a high p(y). The resulting large KL-divergence ensures distinct distributions, contributing to a high Inception Score (IS).

FID (Heusel et al., 2017) - Frechet Inception Distance (FID) stands out as a prominent quantitative metric in the realm of image generation, particularly in evaluating the performance of generative models. Introduced by Heusel et al. in 2017, FID calculates the Frechet distance between feature vectors of synthetic and real-world images. The primary goal when using FID as a metric is to achieve a low score, indicative of high-quality generated images that closely resemble real ones. Maintaining a balance is essential to ensure that the pursuit of a low FID score does not inadvertently sacrifice the diversity and richness required in the generated dataset.

3.1 Comparison of Text-to-Image (TTI) Models

While all models achieve satisfactory quality, nuances in performance become evident upon closer examination. For example, early diffusion model GLIDE exhibits occasional information loss, resulting in misalignment with text prompts. In contrast, models like DALLE-2 (Marcus et al., 2022), Stable-Diffusion (Yang et al., 2022), and GALIP showcase exceptional detailing and color rendition, although some outputs may feature blurred objects or unrealistic scenes. Notably, Stable-Diffusion and GALIP face challenges when synthesizing images with faces. Overall, the comparison highlights the progress in TTI models, with GAN TTI models showing promise for future applications due to their compact model size and computational efficiency.

Table 1. Comparison of the text to image methods

Method	Data Size	IS Evaluation	FID Evaluation	Model Size
AttnGAN (Xu et al., 2017)	120K	20.80	35.49 *	13M
StyleGAN (Karras et al., 2018)	120K	20.80	35.49 *	-
Obj-GAN (Li et al., 2019)	120K	24.09	36.52 *	34M
Control-GAN (Shoshan et al., 2021)	120K	23.61	33.10 *	-
GigaGAN (Kang et al., 2023)	-	-	10.24	650M
GALIP (Tao et al., 2023)	3M-12M	-	12.54	240M
DALLE (Ramesh, Pavlov, Goh, Gray, Voss, Radford, Chen, & Sutskever, 2021)	250M	-	27.5	12B
Cogview (Ding et al., 2021)	300M	-	27.1	4B
Make-A-Scene (Gafni et al., 2022)	35M	-	11.84	4B
GLIDE (Nichol, Dhariwal, Ramesh, Shyam, Mishkin, McGrew, Sutskever, & Chen, 2021)	250M	-	12.24	5B
VQ-diffusion-F	>7M	-	13.86*	370M
DALLE-2 (Marcus et al., 2022)	250M	-	10.39	5.2B
Imagen (Saharia et al., 2022)	~860M	-	7.27	7.6B
LDM (Rombach, Blattmann, Lorenz, Esser, & Ommer, 2021)	400M	30.29	12.63	1.45B
Shift Diffusion (Rombach, Blattmann, Lorenz, Esser, & Ommer, 2021)	900M	-	10.88	-
Re-Imagen (Chen et al., 2022)	50M	-	6.88	~8B
ControlNet (Zhang, Rao, & Agrawala, 2023)	-	-	-	~2.2B

*: no zero-shot results found, use standard results instead.

Figure 11. Different models working for the same prompt

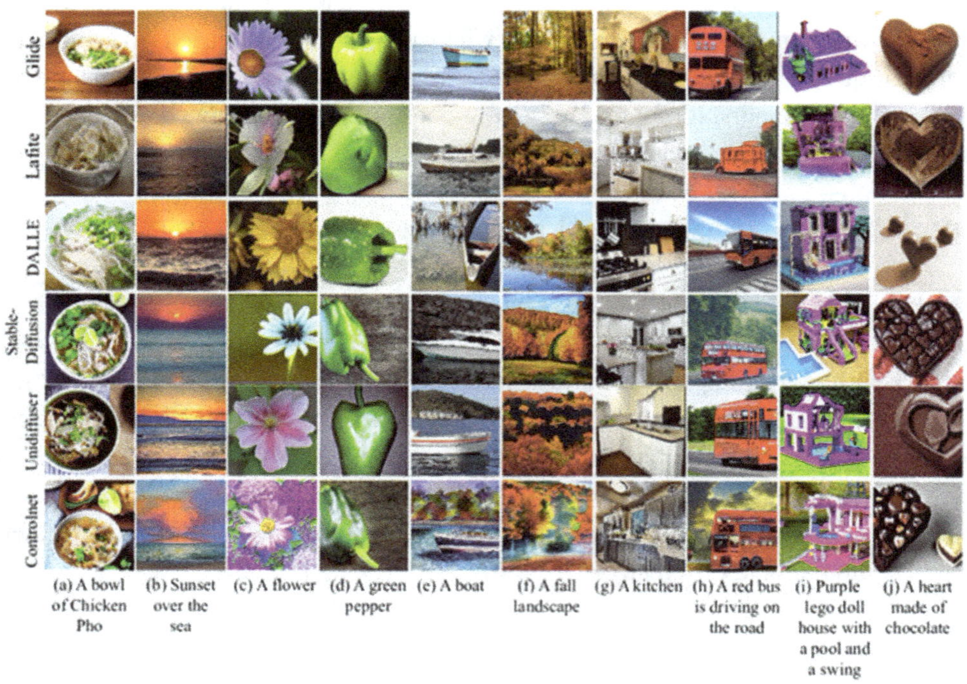

APPLICATIONS BEYOND TEXT-TO-IMAGE GENERATION

4.1 Text-Guided Creative Generation

4.1.1 Visual Art Generation

The text explores advancements in generative art, highlighting techniques like Multimodal Guided Artwork Diffusion (MGAD) (Huang, Tang, Dong et al, 2022) and DiffStyler (Huang, Zhang, Tang et al, 2022), which refine the generative process through multimodal guidance and dual diffusion models. Other approaches focus on creativity improvement through textual conditions and retraining models with datasets like Wikiart. Methods for personalized text-to-image generation, extension to Scalable Vector Graphics (SVGs), and efficient computation using retrieval-augmented diffusion models. Additionally, fine-grained style features are addressed with supervised and self-style guidance methods, contributing to the generation of diverse and high-quality digital artworks.

4.1.2 3D Generation

The text discusses advancements in 3D object synthesis, emphasizing the increased complexity compared to 2D image synthesis. DeepFusion (Li, Yu, Meng et al, 2022) is highlighted as the first successful application of diffusion models to 3D object synthesis, utilizing a randomly initialized NeRF (Mildenhall et al., 2020) with distillation from a pre-trained 2D diffusion model. However, Magic3D (Lin et al., 2022) criticizes DeepFusion for low-resolution image supervision and slow optimization of NeRF, proposing a coarse-to-fine optimization strategy for higher resolution results. Magic3D accelerates the process with a sparse 3D hash grid structure. Another approach, 3DDesigner (Li, Zheng, Wang et al, 2022), addresses cross-view consistency in 3D object generation. Using low-resolution NeRF-based conditions as priors, a two-stream asynchronous diffusion module enhances consistency, resulting in 360-degree consistent outcomes.

4.1.3 Video Generation and Story Visualization

In the realm of text-to-video diffusion models, two notable pioneering works have emerged: Make-A-Video (Singer, Polyak, Hayes, Yin, An, Zhang, & Hu, 2022) and Video Imagen (Singer, Polyak, Hayes, Yin, An, Zhang, & Hu, 2022), each introducing innovative approaches to advance the field. Make-A-Video takes a groundbreaking approach by adapting pre-trained text-to-image diffusion models to the text-to-video context. This adaptation involves integrating temporal information into the existing models. To enhance visual quality, the method further incorporates spatial super-resolution models and frame interpolation models. Notably, Make-A-Video achieves high-quality video generation through the integration of these additional components. Additionally, the method employs pre-trained text-to-image models and utilizes unsupervised learning on video data, enabling accelerated training of a text-to-video model without the dependency on paired text-video datasets. On the other hand, Video Imagen (Singer, Polyak, Hayes, Yin, An, Zhang, & Hu, 2022) takes a different route by extending an existing video diffusion model to the text-to-video domain. This approach leverages insights from recent advancements in text-to-image generation, highlighting the transferability of findings from text-to-image to text-to-video tasks. Furthermore, Video Imagen underscores the bidirectional relationship between video diffusion models and general diffusion models.

Collectively, these pioneering works, Make-A-Video and Video Imagen, contribute novel methodologies to the evolving landscape of text-to-video generation, showcasing advancements in model design, training efficiency, and the transferability of insights across related domains.

4.2 Text-Guided Image Editing

4.2.1 General Image Editing

DiffusionCLIP (Choi et al., 2023) pioneers the integration of diffusion models (DM) to address image inversion challenges. It utilizes a pre-trained DM to convert input images to the latent space and then fine-tunes it with a loss comprising a local directional CLIP (Radford et al., 2021) loss and an identity loss, achieving superior performance for in-domain and out-of-domain manipulations. LDEdit (Chandramouli & Gandikota, 2022) avoids fine-tuning by combining deterministic forward diffusion in the latent space with a reverse process conditioned on the target text, showcasing a versatile image editing framework. Prompt-to-Prompt introduces a cross-attention map during diffusion, enhancing the relation between image pixels and text prompts to ensure consistent output for modified text prompts. DiffusionIT (Ho, Jain, & Abbeel, 2020) presents an unsupervised image translation method that disentangles style and content representation. CycleDiffusion (Wu, 2022) reformulates the latent space of diffusion models, unifying them with GANs for guided generation. Direct Inversion encodes images to corresponding noise vectors and generates edited images without optimization or fine tuning. EDICT (Wallace et al., 2022) maintains coupled noise vectors for improved inversion quality, while Null-text Inversion optimizes DDIM inversion for high-fidelity editing results in real images by addressing error accumulation issues.

4.2.2 Image Editing With Masks

Addressing the challenge of local (masked) image editing, Blended Diffusion (Avrahami et al., 2021) leverages a pre-trained CLIP (Radford et al., 2021) model and integrates two loss terms to align the masked image with a text caption while maintaining coherence in the unmasked region. This approach spatially blends the noisy image with local text-guided diffusion in a progressive manner, ensuring a seamless transition between the edited and original content. The integration of LDM significantly speeds up localized text-driven image editing, especially when considering a multi-stage variant designed for super high-resolution settings. It's essential to emphasize that the application of these techniques necessitates the use of manually crafted masks for precise and targeted editing.

Conversely, DiffEdit (Couairon et al., 2022) presents an innovative approach to mask generation by automatically leveraging the disparity in noise estimates between the query and reference text conditions. This process is automatic and relies on discerning the differences in noise estimates between the query and reference text conditions. By leveraging these disparities, DiffEdit (Couairon et al., 2022) is able to infer masks that precisely identify the regions of interest in the image.This automated mask-generation process streamlines the editing workflow and eliminates the necessity for manually specifying masks, enhancing efficiency and user convenience.

4.2.3 Model Training With a Single Image

The Single Denoising Diffusion Models (SinDDM) (Singer, Polyak, Hayes, Yin, An, Zhang, & Hu, 2022) introduce a hierarchical diffusion model inspired by the multi-scale SinGAN (Wang, Bao, Zhou, Chen, Chen, Yuan, & Li, 2022). This innovative model is constructed with a convolutional denoiser that undergoes training on a variety of image scales, each intentionally corrupted by multiple levels of noise. Unlike SDEdit (Meng et al., 2021), SinDDM exhibits the capability to generate images with diverse dimensions. In contrast, the Single-image Diffusion Model (SinDiffusion) (Wang, Bao, Zhou, Chen, Chen, Yuan, & Li, 2022) takes a different approach by training on a single image at a single scale, thus avoiding error accumulation. Furthermore, SinDiffusion introduces a novel patch-level receptive field mechanism. This design choice encourages the model to learn patch statistics instead of memorizing the entire image, a strategic departure from conventional diffusion models that contributes to improved performance and efficiency. In a distinct strategy, UniTune refines a pre-trained large text-to-image diffusion model (e.g., Imagen [Saharia et al., 2022]) on a single image, as opposed to training the model from scratch. This fine-tuning process capitalizes on the wealth of knowledge embedded in pre-existing models, allowing for efficient adaptation to specific images.

4.2.4 3D Object Editing

The methodology employed by 3DDesigner (Li, Zheng, Wang et al, 2022) involves a meticulous process to generate corresponding text embeddings. This method generates a corresponding text embedding through a two-step process. Initially, it acquires blended noises using 2D local editing, and subsequently maps these blended noises to a view-independent text embedding space. The subsequent step enables the generation of comprehensive 360-degree results based on the acquired text embedding. On a different note, DATID-3D (Kim & Chun, 2022) focuses on text-guided domain adaptation of 3D objects, addressing three key limitations: catastrophic diversity loss, inferior text-image correspondence, and poor image quality. To address these challenges, DATID-3D adopts a multi-step strategy. Initially, it leverages diffusion models to obtain a diverse set of pose-aware target images. The obtained images are then rectified using an improved CLIP (Radford et al., 2021) and filtering process. When evaluated against the state-of-the-art 3D generator, EG3D (Chan et al., 2021), DATID-3D demonstrates its effectiveness by achieving high-resolution target results.

4.3 Generative AI in the Metaverse

Generative AI emerges as a transformative force within the metaverse (Lv, 2022), a collective virtual realm amalgamating augmented reality (AR), virtual reality (VR), and the internet. Within this expansive digital landscape, Generative AI algorithms assume a pivotal role in crafting diverse and authentically immersive content, encompassing virtual terrains, characters, and objects. These algorithms demonstrate remarkable proficiency in generating lifelike textures, intricate animations, and responsive interactions, thus contributing depth and sophistication to the metaverse. Whether tasked with the automatic generation of intricate 3D models, the synthesis of natural language interactions, or the conception of visually striking environments, Generative AI stands as a cornerstone for rendering the metaverse a compelling and ever-evolving space, dynamically adapting to user engagement.

Beyond static content creation, Generative AI's influence within the metaverse extends to real-time adaptability and personalization, driven by user input and preferences. This dynamic content generation fosters heightened engagement and tailors experiences to individual users, fostering an unparalleled sense of presence and immersion. As the metaverse undergoes continuous evolution, Generative AI is poised to assume an increasingly influential role in pushing the boundaries of creativity, facilitating a metaverse that thrives on user-driven innovation.

FUTURE SCOPE AND CONCLUSION

5.1 Future Outlook

5.1.1 Limitations and Potential Improvement of Current TTI Models

Efforts in advancing Text-to-Image (TTI) models seek to overcome existing limitations and create resource-efficient models for high-fidelity image generation. The current challenge involves a trade-off between sampling efficiency and image quality across TTI models, with leading models requiring 50-200 iterative steps. Autoregressive Transformers excel but demand significant memory resources. GAN-based models show promise but lag slightly behind. Continued research is crucial to address these limitations. Exploring model architectures like GANs, non-autoregressive Transformers, and enhanced Diffusion models with distillation techniques is a promising avenue. Overcoming constraints in these models can contribute to more versatile and efficient TTI generation techniques applicable to diverse computing hardware, including mobile devices.

5.1.2 Beyond TTI: Embrace the Era of AI-Generated Content (AIGC)

5.1.2.1 TTI Applications Under the Influence of AIGC

The advent of AI-generated content (AIGC) (Cao et al., 2023) has exerted a profound influence on various societal and research realms. Modern AIGC models, exemplified by ChatGPT, facilitate easy access to extensive information across diverse subjects, benefiting a broad audience. For writers, ChatGPT proves invaluable in generating ideas for stories, characters, and plotlines. The integration of AIGC models into industry fields holds the potential to significantly enhance efficiency and productivity. Text-to-image (TTI) models, aligning with the AIGC trend, promise diverse applications beyond image generation, including image inpainting, super-resolution, and style transfer. This versatility, exemplified by models like stable-diffusion, Imagen (Saharia et al., 2022), and GigaGAN, reshapes creativity and productivity in art and fashion design, allowing for exploration of new styles and pushing artistic boundaries. Further TTI model development anticipates expanded plugin and software support, fostering a refined ecosystem closely connected to daily life.

5.1.2.2 Extend the Task of TTI

Text-to-image (TTI) techniques, renowned for their ability to generate content based on user inputs, exhibit close associations with other generative tasks leveraging similar model architectures and algorithms. Notably, advancements in video generation involve diffusion techniques, as seen in the video-diffusion model implementing a 3D-UNet structure (Çiçek et al., 2016). This structure processes fixed-length time-framed images, contributing to the creation of video sequences. TTI techniques have successfully extended to diffusion video generation, employing innovations like classifier-free guidance for text-to-video and latent diffusion to enhance sampling efficiency.

Moreover, TTI models find application in 3D generation, whether through Generative Adversarial Networks (GANs) or Diffusion methods. The diffusion technique in 3D generation approximates the distribution of a 3D object's shape by utilizing random Gaussian points within 3D space. This facilitates efficient creation for 3D printing based on user descriptions, streamlining the object creation process without the need for laborious manual design.

However, challenges persist in TTI-based 3D generation, particularly in accurately representing three-dimensional shapes. While TTI models excel in generating 2D images, extending their capabilities to 3D objects necessitates handling additional spatial and structural information. Ongoing research focuses on addressing this complexity, exploring novel model architectures and loss functions to ensure the fidelity and coherence of generated 3D shapes. Despite these challenges, the integration of TTI techniques into video and 3D generation holds tremendous potential, promising advancements in digital art creation and object fabrication.

5.1.3 Uni-ControlNet: Advancing Responsible and Versatile Text-to-Image Models

Uni-ControlNet (Zhao et al., 2023) responds to the rising necessity for enhanced control modes in generative models, going beyond mere textual descriptions. It offers a unified framework that enables the concurrent use of various local controls such as edge maps, depth maps, and segmentation masks, along with global controls like CLIP image embeddings. By incorporating these elements in a flexible and composable manner within a single model, Uni-ControlNet demonstrates its superiority over existing methods.In terms of controllability, Uni-ControlNet surpasses current approaches by allowing for precise manipulation of multiple parameters, offering a nuanced level of control over the generated outputs. Uni-ControlNet not only addresses the growing need for diverse control modes but also outperforms existing methods in controllability, generation quality, and composability, making it a promising advancement in the field of generative modeling.

Additionally, addressing potential negative social impacts through responsible deployment practices and ethical regulations is crucial. Implementing features such as special flags in generated images to enhance transparency represents a forward-looking approach to mitigate misuse or abuse. The on-going evolution of Uni-ControlNet holds promise not only for empowering creative professionals but also for establishing ethical standards in the deployment of advanced AI image generation models.

5.3 Conclusion

In conclusion, this survey illuminates the incredible evolution of text-to-image synthesis within generative intelligence, showcasing the unprecedented strides made by models such as generative adversarial networks (GANs), diffusion models etc. The exploration reveals a vast landscape of possibilities, hinting at the expansive potential for future developments in artificial intelligence. The study emphasizes generative AI's profound impact on creativity, where technological advancements, especially through GANs, have not only streamlined content creation but have also fostered collaborative partnerships between AI and human artists. AI graphic design tools have revolutionized visual design and proving invaluable for a myriad of professionals. For content marketers, GenAI tools allow for rapid exchange of ideas and creation of visually captivating graphics through platforms like App Icons AI and Canva. Graphic designers are using tools like PicsArt and Jasper to create original notes, and finding inspiration. Product designers employ AI-driven platforms like Planner 5D and Adobe Firefly to explore innovative design possibilities and refine concepts, thereby enhancing the efficiency of their workflow. Similarly, architects utilize AI technologies offered by platforms like Vizcom and Canva to derive inspiration, analyze site options. By streamlining workflows and fostering seamless collaboration, AI tools play a pivotal role in expediting design processes while simultaneously nurturing creativity and innovation. Real-life text-to-image models have moved beyond theoretical discussions, leading to tangible applications in the realm of art creation.

REFERENCES

AI. (n.d.). https://ai.plainenglish.io/the-complete-timeline-of-text-to-image-evolution-b63298234ed6

Avrahami, O., Lischinski, D., & Fried, O. (2021). *Blended diffusion for text-driven editing of natural images.* arXiv:2111.14818v2 [cs.CV]

Barratt, S., & Sharma, R. (2018). A Note on the Inception Score. *arXiv [stat.ML].* arXiv. http://arxiv.org/abs/1801.01973

BieF.YangY.ZhouZ.GhanemA.ZhangM.YaoZ.WuX. (2023). RenAIssance: A Survey into AI Text-to-Image Generation in the Era of Large Model. *arXiv [cs.CV].* https://arxiv.org/abs/2309.00810

Cao, Y., Li, S., Liu, Y., Yan, Z., Dai, Y., Yu, P. S., & Sun, L. (2023). A Comprehensive Survey of AI-Generated Content (AIGC): A History of Generative AI from GAN to ChatGPT. *arXiv [cs.AI].* arXiv. http://arxiv.org/abs/2303.04226

Caporusso, N. (2023). Generative Artificial Intelligence and the Emergence of Creative Displacement Anxiety [Review]. *Research Directs in Psychology and Behavior.*, *3*(1). Advance online publication. doi:10.53520/rdpb2023.10795

Chan, E. R., Lin, C. Z., Chan, M. A., Nagano, K., Pan, B., De Mello, S., & Gallo, O. (2021). Efficient Geometry-Aware 3D Generative Adversarial Networks. *arXiv [cs.CV].* arXiv. http://arxiv.org/abs/2112.07945

Chandramouli, P., & Gandikota, K. V. (2022). LDEdit: Towards Generalized Text Guided Image Manipulation via Latent Diffusion Models. *arXiv [cs.CV].* arXiv. http://arxiv.org/abs/2210.02249

Chen, W., Hu, H., Saharia, C., & Cohen, W. W. (2022). Re-Imagen: Retrieval-Augmented Text-to-Image Generator. *arXiv [cs.CV].* arXiv. http://arxiv.org/abs/2209.14491

Choi, J., Choi, Y., Kim, Y., Kim, J., & Yoon, S. (2023). Custom-Edit: Text-Guided Image Editing with Customized Diffusion Models. *arXiv [cs.CV].* arXiv. http://arxiv.org/abs/2305.15779

Çiçek, Ö., Abdulkadir, A., Lienkamp, S. S., Brox, T., & Ronneberger, O. (2016). 3D U-Net: Learning Dense Volumetric Segmentation from Sparse Annotation. *ArXiv.* /abs/1606.06650

Couairon, G., Verbeek, J., Schwenk, H., & Cord, M. (2022). DiffEdit: Diffusion-Based Semantic Image Editing with Mask Guidance. *arXiv [cs.CV]*. arXiv. http://arxiv.org/abs/2210.11427

Ding, M., Yang, Z., Hong, W., Zheng, W., Zhou, C., & Da Yin, J. L. (2021). CogView: Mastering Text-to-Image Generation via Transformers. *arXiv [cs.CV]*. arXiv. http://arxiv.org/abs/2105.13290

Elasri, M., Elharrouss, O., Al-ma'adeed, S., & Tairi, H. (2022). Image Generation: A Review. *Neural Processing Letters, 54*. Advance online publication. doi:10.1007/s11063-022-10777-x

Esser, P., Rombach, R., & Ommer, B. (2021). Taming transformers for high-resolution image synthesis. *Proceedings of the IEEE/CVF Conference on Computer Vision and Pattern Recognition*, 12873–12883.

Foster, D. (2019). *Generative deep learning: teaching machines to paint, write, compose, and play*. O'Reilly Media.

Gafni, O., Polyak, A., Ashual, O., Sheynin, S., Parikh, D., & Taigman, Y. (2022). Make-A-Scene: Scene-Based Text-to-Image Generation with Human Priors. *arXiv [cs.CV]*. arXiv. doi:10.1007/978-3-031-19784-0_6

Goodfellow, I. J., Pouget-Abadie, J., Mirza, M., Xu, B., Warde-Farley, D., Ozair, S., Courville, A., & Bengio, Y. (2014). Generative Adversarial Networks. *arXiv [stat.ML]*. arXiv. http://arxiv.org/abs/1406.2661

GPT-2. (n.d.). Accessed November 26, 2023. https://paperswithcode.com/method/gpt-2

Gregor, K., Danihelka, I., Graves, A., Rezende, D., & Wierstra, D. (2015). Draw: A recurrent neural network for image generation. In *International conference on machine learning* (pp. 1462–1471). PMLR.

Heusel, M., Ramsauer, H., Unterthiner, T., Nessler, B., & Hochreiter, S. (2017). GANs Trained by a Two Time-Scale Update Rule Converge to a Local Nash Equilibrium. *arXiv [cs.LG]*. arXiv. http://arxiv.org/abs/1706.08500

Ho, J., Jain, A., & Abbeel, P. (2020). Denoising diffusion probabilistic models. *Advances in Neural Information Processing Systems, 33*, 6840–6851.

Huang, N., Tang, F., Dong, W., & Xu, C. (2022). Draw Your Art Dream: Diverse Digital Art Synthesis with Multimodal Guided Diffusion. *arXiv [cs.CV]*. arXiv. doi:10.1145/3503161.3548282

Huang, N., Zhang, Y., Tang, F., Ma, C., Huang, H., Zhang, Y., Dong, W., & Xu, C. (2022). DiffStyler: Controllable Dual Diffusion for Text-Driven Image Stylization. *arXiv [cs.CV]*. arXiv. http://arxiv.org/abs/2211.10682

Kang, M., Zhu, J.-Y., Zhang, R., Park, J., Shechtman, E., Paris, S., & Park, T. (2023). Scaling up GANs for Text-to-Image Synthesis. *arXiv [cs.CV]*. arXiv. doi:10.1109/CVPR52729.2023.00976

Karras, T., Laine, S., & Aila, T. (2018). A Style-Based Generator Architecture for Generative Adversarial Networks. *arXiv [cs.NE]*. arXiv. http://arxiv.org/abs/1812.04948

Kim, G., & Chun, S. Y. (2022). DATID-3D: Diversity-Preserved Domain Adaptation Using Text-to-Image Diffusion for 3D Generative Model. *arXiv [cs.CV]*. arXiv. http://arxiv.org/abs/2211.16374

Li, G., Zheng, H., Wang, C., Li, C., Zheng, C., & Tao, D. (2022). 3DDesigner: Towards Photorealistic 3D Object Generation and Editing with Text-guided Diffusion Models. *ArXiv*. /abs/2211.14108

Li, W., Zhang, P., Zhang, L., Huang, Q., He, X., Lyu, S., & Gao, J. (2019). Object-Driven Text-to-Image Synthesis via Adversarial Training. *arXiv [cs.CV]*. arXiv. doi:10.1109/CVPR.2019.01245

Li, Y., Yu, A. W., Meng, T., Ben Caine, J. N., Peng, D., & Shen, J. (2022). DeepFusion: Lidar-Camera Deep Fusion for Multi-Modal 3D Object Detection. *arXiv [cs.CV]*. arXiv. doi:10.1109/CVPR52688.2022.01667

Lin, C.-H., Gao, J., Tang, L., Takikawa, T., Zeng, X., Huang, X., Kreis, K., Fidler, S., Liu, M.-Y., & Lin, T.-Y. (2022). Magic3D: High-Resolution Text-to-3D Content Creation. *arXiv [cs.CV]*. arXiv. http://arxiv.org/abs/2211.10440

LinT.-Y.MaireM.BelongieS.BourdevL.GirshickR.HaysJ.PeronaP.RamananD.ZitnickC. L.DollárP. (2014). Microsoft COCO: Common Objects in Context. *arXiv [cs.CV]*. doi:10.1007/978-3-319-10602-1_48

Lv, Z. (2022). Generative artificial intelligence in the metaverse era. *Cognitive Robotics*, *3*, 208–217. doi:10.1016/j.cogr.2023.06.001

Mansimov, E., Parisotto, E., Ba, J. L., & Salakhutdinov, R. (2015). Generating Images from Captions with Attention. *arXiv [cs.LG]*. arXiv. http://arxiv.org/abs/1511.02793

Marcus, G., Davis, E., & Aaronson, S. (2022). A Very Preliminary Analysis of DALL-E 2. *arXiv [cs.CV]*. arXiv. http://arxiv.org/abs/2204.13807

Meng, C., He, Y., Song, Y., Song, J., Wu, J., Zhu, J.-Y., & Ermon, S. (2021). SDEdit: Guided Image Synthesis and Editing with Stochastic Differential Equations. *arXiv [cs.CV]*. arXiv. http://arxiv.org/abs/2108.01073

Midjourney. (2023). https://www.midjourney.com/

Mildenhall, Srinivasan, Tancik, Barron, Ramamoorthi, & Ng. (2020). NeRF: Representing Scenes as Neural Radiance Fields for View Synthesis. *arXiv [cs.CV]*. arXiv. http://arxiv.org/abs/2003.08934

Nichol, A., Dhariwal, P., Ramesh, A., Shyam, P., Mishkin, P., McGrew, B., Sutskever, I., & Chen, M. (2021). Glide: Towards photorealistic image generation and editing with text-guided diffusion models. *arXiv preprint arXiv:2112.10741.*

OpenA. I. (2023). *Dall-e-2*. https://openai.com/product/dall-e-2

Papers With Code. (n.d.). https://paperswithcode.com/sota/text-to-image-generation-on-coco?tag_filter=246

Radford, A., Kim, J. W., Hallacy, C., Ramesh, A., Goh, G., Agarwal, S., & Sastry, G. (2021). Learning Transferable Visual Models From Natural Language Supervision. *arXiv [cs.CV]*. arXiv. http://arxiv.org/abs/2103.00020

Ramesh, A., Pavlov, M., Goh, G., Gray, S., Voss, C., Radford, A., Chen, M., & Sutskever, I. (2021). Zero-shot text-to-image generation. In *The International Conference on Machine Learning* (pp. 8821–8831). PMLR.

Rauniyar, A., Raj, A., Kumar, A., Kandu, A. K., Singh, A., & Gupta, A. (2023). Text to Image Generator with Latent Diffusion Models. *2023 International Conference on Computational Intelligence, Communication Technology and Networking (CICTN),* 144-148, 10.1109/CICTN57981.2023.10140348

Reed, S., Akata, Z., Yan, X., Logeswaran, L., Schiele, B., & Lee, H. (2016). Generative adversarial text to image synthesis. In *The International conference on machine learning* (pp. 1060–1069). PMLR.

Rombach, R., Blattmann, A., Lorenz, D., Esser, P., & Ommer, B. (2021). High-Resolution Image Synthesis with Latent Diffusion Models. *arXiv [cs.CV].* arXiv. http://arxiv.org/abs/2112.10752

Rombach, R., Blattmann, A., Lorenz, D., Esser, P., & Ommer, B. (2022). High-resolution image synthesis with latent diffusion models. *Proceedings of the IEEE/CVF Conference on Computer Vision and Pattern Recognition*, 10684–10695. 10.1109/CVPR52688.2022.01042

Saharia, C., Chan, W., Saxena, S., Li, L., Whang, J., Denton, E., & Seyed, K. S. G. (2022). Photorealistic Text-to-Image Diffusion Models with Deep Language Understanding. *arXiv [cs.CV].* arXiv. http://arxiv.org/abs/2205.11487

Shoshan, A., Bhonker, N., Kviatkovsky, I., & Medioni, G. (2021). GAN-Control: Explicitly Controllable GANs. *arXiv [cs.CV].* arXiv. doi:10.1109/ICCV48922.2021.01382

Singer, U., Polyak, A., Hayes, T., Yin, X., An, J., Zhang, S., & Hu, Q. (2022). Make-A-Video: Text-to-Video Generation without Text-Video Data. *arXiv [cs.CV].* arXiv. http://arxiv.org/abs/2209.14792

Singer, U., Polyak, A., Hayes, T., Yin, X., An, J., Zhang, S., & Hu, Q. (2022). Make-A-Video: Text-to-Video Generation without Text-Video Data. *arXiv [cs.CV].* arXiv. http://arxiv.org/abs/2209.14792

Sohl-Dickstein, J., Weiss, E., Maheswaranathan, N., & Ganguli, S. (2015). Deep unsupervised learning using nonequilibrium thermodynamics. In *The International Conference on Machine Learning* (pp. 2256–2265). PMLR.

Song, Y., & Ermon, S. (2019). Generative Modeling by Estimating Gradients of the Data Distribution. *ArXiv*. /abs/1907.05600

Tao, M., Bao, B.-K., Tang, H., & Xu, C. (2023). GALIP: Generative Adversarial CLIPs for Text-to-Image Synthesis. *arXiv [cs.CV].* arXiv. doi:10.1109/CVPR52729.2023.01366

Verma, P., Adam, V., & Solin, A. (2023). Variational Gaussian Process Diffusion Processes. *arXiv [cs.LG].* arXiv. http://arxiv.org/abs/2306.02066

Voynov, Abernan, & Cohen-Or. (2022). *Sketchguided text-to-image diffusion models.* Academic Press.

Wallace, B., Gokul, A., & Naik, N. (2022). *EDICT: Exact diffusion inversion via coupled transformations.* arXiv:2211.12446v2 [cs.CV]

Wang, Zhang, Zhang, Hao, Chen, Chen, & Wen. (2022). *Pretraining is all you need for image-to-image translation.* Academic Press.

Wang, J., Duan, H., Liu, J., Chen, S., Min, X., & Zhai, G. (2023). *AIGCIQA2023: A Large-scale Image Quality Assessment Database for AI Generated Images: from the Perspectives of Quality.* Authenticity and Correspondence.

Wang, W., Bao, J., Zhou, W., Chen, D., Chen, D., Yuan, L., & Li, H. (2022). SinDiffusion: Learning a Diffusion Model from a Single Natural Image. *arXiv [cs.CV].* arXiv. http://arxiv.org/abs/2211.12445

Wu, C. H. (2022). Unifying Diffusion Models' Latent Space, with Applications to CycleDiffusion and Guidance. *ArXiv*. /abs/2210.05559

Xu, T., Zhang, P., Huang, Q., Zhang, H., Gan, Z., Huang, X., & He, X. (2017). AttnGAN: Fine-Grained Text to Image Generation with Attentional Generative Adversarial Networks. *arXiv [cs.CV].* arXiv. http://arxiv.org/abs/1711.10485

Yang, L., Zhang, Z., Song, Y., Hong, S., Xu, R., Zhao, Y., Zhang, W., Cui, B., & Yang, M.-H. (2022). Diffusion Models: A Comprehensive Survey of Methods and Applications. *arXiv [cs.LG].* arXiv. http://arxiv.org/abs/2209.00796v11

Zhang, H., Xu, T., Li, H., Zhang, S., Wang, X., Huang, X., & Metaxas, D. (2016). StackGAN: Text to Photo-Realistic Image Synthesis with Stacked Generative Adversarial Networks. *arXiv [cs.CV].* arXiv. http://arxiv.org/abs/1612.03242

Zhang, H., Xu, T., Li, H., Zhang, S., Wang, X., Huang, X., & Metaxas, D. (2017). StackGAN++: Realistic Image Synthesis with Stacked Generative Adversarial Networks. *arXiv [cs.CV].* arXiv. doi:10.1109/ICCV.2017.629

Zhang, H., Xu, T., Li, H., Zhang, S., Wang, X., Huang, X., & Metaxas, D. N. (2017). Stackgan: Text to photo-realistic image synthesis with stacked generative adversarial networks. *Proceedings of the IEEE international conference on computer vision*, 5907–5915. 10.1109/ICCV.2017.629

ZhangL.RaoA.AgrawalaM. (2023). Adding Conditional Control to Text-to-Image Diffusion Models. *arXiv [cs.CV].* doi:10.1109/ICCV51070.2023.00355

Zhao, S., Chen, D., Chen, Y.-C., Bao, J., Hao, S., Yuan, L., & Wong, K.-Y. K. (2023). Uni-ControlNet: All-in-One Control to Text-to-Image Diffusion Models. *arXiv [cs.CV].* arXiv. http://arxiv.org/abs/2305.16322

Zhu, J.-Y., Park, T., Isola, P., & Efros, A. A. (2017). Unpaired Image-to-Image Translation Using Cycle-Consistent Adversarial Networks. *arXiv [cs.CV].* arXiv. doi:10.1109/ICCV.2017.244

Chapter 3
Generative AI and Generative Pre-Trained Transformer Applications: Challenges and Opportunities

Albérico Travassos Rosário
https://orcid.org/0000-0003-4793-4110
GOVCOPP, IADE, Universidade Europeia, Portugal

ABSTRACT

Generative AI, such as generative pre-trained transformer (GPT), has seen rapid advancements in recent years, offering a wide range of applications, but it also presents several challenges and opportunities. GPT can automate content generation for various industries, including journalism, marketing, and entertainment, reducing the need for manual content creation. Generative AI can personalize content and recommendations in e-commerce, streaming services, and more, enhancing user experiences. Generative AI, such as GPT, offers immense potential across various sectors but requires careful management to address bias, ethics, and quality control challenges. As technology evolves, finding the right balance between control and creativity will be crucial for maximizing its benefits while minimizing risks. Based on the above, the authors systematically review the bibliometric literature on how Generative AI and generative pre-trained transformer applications challenge opportunities using the Scopus database by analysing 49 academic and/or scientific documents.

INTRODUCTION

Generative AI has emerged as a disruptive and transformative innovation in recent years, applicable in multiple industries. According to Bandi et al. (2023), the global market value for generative AI was US$10.79 billion in 2022. It is projected to reach US$118.06 billion by 2032, growing at a compound annual growth rate (CAGR) of 27.02%.

DOI: 10.4018/979-8-3693-1950-5.ch003

Brynjolfsson and Raymond (2023) define generative AI as a class of machine-learning technologies that analyze patterns in existing data to generate content in the form of texts, images, videos, or music. It involves developing models and algorithms that can generate synthetic data comparable to real-life data. In addition, generative AI is trained on massive data to produce output based on users' commands or prompts (Bandi et al., 2023). This innovation has gained attraction recently due to the launch of various tools, including ChatGPT, DALL-E, and GitHub Copilot. As a result, the global adoption of generative AI has revolutionized multiple fields, from creative arts to neural language processing, computer vision, health, finance, and research (Sætra, 2023). Businesses and individual users are utilizing it for various purposes, such as creating content, detecting anomalies, and augmenting data.

The rapid development of generative AI has resulted from large-scale data generation and the advancements of deep learning techniques.

Generative pre-trained transformer (GPT), on the other hand, is a deep learning model pre-trained using massive amounts of text data to perform various tasks such as language generation and modeling, text classification, sentiment analysis, and machine translation. Companies and individual users leverage GPT tools for multiple applications. For example, its natural language understanding (NLU) and natural language generation (NLG) capabilities are used in creative content writing or in chatbots and virtual assistants to answer questions (Yenduri et al., 2023). NLU enables GPT systems to analyze and understand text meanings, including identifying relations and structure in sentences. NLG facilitates the creation of text output. GPT can also be used to generate code in various programming languages, including JavaScript and Python (Aydın & Erdem, 2022). In addition, GPT can be used to translate text from one language to another and provide summaries or briefs of articles, research papers, and reports. The wide application of GPT has led to its adoption in numerous fields, including marketing, healthcare, entertainment, travel, and e-commerce.

Generative AI and GPT provide numerous opportunities to improve productivity and performance. For example, e-commerce and streaming platforms can leverage these innovations to provide personalized content and recommendations. They can also be integrated into chatbots and virtual assistants to ensure 24/7 access to customer support, thereby improving a brand's responsiveness and enhancing customer satisfaction. Brynjolfsson and Raymond (2023) found that generative AI increased productivity by 14%. However, generative AI and GPT face numerous challenges, including the potential for misuse, bias, and data inaccuracies. For example, GPT tools require large amounts of data for pre-training and tuning to perform certain tasks. This means that the use of biased or inaccurate data can affect the accuracy of its outputs. Therefore, this systematic review synthesizes data from 49 sources, analyzing the origins and development of generative AI and GPT, their applications, and associated opportunities and challenges.

METHODOLOGICAL APPROACH

The investigator carried out a methodical bibliometric literature review to assess the influence of Generative AI and the applications of Generative Pre-trained Transformers. This approach encompasses the organized identification, examination, and integration of pertinent scholarly literature. It facilitated the acquisition of a thorough comprehension of the current knowledge about the research subject, unveiling pivotal trends and patterns in the literature. Applied to Generative AI and Generative Pre-trained Transformer Applications, this methodology has the potential to unveil the emergence and development

Table 1. Process of systematic LRSB

Fase	Step	Description
Exploration	Step 1	formulating the research problem
	Step 2	searching for appropriate literature
	Step 3	critical appraisal of the selected studies
	Step 4	data synthesis from individual sources
Interpretation	Step 5	reporting findings and recommendations
Communication	Step 6	Presentation of the LRSB report

Source: adapted Rosário and Dias (2023), Rosário et al. (2023), Raimundo and Rosário (2022).

of novel technologies, their ongoing effects, and the strategies businesses employ to navigate through disruptions.

Furthermore, the systematic bibliometric literature review serves as a valuable tool for evaluating the methodologies employed in studies related to Generative AI and Generative Pre-trained Transformer Applications. By critically assessing the various research approaches and methodologies used across the literature, the researcher can identify strengths, weaknesses, and gaps in the existing body of knowledge. This insightful analysis contributes to the refinement of future research directions and methodologies within the field, fostering a more robust and informed academic discourse (Rosário & Dias, 2023; Raimundo & Rosário, 2202). Additionally, the findings of this comprehensive literature review can offer practical insights for industry professionals and policymakers. Understanding the historical context and current state of Generative AI and Generative Pre-trained Transformer Applications allows stakeholders to make informed decisions about technology adoption, investment strategies, and policy development. By elucidating key trends and patterns, the research provides a valuable resource for those seeking to anticipate and adapt to the dynamic landscape of artificial intelligence, ultimately contributing to more effective decision-making in both academic and practical realms.

In contrast to conventional literature reviews, the LRSB adopts a thorough approach in examining the published literature about the research topic (Rosário & Dias, 2023; Raimundo & Rosário, 2202). This method aims to condense the number of articles, concentrating on the most relevant ones. Additionally, the researcher furnishes an audit trail, enabling readers to evaluate the research's methodologies, conclusions, and the quality of the amalgamated studies.

Consequently, the LRSB encompasses a meticulous screening and selection of information sources to ensure the precision and validity of the presented data. This process unfolds through three phases and six steps, as delineated by Rosário and Dias (2023), Rosário et al. (2023), and Raimundo and Rosário (2022), as illustrated in Table 1.

The investigators utilized the Scopus database to pinpoint and choose reputable sources esteemed in academic and scientific communities. It is crucial to underscore that this study has limitations since it concentrated solely on the Scopus database, overlooking other academic and scientific databases. For literature searches extending through 2023, it is imperative to take into account peer-reviewed scientific and academic publications.

To conduct the research, the researcher conducted an extensive literature search on the Scopus database. For the initial search, the researcher used the keywords "generative AI," which resulted in 1,048 sources. To ensure that the sources used were relevant to the research topic, the researcher limited the

Table 2. Screening methodology

Database Scopus	Screening	Publications
Meta-search	Keyword: generative AI	1,048
First Inclusion Criterion	Keyword: generative AI Exact keywords: GPT, ChatGPT, GPT-3, GPT-4	260
Second Inclusion Criteria	Keyword: generative AI Exact keywords: GPT, ChatGPT, GPT-3, GPT-4 Subject area: business, management and accounting Duplicates removed	49
Screening	Keyword: generative AI Exact keywords: GPT, ChatGPT, GPT-3, GPT-4 Subject area: business, management and accounting Published until January 2024	

Source: own elaboration

search to the exact keywords "ChatGPT," "GPT," "GPT-3," and "GPT-4." In addition, duplicates were removed, and abstracts and conclusions of selected papers were carefully screened. This process reduced the document results to 260.

The researcher meticulously reviewed these results to ensure they directly addressed the research topic. As part of the inclusion criteria, papers published in English were selected to ensure accessibility and language consistency. Finally, the search was limited to the subject area "Business, Management and Accounting," reducing the number of results to 49. These documents include peer-reviewed publications in journals and conferences, which enables the presentation of a comprehensive and insightful analysis of the application of generative AI and GPT (Table 2).

We applied content and thematic analysis techniques to detect, investigate, and present various documents as outlined by Rosário and Dias (2023), Rosário et al. (2023), and Raimundo and Rosario (2022).

Following this, the 49 scientific and academic documents, cataloged in Scopus, underwent both narrative and bibliometric analysis to delve into the content and potentially uncover recurring themes that directly addressed the research inquiries, as outlined by Rosário and Dias (2023), Rosário et al. (2023), and Raimondo and Rosario (2022).

This whole process resulted in 49 documents, classified as 45 articles, 3 conference papers, and 1 book.

PUBLICATION DISTRIBUTION

Peer-reviewed articles on Generative AI and Generative Pre-trained Transformer applications until January 2024. The year 2023 had the highest number of peer-reviewed publications on the subject, reaching 48 (Figure 1). Investigations into this subject are still scarce.

Figure 2 shows the countries with the most active scientific output in research areas, focusing on the USA, UK, and India, which have the most publications.

Table 3 and Figure 2 show the top 10 countries that have made the most noteworthy scientific contributions in the fields under study. This analysis aims to understand whether these countries prioritize utilizing artificial intelligence in the consumer behavior process in a business or if they emphasize boosting their productivity.

Figure 1. Documents by year (own elaboration)

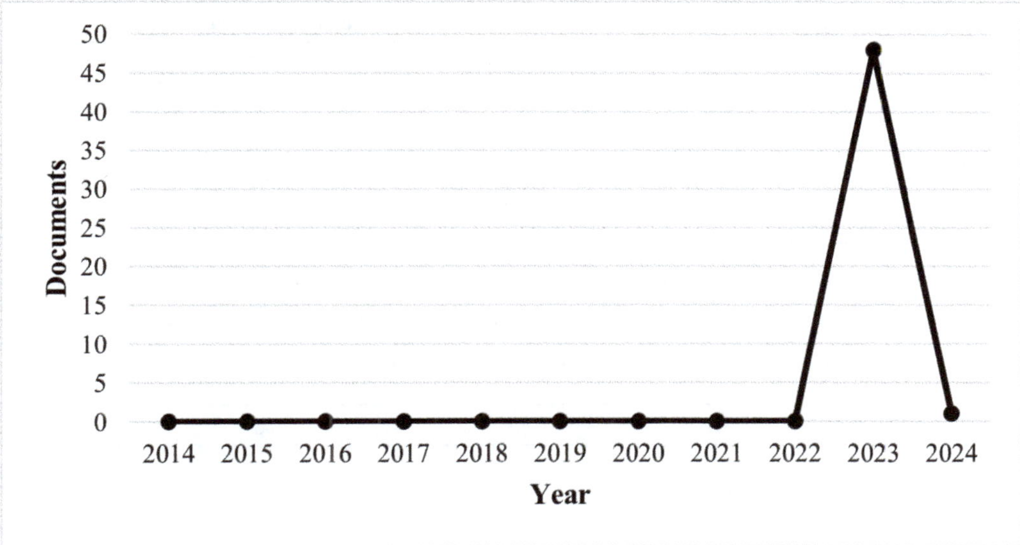

Figure 2. Scientific production by country

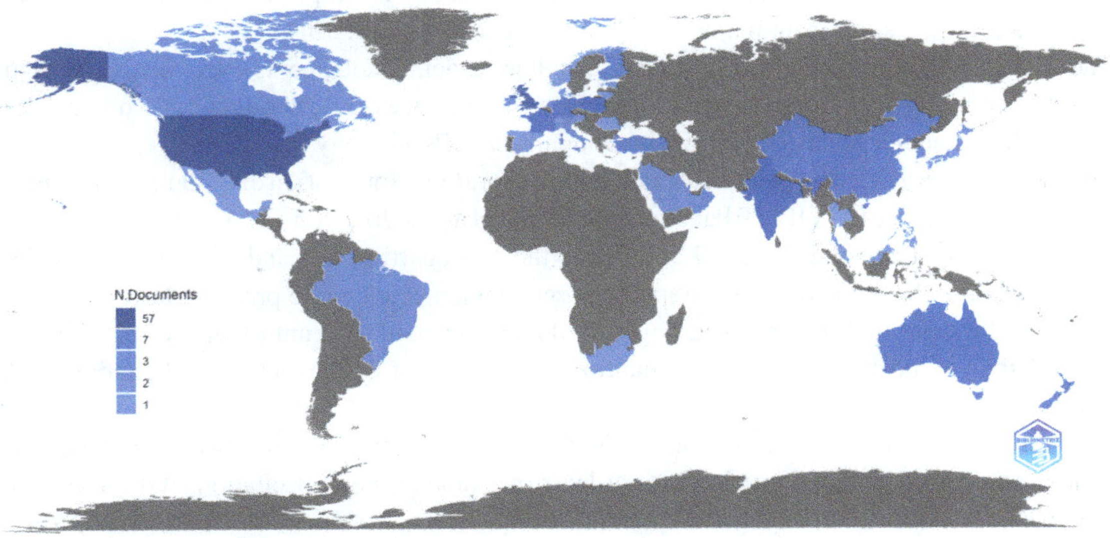

The publications were sorted out as follows: International Journal Of Information Management (4); Journal Of Business Strategy (3); Issues In Information Systems (3); Computer Law And Security Review (3); and with 2 (International Journal Of Production Research; International Journal Of Management Education; Economics And Business Review; Applied Marketing Analytics; Annual Conference On Innovation And Technology In Computer Science Education Iticse); and the remaining publications with 1 document.

In Table 4 we analyze the Scimago Journal & Country Rank (SJR), the best quartile and the H index by IJournal Of IInternational Journal Of Research In Marketing is the most quoted publication with 3,900

Table 3. Top 10 countries by number of publications

Country	Number of Publications
USA	57
UK	43
INDIA	18
POLAND	17
FRANCE	14
GERMANY	11
AUSTRALIA	10
CHINA	8
NEW ZEALAND	7
TURKEY	6

Source: own elaboration

(SJR), Q1 and H index 115. There is a total of 17 publications in Q1, 8 publications in Q2, 1 publication Q3 and 3 publications in Q4. Publications from best quartile Q1 represent 49% of the 35 publications titles; best quartile Q2 represents 23%, best Q3 represents 3% and best Q4 represents 9% of each of the titles of 35 publications. Finally, 6 publications without indexing data represent 17% of publications. As shown in Table 4, the significant majority of publications do have quartile Q1.

The subject areas covered by the 49 scientific and/or academic documents were: Business, Management and Accounting (49); Social Sciences (22); Decision Sciences (11); Economics, Econometrics and Finance (10); Computer Science (10); Engineering (4); and Psychology (1).

The most quoted article was "Implementation Guide for Rapid Integration of an Outpatient Telemedicine Program During the COVID-19 Pandemic" by Smith et al. (2020), with 127 quotes published Journal of the American College of Surgeons 1,530 (SJR), the best quartile (Q1) and with H index (195), this paper is to explore the guide on how to rapidly integrate telemedicine into practice during a pandemic.

In Figure 3 we can analyze citation changes for documents published until January 2024. The period 2014-2024 shows a positive net growth in citations with an R2 of 21%, reaching 594 citations in January 2024.

The h-index is used to determine the productivity and impact of a published work based on the maximum number of included articles with at least the same number of citations. Of the documents considered for h-index, 8 were cited at least 8 times.

Citations of all scientific and/or academic documents from the period ≤2013 to until January 2024, with a total of 1288 citations, of the 99 documents 10 were not cited. The self-citation of documents in the period ≤2014 to January 2024 was self-cited 1176 times.

Using the primary keywords, the bibliometric study delved into and uncovered markers of the scientific and/or academic information's dynamics and evolution within documents, as depicted in Figure 4. These findings were extracted utilizing the scientific software VOSviewe, with a focus on identifying the primary search keywords "generative AI, GPT, ChatGPT, GPT-3 and GPT-4".

This study is rooted in scientific and academic documents that explore the potential of Generative AI and Generative Pre-trained Transformer applications. In Figure 5, we can scrutinize the interconnected keywords. This enables us to emphasize the interrelationships among keywords within each scientific

Table 4. Scimago journal & country rank impact factor

Title	SJR	Best Quartile	H Index
International Journal Of Research In Marketing	3,900	Q1	115
Journal Of Travel Research	3,250	Q1	159
Journal Of Business Logistics	3,140	Q1	90
International Journal Of Production Economics	3,030	Q1	214
International Journal Of Production Research	2,980	Q1	170
International Journal Of Contemporary Hospitality Management	2,500	Q1	113
International Journal Of Information Management	2,480	Q1	20
Human Resource Management Journal	2,340	Q1	108
Tourism Review	1,880	Q1	48
Technology In Society	1,490	Q1	69
Review Of Managerial Science	1,310	Q1	41
International Journal Of Management Education	1,060	Q1	44
Journal Of Marketing Analytics	0,790	Q1	16
Journal Of Marketing Education	0,740	Q1	63
Computer Law And Security Review	0,720	Q1	49
International Journal Of Public Administration	0,690	Q2	52
Publications	0,630	Q1	21
Intelligent Systems In Accounting Finance And Management	0,630	Q2	16
Entrepreneurial Business And Economics Review	0,540	Q1	21
Administrative Sciences	0,530	Q2	28
Journal Of Place Management And Development	0,470	Q2	34
Journal Of Business Strategy	0,450	Q2	45
Journal Of Property Investment And Finance	0,440	Q2	39
Entrepreneurship Education And Pedagogy	0,400	Q2	14
Journal Of Corporate Accounting And Finance	0,30	Q2	19
Central European Management Journal	0,220	Q3	10
Journal Of Distribution Science	0,200	Q4	13
Economics And Business Review	0,170	Q4	4
Applied Marketing Analytics	0,120	Q4	4
Annual Conference On Innovation And Technology In Computer Science Education Iticse	0	-*	32
Issues In Information Systems	-*	-*	-*
Transformative AI Responsible Transparent And Trustworthy AI Systems	-*	-*	-*
Journal Of Work Applied Management	-*	-*	-*
Journal Of Hospitality And Tourism Management	-*	-*	-*
36th Bled Econference Digital Economy And Society The Balancing Act For Digital Innovation In Times Of Instability Bled 2023 Proceedings	-*	-*	-*

Note: *data not available.
Source: own elaboration

Figure 3. Evolution of citations between 2014 and 2024 (own elaboration)

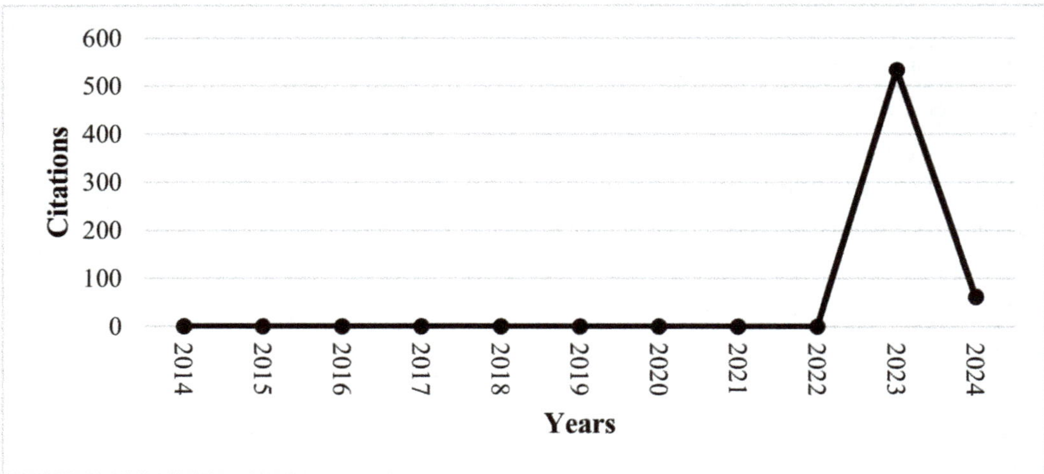

Figure 4. Network of all keywords

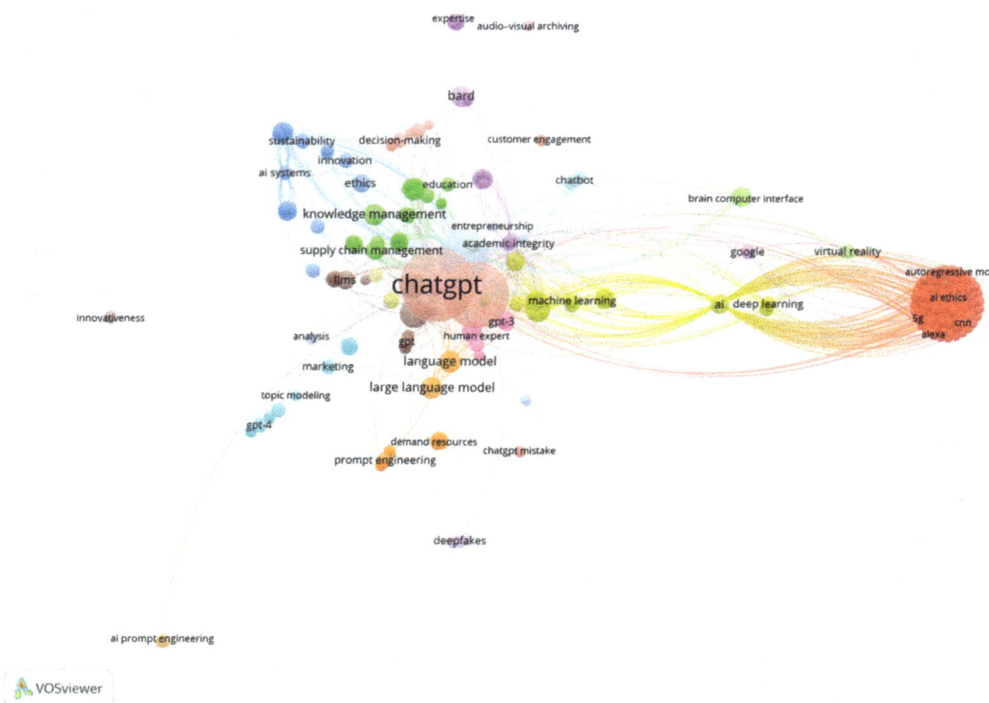

Figure 5. Network of linked keywords

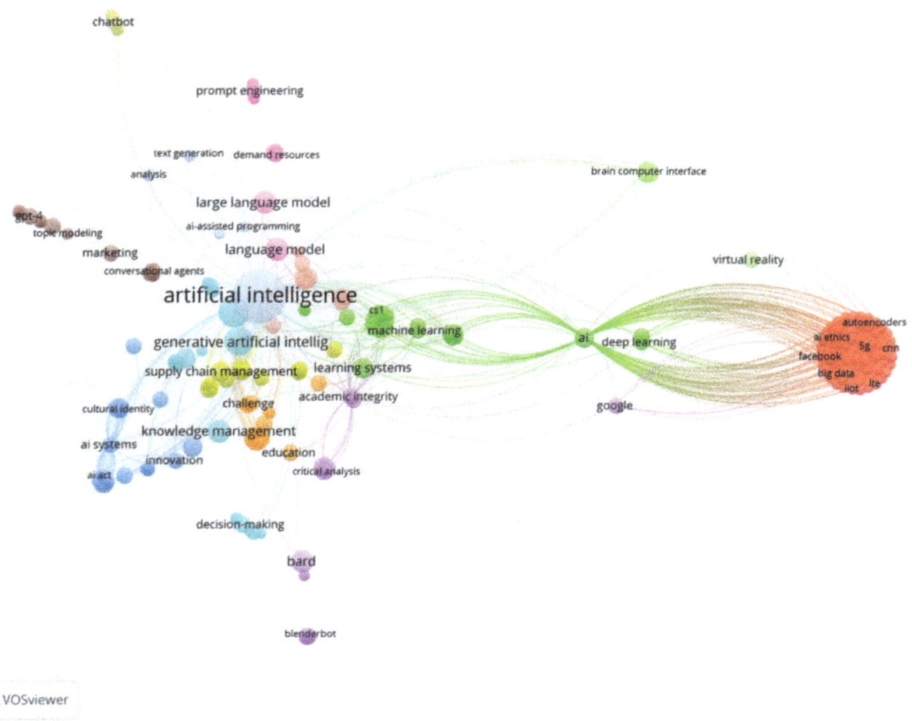

article, aiding in the identification of subjects explored in the studies and providing insights into future research trends. The main lines of research are divided into 3 large clusters, in order of magnitude: (i) red cluster with an interconnection of 81 topics; (ii) green cluster with an interconnection of 37 topics; and (iii) blue cluster with an interconnection of 37 topics. Moreover, Figure 6 reveals a substantial volume of co-citations and units for cited reference analysis.

THEORETICAL PERSPECTIVES

In recent years, the emergence and adoption of generative AI and GPT have changed traditional workflows. These innovations have a remarkable capability to use pre-existing data to comprehend and generate human-like texts, images, and videos (Buckley, 2023). As a result, businesses are integrating them into their core systems, thereby affecting different professions and operations. The collaborative synergy between human expertise and generative AI capabilities is redefining how industries operate, fostering innovation and efficiency across professional domains (Dalalah & Dalalah, 2023). As businesses increasingly integrate generative AI and GPT into their operations, the ripple effects of these innovations are reshaping the future of work. This emphasizes the need for a harmonious collaboration between human innovation and machine intelligence (Dwivedi et al., 2023). This literature review section provides an in-depth analysis of generative AI and GPT and the opportunities and challenges resulting from their application in business.

Figure 6. Network of co-citation

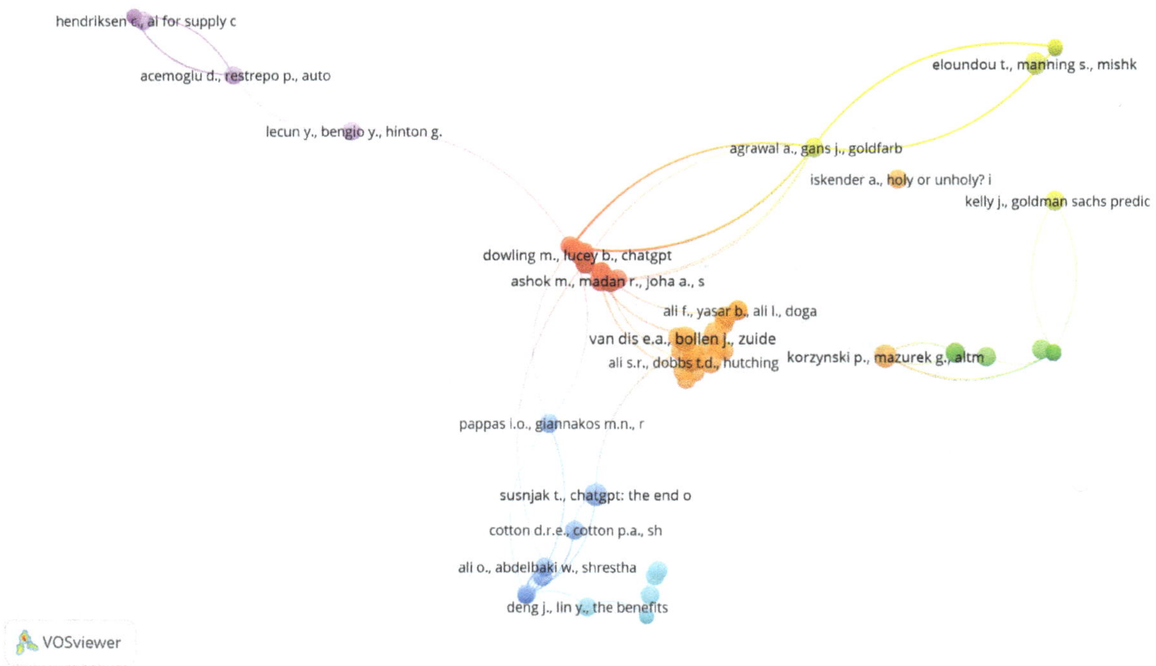

Generative AI and Generative Pre-Trained Transformer (GPT)

Generative AI has become a popular topic due to its accessibility and ability to produce creative, realistic results. While the concept has existed for decades, generative AI experienced explosive growth in 2022 following the launch of OpenAI's generative pre-trained transformer, ChatGPT. ChatGPT had a record-breaking growth after signing one million users in five days and reaching 100 million users in just two months, making it one of the fastest-growing consumer tools (Kanbach et al., 2023). To provide perspective, it took TikTok nine months and Instagram two and a half years to reach 100 million users. The making of ChatGPT, DALL-E2, and Midjourney accessible to end customers in 2022 set a milestone for the use of generative AI. These large language models (LLMs) enable audiences to create human-like textual content, realistic images, and music. Their adoption has had far-reaching implications in various industries, including marketing, education, medicine, software development, art, and music, among others. Before diving into the complex applications of these generative AI, it is important to understand its meaning and origins.

The term generative refers to the ability to produce or create something. When applied in AI, this definition means that technically, every AI model is generative since they all generate or create something, whether it is internal rules, numerical predictions, or content generation. However, García-Peñalvo and Vázquez-Ingelmo (2023) explain that not all AI models are considered generative. The authors indicate that generative AI models create "fresh, human-like material that can be engaged with and consumed, rather than just numerical forecasts or internal rules" (p.7). In this, although decision tree models are based on AI, they are classified as discriminative models rather than generative models. While generative AI focuses on creating high-quality, human-like materials, discriminative AI models are trained to use incoming data to predict probabilities. Walczak and Cellary (2023, p.73) define generative AI as a "type of machine learning models that focus on generating novel data instances, often by learning the latent structure and distribution of a given dataset." In this regard, generative AI is trained on a diverse dataset to identify hidden patterns or features within data that are explicitly labeled or identified. This allows the model to create new instances of data that resemble the characteristics of the original dataset. Kanbach et al. 92023) define it as a type of AI used to generate texts, synthetic data, code, images, video, and audio. The ability to uncover and learn latent structures enables generative AI to create new and meaningful data instances, making it valuable for tasks like image synthesis, text generation, music composition, and other applications that require novel and coherent content.

Enabling Technologies

Developing and implementing generative AI models requires various technologies that make up the infrastructure and systems. For example, GPT as a language model requires the integration of multiple innovations, such as natural language processing (NLP) frameworks, cloud computing, and advanced neural network architectures (Dwivedi et al., 2023). These technologies provide the generative AI model with distinct functionalities and capabilities that contribute to its overall performance. According to Bandi et al. (2023), building generative AI models, such as transformers, including GPT, generative adversarial networks (GANs), and variational autoencoders (VAEs), involves various stages that must be approached in a systematic way to achieve the desired results. Although the stages vary depending on the models, the authors identify eight common phases, as shown in Figure 7. Specific technologies are required in each of these stages, indicating the significance of understanding the enabling technologies that support generative AI, including GPT.

Figure 7. The implementation stages of generative AI (Bandi et al., 2023)

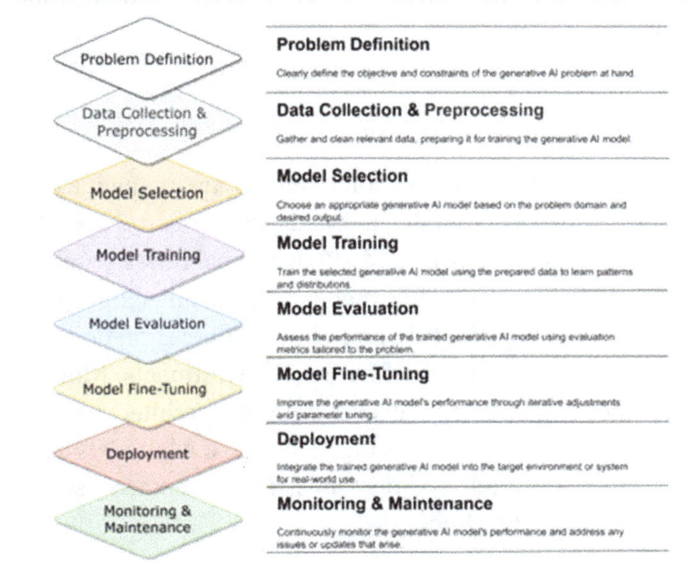

Artificial Intelligence (AI)

AI serves as the foundational enabling technology for generative AI models, including GPT. Yenduri et al. (2023, p.8) define AI as the "simulation of intelligent behaviors in machines that are programmed to learn from their experience to reason, understand natural language, and perceive their environment." AI in GPT is used to enable the machine to understand and react to human language, thereby improving its language generation capabilities. According to Budhwar et al. (2023), generative models are a subset of AI that leverages neural networks and deep learning architectures to learn complex representations and generate novel content. For this reason, the sophistication of generative algorithms is intricately tied to advancements in AI research (Earley, 2023). The interplay of machine learning techniques, neural network architectures, and optimization algorithms within the broader AI framework empowers generative AI models to comprehend, interpret, and synthesize information.

Big Data

Most digital systems are embedded with data-collecting tools such as web scraping tools, sensors, microphones, and cameras. These devices facilitate the collection of large amounts of structured and unstructured data gathered from diverse sources, including social media and transaction-based systems (Jackson et al., 2023). This vast data is referred to as big data. The immense size and diversity of datasets in big data allow AI systems to discern intricate patterns, facilitating the generation of more nuanced and contextually relevant outputs. Moreover, big data enables the training of large-scale models, such as GPT-3, by exposing them to a vast array of linguistic and contextual scenarios (Korzynski et al., 2023). For example, Yenduri et al. (2023) explain that GPT models are trained using trillions of data collected from diverse sources, such as articles, books, social media platforms, and websites. The diversity of this training data enables GPT models to capture patterns such as differences in language use and structures. This makes them more effective and accurate when carrying out NLP tasks such as summarizing or translating texts and answering questions. Therefore, this data-centric approach empowers generative AI to surpass traditional models in understanding and reproducing complex information, advancing its capabilities across various applications.

Cloud Computing

Cloud computing ensures on-demand access to computer resources, such as storage, applications, and processing power, which are availed through the internet. According to Xu et al. (2024), cloud platforms provide the substantial computational power and storage capabilities required to meet the resource-intensive nature of training large-scale generative models. As a result, cloud-based infrastructure enables researchers and developers to access powerful computing resources on demand (Yenduri et al., 2023). This helps mitigate the need for substantial local hardware investments. Moreover, cloud environments facilitate collaboration by allowing seamless sharing of model architectures and datasets (Wang et al., 2023). The scalability of cloud resources ensures that generative AI models can be deployed on a global scale, accommodating varying workloads and demands. These characteristics enable the accessibility and democratization of generative AI technologies.

Edge Computing

In generative AI, edge computing emerges as a critical enabler by addressing the challenges associated with real-time processing and low-latency requirements. Edge computing involves the decentralization of computational processes by bringing the computational resources closer to the data source (Xu et al., 2024). As a result, there is less need for users and servers to communicate over long distances, reducing the use of bandwidth and lowering latency (Yenduri et al., 2023). This is particularly advantageous for generative AI models deployed in applications requiring rapid response times, such as natural language processing in conversational agents or real-time image and video generation. Some edge servers and devices feature accelerators such as graphics processing units (GPUs) and field-programmable gate arrays (FPGAs), which improve the models' processing power (Wang et al., 2023). In addition, the integration of these technologies helps accelerate the speed of training these generative AI models. Furthermore, edge computing reduces the reliance on centralized data centers, thus enhancing the efficiency of generative AI applications. It ensures timely and contextually relevant outputs in scenarios where immediate processing is imperative.

Human-Computer Interactions

Human-computer Interactions (HCI) is concerned with how machines and humans communicate. The symbiotic relationship between generative AI and HCI emphasizes the technology's user-centric applications. Yenduri et al. (2023) explain that HCI principles guide the design and integration of generative models into user interfaces, enhancing user experiences and facilitating seamless interactions. For example, HCI is integrated into GPT models to enable designers to build more effective input systems, like natural language interfaces, that enhance users' ability to easily and accurately communicate with the model (Spennemann, 2023; Niszczota & Conway, 2023). This enabling technology can be used to evaluate generative AI model's real-time responses to users and identify areas that need improvements. Therefore, it can help improve the model's reliability and accuracy. Moreover, incorporating generative AI into HCI frameworks enables it to comprehend and respond to user inputs more intelligently (Karakose et al., 2023). This helps create a more natural and intuitive interface. The use of generative models in areas such as virtual assistants, chatbots, and content creation tools reflects the significance of HCI in tailoring generative AI technologies to align with human needs and preferences.

5G and Beyond Networks

The 5G and beyond networks represent a paradigm shift in connectivity, providing the high bandwidth and low latency necessary for the effective deployment of generative AI applications. This latest generation of cellular networks enables simultaneous connection of multiple devices (Hughes et al., 2019). The increased data transfer speeds and reduced communication delays afforded by these networks are particularly consequential for real-time interactions and data-intensive generative tasks (Figure 8) (Yenduri et al., 2023). For instance, applications like augmented reality, autonomous vehicles, and remote collaborative environments heavily rely on the capabilities of 5G networks to support the seamless integration of generative AI (Maksymyuk et al., 2018). The convergence of generative AI and advanced networking technologies promises transformative innovations in diverse sectors, amplifying the impact and ubiquity of generative models in future technological applications.

Figure 8. Summary of the enabling technologies of generative AI and GPT (Yenduri et al., 2023)

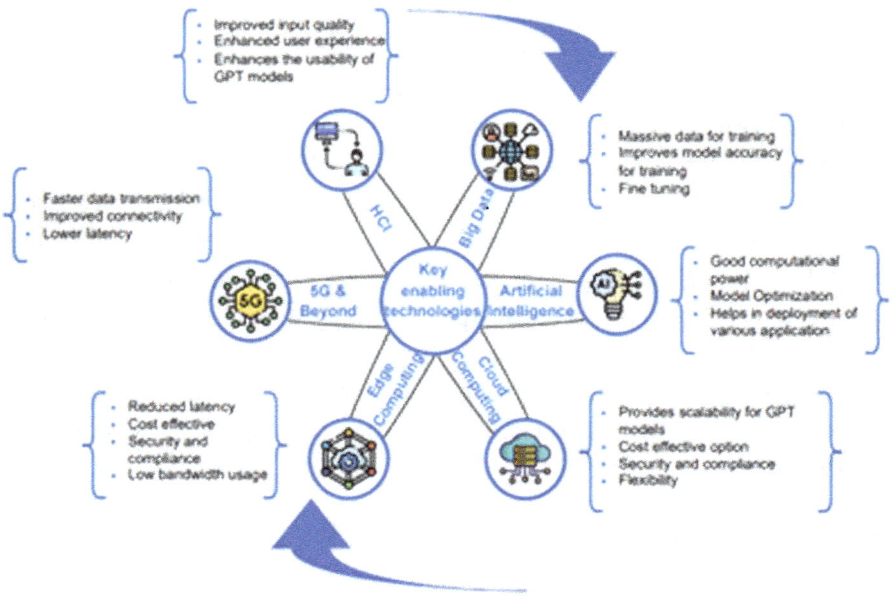

Generative AI and GPT Opportunities Across Various Industries

Generative AI and GPT have made significant progress following the integration of advanced technologies. As a result, they have enormous impacts on various fields, including e-commerce, education, marketing, accounting, supply chains and logistics, travel and tourism. This section provides valuable insights into the opportunities created by applying generative AI and GPT in these industries.

Marketing and Market Research Analysis

Generative AI offers a range of opportunities for innovation and efficiency in marketing and marketing analysis. For instance, it can be used in marketing to comprehend and generate human-like language needed to create compelling and personalized content (Buckley, 2023). This opportunity is particularly valuable in crafting targeted advertisements and promotional material with tailored messaging for specific demographics. Besides, GPT's natural language processing prowess facilitates sentiment analysis on a nuanced level, enabling marketers to gauge consumer reactions with greater accuracy and depth (Earley, 2023). In market research analysis, generative AI's capacity to process and interpret vast datasets is instrumental. This technology can analyze consumer behavior, preferences, and trends, providing businesses with insightful market intelligence (Guha et al., 2023). As a result, this data-driven approach enhances decision-making processes by offering comprehensive and up-to-date information for strategic planning.

The automation of tasks such as survey analysis and sentiment extraction from social media platforms allows market researchers to focus on higher-order analysis and strategy formulation. Moreover, the integration of generative AI into market research tools streamlines the generation of reports and insights, enabling faster turnaround times (Kshetri et al., 2023). The synthesized information aids in understanding market dynamics, forecasting trends, and identifying emerging opportunities (Zhou et al., 2023). The collaborative potential of generative AI in marketing and market research opens avenues for interdisciplinary research, bringing together expertise in data science, linguistics, and business strategy.

Human Resource Management

Generative AI presents diverse opportunities for optimization and innovation across various facets of human resource management. For instance, generative AI models can be used in talent acquisition to automate certain aspects of the recruitment process (Budhwar et al., 2023). GPT-based systems can efficiently screen resumes, analyze candidate profiles, and even conduct preliminary assessments, streamlining the initial stages of the hiring process. This automation expedites recruitment timelines and reduces the potential for bias in candidate evaluation, thereby promoting a more equitable and inclusive hiring environment (Karakose et al., 2023; Yenduri et al., 2023). In addition, generative AI can be used in employee training and development. The technology enables companies to create personalized and adaptive learning materials. GPT's natural language generation capabilities allow the creation of training content tailored to individual employee needs, enhancing the effectiveness of learning initiatives (Triantoro et al., 2023). Furthermore, generative models can assist in the creation of realistic job previews and immersive training simulations. This provides employees with hands-on experiences that contribute to skill development and performance improvement.

Generative AI introduces innovations in employee engagement and communication. For example, GPT-powered chatbots can serve as virtual assistants, handling routine HR queries, providing information on company policies, and assisting in onboarding processes (Budhwar et al., 2023). This application enhances the efficiency of HR operations and improves the overall employee experience by ensuring prompt and accurate responses to inquiries. In addition, the integration of generative AI in HR analytics enhances decision-making processes (Triantoro et al., 2023). GPT's ability to process and analyze large volumes of HR data facilitates predictive analytics for talent management, succession planning, and workforce optimization (Yenduri et al., 2023). This data-driven approach empowers HR professionals to make strategic decisions based on a comprehensive understanding of organizational dynamics, employee performance, and market trends.

Property Valuation Reports in Real Estate

The complexity of factors influencing property values, including market trends, neighborhood dynamics, and property features, makes valuation a nuanced and data-intensive process. Generative AI provides natural language processing capabilities that can be leveraged to analyze vast datasets and generate comprehensive and accurate property valuation reports (Cheung, 2023). One key advantage of using generative AI in property valuation is its ability to assimilate diverse and dynamic data sources. For instance, GPT can process information from real estate listings, historical property transactions, economic indicators, and geographic data to develop a holistic understanding of the factors influencing property values (Ma & Huang, 2023). Moreover, generative models can help reduce human bias in property valuation reports. The reliance on data-driven insights in these models mitigates subjective judgments that can sometimes affect human appraisals (Cheung, 2023). Traditional property valuation processes can be time-consuming, particularly in markets with high transaction volumes. Generative AI expedites this process by automating the analysis of extensive datasets providing timely and accurate valuation reports (Ma & Huang, 2023). This efficiency benefits property owners and investors and contributes to more informed decision-making in a dynamic real estate market. Moreover, integrating generative AI in property valuation supports risk management strategies. This innovation can analyze market trends, assess potential risks, and provide insights into future property value fluctuations (O'Leary, 2023). Real estate professionals can leverage this proactive approach to risk analysis to make informed decisions regarding property investments and portfolio management.

Education and Academic Research

The adoption of generative AI in education and academic research has redefined knowledge dissemination, content creation, and research methodologies. In education, generative AI facilitates the development of intelligent tutoring systems, personalized learning experiences, and innovative educational content generation (Lim et al., 2023). For instance, educators can use generative AI models to create customized learning materials by tailoring content to individual student needs (Guha et al., 2023). GPT's natural language processing capabilities enable them to generate adaptive quizzes, educational content, and interactive learning modules (Winkler et al., 2023). This personalized approach enhances student engagement, addresses diverse learning styles, and supports individualized skill development.

Generative AI is used in academic research to streamline literature reviews, synthesize data, and create content. For example, GPT's ability to process vast amounts of information allows researchers to conduct literature reviews faster, extracting relevant insights from multiple academic sources (Passmore & Tee, 2023). In addition, generative AI models aid in generating coherent and contextually relevant research papers, fostering efficiency in the academic writing and publishing process. It also supports interdisciplinary collaboration by facilitating the integration of diverse datasets and methodologies (Peres et al., 2023; Lim et al., 2023). In fields where research involves complex data analysis and interpretation, such as data science and computational biology, generative models enable researchers to create hypotheses, explore data patterns, and formulate research questions (Willey et al., 2023). These models assist in developing educational resources that cater to diverse learning needs and accommodate different linguistic preferences. This inclusivity extends to research, where generative models can aid in translating and summarizing research findings, making academic content more accessible to a global audience.

Software Engineering

Generative AI alters traditional approaches to code generation, optimization, and problem-solving. One of the significant contributions of generative models in this field is the automated generation of code snippets and functions (Reeves et al., 2023). GPT's natural language processing capabilities enable it to understand and generate coherent code based on textual prompts, significantly expediting the coding process for developers (Daun & Brings, 2023). This enhances productivity and assists programmers, especially those newer to coding, by providing valuable suggestions and examples. Furthermore, generative AI supports code optimization by proposing alternative algorithms and approaches (Reeves et al., 2023). GPT can analyze existing codebases, identify inefficiencies, and generate optimized versions. This aspect of generative AI streamlines the development process and helps create robust and scalable software applications.

The integration of generative AI in software engineering encompasses documentation and communication. GPT can assist in automatically generating documentation for codebases, making software projects more comprehensible and maintainable (Rose et al., 2023). This is particularly valuable in collaborative software development environments where clear documentation is crucial for effective collaboration and knowledge transfer. Moreover, generative AI contributes to software testing by generating diverse test cases and scenarios (Reeves et al., 2023). GPT can simulate different inputs, edge cases, and error conditions, aiding in the identification of potential bugs and vulnerabilities. The collaborative potential of generative AI in software engineering is exemplified by its role in fostering human-machine collaboration (Daun & Brings, 2023). Developers can leverage generative models to brainstorm ideas, troubleshoot issues, and refine their coding practices. This collaboration enhances creativity, problem-solving, and overall software development proficiency.

Operations and Supply Chain Management

Generative AI offers innovative solutions for efficiency, decision-making, and adaptability in operations and supply chain management. In the context of operations, generative models can enhance decision support systems by processing vast datasets related to production, inventory, and logistics (Fosso Wamba et al., 2023). GPT's natural language understanding capabilities enable it to analyze complex operational scenarios, providing valuable insights for optimizing resource allocation, production schedules, and supply chain strategies. Supply chain management is characterized by an intricate network of processes (Richey et al., 2023). As a result, it benefits significantly from the integration of generative AI. For example, companies can use GPT-based models to forecast demand by analyzing historical data, market trends, and external factors (Fosso Wamba et al., 2023). This facilitates accurate predictions, enabling organizations to optimize inventory levels, reduce carrying costs, and mitigate the risk of stockouts or overstock situations. In addition, generative AI can support risk management within supply chains (Hirsch, 2023a). In this regard, generative AI models can process and interpret a diverse range of data sources, including geopolitical events, economic indicators, and environmental factors. This application can help assess potential risks and recommend mitigation strategies, resulting in resilient supply chain operations.

The implementation of generative AI in operations and supply chain management supports logistics optimization. For instance, GPT can assist in route planning, warehouse management, and distribution strategies by considering various factors such as transportation costs, delivery times, and inventory levels (Fosso Wamba et al., 2023). This optimization leads to cost reduction, improved delivery performance, and enhanced customer satisfaction. The human-machine collaboration facilitated by generative AI empowers professionals to focus on strategic decision-making while automating routine and data-intensive tasks (Karakose et al., 2023). This collaboration enhances the agility of supply chain operations, allowing for quicker adaptation to market dynamics and changes in demand.

Tourism Decision-Making

Generative AI provides new ways of promoting destinations, personalizing travel experiences, and formulating strategic decisions within the tourism industry. One major application of generative AI is the provision of personalized travel recommendations (Kim et al., 2023). Generative models can analyze vast datasets, including traveler preferences, historical trends, and cultural nuances, to generate tailored suggestions for individuals or groups. This enhances the overall travel experience and facilitates destination marketing by providing targeted and appealing recommendations (Wong et al., 2023). In addition, predictive analytics powered by generative AI can improve tourism decision-making. GPT-based models can analyze historical data, booking patterns, and external factors to forecast future trends in tourism demand (Dwivedi et al., 2023). This foresight enables tourism businesses and destinations to anticipate peak periods, optimize resource allocation, and tailor marketing strategies to capitalize on emerging opportunities.

Businesses and professionals in the tourism industry can leverage generative to create relevant content, such as travel narratives, promotional materials, and social media content. This content creation capability streamlines marketing efforts and ensures a consistent and engaging portrayal of destinations, leading to positive perceptions and increased visitor interest (Kim et al., 2023; Salah et al., 2023). Moreover, chatbots powered by generative AI enhance customer interactions in the tourism sector. These virtual assistants can provide real-time information on travel itineraries, local attractions, and accommodation options (Dwivedi et al., 2023). The conversational abilities of generative models contribute to a more natural and responsive interaction, enhancing customer satisfaction and facilitating efficient decision-making for travelers (Hirsch, 2023b). Besides, the ability to analyze diverse sources of information, including geopolitical events, weather patterns, and health-related data, using generative models can enhance risk mitigation strategies.

Human-AI Collaboration

Human-AI collaboration represents a transformative paradigm in which humans and AI work together synergistically to achieve enhanced creativity, problem-solving, and productivity. This collaboration acknowledges the strengths of both human intelligence and AI capabilities and aims to leverage their combined potential across various domains (Karakose et al., 2023). For instance, generative AI models assist humans in creative processes such as content creation, design, and storytelling. GPT's ability to generate content serves as a valuable tool for inspiration and ideation (Zhao & Wang, 2023). This collaboration enhances creativity by providing a constant flow of ideas, suggestions, and alternatives, thereby accelerating the creative process (Triantoro et al., 2023). Human-AI collaboration can be applied to problem-solving to enable more effective and efficient solutions. Human experts can leverage the analytical and pattern recognition capabilities of generative AI models to gain insights, generate hypotheses, and explore alternative approaches (Ali et al., 2023). This collaboration is applicable in multiple other fields, including data analysis, research, and software engineering, where the combination of human intuition and AI-driven analysis yields more innovative solutions.

Human-AI collaboration is instrumental in knowledge dissemination and decision-making. Generative models contribute to natural language understanding, enabling more effective communication between humans and AI systems (Ritala et al., 2023). This is particularly valuable in applications such as customer support, where chatbots powered by generative AI can engage in conversations with users to enhance their experience. The integration of generative AI in collaborative workflows also leads to advancements in interdisciplinary research (Triantoro et al., 2023). Professionals from diverse fields can collaborate with generative models to explore new ideas and analyze complex datasets. This multidisciplinary collaboration fosters innovation by combining domain-specific expertise with the analytical power of AI-driven insights.

Challenges of Generative AI and GPT

The use of generative AI and GPT models is associated with multiple challenges that hinder optimal application. For example, the quality of data and potential misuse is a major challenge related to ChatGPT usage (Kim et al., 2023). In addition, generative AI infrastructure requires a lot of resources and is associated with high energy consumption. This can be a limiting factor, especially for SMEs with limited budgets. Other major factors identified in the research include ethical concerns, issues related to content authorship and originality, data inaccuracies, potential bias, and security and privacy concerns.

Ethical Concerns

Generative AI and GPT models have raised numerous ethical challenges. For instance, the significant use of AI technologies increases the risk of spreading inaccurate information and deceptive narratives (Stahl & Eke, 2024). In addition, the lack of transparency and accountability in the development and deployment of generative AI poses ethical issues (Banafa, 2023). The automation of various tasks has led to workforce displacement, causing major ethical concerns. GPT models' ability to generate highly context-aware and human-like text raises the risk of unintentionally disclosing confidential information or creating content that poses privacy threats (Stahl & Eke, 2024). Additionally, the advent of deepfakes driven by generative AI raises ethical questions about the potential misuse of realistic and deceptive content for malicious purposes.

Content Originality and Authorship

The vast capabilities of generative AI and GPT models to generate diverse and coherent text raise questions about the authenticity of the content produced. The challenge lies in distinguishing between content created by human authors and that generated by AI, blurring the lines of authorship (Walczak & Cellary, 2023). This issue has implications for intellectual property rights, academic integrity, and the recognition of human creative contributions (Fenwick & Jurcys, 2023). As AI-generated content becomes more prevalent, addressing the question of authorship and establishing mechanisms to protect original human-authored work is a critical concern.

Potential Bias and Data Inaccuracies

Generative AI and GPT models are trained on extensive datasets, which raises concerns regarding potential bias and data inaccuracies. The information embedded in these datasets can inadvertently introduce biases, reflecting historical prejudices and societal inequities. This increases the risk of perpetuating and amplifying these biases in the generated content, thereby reinforcing stereotypes or discriminatory patterns. Moreover, the accuracy of generative AI depends on the quality and representativeness of the training data (Levantino, 2023). Therefore, inaccuracies within the training data can lead to the generation of content that lacks factual correctness. This challenge is particularly high when the training data exhibits disparities or inaccuracies in capturing diverse perspectives, experiences, or contexts.

Inaccuracies in AI Detection Tools

The use of AI detection tools to discern AI-generated content presents a notable challenge due to the potential for inaccuracies. As generative AI models like GPT advance, developing detection tools that reliably differentiate between AI-generated and human-authored content has become increasingly complex (Dalalah & Dalalah, 2023). This has resulted in multiple cases of false positives and false negatives, both instances of misclassification. False positives occur when human-generated content is incorrectly attributed to AI. This leads to unwarranted skepticism and mistrust. Conversely, false negatives occur when AI-generated content is not detected. These issues challenge the credibility of AI detection tools, which are particularly important in contexts where the accurate identification of authorship is critical, such as academic research or creative practices (Laker & Sena, 2023). For instance, the failure to identify AI-generated content in educational settings may undermine the trustworthiness of research outputs and compromise the principles of intellectual honesty.

CONCLUSION

Generative AI and GPT are disruptive innovations adopted in multiple industries for various applications, such as generating content, creating AI images, and composing music and video content. The launching of OpenAI's ChatGPT for end users increased the popularity of generation AI, resulting in the building and deployment of multiple AI-based tools. Companies and individual users are leveraging generative AI to improve productivity and efficiency. For example, GPT models can be used for sentiment analysis, language translation, content creation, and text classification. As a result, generative AI and GPT have created opportunities across various industries ranging from marketing, education, health, travel, and tourism. These opportunities include improved efficiency and innovation in marketing and marketing analysis, human resource management, property valuation, and education and academic research. In addition, generative AI has had a significant impact on various professions, such as software engineering. Developers can input prompts on GPT to generate and optimize codes. Leveraging these AI tools enables businesses to create resilient and transparent supply chains for better performance and operational efficiency. They also enhance tourism decision-making by empowering companies and travelers with the appropriate information needed to make decisions. These opportunities are often optimized through human-AI collaborations that leverage user and machine intelligence to deliver certain outcomes.

Despite the opportunities generative AI and GPT create, these innovations present numerous challenges. For instance, they are trained on pre-existing large amounts of data, which increases the risks of bias and data inaccuracies. If the data used to train the models is inaccurate, the outputs will be incorrect, thereby leading to misinformation and misguided decision-making. In addition, these AI systems can be manipulated for malicious purposes. With the blurred lines between AI-generated and human-written content, originality and authorship have become major challenges. This challenge has had a significant impact on academic integrity and intellectual property. Although AI models are trained using pre-existing data, there have been concerns about the lack of recognition of human creative contributions. Finally, unintentional disclosure of personal, confidential data is a major challenge with generative AI tools. There is a need to implement appropriate measures that safeguard the privacy and security of users. As technologies advance, breakthroughs in generative AI and GPT models will continue to enhance their adoption and applications. Therefore, it is important to develop and implement solutions addressing these problems to mitigate their potential risks.

Generative AI, particularly exemplified by Generative Pre-trained Transformers, has significant theoretical and practical implications across various domain. Aspects to consider: (i) GPT models learn rich hierarchical representations of data, capturing complex patterns and relationships. This has implications for understanding how neural networks can encode and manipulate information; (ii) pre-training on vast datasets allows models to generalize well to a wide range of tasks, showcasing the potential for transfer learning. The theoretical understanding of how this knowledge transfer occurs is a key area of interest; (iii) GPT models demonstrate an impressive ability to understand and generate human-like text. The theoretical implications involve insights into natural language understanding, syntax, semantics, and even pragmatics; (iv) generative AI has shown a capacity for creative generation, including text, art, and more. This raises questions about machine creativity, the nature of imagination in artificial systems, and the potential for AI-driven creative collaboration; (v) the theoretical implications of AI ethics become more prominent with generative models, considering concerns like bias, fairness, and the responsible use of technology; (vi) GPT models excel in NLP tasks like text completion, summarization, translation, and sentiment analysis. Applications include chatbots, content generation, and language translation services; (vii) generative AI has practical applications in content creation for various media, including text, images, and music. This can enhance creative workflows, automate content generation, and even assist in design tasks; (viii) GPT-based models have potential in analyzing medical data, assisting in diagnostics, and even contributing to drug discovery by understanding complex biological relationships.

In conclusion, the theoretical and practical implications of Generative AI, especially in the context of models like GPT, span a wide range of fields, opening up new possibilities and challenges in both understanding artificial intelligence and applying it to solve real-world problems.

The field of Generative AI, especially with the advent of models like Generative Pre-trained Transformers (GPT), has seen significant advancements. Potential future lines of research in Generative AI and applications of models like GPT: (i) methods for fine-tuning pre-trained generative models like GPT for specific industries or domains. This could enhance the model's performance in generating content relevant to particular fields such as medicine, law, finance, etc; (ii) the integration of vision and language in generative models. This could involve creating models that generate both text and image content coherently, enabling more versatile applications in areas like content creation and storytelling; (iii) research ways to identify and mitigate biases present in generated content. Understanding and addressing bias in generative models is crucial to ensure fair and ethical use in various applications, including content creation and decision-making systems; (iv) investigate methods for enabling dynamic and interactive content generation. This could involve generating content that evolves based on user interactions or real-time changes in input conditions, expanding the utility of generative models in dynamic environments; (v) techniques to enhance the multilingual capabilities of generative models. This includes improving language translation, cross-language content generation, and understanding the nuances of different languages in the generative process; and (vi) develop methods to make generative models more interpretable and explainable. Understanding how these models arrive at specific outputs is crucial for building trust and ensuring accountability, especially in sensitive applications like healthcare or legal document generation.

As technology continues to advance, these research directions in Generative AI and applications of models like GPT aim to push the boundaries of what is possible, addressing challenges and unlocking new possibilities for creative, responsible, and ethical use of generative technologies.

ACKNOWLEDGMENT

I would like to express gratitude to the Editor and the Arbitrators. They offered extremely valuable suggestions or improvements. The GOVCOPP Research Center of the University of Aveiro supported the author.

REFERENCES

Ali, O., Murray, P., Momin, M., & Al-Anzi, F. S. (2023). The knowledge and innovation challenges of ChatGPT: A scoping review. *Technology in Society*, *75*, C7–C102402. doi:10.1016/j.techsoc.2023.102402

Aydın, N., & Erdem, O. A. (2022, December). A Research on the New Generation Artificial Intelligence Technology Generative Pretraining Transformer 3. In *2022 3rd International Informatics and Software Engineering Conference (IISEC)* (pp. 1-6). IEEE. http://dx.doi.org/10.1109/IISEC56263.2022.9998298

Banafa, A. (2023). *Transformative AI: Responsible, Transparent, and Trustworthy AI Systems*. River Publishers.

Bandi, A., Adapa, P. V. S. R., & Kuchi, Y. E. V. P. K. (2023). The power of generative ai: A review of requirements, models, input–output formats, evaluation metrics, and challenges. *Future Internet*, *15*(8), 260. doi:10.3390/fi15080260

Brynjolfsson, E., Li, D., & Raymond, L. R. (2023). *Generative AI at work* (No. w31161). National Bureau of Economic Research. https://www.nber.org/system/files/working_papers/w31161/w31161.pdf

Buckley, A. (2023). Generative AI: A master or servant of market research analysis? *Applied Marketing Analytics*, *9*(2), 145–152.

Budhwar, P., Chowdhury, S., Wood, G., Aguinis, H., Bamber, G. J., Beltran, J. R., Boselie, P., Lee Cooke, F., Decker, S., DeNisi, A., Dey, P. K., Guest, D., Knoblich, A. J., Malik, A., Paauwe, J., Papagiannidis, S., Patel, C., Pereira, V., Ren, S., ... Varma, A. (2023). Human resource management in the age of generative artificial intelligence: Perspectives and research directions on ChatGPT. *Human Resource Management Journal*, *33*(3), 606–659. doi:10.1111/1748-8583.12524

Cheung, K. S. (2023). Real Estate Insights Unleashing the potential of ChatGPT in property valuation reports: The "Red Book" compliance Chain-of-thought (CoT) prompt engineering. *Journal of Property Investment & Finance*. Advance online publication. doi:10.1108/JPIF-06-2023-0053

Dalalah, D., & Dalalah, O. M. A. (2023). The false positives and false negatives of generative AI detection tools in education and academic research: The case of ChatGPT. *International Journal of Management Education, 21*(2). doi:10.1016/j.ijme.2023.100822

Daun, M., & Brings, J. (2023). How ChatGPT Will Change Software Engineering. *Education. Annual Conference on Innovation and Technology in Computer Science Education, ITiCSE.*

Dwivedi, Y. K., Hughes, L., Bhadeshia, H. K. D. H., Ananiadou, S., Cohn, A. G., Cole, J. M., . . . Wang, X. (2023). Artificial intelligence (AI) futures: India-UK collaborations emerging from the 4th Royal Society Yusuf Hamied workshop. *International Journal of Information Management.* 10.1016/j.ijinfomgt.2023.102725

Dwivedi, Y. K., Kshetri, N., Hughes, L., Slade, E. L., Jeyaraj, A., Kar, A. K., Baabdullah, A. M., Koohang, A., Raghavan, V., Ahuja, M., Albanna, H., Albashrawi, M. A., Al-Busaidi, A. S., Balakrishnan, J., Barlette, Y., Basu, S., Bose, I., Brooks, L., Buhalis, D., ... Wright, R. (2023). "So what if ChatGPT wrote it?" Multidisciplinary perspectives on opportunities, challenges and implications of generative conversational AI for research, practice and policy. *International Journal of Information Management, 71*, C7–C102642. doi:10.1016/j.ijinfomgt.2023.102642

Dwivedi, Y. K., Pandey, N., Currie, W., & Micu, A. (2023). Leveraging ChatGPT and other generative artificial intelligence (AI)-based applications in the hospitality and tourism industry: Practices, challenges and research agenda. *International Journal of Contemporary Hospitality Management.* Advance online publication. doi:10.1108/IJCHM-05-2023-0686

Earley, S. (2023). What executives need to know about knowledge management, large language models and generative AI. *Applied Marketing Analytics, 9*(3), 215–229.

Fenwick, M., & Jurcys, P. (2023). Originality and the future of copyright in an age of generative AI. *Computer Law & Security Report, 51*, C7–C105892. doi:10.1016/j.clsr.2023.105892

Fosso Wamba, S., Guthrie, C., Queiroz, M. M., & Minner, S. (2023). ChatGPT and generative artificial intelligence: An exploratory study of key benefits and challenges in operations and supply chain management. *International Journal of Production Research*, 1–21. Advance online publication. doi:10.1080/00207543.2023.2294116

Fosso Wamba, S., Queiroz, M. M., Chiappetta Jabbour, C. J., & Shi, C. V. (2023). Are both generative AI and ChatGPT game changers for 21st-Century operations and supply chain excellence? *International Journal of Production Economics, 265*, C7–C109015. doi:10.1016/j.ijpe.2023.109015

García-Peñalvo, F., & Vázquez-Ingelmo, A. (2023). What do we mean by GenAI? a systematic mapping of the evolution, trends, and techniques involved in generative AI. *International Journal of Interactive Multimedia and Artificial Intelligence, 8*(4), 7–16. doi:10.9781/ijimai.2023.07.006

Guha, A., Grewal, D., & Atlas, S. (2023). Generative AI and Marketing Education: What the Future Holds. *Journal of Marketing Education.* Advance online publication. doi:10.1177/02734753231215436

Hirsch, P. B. (2023a). At the crossroads: Generative AI and corporate risk management. *The Journal of Business Strategy, 44*(6), 426–429. doi:10.1108/JBS-09-2023-0196

Hirsch, P. B. (2023b). Cui bono: A conversation with ChatGPT. *The Journal of Business Strategy, 44*(4), 238–241. doi:10.1108/JBS-05-2023-0088

Hughes, B., Bothe, S., Farooq, H., & Imran, A. (2019, February). Generative adversarial learning for machine learning empowered self-organizing 5G networks. In 2019 international conference on computing, networking and communications (ICNC) (pp. 282-286). IEEE.

Jackson, I., Jesus Saenz, M., & Ivanov, D. (2023). From natural language to simulations: Applying AI to automate simulation modelling of logistics systems. *International Journal of Production Research*. Advance online publication. doi:10.1080/00207543.2023.2276811

Kanbach, D. K., Heiduk, L., Blueher, G., Schreiter, M., & Lahmann, A. (2023). The GenAI is out of the bottle: Generative artificial intelligence from a business model innovation perspective. *Review of Managerial Science*. Advance online publication. doi:10.1007/s11846-023-00696-z

Karakose, T., Demirkol, M., Yirci, R., Polat, H., Ozdemir, T. Y., & Tülübaş, T. (2023). A conversation with ChatGPT about digital leadership and technology integration: comparative analysis based on human–AI collaboration. *Administrative Sciences, 13*(7). doi:10.3390/admsci13070157

Kim, J. H., Kim, J., Kim, S. S., & Hailu, T. B. (2023). Effects of AI ChatGPT on travelers' travel decision-making. *Tourism Review*. Advance online publication. doi:10.1108/TR-07-2023-0489

Kim, J. H., Kim, J., Park, J., Kim, C., Jhang, J., & King, B. (2023). When ChatGPT gives incorrect answers: The impact of inaccurate information by Generative AI on tourism decision-making. *Journal of Travel Research*. Advance online publication. doi:10.1177/00472875231212996

Korzynski, P., Mazurek, G., Altmann, A., Ejdys, J., Kazlauskaite, R., Paliszkiewicz, J., Wach, K., & Ziemba, E. (2023). Generative artificial intelligence as a new context for management theories: Analysis of ChatGPT. *Central European Management Journal, 31*(1), 3–13. doi:10.1108/CEMJ-02-2023-0091

Kshetri, N., Dwivedi, Y. K., Davenport, T. H., & Panteli, N. (2023). Generative artificial intelligence in marketing: Applications, opportunities, challenges, and research agenda. *International Journal of Information Management*. doi:10.1016/j.ijinfomgt.2023.102716

Laker, L. F., & Sena, M. (2023). Accuracy and detection of student use of ChatGPT in business analytics courses. *Issues in Information Systems, 24*(2), 153–163. doi:10.48009/2_iis_2023_113

Levantino, F. P. (2023). Generative and AI-powered oracles: "What will they say about you?" *Computer Law & Security Report, 51*, C7–C105898. doi:10.1016/j.clsr.2023.105898

Lim, W. M., Gunasekara, A., Pallant, J. L., Pallant, J. I., & Pechenkina, E. (2023). Generative AI and the future of education: Ragnarök or reformation? A paradoxical perspective from management educators. *International Journal of Management Education, 21*(2). doi:10.1016/j.ijme.2023.100790

Ma, J., & Huang, K. (2023). ChatGPT in Real Estate. In A. I. Beyond (Ed.), *ChatGPT, Web3, and the Business Landscape of Tomorrow* (pp. 219–242). Springer Nature Switzerland. doi:10.1007/978-3-031-45282-6_8

Maksymyuk, T., Gazda, J., Luntovskyy, A., & Klymash, M. (2018, September). Artificial intelligence based 5G coverage design and optimization using deep generative adversarial neural networks. In *2018 International Conference on Information and Telecommunication Technologies and Radio Electronics (UkrMiCo)* (pp. 1-4). IEEE. 10.1109/UkrMiCo43733.2018.9047611

Niszczota, P., & Conway, P. (2023). Judgements of research co-created by Generative AI: Experimental evidence. *Economics and Business Review, 9*(2), 101–114. doi:10.18559/ebr.2023.2.744

O'Leary, D. E. (2023). Enterprise large language models: Knowledge characteristics, risks, and organizational activities. *International Journal of Intelligent Systems in Accounting Finance & Management, 30*(3), 113–119. doi:10.1002/isaf.1541

Passmore, J., & Tee, D. (2023). The library of Babel: Assessing the powers of artificial intelligence in knowledge synthesis, learning and development and coaching. *Journal of Work-Applied Management*. Advance online publication. doi:10.1108/JWAM-06-2023-0057

Peres, R., Schreier, M., Schweidel, D., & Sorescu, A. (2023). Editorial: On ChatGPT and beyond: How generative artificial intelligence may affect research, teaching, and practice. *International Journal of Research in Marketing, 40*(2), 269–275. doi:10.1016/j.ijresmar.2023.03.001

Raimundo, R., & Rosário, A. T. (2022). Cybersecurity in the Internet of Things in Industrial Management. *Applied Sciences (Basel, Switzerland), 12*(3), 1598. doi:10.3390/app12031598

Reeves, B., Sarsa, S., Prather, J., Denny, P., Becker, B. A., Hellas, A., ... Leinonen, J. (2023). Evaluating the performance of code generation models for solving parsons problems with small prompt variations. *Annual Conference on Innovation and Technology in Computer Science Education, ITiCSE.* 10.1145/3587102.3588805

Richey, R. G. Jr, Chowdhury, S., Davis-Sramek, B., Giannakis, M., & Dwivedi, Y. K. (2023). Artificial intelligence in logistics and supply chain management: A primer and roadmap for research. *Journal of Business Logistics, 44*(4), 532–549. doi:10.1111/jbl.12364

Ritala, P., Ruokonen, M., & Ramaul, L. (2023). Transforming boundaries: How does ChatGPT change knowledge work? *The Journal of Business Strategy*. Advance online publication. doi:10.1108/JBS-05-2023-0094

Rosário, A. T., & Dias, J. C. (2023). How Industry 4.0 and Sensors Can Leverage Product Design: Opportunities and Challenges. *Sensors (Basel), 23*(3), 1165. doi:10.3390/s23031165 PMID:36772206

Rosário, A. T., Lopes, P. R., & Rosário, F. S. (2023). Metaverse in Marketing: Challenges and Opportunities. In A. Khang, V. Shah, & S. Rani (Eds.), *Handbook of Research on AI-Based Technologies and Applications in the Era of the Metaverse* (pp. 204–227). IGI Global. doi:10.4018/978-1-6684-8851-5.ch010

Rose, K., Massey, V., Marshall, B., & Cardon, P. (2023). IS professors' perspectives on AI-assisted programming. *Issues in Information Systems, 24*(2), 178–190. doi:10.48009/2_iis_2023_115

Sætra, H. S. (2023). Generative AI: Here to stay, but for good? *Technology in Society, 75*, 102372. doi:10.1016/j.techsoc.2023.102372

Salah, M., Abdelfattah, F., & Al Halbusi, H. (2023). Generative Artificial Intelligence (ChatGPT & Bard) in public administration research: A double-edged sword for street-level bureaucracy studies. *International Journal of Public Administration*, 1–7. Advance online publication. doi:10.1080/01900692.2023.2274801

Spennemann, D. H. R. (2023). Children of AI: A protocol for managing the born-digital ephemera spawned by Generative AI language models. *Publications, 11*(3). doi:10.3390/publications11030045

Stahl, B. C., & Eke, D. (2024). The ethics of ChatGPT – Exploring the ethical issues of an emerging technology. *International Journal of Information Management*, *74*, C7–C102700. doi:10.1016/j.ijinfomgt.2023.102700

Triantoro, T., Przegalinska, A., & Kovbasiuk, A. (2023). Human-AI collaboration in the contemporary workplace: the job demands-resources model perspective. *36th Bled eConference: Digital Economy and Society: The Balancing Act for Digital Innovation in Times of Instability, BLED 2023 – Proceedings*.

Walczak, K., & Cellary, W. (2023). Challenges for higher education in the era of widespread access to Generative AI. *Economics and Business Review*, *9*(2), 71–100. doi:10.18559/ebr.2023.2.743

Wang, Y. C., Xue, J., Wei, C., & Kuo, C. C. J. (2023). *An Overview on Generative AI at Scale with Edge-Cloud Computing*. https://arxiv.org/pdf/2306.17170.pdf

Willey, L., White, B. J., & Deale, C. S. (2023). Teaching AI in the college course: Introducing the AI prompt development life cycle (PDLC). *Issues in Information Systems*, *24*(2), 123–138. doi:10.48009/2_iis_2023_111

Winkler, C., Hammoda, B., Noyes, E., & Van Gelderen, M. (2023). Entrepreneurship education at the dawn of generative artificial intelligence. *Entrepreneurship Education and Pedagogy*, *6*(4), 579–589. doi:10.1177/25151274231198799

Wong, I. A., Lian, Q. L., & Sun, D. (2023). Autonomous travel decision-making: An early glimpse into ChatGPT and generative AI. *Journal of Hospitality and Tourism Management*, *56*, 253–263. doi:10.1016/j.jhtm.2023.06.022

Xu, M., Du, H., Niyato, D., Kang, J., Xiong, Z., Mao, S., Han, Z., Jamalipour, A., Kim, D. I., Shen, X., Leung, V. C. M., & Poor, H. V. (2024). Unleashing the power of edge-cloud generative ai in mobile networks: A survey of aigc services. *IEEE Communications Surveys and Tutorials*, 1. Advance online publication. doi:10.1109/COMST.2024.3353265

Yenduri, G., Ramalingam, M., Chemmalar Selvi, G., Supriya, Y., Srivastava, G., Maddikunta, P. K. R., . . . Athanasios, V. (2023). GPT (Generative Pre-trained Transformer)–A Comprehensive Review on Enabling Technologies, Potential Applications, Emerging Challenges, and Future Directions. *arXiv preprint arXiv:2305.10435,* 1-40. https://doi.org//arXiv.2305.10435 doi:10.48550

Zhao, J., & Wang, X. (2023). Unleashing efficiency and insights: Exploring the potential applications and challenges of ChatGPT in accounting. *Journal of Corporate Accounting & Finance*. Advance online publication. doi:10.1002/jcaf.22663

Zhou, W., Zhang, C., Wu, L., & Shashidhar, M. (2023). ChatGPT and marketing: Analyzing public discourse in early Twitter posts. *Journal of Marketing Analytics*, *11*(4), 693–706. doi:10.1057/s41270-023-00250-6

ADDITIONAL READING

Awan, U., Shamim, S., Khan, Z., Zia, N. U., Shariq, S. M., & Khan, M. N. (2021). Big data analytics capability and decision-making: The role of data-driven insight on circular economy performance. *Technological Forecasting and Social Change*, *168*, C7–C120766. doi:10.1016/j.techfore.2021.120766

Chen, H., Chiang, R. H. L., & Storey, V. C. (2012). Business intelligence and analytics: From big data to big impact. *Management Information Systems Quarterly*, *36*(4), 1165–1188. doi:10.2307/41703503

Du, H., Teng, S., Chen, H., Ma, J., Wang, X., Gou, C., Li, B., Ma, S., Miao, Q., Na, X., Ye, P., Zhang, H., Luo, G., & Wang, F. Y. (2023). Chat With ChatGPT on Intelligent Vehicles: An IEEE TIVPerspective. *IEEE Transactions on Intelligent Vehicles*, *8*(3), 2020–2026. doi:10.1109/TIV.2023.3253281

Dwivedi, Y. K., Kshetri, N., Hughes, L., Slade, E. L., Jeyaraj, A., Kar, A. K., Baabdullah, A. M., Koohang, A., Raghavan, V., Ahuja, M., Albanna, H., Albashrawi, M. A., Al-Busaidi, A. S., Balakrishnan, J., Barlette, Y., Basu, S., Bose, I., Brooks, L., Buhalis, D., ... Wright, R. (2023). "So what if ChatGPT wrote it?" Multidisciplinary perspectives on opportunities, challenges and implications of generative conversational AI for research, practice and policy. *International Journal of Information Management*, *71*, 102642. Advance online publication. doi:10.1016/j.ijinfomgt.2023.102642

Rosário, A., Moniz, L. B., & Cruz, R. (2021). Data science applied to marketing: A literature review. *Journal of Information Science and Engineering*, *37*(5), 1067–1081. doi:10.6688/JISE.202109_37(5).0006

KEY TERMS AND DEFINITIONS

Artificial Intelligence: Simulation of human intelligence processes by machines, especially computer systems.

Big Data: Area of knowledge that studies how to treat, analyze and obtain information from very large data sets.

Compound Annual Growth Rate (CAGR): Is the rate of return (RoR) that would be required for an investment to grow from its beginning balance to its ending balance, assuming the profits were reinvested at the end of each period of the investment's life span.

DALL-E: Is an artificial intelligence program that creates images from textual descriptions.

Generative Pre-Trained Transformer (GPT): Interactive experience that enhances the real world with computer-generated perceptual information.

GitHub Copilot: Is an artificial intelligence tool developed by GitHub in conjunction with OpenAI, in order to assist users of integrated development environments such as Visual Studio Code, Visual Studio, Neovim and JetBrains by suggesting code for automatic completion.

Machine Learning: Is a field of study in artificial intelligence concerned with the development and study of statistical algorithms that can learn from data and generalize to unseen data, and thus perform tasks without explicit instructions.

Natural Language Generation (NLG): Is the use of artificial intelligence (AI) programming to produce written or spoken narratives from a data set.

Natural Language Processing: A branch of artificial intelligence that enables computers to comprehend, generate, and manipulate human language.

Natural Language Understanding (NLU): Is the ability of a computer to understand human language.

Section 2

Applied Artmaking With A-GAI

Chapter 4
The Human-Machine Nexus With Art-Making Generative AIs

Pankaj Bhambri
https://orcid.org/0000-0003-4437-4103
Guru Nanak Dev Engineering College, Ludhiana, India

Alex Khang
https://orcid.org/0000-0001-8379-4659
Global Research Institute of Technology and Engineering, USA

ABSTRACT

The chapter delves into the dynamic interplay between human creativity and artificial intelligence, exploring the transformative landscape of art creation facilitated by generative AI tools. As the realms of technology and artistic expression converge, this chapter navigates the intricate relationship between human artists and machine-generated algorithms. It scrutinizes how generative AI tools serve not as replacements for human ingenuity but as collaborators, augmenting the creative process and challenging conventional notions of authorship in the realm of art. Through a comprehensive examination of case studies and examples, the chapter illustrates the symbiotic fusion of human intuition, emotion, and conceptualization with the computational capabilities of AI, shedding light on the profound implications for the future of artistic endeavors.

1. INTRODUCTION

Generative AI, namely through the utilization of generative models, has fundamentally transformed the field of artificial intelligence by empowering machines to produce text, images, as well as code that closely resembles human creations. The aforementioned models are trained using extensive datasets and can produce a wide range of information that is relevant to the given context. Generative AI in the realm of natural language enables the production of coherent and contextually suitable replies, rendering it valuable for endeavors such as content generation, language interpretation, and even conversational

DOI: 10.4018/979-8-3693-1950-5.ch004

bots. The capabilities of generative AI raise exciting possibilities for human-AI collaboration, as it can assist humans in various creative and cognitive tasks.

Human-machine collaboration is an evolving paradigm that emphasizes leveraging the strengths of both humans and machines to achieve more than what either could accomplish alone. Generative AI plays a crucial role in this collaboration by enhancing the creative capacities of humans and automating certain aspects of complex tasks. For instance, in content creation, writers can use generative AI to generate ideas, suggest improvements, or even draft sections of text, allowing them to focus on higher-level aspects of their work. In this way, generative AI becomes a collaborative tool, augmenting human capabilities and facilitating more efficient and innovative workflows.

However, the collaboration between generative AI and humans also poses challenges, including ethical considerations, bias in model outputs, and the potential displacement of certain jobs (Ha & Schmidhuber, 2018). Striking the right balance between the strengths of AI and human intuition is crucial for the effective and responsible integration of generative AI into various domains. Efforts should be directed towards developing transparent and explainable AI systems, ensuring that humans can understand and trust the outputs of generative models. Ultimately, successful human-machine collaboration in the era of generative AI requires a thoughtful approach that maximizes the benefits while addressing the associated challenges.

2. KEY CONCEPTS

Generative AI encompasses a set of technologies that enable machines to generate new content, such as text, images, or even entire virtual environments, autonomously (Schneider & Fischer, 2019). Generative AI is fundamentally based on sophisticated algorithms, frequently utilizing deep learning methods such as generative adversarial networks, also known as GANs or recurrent neural networks of neurons (RNNs). These algorithms are trained on vast datasets to understand patterns and relationships, allowing the model to create novel outputs that mimic the input data. The key concept of generative AI lies in its ability to produce content that goes beyond mere replication, introducing an element of creativity and innovation. This technology has diverse applications, from generating realistic images to composing music or crafting written content. As generative AI continues to advance, ethical considerations and responsible deployment become crucial to ensure that the generated content aligns with societal norms and values.

Human-machine collaboration represents a fundamental shift in the way artificial intelligence interacts with human users. Rather than replacing human involvement, these systems are designed to work alongside humans, leveraging each other's strengths to achieve enhanced outcomes. In the context of generative AI, collaboration involves humans guiding and refining the outputs generated by the machine (Tan et al., 2019). This synergy capitalizes on the creativity, intuition, and contextual understanding that humans possess while harnessing the computational power and pattern recognition capabilities of the AI. Effective human-machine collaboration requires transparent interfaces, clear communication channels, and iterative feedback loops. Striking the right balance between automation and human intervention ensures that generative AI not only enhances productivity but also aligns with human values and objectives (Zhu et al., 2017). The collaboration fosters a symbiotic relationship where the strengths of both humans and machines are leveraged to achieve outcomes that neither could accomplish independently.

2.1 Optimal Balance Between Humans and Machines in Co-Collaboration

Attaining the ideal equilibrium between humans and machines in collaborative work is a complex and dynamic task that necessitates thoughtful evaluation of the unique capabilities of each participant (Russell & Norvig, 2010). On one side, machines, driven by sophisticated technologies like artificial intelligence and automation, demonstrate exceptional proficiency and effectiveness in managing repetitive and data-intensive jobs. They are essential for handling substantial amounts of data, performing intricate computations, and carrying out repetitive tasks at an unparalleled pace compared to human equivalents (Goodfellow et al., 2016). However, humans contribute distinctive attributes to the collaborative setting, such as creativity, emotional intelligence, critical thinking, and flexibility. These qualities empower individuals to handle uncertainty, exercise moral discernment, and promote creativity, areas in which robots may be lacking. Hence, achieving the ideal equilibrium entails deliberately allocating tasks according to the individual strengths of each collaborator, cultivating a mutually beneficial relationship that harnesses the superior qualities of both humans and machines.

In a successful co-collaboration, the synergy between humans and robots goes beyond just dividing tasks and includes efficient communication, shared comprehension, and ongoing learning (Domingos, 2015). Humans bring valuable contributions to collaborative efforts by providing contextual awareness, ethical concerns, and the ability to interpret complicated social cues. This ensures that the collaborative efforts are in line with broader organizational aims and societal ideals. Simultaneously, machines provide efficiency, scalability, and data-driven insights that improve decision-making processes (Murphy, 2012). The crucial factor lies in fostering a cooperative atmosphere that promotes transparent communication, confidence, and a collective understanding of objectives. Moreover, cultivating a culture that emphasizes ongoing education is essential, given the quick pace of technological advancements (Chollet, 2018). This necessitates the need for both humans and machines to adjust and enhance their skills. By acknowledging the distinct abilities of each collaborator and cultivating a collaborative environment that welcomes variety and innovation, organizations may successfully negotiate the intricacies of the contemporary work environment and fully utilize the potential of human-machine co-collaboration.

2.2 Machine Learning, Neural Networks, and Algorithms

Generative AI and human-machine collaboration involve the integration of various technologies, each playing distinct roles. Machine Learning (ML), Neural Networks, and Algorithms are key components contributing to the capabilities of Generative AI and facilitating effective collaboration between machines and humans. Here's an overview of their roles:

- Machine Learning: ML is the foundational technology behind Generative AI. It enables machines to learn patterns and relationships from data, allowing them to generate new content, such as images, text, or other forms of media (Reed et al., 2016). ML algorithms analyze and interpret large datasets, identifying patterns and making predictions. In collaboration with humans, ML can enhance decision-making by providing insights, predictions, and automation of repetitive tasks.
- Neural Networks: Neural networks, particularly deep neural networks, are a specific category of machine learning that plays a vital role in generative models such as GANs (Generative Adversarial Networks) and Recurrent Neural Networks (RNNs). They excel in capturing complex patterns and generating realistic content (Nilsson, 1998). Neural Networks contribute to natural language pro-

cessing, image recognition, and other tasks where human-like understanding and generation are required. They assist in translating human inputs into meaningful machine actions.

- Algorithms: Algorithms, including optimization algorithms and reinforcement learning algorithms, are essential for training generative models. They guide the learning process, adjusting model parameters to improve performance. Algorithms are of utmost importance in the process of decision-making, optimizing, and resource allocation. They enhance collaboration by automating repetitive decisions and procedures, enabling humans to concentrate on activities that demand creativity, analytical reasoning, and emotional acumen.

2.3 Applications of Generative AI in Artistic Expression

Generative AI has found exciting applications in the realm of artistic expression, transforming the way artists create, explore, and push the boundaries of their craft. Here are some notable applications of Generative AI in art:

- Generative Adversarial Networks (GANs) for Image Generation: GANs can be employed for style transfer, allowing artists to apply the characteristics of famous paintings or unique styles to their artwork (Yampolskiy, 2018). GANs can generate realistic images based on given prompts, opening up new possibilities for creating unique and imaginative visuals.
- Text-to-Image Generation: OpenAI's DALL-E and similar models can create visuals by interpreting written descriptions, allowing artists to visually manifest conceptual ideas expressed in language.
- Music Composition: AI models, particularly Recurrent Neural Networks (RNNs), can compose music in various styles, mimicking the patterns and structures present in training datasets (Bishop, 2006).
- Harmony and Melody Generation: AI algorithms can assist musicians in creating harmonies and melodies, providing inspiration and expanding the creative process.
- Generative Design in Visual Arts: Generative algorithms can be used to create algorithmic or procedural art, generating intricate patterns, shapes, and visual structures that may be challenging for humans to conceive. AI-powered tools can assist in creating unique and aesthetically pleasing typography, offering new possibilities for graphic design and digital art.
- Interactive Art Installations: Artists can use Generative AI to create interactive installations that respond to human input or environmental cues, allowing for dynamic and engaging art experiences (Zhang et al., 2018).
- Animation and Video Production: AI models can assist in generating realistic and expressive character animations, reducing the manual labor involved in frame-by-frame animation. Generative models can be used to synthesize video content, opening up possibilities for creating visually stunning and unique video effects.
- Collaboration Between Artists and AI: Artists can collaborate with AI systems, using them as creative partners in the art-making process. This collaborative approach can lead to the creation of novel and unexpected artworks.
- Art Market and NFTs: Generative AI has been employed to produce distinct digital assets for use in the Non-Fungible Token (NFT) marketplace, enabling artists to convert and trade AI-generated artworks.

- Storytelling and Creative Writing: Natural Language Processing (NLP) models can assist writers by generating story ideas, dialogue, or even entire narratives, fostering creativity in the writing process.

3. THE CREATIVE PROCESS WITH GENERATIVE AIS

Traditionally, the creative process relied heavily on human intuition, experience, and inspiration (Bhambri & Hans, 2010). However, with the advent of Generative AI, artists now can collaborate with intelligent algorithms that can generate novel ideas, designs, and compositions (S. Thrun et al., 2005). These AI models, often based on advanced neural networks, learn from vast datasets of existing creative works and can autonomously produce new, innovative pieces. The creative process with Generative AI involves a dynamic interplay between human creativity and machine-generated suggestions, fostering a symbiotic relationship where the AI augments human potential by offering alternative perspectives, styles, or elements that might not have been considered otherwise. This collaboration enables artists to explore new realms of creativity, pushing the boundaries of traditional artistic expression.

Generative AI also introduces an element of unpredictability and serendipity into the creative process. Artists can input certain parameters or seed ideas, and the AI responds with unexpected and sometimes serendipitous outputs (OpenAI, 2019). This element of surprise can lead to the discovery of unique concepts or aesthetic combinations, sparking inspiration in unexpected ways. The iterative nature of working with Generative AI allows artists to refine and evolve their ideas over time, creating a continuous loop of feedback and adaptation. Ultimately, the creative process with Generative AI is characterized by a dynamic synergy between human intuition, imagination, and the computational capabilities of AI, leading to the emergence of entirely new forms of artistic expression that blend the boundaries between human and machine creativity.

3.1 Exploring Algorithmic Creativity

Exploring algorithmic creativity in Generative AIs involves investigating how these algorithms can be used to generate novel and imaginative outputs across various domains. Algorithmic creativity in Generative AIs can be applied to fields such as art, music, literature, and design. Here are key aspects of exploring algorithmic creativity in Generative AIs:

- Generative Adversarial Networks: GANs are a widely used category of generative algorithms including a generator with a discriminator. The primary objective of the generator is to produce data that closely resembles genuine data, whereas the discriminator's main task is to accurately differentiate between real data and the generated data (Goodfellow et al., 2014). GANs can be employed to produce imaginative results, such as authentic photos, through the process of acquiring knowledge from a dataset. The training process promotes the generation of varied and original content, rendering GANs excellent instruments in algorithmic creation.
- Recurrent Neural Networks and Long Short-Term Memory (LSTM) Networks: RNNs and LSTMs are neural network architectures that excel in processing sequential input. These applications, such as natural language processing and music production, have broad usage in various creative contexts (Elgammal et al., 2017). These networks can learn sequential patterns and generate coherent

sequences. In literature, RNNs can generate text in the style of a given author, while in music, they can compose melodies that follow a specific genre.

- Evolutionary Algorithms: Evolutionary algorithms draw inspiration from the mechanism of natural selection (Hinton et al., 2012). These processes entail the advancement of a group of potential solutions over multiple cycles of selection, mutation, and crossover. These algorithms can be applied to creative tasks by evolving solutions over time. For example, evolutionary algorithms can be used to evolve visual designs, architectural structures, or even game strategies.
- Algorithmic Design and Procedural Generation: Algorithmic design involves using algorithms to generate creative designs, patterns, or structures. Procedural generation refers to the creation of content algorithmically, often used in video games and simulations. Algorithms can be programmed to generate aesthetically pleasing designs, architectural plans, or even entire virtual worlds. Procedural generation enables the creation of diverse and dynamic content in games and simulations.
- Transfer Learning and Style Transfer: Transfer learning entails utilizing acquired knowledge from one job to enhance performance on another (LeCun et al., 2015). Style transfer algorithms provide the capability to transfer the artistic style from one image to another. Transfer learning allows models trained on one dataset to be fine-tuned for creative tasks with limited data. Style transfer can be applied to images, videos, or even text to create unique and artistic variations.

3.2 Examples of Artistic Collaboration With AI

Artistic collaboration with AI involves the integration of artificial intelligence tools and algorithms into the creative process, often working in tandem with human artists to produce unique and innovative artworks. Here are some notable examples of artistic collaboration with AI:

- Google's Magenta Studio: Magenta Studio, developed by Google's Magenta project, explores the intersection of AI and creativity in the music domain (Radford et al., 2015). It offers tools like the AI-powered plugin "AIVA" (Artificial Intelligence Virtual Artist), which assists musicians in generating musical ideas and harmonies.
- DALL-E by OpenAI: OpenAI's DALL-E is a generative model that can generate images from textual prompts. Artists and designers have collaborated with DALL-E to create surreal and imaginative visuals based on textual descriptions, showcasing the potential for AI in visual art creation.
- AI Dungeon: AI Dungeon is an interactive storytelling platform that uses OpenAI's GPT (Generative Pre-trained Transformer) models. Writers and users can collaborate with the AI to create dynamic and evolving narratives by providing text-based prompts. The AI responds to these prompts, generating the next steps in the story.
- AICAN: AICAN is an AI program developed by artist and researcher Ahmed Elgammal. AICAN uses deep learning algorithms to analyze art history data and then generates original artworks. The collaboration involves the artist shaping the training process and selecting the most interesting outputs.
- The Next Rembrandt: In this project, Microsoft and ING collaborated to create a new painting in the style of Rembrandt. Analyzing the artist's existing works, the team used machine learning algorithms to generate a new piece that emulated Rembrandt's techniques and style.

- IBM Watson Beat: Watson Beat is an AI system developed by IBM that collaborates with musicians. It analyzes the emotional content of a story or narrative and generates original musical compositions to match the emotional tone. This collaborative effort between AI and musicians enhances the creative process of composing music.
- Edmond de Belamy: The artwork "Edmond de Belamy" was produced by the Parisian art collective Obvious utilizing Generative Adversarial Networks (GANs). The AI-generated picture was created as a means of investigating the convergence of art and technology, questioning conventional ideas about authorship and creativity.
- AI-Generated Ballet: Choreographer Wayne McGregor collaborated with Google Arts and Culture and Google's Magenta project to create "Living Archive," an AI-generated ballet. The performance incorporated AI-generated visuals and music, showcasing the potential for AI in shaping the future of dance and performing arts.
- AI-Generated Poetry: Poets and writers have experimented with AI tools to generate poetry. OpenAI's GPT models, for example, have been used to generate verses in specific styles or to provide inspiration for human poets.

4. HUMAN-MACHINE INTERACTION IN ART-MAKING

Human-machine interaction in art-making represents a dynamic interplay between human creativity and the capabilities of AI technologies, fostering a collaborative and innovative approach to artistic expression (Garg & Bhambri, 2011). This interaction is characterized by a symbiotic relationship where artists leverage the computational power and unique algorithms of AI systems to augment their creative processes. AI tools can serve as catalysts for inspiration, providing artists with novel ideas, visualizations, or musical compositions. Through intuitive interfaces and interactive platforms, artists can engage with AI systems in real time, shaping the evolution of the artwork and influencing the output based on their artistic intent.

Furthermore, human-machine interaction in art-making introduces a new dimension of exploration and experimentation (Bansal et al., 2012). Artists may use AI algorithms to break creative boundaries, generating unexpected outcomes that challenge traditional notions of artistic authorship. The collaboration extends beyond mere tool usage, as artists and AI engage in a co-creative dialogue, each influencing and responding to the other. This interaction also highlights the importance of interpretability and explainability in AI, as artists seek to understand and guide the underlying algorithms to align with their artistic vision (Karras et al., 2018). Overall, the evolving landscape of human-machine interaction in art-making signifies a transformative shift in the creative process, where technology becomes an integral part of the artist's toolkit, fostering a rich and dynamic exchange between human ingenuity and machine intelligence.

4.1 The Dialogue Between Humans and Machine

The dialogue between humans and machines within the human-machine nexus in art-making, particularly with generative AIs, signifies a transformative shift in the creative process. As artists collaborate with these intelligent systems, a dynamic exchange of ideas unfolds, blurring the traditional boundaries between creator and creation. Generative AIs, such as GANs or language models, become creative companions, capable of understanding human inputs, interpreting artistic styles, and generating novel outputs.

This collaboration is not a one-way street; it involves a reciprocal conversation where humans guide the algorithms with their intentions, preferences, and aesthetics, while the AI responds by offering suggestions, exploring uncharted territories, and even challenging preconceived notions of artistic expression.

The human-machine dialogue extends beyond mere tool usage; it involves a co-creative relationship where artists and generative AIs influence each other iteratively. Artists introduce the nuances of emotion, context, and cultural significance, injecting a human touch into the algorithms' output. Simultaneously, the algorithms contribute by offering unexpected insights, suggesting alternative creative paths, and pushing artists to reconsider conventional approaches. This symbiotic interaction fosters a continuous learning loop, where the human artist and the machine collaboratively evolve, creating a fusion of human creativity and artificial intelligence. In the human-machine nexus of art-making with generative AIs, the dialogue becomes a dance of inspiration and innovation, resulting in artworks that reflect the harmonious convergence of human imagination and computational capabilities.

4.2 Challenges and Opportunities in Collaborative Art-Making

Collaborative art-making involving humans and AI presents a unique set of challenges and opportunities that shape the landscape of creative expression (Abrol et al., 2005). One significant challenge is the potential loss of individual agency and authorship as AI algorithms contribute to the artistic process. Artists grapple with questions of identity and originality, navigating the fine line between co-creation and relinquishing creative control. The challenge lies in striking a balance that allows for meaningful collaboration while preserving the artist's distinct voice and vision (Lucic et al., 2018). Ethical considerations also emerge, including the responsible use of AI, addressing biases in training data, and ensuring transparency in the collaborative process to maintain the integrity of the artistic endeavor.

On the flip side, collaborative art-making with AI opens up unprecedented opportunities for innovation and exploration (Nguyen et al., 2015). AI tools provide artists with new mediums, enabling the generation of novel forms of expression and pushing the boundaries of traditional art disciplines. The fusion of human creativity and machine intelligence offers opportunities for cross-disciplinary collaboration, fostering the emergence of entirely new art forms that bridge the gap between technology and the arts. Additionally, AI's ability to analyze vast datasets and identify patterns can serve as a source of inspiration, helping artists discover new perspectives and unconventional approaches. The collaborative process becomes a conduit for artistic evolution, offering artists the chance to engage with cutting-edge technologies and redefine the landscape of contemporary art. The dynamic interplay between challenges and opportunities in collaborative art-making catalyzes pushing the limits of creativity and contributing to the evolution of artistic expression in the digital age.

4.3 Shaping Artistic Intentions Through AI Assistance

Shaping artistic intentions through AI assistance involves a collaborative process where artists leverage artificial intelligence tools to refine, expand, or challenge their creative vision. AI can serve as a valuable assistant by offering insights, suggesting alternative approaches, and facilitating the realization of artistic intentions. One of the primary ways AI contributes to shaping artistic intentions is through its ability to analyze vast datasets, identify patterns, and provide artists with inspiration drawn from a wide array of sources. This assistance can spark new ideas, enabling artists to explore uncharted territories and infuse their work with fresh perspectives. AI also plays a crucial role in refining artistic details and optimizing the creative process. For instance, in visual arts, generative models like GANs can assist artists in creating intricate designs or refining aesthetic elements (Salimans et al., 2016). In music composition, AI algorithms can analyze musical patterns, helping artists fine-tune melodies or harmonies to achieve specific emotional or thematic intentions. This collaborative relationship empowers artists to experiment with different styles, genres, or techniques, enriching their creative toolkit.

However, the use of AI assistance in shaping artistic intentions is not without its challenges (Vaswani et al., 2017). Artists must grapple with questions of agency, ensuring that the technology enhances rather than eclipses their unique voice and intent. Striking a balance between the interpretative abilities of AI and the artist's expression is crucial to maintaining the authenticity of the work. Ethical considerations, such as addressing biases in training data and being transparent about the role of AI in the creative process, also come to the forefront. Ultimately, the synergy between human artistic intuition and AI capabilities creates a collaborative environment where intentions are refined, expanded, and redefined. The dialogue between artist and machine allows for a dynamic exchange of ideas, pushing the boundaries of traditional artistic practices and contributing to the evolution of creative expression. In this way, AI assistance becomes a tool for artists to navigate the complexities of their intentions, offering a bridge between the traditional and the cutting-edge in the ever-evolving landscape of contemporary art.

5. ETHICAL CONSIDERATIONS IN AI-GENERATED ART

Ethical considerations in AI-generated art encompass a range of concerns that arise from the intersection of technology and creative expression (McCosker et al., 2017). One significant issue involves transparency and attribution, as artists collaborating with AI must be clear about the role of algorithms in the creative process, ensuring proper credit and acknowledgment. Addressing biases in training data is crucial to prevent the perpetuation of societal prejudices in AI-generated artworks. Ethical considerations also extend to the responsible use of AI, particularly in cases where the technology might be exploited for malicious purposes, such as deepfake art or the creation of deceptive visual content. Moreover, privacy concerns may arise when AI algorithms are trained on publicly available images without explicit consent. As AI-generated art becomes more prevalent, establishing ethical guidelines and standards becomes imperative to navigate the complex landscape of creativity, ensuring that the collaboration between humans and machines upholds principles of fairness, transparency, and respect for individual rights.

Shaping artistic intentions through AI assistance involves a collaborative process where artists leverage artificial intelligence tools to refine, expand, or challenge their creative vision. AI can serve as a valuable assistant by offering insights, suggesting alternative approaches, and facilitating the realization of artistic intentions. One of the primary ways AI contributes to shaping artistic intentions is through its ability to analyze vast datasets, identify patterns, and provide artists with inspiration drawn from a wide array of sources. This assistance can spark new ideas, enabling artists to explore uncharted territories and infuse their work with fresh perspectives.

AI also plays a crucial role in refining artistic details and optimizing the creative process. For instance, in visual arts, generative models like GANs can assist artists in creating intricate designs or refining aesthetic elements. In music composition, AI algorithms can analyze musical patterns, helping artists fine-tune melodies or harmonies to achieve specific emotional or thematic intentions. This collaborative relationship empowers artists to experiment with different styles, genres, or techniques, enriching their creative toolkit.

However, the use of AI assistance in shaping artistic intentions is not without its challenges (Kingma & Ba, 2014). Artists must grapple with questions of agency, ensuring that the technology enhances rather than eclipses their unique voice and intent. Striking a balance between the interpretative abilities of AI and the artist's expression is crucial to maintaining the authenticity of the work. Ethical considerations, such as addressing biases in training data and being transparent about the role of AI in the creative process, also come to the forefront.

Ultimately, the synergy between human artistic intuition and AI capabilities creates a collaborative environment where intentions are refined, expanded, and redefined (Jahanian & Balakrishnan, 2018). The dialogue between artist and machine allows for a dynamic exchange of ideas, pushing the boundaries of traditional artistic practices and contributing to the evolution of creative expression. In this way, AI assistance becomes a tool for artists to navigate the complexities of their intentions, offering a bridge between the traditional and the cutting-edge in the ever-evolving landscape of contemporary art.

6. CASE STUDIES AND EXAMPLES

Numerous case studies and projects showcase the integration of AI into artistic practices. Notable projects include "Edmond de Belamy" by Obvious, where a Generative Adversarial Network (GAN) was employed to create a unique artwork sold at auction. "AI Dungeon" by Latitude, a text-based adventure game powered by OpenAI's GPT-3, exemplifies how users can collaboratively craft narratives with AI. Additionally, Google's "Magenta Studio" provides musicians with tools like "AIVA" to explore AI-generated compositions. These case studies illustrate the diverse applications of AI in art across different mediums.

6.1 Impact on Traditional Artistic Practices

The integration of AI has significantly impacted traditional artistic practices (Singh & Bhambri, 2007). In visual arts, AI tools challenge conventional notions of authorship and originality, pushing artists to reconsider their role in the creative process. The use of algorithms for generative design and style transfer introduces new methods for visual expression. In music, AI assists in composition and offers novel approaches to sound creation. While AI contributes to efficiency and inspiration, it also raises questions about the preservation of human creativity and the ethical implications of automated art-making.

6.2 User Experiences and Feedback

User experiences and feedback highlight both the excitement and challenges of AI in art. Artists often express enthusiasm about the possibilities AI unlocks, enabling them to explore new styles and break creative boundaries (Selvaraju et al., 2017). However, concerns about loss of artistic control, ethical considerations, and the potential for AI to replicate existing biases are also voiced. Users engaging with AI-generated content report a mix of fascination and unease, emphasizing the need for responsible AI practices. As the field evolves, ongoing user feedback contributes to refining AI tools and ensuring a positive and ethically sound user experience. Collaborations between artists and AI platforms often lead to a nuanced understanding of the capabilities and limitations of these technologies, shaping the ongoing dialogue in the intersection of art and artificial intelligence.

7. CONCLUSION

In conclusion, the exploration of the human-machine nexus within art-making generative AIs has unveiled a dynamic synergy between human creativity and artificial intelligence. The collaborative process between artists and AI technologies marks a transformative era in artistic expression, challenging traditional paradigms and fostering new possibilities. Throughout this chapter, we delved into the reciprocal dialogue between humans and machines, emphasizing the co-creative relationship that emerges when artists leverage generative AI tools. From visual arts to music composition, storytelling, and beyond, the chapter highlighted how AI assistance shapes artistic intentions, offering novel insights, enhancing efficiency, and contributing to the evolution of creative practices.

The significance of generative AI in artistic exploration lies in its capacity to push the boundaries of imagination and redefine the creative process. As artists continue to experiment with AI-generated content, the field becomes a playground for innovation, inviting cross-disciplinary collaborations and novel forms of expression. The ethical considerations and user feedback underscore the need for responsible AI practices and an ongoing conversation about the ethical implications of integrating AI into the art-making process. Looking ahead, the future of art-making with AI promises a fascinating landscape where human ingenuity and computational capabilities converge to produce artworks that challenge, inspire, and reflect the evolving nature of creativity in the digital age. The human-machine nexus, facilitated by generative AIs, paves the way for a harmonious coexistence where technology becomes a catalyst for artistic exploration rather than a replacement for human expression.

REFERENCES

Bhambri, P., & Hans, S. (2010). Evaluation of Integrated Development Environments for Embedded System Design. *Apeejay Journal of Management and Technology*, *5*(2), 138–146.

Bishop, C. M. (2006). *Pattern Recognition and Machine Learning*. Springer.

Chollet, F. (2018). *Deep Learning with Python*. Manning Publications.

Domingos, P. (2015). *The Master Algorithm: How the Quest for the Ultimate Learning Machine Will Remake Our World.* Basic Books.

Elgammal, A., Liu, B., Elhoseiny, M., & Marey, M. (2017). To hide or not to hide: A transparent 3D model of deep neural networks. *Proceedings of the IEEE Conference on Computer Vision and Pattern Recognition (CVPR).*

Garg, D., & Bhambri, P. (2011). A novel approach for fusion of multimodality medical images. *CiiT International Journal of Digital Image Processing, 3*(10), 576-580.

Goodfellow, I., Bengio, Y., & Courville, A. (2016). *Deep Learning*. MIT Press.

Goodfellow, I., Pouget-Abadie, J., Mirza, M., Xu, B., Warde-Farley, D., Ozair, S., . . . Bengio, Y. (2014). Generative adversarial nets. *Advances in neural information processing systems (NeurIPS).*

Ha, D., & Schmidhuber, J. (2018). *World models.* arXiv preprint arXiv:1803.10122.

Hinton, G., Deng, L., Yu, D., Dahl, G. E., Mohamed, A. R., Jaitly, N., Senior, A., Vanhoucke, V., Nguyen, P., Sainath, T., & Kingsbury, B. (2012). Deep neural networks for acoustic modeling in speech recognition: The shared views of four research groups. *IEEE Signal Processing Magazine*, *29*(6), 82–97. doi:10.1109/MSP.2012.2205597

Jahanian, A., & Balakrishnan, G. (2018). *On the "steerability" of generative adversarial networks.* arXiv preprint arXiv:1812.00073.

Karras, T., Aila, T., Laine, S., & Lehtinen, J. (2018*). Progressive growing of GANs for improved quality, stability, and variation.* arXiv preprint arXiv:1710.10196.

Kingma, D. P., & Ba, J. (2014). *Adam: A method for stochastic optimization.* arXiv preprint arXiv:1412.6980.

LeCun, Y., Bengio, Y., & Hinton, G. (2015). Deep learning. *Nature*, *521*(7553), 436–444. doi:10.1038/nature14539 PMID:26017442

Lucic, M., Kurach, K., Michalski, M., Gelly, S., & Bousquet, O. (2018). Are GANs created equal? A large-scale study. Advances in neural information processing systems (NeurIPS).

McCosker, A., Wilken, R., & Wilken, R. (2017). Rethinking 'ethics' in data science: Towards a speculative ethics for big data research. *Proceedings of the 2017 Data Science Conference.*

Murphy, K. P. (2012). *Machine Learning: A Probabilistic Perspective.* MIT Press.

Nguyen, A., Yosinski, J., & Clune, J. (2015). Deep neural networks are easily fooled: High confidence predictions for unrecognizable images. *Proceedings of the IEEE Conference on Computer Vision and Pattern Recognition (CVPR).* 10.1109/CVPR.2015.7298640

Nilsson, N. J. (1998). *Artificial Intelligence: A New Synthesis.* Morgan Kaufmann.

Open, A. I. (2019). *GPT-2: Language Models are Few-Shot Learners.* Retrieved from https://openai.com/research/gpt-2

Radford, A., Metz, L., & Chintala, S. (2015). *Unsupervised representation learning with deep convolutional generative adversarial networks.* arXiv preprint arXiv:1511.06434.

Reed, S. E., Akata, Z., Yan, X., Logeswaran, L., Schiele, B., & Lee, H. (2016). Generative adversarial text-to-image synthesis. *Proceedings of the 33rd International Conference on Machine Learning (ICML).*

Russell, S., & Norvig, P. (2010). *Artificial Intelligence: A Modern Approach* (3rd ed.). Prentice Hall.

Salimans, T., Goodfellow, I., Zaremba, W., Cheung, V., Radford, A., & Chen, X. (2016). Improved techniques for training GANs. Advances in neural information processing systems (NeurIPS).

Schneider, M., & Fischer, M. (2019). A survey of digital art history. arXiv preprint arXiv:1906.02102.

Selvaraju, R. R., Cogswell, M., Das, A., Vedantam, R., Parikh, D., & Batra, D. (2017). Grad-CAM: Visual explanations from deep networks via gradient-based localization. *Proceedings of the IEEE International Conference on Computer Vision (ICCV).* 10.1109/ICCV.2017.74

Singh, P., & Bhambri, P. (2007). Alternate Organizational Models for Ports. *Apeejay Journal of Management and Technology*, *2*(2), 9–17.

Tan, H., Chan, C., Aggarwal, V., & Gupta, D. (2019). Deep neural network models for computational microscopy. *Proceedings of the IEEE Conference on Computer Vision and Pattern Recognition (CVPR).*

Thrun, S., Burgard, W., & Fox, D. (2005). *Probabilistic Robotics.* MIT Press.

Vaswani, A., Shazeer, N., Parmar, N., Uszkoreit, J., Jones, L., Gomez, A. N., . . . Polosukhin, I. (2017). Attention is all you need. Advances in neural information processing systems (NeurIPS).

Yampolskiy, R. V. (2018). *Artificial intelligence in art.* arXiv preprint arXiv:1803.09518.

Zhang, H., Xu, T., Li, H., Zhang, S., Wang, X., Huang, X., & Metaxas, D. (2018). StackGAN++: Realistic image synthesis with stacked generative adversarial networks. *IEEE Transactions on Pattern Analysis and Machine Intelligence.*

Zhu, J. Y., Park, T., Isola, P., & Efros, A. A. (2017). Unpaired image-to-image translation using cycle-consistent adversarial networks. *Proceedings of the IEEE International Conference on Computer Vision (ICCV).* 10.1109/ICCV.2017.244

Chapter 5
Children's Book Visualizations From an Artmaking Generative AI

Shalin Hai-Jew
https://orcid.org/0000-0002-8863-0175
Hutchinson Community College, USA

ABSTRACT

How would a well-known artmaking generative AI (A-GAI) go about illustrating children's books? This chapter uses multiple prompting approaches to elicit children's book illustrations for known stories and more original plots to identify some early visual patterns from Deep Dream Generator. The research explores a variety of questions around the quality of the output images in conveying visual meaning in the children's book space (albeit using fictional prompts). This exploratory work provides some early and preliminary insights into this space, including in how to set up a light experiment using an A-GAI.

INTRODUCTION

Adults who grew up reading children's books of various types may think of such books fondly given how they extended the world of the child by offering characters, adventures, varied perspectives, humor, and insights…and by extending the power of language. For adults who have read children's books in their childhood, they may have a mental abstraction of what the visuals from children's books look like. Some visuals here may be captured in a Google Image Search (Figure 1).

Children's literature is defined as "the totality of spoken and written products formed with an aesthetic concern that contribute to the development, interests, needs, pleasure, emotions and ideas of individuals between the ages of 2 – 15" (Sinan, Demir, & Dogan, 2017, p. 133). [Some suggest that children's literature are for any under 16.] Children's literature "started to develop once children had been accepted as individuals" (Sinan, Demir, & Dogan, 2017, p. 133).

Children's picturebooks are "profusely illustrated books in which the illustrations are, to varying degrees, essential to the enjoyment and understanding of the story" (Tomlinson & Lynch-Brown, 1996,

DOI: 10.4018/979-8-3693-1950-5.ch005

Figure 1. Children's books (in terms of Google Image search)

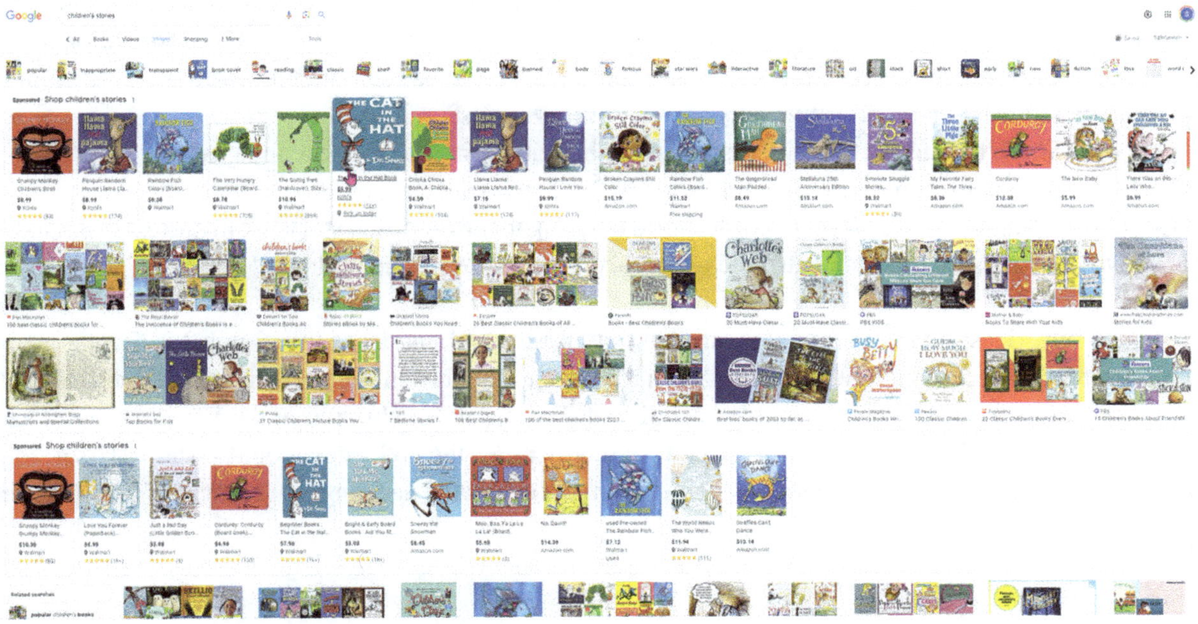

as cited in Fang, 1996, p. 130). It is hard to say when picturebooks originated, but one of the first ones hails from 1658 in terms of a book by John Amos Comenius (titled *Orbis Sensualium Pictus*, a children's encyclopedia illustrated with woodcuts) ("John Amos Comenius," Wikipedia, Dec. 19, 2023). Picturebooks have traditionally included images as augmentation to text, but some books have few to no text and the rest as pictures in some present iterations (Karaman, n.d., n.p.). Picturebooks enable young readers to look at pictures even if they cannot read yet (Karaman, n.d., n.p.). It is important to understand the relationship of illustration to print in children's books. One researcher suggests that visuals in children's books "expand, explain, interpret, or decorate a written text" (Bodmer, 1992, p. 72, as cited in Fang, 1996, p. 131). A later work explains the complementary and augmentary role of visuals:

The characters in picture books must have specific traits that make them appealing to the child reader and that meet the demands of the short format. Since a short story does not normally allow for more fully developed characters, illustrations help develop the characters by depicting situations and emotions immediately familiar and credible to the children. (Fang, 1996, p. 132)

Visuals in children's books may "correspond to aesthetic sensitiveness" (Sinan, Demir, & Dogan, 2017, p. 143). The current period has been referred to as the digital age in literary education, which requires readers to develop a new set of reading skills" (Pokrivcakova, 2017, p. 11).

This work explores how artmaking generative AIs (A-GAIs) may be used to create visuals. Artmaking generative AIs are tools that were trained on "big data" using artificial neural networks. From the training, the model acquires weights across various nodes as it "learns" the visuals. These models are fine-tuned for particular outputs.

This research work is based around a particular use case, of eliciting images for children's literature. The interrelated research questions being explored include the following:

RQ1. How does the studied generative AI apparently tailor visuals for children?
RQ2. How well does/do the synthetic image(s) convey the message that is inherent to the textual prompt?
RQ3. Are there any obvious emulative styles from known children's book artists? Is there emulation from originals, through "memorization," "data leakage," "hallucination" or other forms of repetition?
RQ4. Is there visual communicative range in the visualizations?
RQ5. What is the balance between realism and the imaginary in the synthetic images?
RQ6. Are the images "child safe"? "Child friendly"? How so or how not?
RQ7. Do the synthetic images contribute to world building in the proposed story (from the text prompts)?
RQ8. Do the synthetic images contribute to character embodiment and building?

Ultimately, does the artmaking generative AI offer a throughline from the visuals? Is there a form of understood style, a childlike sensibility? What comes to the fore in the synthetic generated images? What may be seen of the generative AI capability of illustrating for children in the 8 – 12 range? That age range would include those in third through sixth grades (in the U.S. educational system). [As a side note, the age range selected for this study comes from the estimated age range for readers of the fairytale "Hansel and Gretel."]

REVIEW OF THE LITERATURE

In the academic research literature, children's literature is used for teaching and learning for both children and adults. The basic elements of a story include "setting, character, and plot" (Golden, 1984, p. 578). These are each interrelated and affect the other elements. Elementary narration links causations between described events as experienced by a single major protagonist; however, such approaches may not be aligned with how children may necessarily sense-make from storytellng (Nicolopoulou, 2008, p. 299).

Often, children's literature features repeating elements (Gannon, 1987, p. 2), such as text, images, symbols, characters, and other aspects. Repetition benefits young readers:

It clarifies the structure of narrative for young readers, and helps them to remember what they have read. It adds rhythm and the mysterious charm of ritual to the simplest of verbal formulas. It offers the pleasure of extended suspense and delayed gratification to even the youngest audience. But repetition—whether in the sequence of events which makes up a story—or in the patterning of the textual discourse which presents that story—is also a powerful means of generating meaning in fiction. (Gannon, 1987, p. 2)

Visuals may help depict different points of view since a story may be told through the eyes of different characters (Fang, 1996, p. 132). Some visuals reinforce a story without adding new information per se (Fang, 1996, p. 136). Perhaps images may offer a throughline to the children's story, given that picture books have a "jumpy rhythm" vs. a smooth linear structure (Fang, 1996, p. 137). Images may provide "mental scaffolds" to enhance comprehension (Fang, 1996, p. 138), given children's short attention spans, limited vocabulary, and stops-and-starts to reading. Visuals in children's books may offer some early aesthetic education in terms of what is seen as culturally and historically artful (Fang, 1996). Visuals in children's literature may serve as aide-mémoire or cognitive scaffolding for memory. One work suggests that visual images and written language are interrelated in three main ways in the studied multimodal novels for middle school readers: "visual enhancement of written language, as visual and verbal construction of narrative, or as word-image fragmentary construction of narrative" (Reid & Serafini, 2018, p. 33). In other words, the visuals and attendant semiotics interrelate closely with the text for meaning making.

Yet another work describes how visual descriptors convey meaning in a kind of code:

In a formulaic novel, blond hair is likely to indicate innocence, while dark hair will indicate evil. In a realistic novel, the color of hair does not necessarily imply moral qualities. Yet, even in realistic modes, certain external traits, such as moles, crooked teeth, or extreme facial hair are often ascribed to evil characters. (Nikolajeva, 2001, p. 444)

Outside features may describe something of the internal states of the individual characters.

At present, children's literature is a socially fought-over space, given differing goals for society's children and youth, often values-based and learnings based. Children's stories are told as both stories to emulate [as in didactic works where characters serve as "mouthpieces for the author (Nikolajeva, 2001, p. 435)], stories to avoid (such as cautionary tales), and those which do not suggest anything pedagogical at all. Some stories take after songs, poems, jokes, riddles, and other cultural forms. The rhetoric of children's literature is "relaxed, personal, colloquial, anecdotal…gently positive" (Hunt, 1984 – 1985, p. 192). They are described as follows:

Simple but not necessarily simplistic; action-oriented rather than character-oriented; presented from the viewpoint of innocence; optimistic and with happy endings; didactic; repetitious in diction and structure. (Nodelman, 1992, p. 190, as cited in Nikolajeva, 1998, p. 221)

There is an expectation of children's literature that they both "entertain" and "inform," foremost, and that they result in "productive time" use and "permanent knowledge" and "visual use" (Sinan, Demir, & Dogan, 2017, p. 135). There is a utilitarian angle. Modern stories for children are told with fewer taboos, enabling engagement on "themes like death, suicide, or drug addiction" (Nikolajeva, 1998, n.p.), homelessness, and others. Complex picturebooks may have an "emotional impact" on young readers (Arizpe, Styles, Mackey, Bromley, Coulthard, & Noble, 2015, p. 146). There needs to be a theme of hope for young readers even in the face of challenges.

Their modalities have changed in the past few decades given advances in technologies, from print to digital to multimodal (including interactive games, films, and others). There are "book-based animated stories" built into multimedia, physical media, television shows, and others (Verhallen, Bus, & de Jong, 2006, p. 410). The stories may be multi-sensory and interactive. Reading "digital-born" content requires multimedia sophistication as this transmedia narrative form "ruptures discursive linearity" (Pokrivcakova, 2017, p. 14). Digital children's literature play important roles in the technology-based literacy instruction space (Ertem, 2013, p. 102). Children's stories have moved from single media t multimedia to web-based hypermedia (web links) to social media (podcasts, blogs, online games, virtual worlds, and others).

The technology enablements and advances in literary techniques have enabled modern children's literature to incorporate "metafictive elements," including "multiple story levels," and "the expansion of visual images and visual design features" (Serafini, Kachorsky, & Reid, 2018, p. 311). Narrative structures may nest in more complex ways. One new term is "metabooks" to label children's picturebooks "that have multiple narrative levels and use portals, narrators, and other visual and literary devices as metaleptic transgressions" (Serafini, Kachorsky, & Reid, 2018, p. 313).

Even with the evolutions, children's books maintain some elements that evoke the past. Still, they are formulaic in their own way. Perhaps there is a form of whimsy, of magic, of talking animals, of right-sized furniture, of a child's concerns. Perhaps the depictions are of a child's world, of a child's sense of justice and agency and power. Perhaps the stories speak to a child's identity, history, culture, and other inheritances. Perhaps present-day children's books are more hard-eyed, with some spillover of adult worlds into the children's ones.

Pedagogical Applications of Children's Literature

The use of children's literature applies to language acquisition at a fundamental level. Understanding story grammars is also important, including plot structures (Norton, Nov. 1992, p. 254), many of which may align with known plots like "rags to riches," "quest," "overcoming the monster," "voyage and return," "mystery," and others.

How well learners may learn from listening to stories and reading depends in part on their age. One group of works involves how well children at different ages can interpret texts, such as their "theory of mind" of respective characters. At younger ages, children tend to focus on action without understanding character motivations or personalities or thinking and the ties of that to the characters' behaviors. Some may have awareness of character thinking only, without relating that to their actions. Some know to combine consciousness and action (Pelletier & Wilde Astington, 2004, p. 5), but these tend to be children who are somewhat older. There are age-related developmental progressions in early-childhood children's understandings of story structures (Khan, Gugiu, Justice, Bowles, Skibbe, & Piasta, 2016).

For younger readers (preschool and first graders, in one study), their recall of story units depends on schemas (like familiar events and logically organized events) "but that with age, children become more flexible in their use of scripts in story recall" (Hudson & Nelson, 1983, p. 625).

How young readers engage with the stories affects their depth of learning. One work observes the various ways that children engage with storytelling, such as dramatizing particular roles or scenes; "talking back" both "to the story or characters"; critiquing or proposing alternate "plots, characters, or settings" placing themselves or friends into the story; or taking over a text by using a story "as a launching pad for the expression of their own creativity" (Sipe, 2002, pp. 477-478).

The study of characters may be revelatory of "human nature and human relationships" that benefit children's awareness (Nikolajeva, 2001, p. 430). When children read, they are expected to empathize with at least one character. The evocation of empathy is used to aid children's "social adjustment" and "social competence" (Cress & Holm, 1998, p. 2). Another study experiments with raising awareness of stereotyping through collaborative digital storytelling, given the negative impacts of such stereotypes to the fabric of society (Rubegni, Landoni, Malinverni, & Jaccheri, 2022, n.p.). An important democratic value is to value people in all their differences and to promote equal treatment.

One work describes the available skills learning:

Some of the most important skills children can gain are: (1) the concept of story; (2) the many strands of plot; (3) comprehension of vocabulary; (4) internalization of character; (5) visualization; (6) natural rhythms and patterns of the language; (7) figures of speech and metaphors; (8) prediction skills; (9) concepts about the world; (10) listening and attending skills; (11) internalizing their culture; and (12) healthy self concept" (Malo & Bullard, 2000, p. 1)

When children "re-story" or retell a story, they reveal their understandings of plot and character. This ability is also age- and development- related: "…children's representation of characters shifted from almost exclusively physical and external portrayals of 'actors' at 3 to increasing inclusion of 'agents' with rudimentary mental states at 4 and of 'persons' with mental representational capacities by 5" (Nicolopoulou & Richner, 2007, p. 412). Older children may move beyond naïve conceptions:

Actors are essentially nonpsychological characters, described exclusively in terms of externally observable actions and characteristics; agents are depicted as having simple psychological capacities; and persons are depicted with more complex mental representational capacities. In its highest levels, our category of 'persons' roughly corresponds to what many theory-of-mind researchers would regard as a full mental agent. The key difference between actors and agents is that for a character to be categorized as an 'agent,' we require the inclusion of some simple perceptual or psychological capacities, including actions marked as intentional and / or capacities to see, feel, communicate, or react physically or emotionally to events, situations, or other characters. The key difference between agents and persons is that to be categorized as a 'person,' a character must be explicitly portrayed as having representational beliefs, desires, or intentions—that is, cognitive or emotional inner states focused on specific things or conditions, as opposed, for example, to generalized emotional moods—that motivate and / or direction actions. (Nicolopoulou & Richner, 2007, p. 417)

Re-storying quality may be assessed by people (manually), or that may be assessed using computational means. One work describes using a computer program—based on statistical and symbolic semantic analysis of narratives—to evaluate how accurately a retold story is in terms of plot (Halpin, 2003). This hybrid model uses "both symbolic and statistical knowledge" (Halpin, 2003, p. 86).

The complexities of characters may be better understood. "External description is the simplest device as readers get a direct portrait of the character" (Nikolajeva, 2003, p. 9); however, the mark of more sophisticated reading is to see into the characters. There is power in retelling stories to enhance story "comprehension, concept of story structure, and oral language complexity" (Morrow, 1985, p. 647).

How young learners tell stories may be analyzed to understand and enhance their conflict resolution strategies (Peirce & Edwards, 1988). An important skill is understanding other people and their intentions, which is a skill that may benefit from better understanding respective characters through "mindreading" (Scalise Sugiyama, 2009, p. 95). This involves understanding character behaviors based on their internal states. In one study, when prompted with a sequence of visuals from which to tell a story (Shapiro & Hudson, 1991), older learners offered work that was relatively more sophisticated.

Beyond re-telling stories, children are brought into the playful learning through drawing and storytelling, too (Wright, 2007). One study found that multimedia enabled children to take on "*multiple roles* (i.e. artist, author, director, scripter, performer and narrator" with a wide range of embodied authoring through "layers of visual and physical action, character development, plot scheme, scenery and running narrative working in harmony, simultaneously" (Wright, 2007, n.p.) Children have developed their sense of narration through computer game authoring, including the making of digital characters in a digital game space (Robertson & Good, June 2004).

Early authorship by young learners is often typified by literary borrowing and emulation (Lancia, 1997). One study found children borrowing in five main ways: taking an entire original plot; using original characters but engaging in new ways; harnessing "*plot devices* such as setting, conflict, language patterns and vocabulary, titles and structural devices"; taking genre elements, and using information from nonfiction sources (Lancia, 1997, pp. 472 - 473).

Children may draw creatively and in explorative ways to "narrate the questions and predicaments they find to be most pressing—about themselves, about others, and about the changing world around them" (Schulte, 2019, p. 15). Their drawings may be studied for "plot holes," defined as "a gap or inconsistency in the storyline of a drawing, a break or fissure that works against the current course of logic that has been established by the drawing's plot" (Schulte, 2019, p. 15). Children's expressive work may be understood as portraying "miniature ecosystems" (Pantaleo, 2005, n.p.) Children create narrative coherence in nonlinear ways. Studying how children tell stories and the patterns that may be found from those tellings are an important approach (Nicolopoulou, 2008).

Benefitting a Range of Children With Varying Needs

Early exposures to reading are thought to benefit all learners. For deaf children, who are supported in their bilingual learning, they benefit from factors like "first language transfer, meta-linguistic awareness, cognitive readiness, motivation, parental interaction and emotional well-being" (Rathmann, Mann, & Morgan, 2007, p. 187). Helping deaf learners acquire complex literacy skills require complex considerations:

Once children are reading simple sentences however, how do we get them interested in exploring and constructing complex narratives? How can deaf children develop the social-cognitive abilities necessary to understand typical multi-character novels? We think that meta-linguistic awareness of how signed narratives are constructed, how to encode shifts in perspective and character motives can feed into the development of the same literacy skills in the written form. (Rathmann, Mann, & Morgan, 2007, p. 195)

At-risk young learners benefit in their story comprehension when the stories are told in sensorially rich ways, through "rich images, music, and sounds" in storytelling through multimedia (Verhallen, Bus, & de Jong, 2006, p. 417).

Children's literature introduces readers to people with different life realities. Studies have explored how those with mental retardation and autism are portrayed in children's books. Earlier studies found a need for "more children's books that include characters with MR/A as an integrated and accepted part of society," including showing them in "helping roles, rather than the recipients of care and protection" (Dyches, Prater, & Cramer, 2001, p. 243). A follow-on study found more accepting and sophisticated depictions:

... characters with developmental disabilities made more deliberate choices, were educated in more inclusive settings, were more accepted in their communities, and served in more helping roles; and more commonly the disability was only one of many character traits. Also, a wide age spectrum was portrayed, and several characterizations represented people from minority races or cultures. (Dyches & Prater, 2005, p. 202)

How diverse individuals are portrayed in children's literature is another area of focus. Diverse picturebooks may awaken minds through textual and visual symbolic thinking. One team writes about "the visual elements in diverse picturebooks as essential resources for critical classroom discussions" (Zapata, Fugit, & Moss, 2017, p. 62).

One research team identified some key themes found in writing about subgroups:

… the key figure is presented as different from the group; the key figure is often only accepted through the mediation of another character who is not considered different or an incident; different figures belong together and not with the figures that belong in the dominant group, and the key figure is an excellent character who might also be brave and unique for several reasons. (Monoyiou & Symeonidou, 2016, p. 588)

The researchers found reproduction of stereotypes of people "who have traditionally experienced oppression by dominant groups" (Monoyiou & Symeonidou, 2016, p. 589).

About Life Skills

Children's stories are used to teach children life skills. For example, solution stories help learners develop problem-solving skills and senses of independence and self-efficacy. In the classroom, pedagogical strategies of "modeling, mindful language, and other proactive strategies" may be used to help children solve "complex functional and social problems" (Kelley, 2018, p. 313). The researcher writes:

A child's approach to a challenging task is not dissimilar from the arc of a narrative plot: a character attempting to solve a problem. Teachers, then, can be seen as playing a supporting role. This study examined how teachers enact that support during children's authentically encountered problems. (Kelley, 2018, p. 316)

In many cases, early reading is social, between parents and children, and teachers and children. There are known benefits of using shared reading contexts to spark conversations between parents and children (Aram, Fine, & Ziv, 2013, p. 111). For older readers, adults reading with children may focus on the plot initially, then draw out socio-cognitive themes in a follow-on reading, then relate the story to the child's life experiences, and then have the child retell the story (Aram, Fine, & Ziv, 2013, p. 114). Structured reading approaches like the prior are found to benefit families with low socio-economic status by empowering the learning from the texts.

Advocating for Social Justice in Children's Literature

Children's books portray global and transnational perspectives. Children's education may be a conduit for improved global understandings of the world and related issues, like global warming (Yoon, 2022, p. 206). They may contribute to understandings of other peoples, nations, and cultures. They may expand readers' world views and support prosocial action (Wiltse, 2015). Researchers advocate reading broadly, beyond traditionalist canons (Tschida, Ryan, & Ticknor, 2014). Visuals may be an important part of evoking history and social change: "Visuals are powerful, forcing viewers to experience and/or witness events, even if only from within" (Gardner, 2017, p. 338). Even novels have become multimodal ones (aka "visual narratives" or "illustrated novel") (Serafini, Kachorsky, & Reid, 2018, p. 315).

Some of the works are "liberatory" and advocate for social justice, for every level of reader. Children's literature is used in higher education for grown-up lessons, in fields such as sociology and early childhood education. There are high ambitions, such as for "racial healing" (Gardner, 2017, p. 341) and other social ideals. Children's literature enables the discovery of others in empathetic ways (Bouley & Godfrey, 2008). The works contribute to "transnational literacy" (Bradford, 2011). Some older works of children's literature are seen as colonial texts, rife with human politics. A critique view is that children's literature has "an imperialist form: its ideological functions of social control have become a routine topic" (Higonnet, 1987, p. 37). The narrative form is seen as manipulative, "to direct the child reader's responses" (Higonnet, 1987, p. 37). Breaking the narrative form, with "mosaic" and narrative ruptures, may break out of traditionalist controls.

Literary critics take on "geocritical" views, such as studying Muslim-themed content in children's books (Abas, Bamanger, Gashan, & Guler, 2021, p. 48). Another liberatory approach involves diversity representations in children's media for a more civil and inclusive world, particularly in democratic societies (Thomas, 2016). The telling and retelling of stories may disrupt the power of single narratives, through a particular power frame. Regardless, it is important to bring critical thinking into play when considering stories, such as "the stories we tell, who is doing the telling, and who gets left out" (Tschida, Ryan, & Ticknor, 2014, p. 28). Literary critique is affected by the multimodalities:

As the texts children and young adult readers encounter continue to evolve in both format, design, and content, literacy researchers and educators will need to conduct more extensive analyses of both multimodal ensembles themselves and the ways readers transact with these complex texts. Better understandings of multimodal texts produced for young readers will foster greater understandings of the ways children and middle-grade readers approach, navigate, and interpret the visual, verbal, and design elements of contemporary texts. (Serafini, Kachorsky, & Reid, 2018, p. 318)

For readers to approach the children's literary texts critically, there is some advice: "...approaching a text as an object of enquiry, rather than focusing on its subject or content, can provide pupils with the room to distance themselves from texts and view them critically" (Arizpe, Styles, Mackey, Bromley, Coulthard, & Noble, 2015, p. 168). Another approach is to learn a visual grammar as a metalanguage, in appreciating picturebooks and other works of children's literature.

One analytical approach involves the study of the plot structures of the most popular children's books of the year in order to understand the social moment (Abrahamson & Shannon, 1983, p. 44).

A Note About Generative AI

Generative AI tools are built based on machine learning using neural networks and a set of large training corpora. The large language model (LLM) is fine-tuned to be able to output images based on text prompts, in a way to resemble human output (McIntyre & Lapata, July 2010, p. 1562). The Deep Dream Generator was created at Google and released in 2015 for public use through a web-facing platform. Version 3 was released in late 2023, including a new inpainting AI feature and smoother work pipelines to experiment using some ten (10) integrated models. (Figure 2)

The lower-cost models include Artistic 2, Artistic, DreamForge, MirageMaker, and Photonic. The PRO models which cost more points include EssenceOfReality, PhotoMage, DigitalDaVinci, Animatron, and AIVision. The low-cost ones are 4 energy points per basic image, and the PRO ones range from 10 – 40 points and are restricted to tree per 24-hour period per user with a free account. The research literature includes some information about the DDG and the underlying computational processing related to the DDG, but there does not seem to be much on the respective integrated models

Figure 2. Ten AI models in the deep dream generator

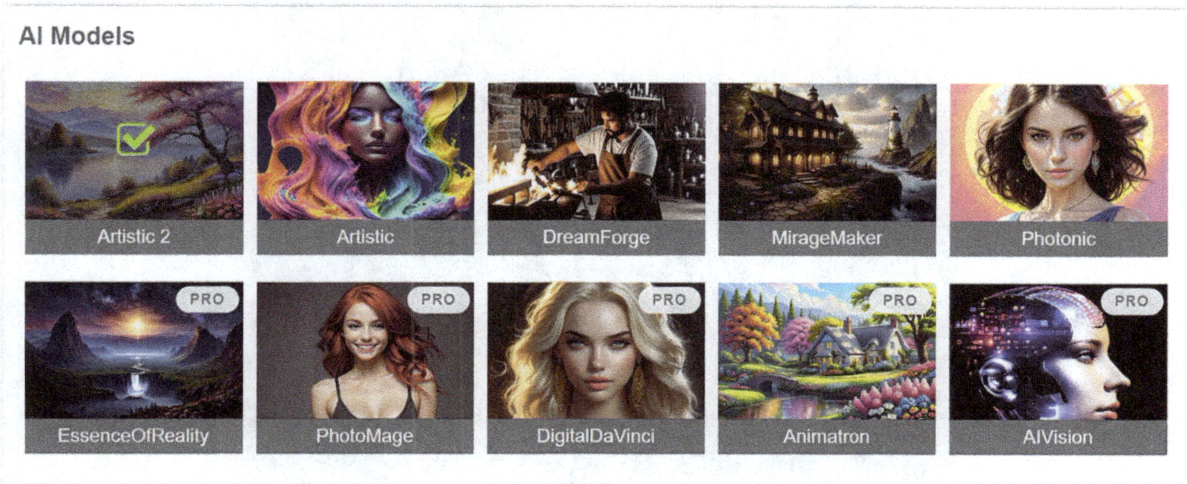

CHILDREN'S BOOK VISUALIZATIONS FROM AN ARTMAKING GENERATIVE AI

Some early work was done to help shape the research approach. First, there were some light explorations using known children's stories to see how the A-GAI would handle those prompts. Then, a dozen text prompts were created for use in this work. This light study is based on a dozen prompts, with two basic modifier tags…and variations only based on the prompts and then the models within the Deep Dream Generator.

Hurdles to Using Known Stories to Prompt the A-GAI

An AI-generated image of the two characters show their sense of fortitude and connection as they are walking into the woods or are in the midst of the woods. (Figure 3)

While known storylines could have been used, many of the models within the Deep Dream Generator disallow the uses of known titles and characters as seeds for the visuals, so a more original approach was used for this research. Also, with some light probes involving "Snow White and the Seven Dwarves" and a "flying elephant" in the context of a children's story prompt, some models may be emulative of a known work while others may go with generics (no Dumbo).

A prompt for "snow white and the seven dwarves" was rejected from one of the models in DDG for not aligning with the model's guidelines. (Figure 4)

The other models enabled some drawing, but these were highly variant and did not show any of the seven dwarves. (Figure 5) [In terms of the modifiers, only "linocut" was applied.] The visuals for Figures 5 and # emulate how a traditional proof sheet might look with comparative images.

The seeding for "Goldilocks and the Three Bears" shows bears but no Goldilocks. (Figure 6) The modifying tags for this were only "linocut" and "pixel art." These 9 thumbnails show images using models from the non-PRO section.

DDG was asked for an illustration for a book about youth achievement in the style of Dr. Seuss for a children's book for ages. The "Dr. Seuss" request did not seem to result in any applied style, perhaps

Figure 3. "Hansel and Gretel" in an important scene as depicted by deep dream generator

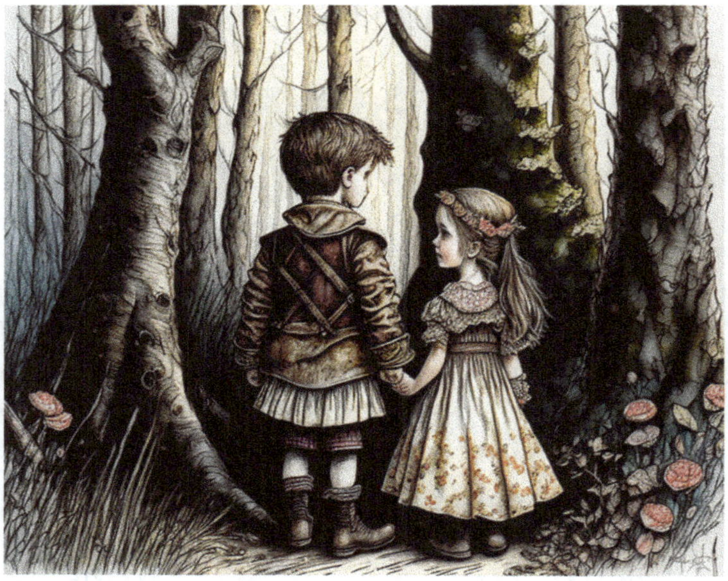

Figure 4. "Snow White and the Seven Dwarves" rejected as a prompt in one of the models in the deep dream generator

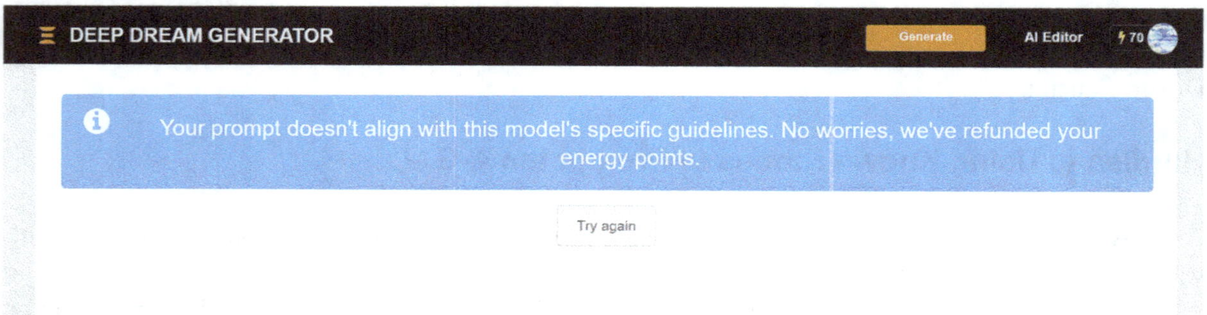

because the books are copyrighted and not available for "training" the large language models. There is a misspelling in the image (but not in the original text prompt). This prompt clearly stretched the capabilities of this technical tool. (Figure 7) The visual was created using the AIVision model, but without any seeding image (the model itself does not take a seeding image).

The Challenges of Text Prompting

The early explorations above made it clear that a prompt for this research would have to be either (1) generated by the researcher or (2) autogenerated by a text-based or multimodal generative AI (like Google's BardAI). It is possible to autogenerate a full children's story in milliseconds using generative AI. One study did find that large language models (LLMs) fall short in terms of generating children's stories to the expected "quality and nuance" found in human-written children's stories (Bhandari &

Figure 5. Variations of "Snow White and the Seven Dwarves" from multiple models in the deep dream generator

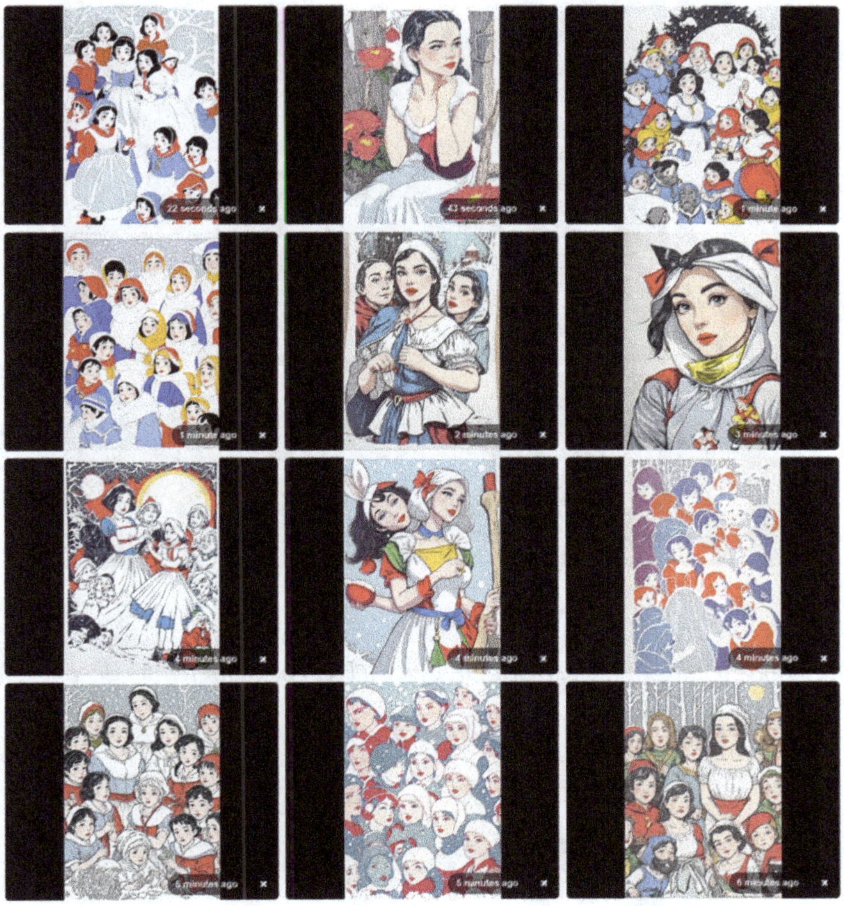

Brennan, 2023, n.p.) In addition, some came up with "toxic text" that would not be suitable for children (Bhandari & Brennan, 2023, n.p.)

For simplicity's sake, the researcher chose to use a human-generated (manual) prompt. The idea was to create some simple "log-lines" in the style of those created for scripts. These include a basic evocation of character and plot and maybe an overview of the entire story, albeit applied to a children's book. First, a list of a dozen log-lines were created, including both fictional and non-fictional sorts of stories.

1. Teen girl discovers her talent for computer coding as she comes into her own
2. A girl and her German shepherd head out to a family cabin in the Alaskan wilds to spend the summer
3. A group of four teenagers form a team to solve crime mysteries
4. A young gymnast or dancer makes his way to the big city and makes it big
5. A young scuba diver has underwater and over-water adventures
6. A multi-generational family makes a life in Chinatown
7. A car racer wins the car race in front of cheering crowds

Figure 6. "Goldilocks and the Three Bears" in an important scene as depicted by deep dream generator

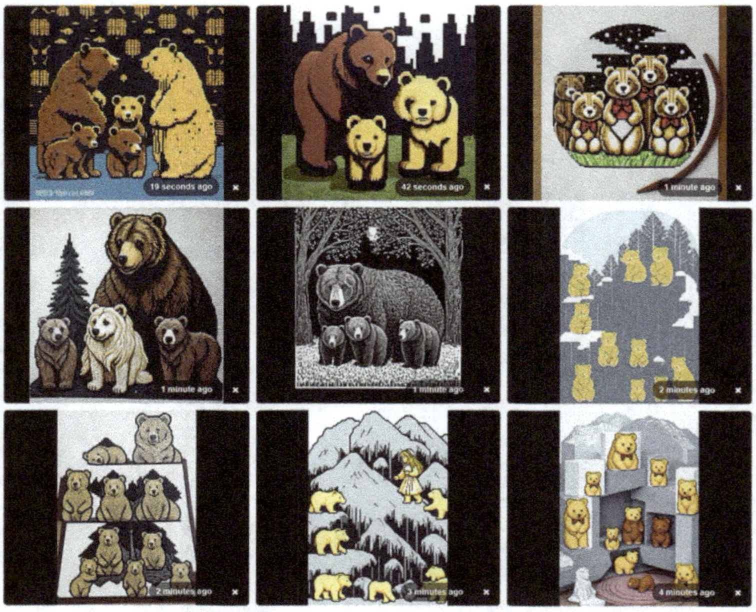

Figure 7. "Youth Achievement" in the style of Dr. Seuss (Fail) as depicted by deep dream generator

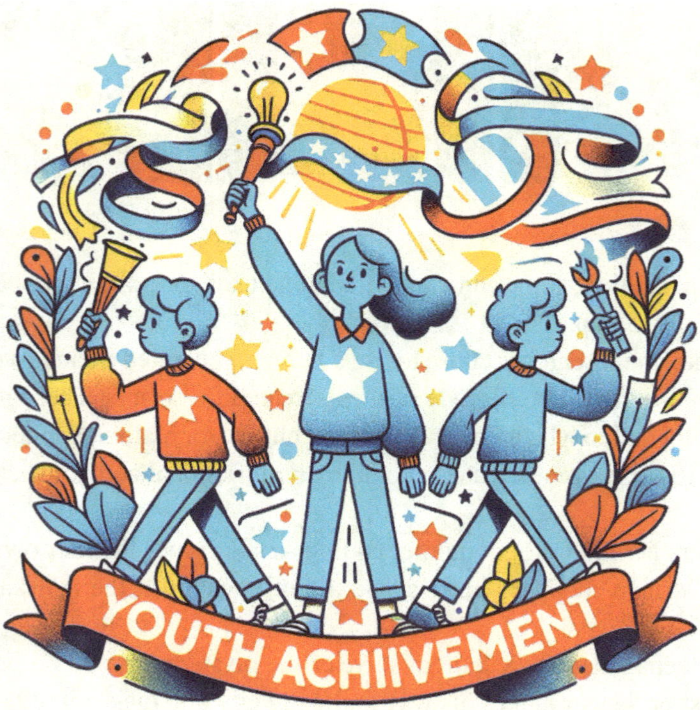

8. A mouse family lives in a sweets shop (pastry, ice cream)
9. Family suffering in Europe during WWII
10. The history of silver smithing
11. A candymaker or chef caters a party
12. Two friends visit a haunted house

A set of modifying tags were selected to emphasize line art looks-and-feels ("linocut" and "high-contrast" for better reproducibility in the print book form). After the text prompt, a phrase was appended: "in a children's book for readers ages 8 – 12." No named artist or illustrator or art school styles were mentioned in the prompts. Single visuals were created from each prompt, using different integrated models within the Deep Dream Generator tool. No seeding images were used for the visuals. This setup means that the models in the A-GAI will manage their own color palettes. Also, the aspect ratio used for all the images was the horizontal one (vs. the vertical, vs. the square).

To understand the output images, it helps to think about what the A-GAI has to figure out. It has to take the semantic elements to understand something of visual contents. It has to take syntactic text to understand the interrelationships between the semantic elements. It has to use the weights in the model from the neural network trained on the large imagesets, the fine-tuning, and the visual to text mapping to generate a visual in a limited 2d plane. [The seeding text prompts are fairly basic in this particular research, but more detailed and specific phraseology will likely result in different visuals.] The visuals were created over multiple days in order to enable the energy points to regenerate. None of the output

Figure 8. "Teen Girl..." prompt in the deep dream generator (with integrated AIVision PRO model)

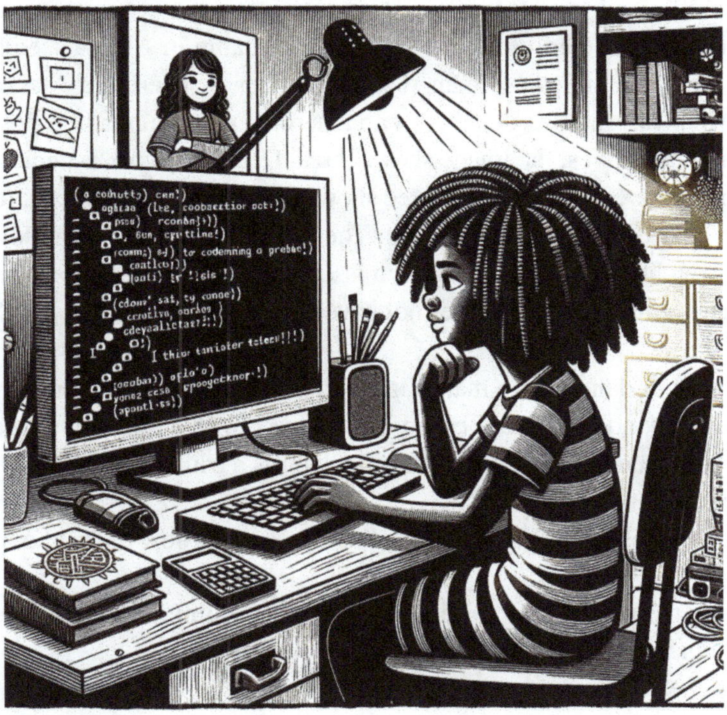

Figure 9. "Family Cabin..." prompt in the deep dream generator (with integrated Artistic 2 model)

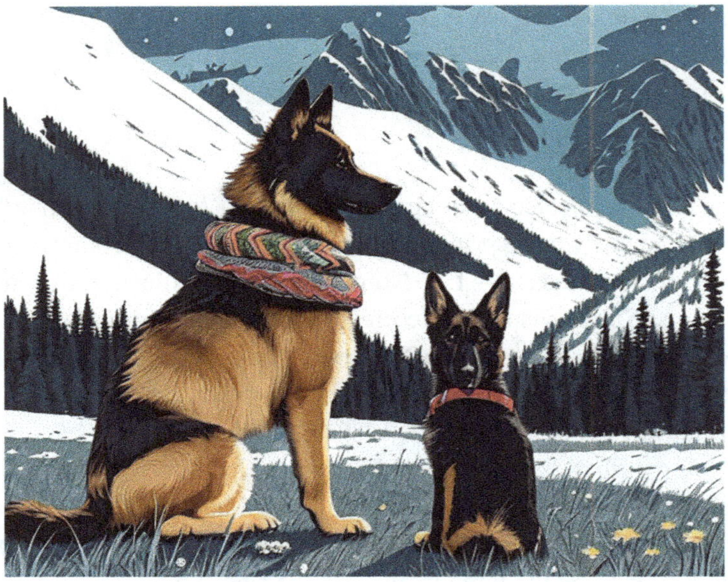

images were re-generated (through "iterations" or "inceptions" in the DDG). None were digitally edited (even though one seemed to have a crooked tilt).

In the first image, a teen girl discovers her talent for coding. This visual was created by the AIVision model in the DDG. The sense of context is evocative, with the desk lamp, books and a calculator on the desk, a friend's photo on the wall, a certificate or article on the wall, and knick-knacks on a shelf. The protagonist is left-handed and of African descent. The character is stylish and engaged. She is a relatable character. (Figure 8)

The image of a young female going to live in the family cabin in Alaska seems to have left off the protagonist. Rather, there is a styled German shepherd and pup. There are Alaskan mountains in the background. The German shepherd is depicted with a heroic and not unnatural pose. (Figure 9)

As to the four young detectives, the image shows three. Detective work is depicted as reading vs. being out in the field somewhere. The group of three shows two males and a female, for a gender mix. The colors and lines seem positive for print processing. The male character in the middle has misconfigured fingers in terms of the right hand. This is a known issue with large language models (LLMs) and how images are created. The female character does not have a book in front of her, but the two male ones do (Figure 10).

As to the young gymnast or dancer who makes it big in NYC, there is a silhouette of a dancer walking on what may be a roof or window ledge. Behind is a blue sky with a gradient turning to white. The big city is evoked in the background. The pose of the character is a triumphant one. The apparent gender is not fully defined (Figure 11).

A young scuba diver has some of the art right, but it is unclear how the scuba diving would breathe in the image (Figure 12).

A scuba diver prompt similar to that in Figure 12 was run with PhotoMage, which results in both a pleasant and more factual image (Figure 13).

Figure 10. "Four Teens..." prompt in the deep dream generator (with integrated artistic model)

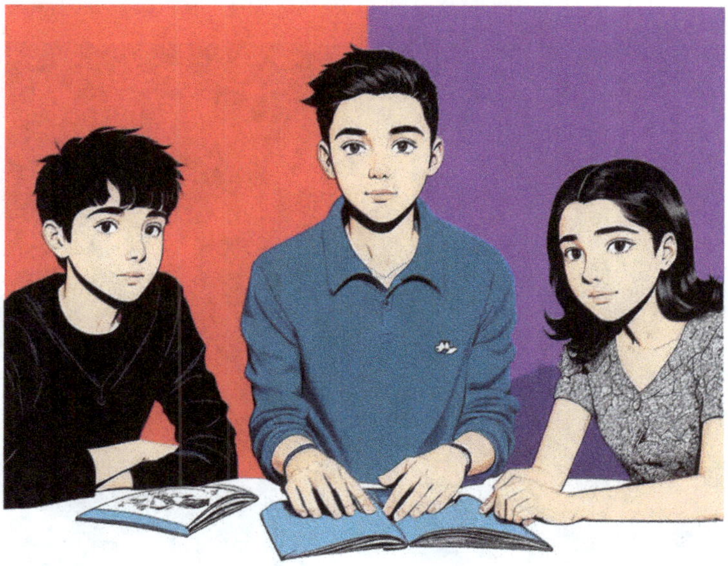

Figure 11. "A Young Gymnast..." prompt in the deep dream generator (with integrated DreamForge model)

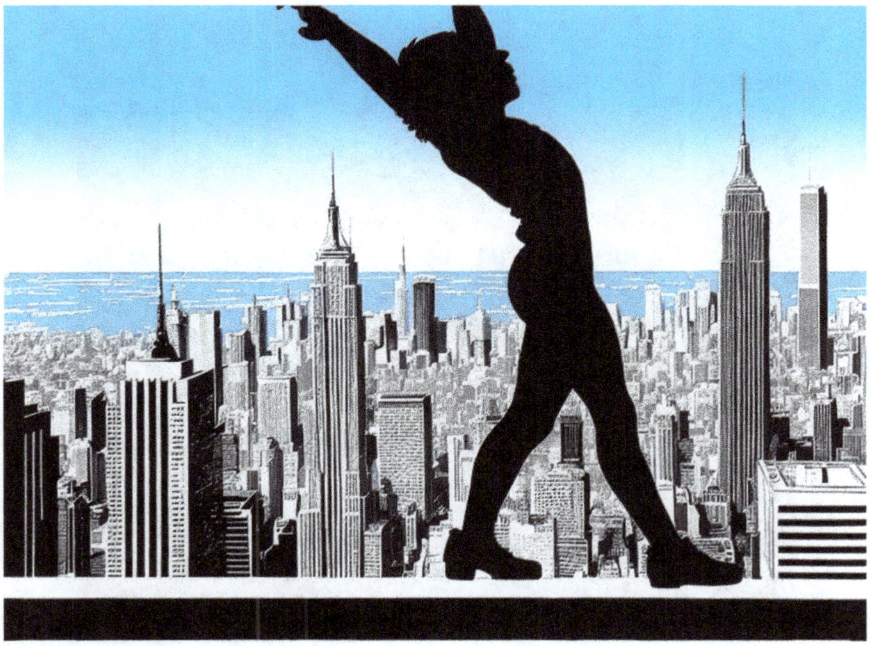

Figure 12. "A Scuba Diver..." prompt in the deep dream generator (with integrated EssenceOfReality PRO model)

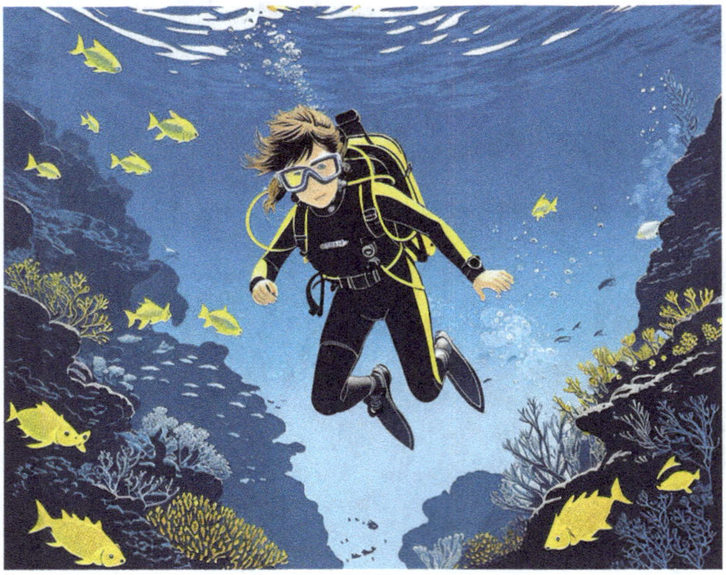

Figure 13. "A Scuba Diver..." prompt in the deep dream generator (with integrated PhotoMage PRO model)

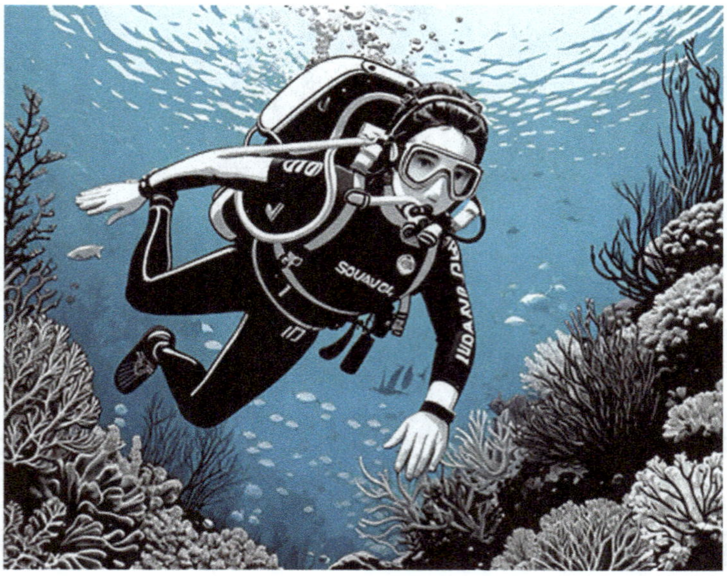

Figure 14. "Chinatown…" prompt in the deep dream generator (with integrated PhotoMage PRO model)

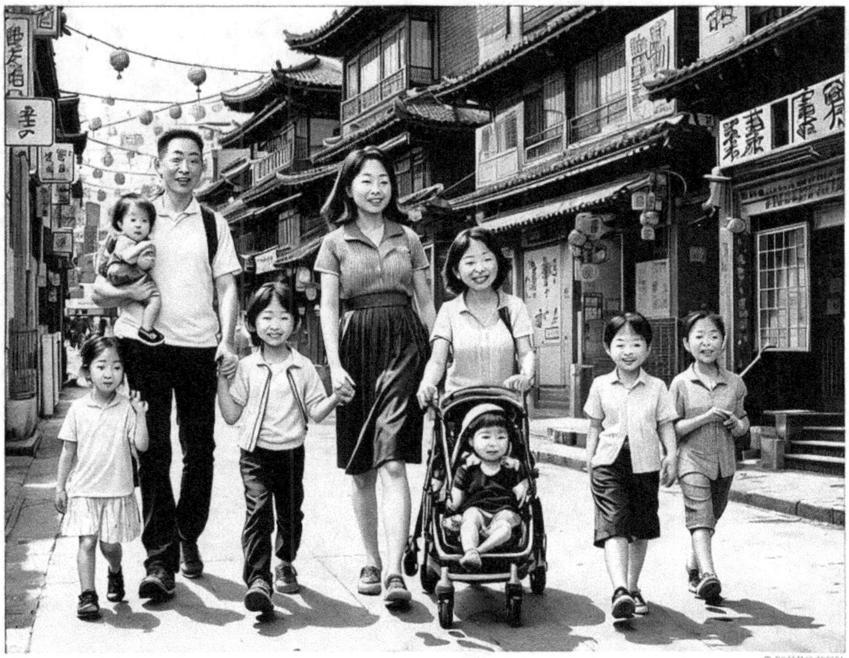

The b/w image of adults and children strolling together happily is an encouraging and positive image. The interrelationships are not particularly clear though, if this were a photo that a viewer is trying to decipher. The children look happy as do the adults. (Figure 14) There may be some racial profiling of the family given that they live in Chinatown, but people of many different races live in various "Chinatowns" and "International Districts."

As to the winner of a car race, the yellow tint is used to color the winning car in the foreground. There are cheering crowds in the background and just the tip of a car behind. There I no driver in the driver's seat, though. In a human-made illustration, perhaps a driver would be helmeted and waving to the crowds from an open window (Figure 15).

The next image is about a mouse family living in a sweets shop. There is unintelligible lettering (gibberish from the AI model) across the top area of the store. The mouse family is nowhere in sight. And the product behind the doors seem very close to where people would enter (Figure 16).

A nonfiction book may address the privations of WWII and the desperate efforts that families took to survive. The first of the two WWII images show children huddled together reading. The war itself may be outside of the room and beyond the consciousness of the clean-cut (and apparently well fed) youth. But there is little in the visual that might evoke this war (Figure 17).

The same prompt was run with the DigitalDaVinci PRO model and came up with a similar image… of a family reading books. (Figure 18) This prompt was run a second time in order to integrate all the models within the 12 prompts. The author had used multiple other models when she ran out of PRO access and decided to include the output images.

The image for the history of silver smithing does not seem particularly historical. There is no depiction of the actual equipment or processes. The protagonist is very childlike and does not have the requisite

Figure 15. "Car Racer…" prompt in the deep dream generator (with integrated Photonic model)

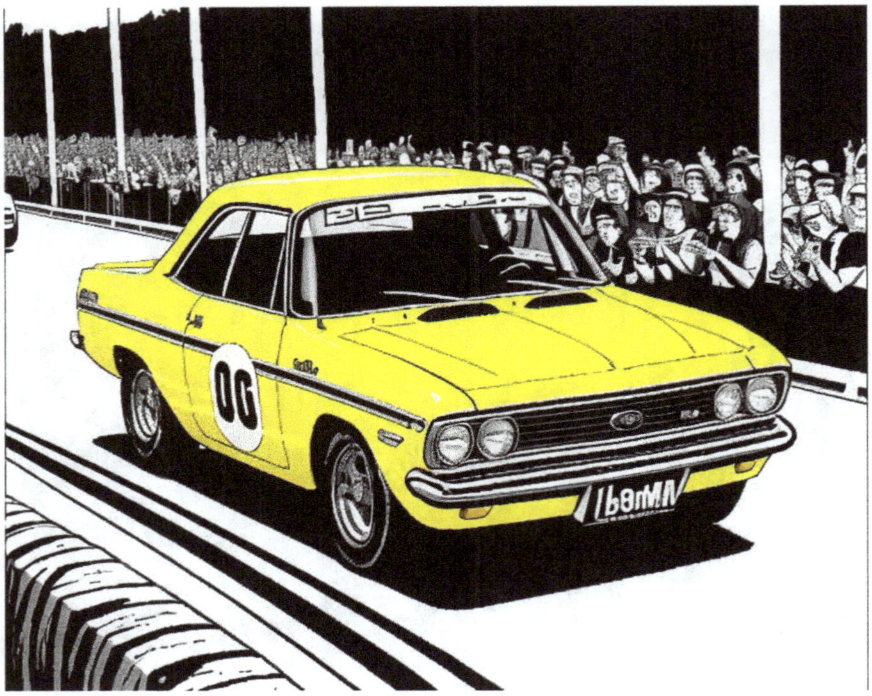

Figure 16. "Mouse Family…" prompt in the deep dream generator (with integrated DreamForge model)

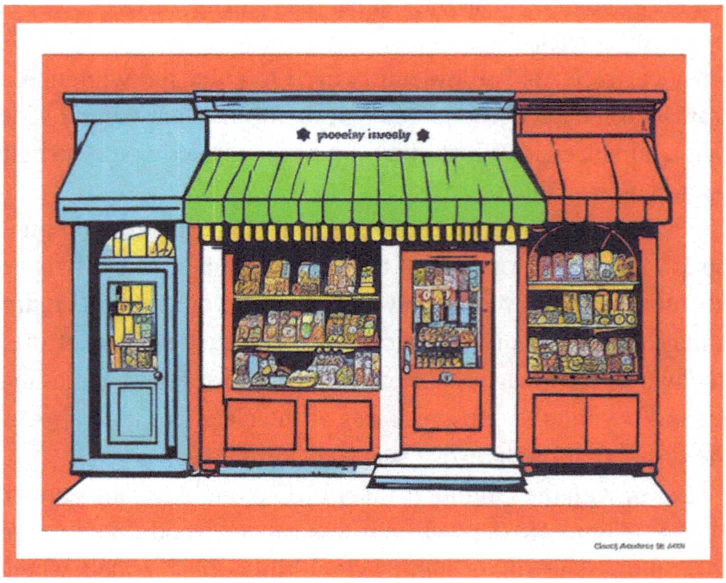

Figure 17. "WWII..." prompt in the deep dream generator (with integrated Artistic 2 model)

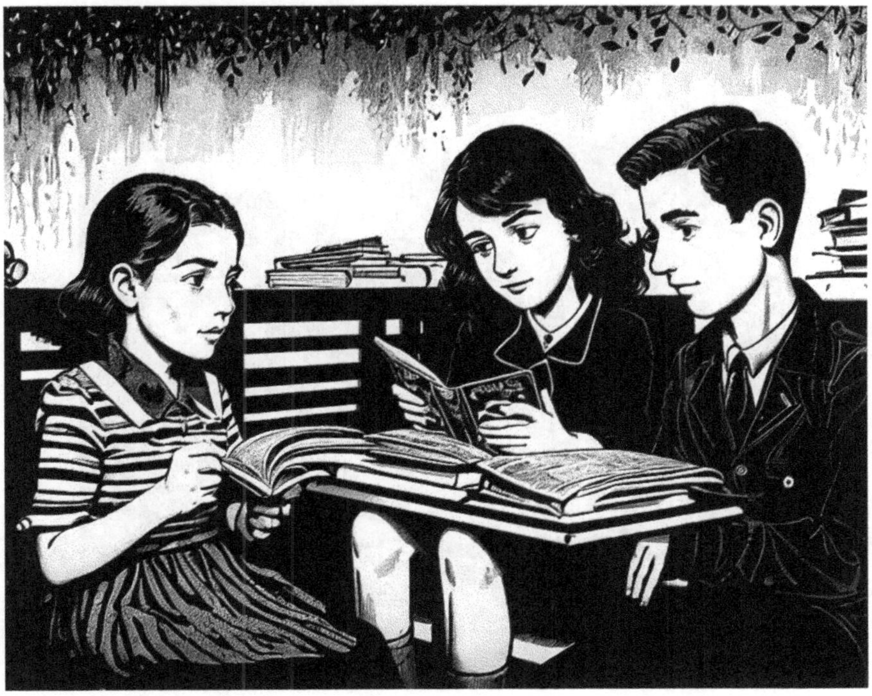

Figure 18. "WWII..." prompt in the deep dream generator (with integrated DigitalDaVinci PRO model)

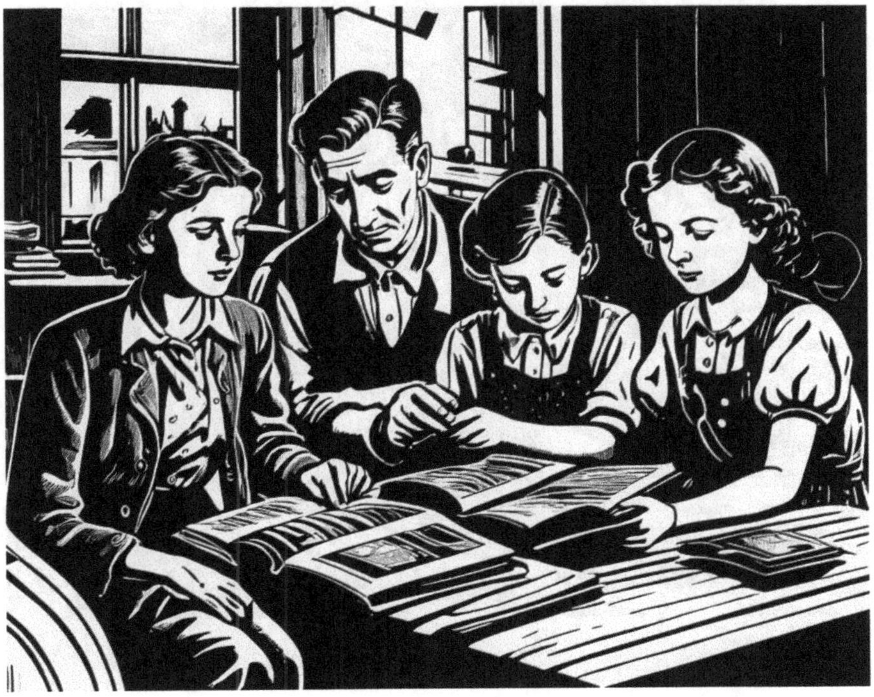

Figure 19. "Silver Smithing…" prompt in the deep dream generator (with integrated Animatron PRO model)

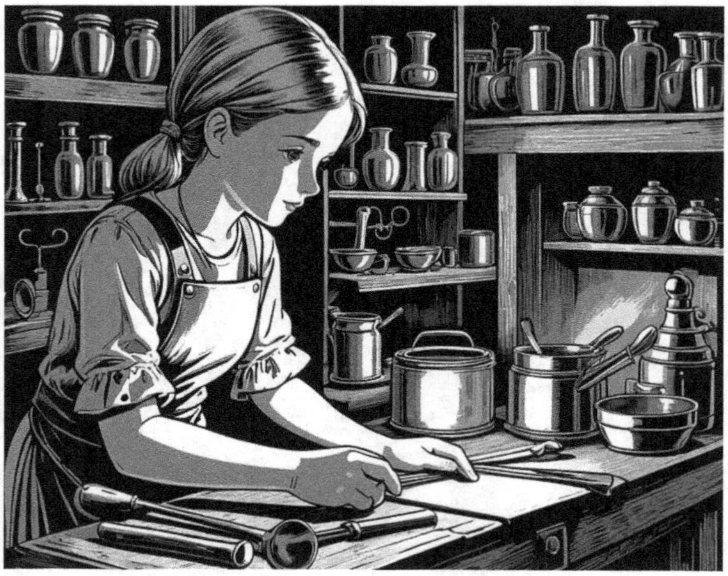

Figure 20. "Party…" Prompt in the deep dream generator (with integrated MirageMaker model)

Figure 21. "Haunted House..." prompt in the deep dream generator (with integrated Photonic model)

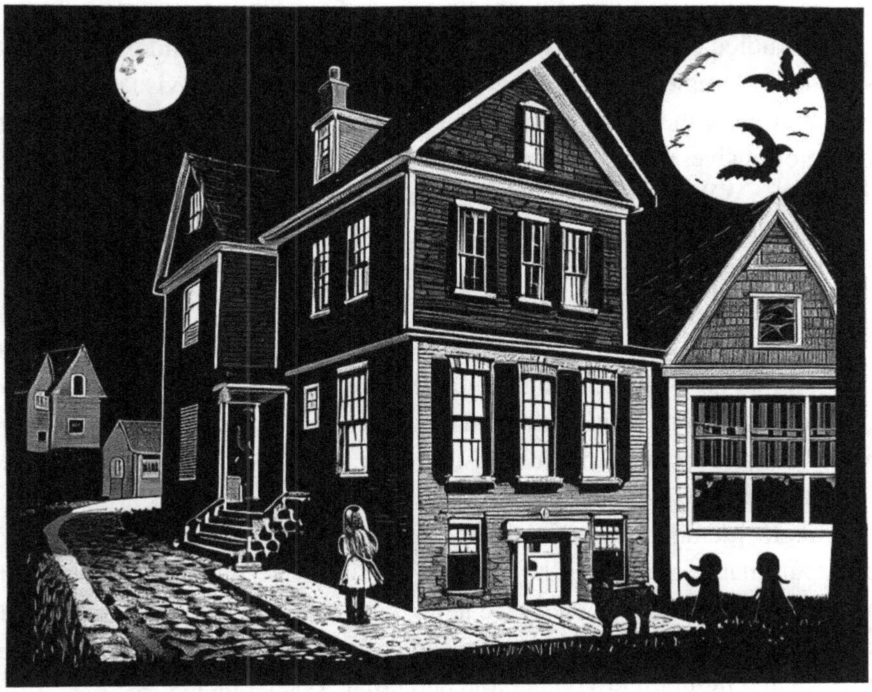

strength to engage in this dangerous work. There is an appeal to the visual though, in terms of evoking a fantastical "can do" approach (Figure 19).

As to a candymaker or chef catering a party, this AI-generated visual shows people in aprons and chefs' hats working on a cupcake pan (Figure 20).

For two friends visiting a haunted house, the generated visual shows a girl in the center front of the image frame...and two children with a dog at the bottom right (in silhouette). Bats are shown flying against the backdrop of a moon. There is a second moon in the night sky at the top left (which is also a common motif in A-GAI tools). The B/W (and some grayscale) work to the atmospherics of a haunted house. There are ways to work visuals into a text, such as suggesting that the girl arrived before her friend (Figure 21).

So after these walk-throughs, what was learned initially?

Research Questions

RQ1. How does the studied generative AI apparently tailor visuals for children?
RQ2. How well does/do the synthetic image(s) convey the message that is inherent to the textual prompt?
RQ3. Are there any obvious emulative styles from known children's book artists? Is there emulation from originals, through "memorization," "data leakage," "hallucination" or other forms of repetition?
RQ4. Is there visual communicative range in the visualizations?
RQ5. What is the balance between realism and the imaginary in the synthetic images?
RQ6. Are the images "child safe"? "Child friendly"? How so or how not?
RQ7. Do the synthetic images contribute to world building in the proposed story (from the text prompts)?

RQ8. Do the synthetic images contribute to character embodiment and building?

RQ1. How does the studied generative AI apparently tailor visuals for children?

The visuals are fairly simple, and the images have a clear location of visual interest or focus. Most show some representation of the protagonists, but a few did not. Many A-GAIs have limitations against portraying anything offensive, with limits on text prompts and limits on what the tool may output. One example here is that the WWII image shows people reading together, without a clear reference to the prompt's evocation of the dreadful second world war and its atrocities and abasements.

RQ2. How well does/do the synthetic image(s) convey the message that is inherent to the textual prompt?

In terms of responsiveness to the text prompts, the results were a mixed bag. Sometimes, semantic elements from the prompt are dropped altogether (the mouse family in the sweet shop, one of the teenage detectives, one of the friends visiting the haunted house, and so on). Some of the layouts seem pro forma. The points of emphasis are sometimes lost.

RQ3. Are there any obvious emulative styles from known children's book artists? Is there emulation from originals, through "memorization," "data leakage," "hallucination" or other forms of repetition?

None of the output images are observably derivative of a known children's book illustrator's works. (A-GAIs are not known to memorize or leak data or hallucinate in the way some of the models that output in text do.) The "style" is more illustrative and generic and less of a styled look-and-feel. There are not the flourishes and humor and vivid colors and other style elements.

RQ4. Is there visual communicative range in the visualizations?

The generated images were from a variety of different models, but the images do not communicate a broad visual range. If the images are placed in a normal curve, most of these would not be more than a standard deviation out from average.

RQ5. What is the balance between realism and the imaginary in the synthetic images?

The output images here read as more imaginary than real. Of course, the modifier tags for "linocut" and "high-contrast" may evoke more of an illustrative feel vs. anything photorealistic. Even so, the depicted contents read as imaginary more than real. (Line art may be used to evoke reality.)

RQ6. Are the images "child safe"? "Child friendly"? How so or how not?

The output images from this small study were generally child friendly. The differences in finger counts, though, may be off-putting for some. Any images used in a publication caliber need to be vetted by humans through a grid-level evaluation at minimum. Then, the visual messaging should also be evaluated from multiple frameworks: cultural, aesthetic, and others.

As a side note, in early January 2024, DDG included a new "Guidelines" at the point when a dream could be published out to the world. Their guidelines read:

Guidelines for publishing dreams

1. *No nudity or sexually suggestive material.*
2. *No hate speech, racist, or discriminatory content.*
3. *No images that depict gore or death in explicit way.*
4. *No violent or explicit content.*
5. *No political messages or symbols.*

These guidelines are in addition to computational means to head off potentially offensive or provocative or unethical contents.

RQ7. Do the synthetic images contribute to world building in the proposed story (from the text prompts)?

World building in an image-sense is too large of a phenomena to assess from a small set of output images for various unrelated prompts. As for fleeting contexts, some visual elements speak to that context. However, the leaning is more towards simplicity vs. complexity in the visual. Text and other multimedia elements may be needed for a full sense of evoked story. (Of course, each story speaks to readers in different ways.)

RQ8. Do the synthetic images contribute to character embodiment and building?

What about the imagery used to evoke personality? Character? As noted earlier, the German shepherd was shown with a heroic pose. In terms of human characters, though, these also look to be fairly generic vs. novel.

Discussion

The A-GAI is a powerful tool that outputs usable visuals for a variety of contexts. In terms of imagery for children's stories, the created images may be useful as reference ones, for compositing and layout. They may be useful for drafty publications. However, the output do not necessarily seem ready yet for prime time or actual "publication." Perhaps a few may be useful after extensive digital image editing. Or perhaps these may be useful for a do-it-yourself work, but as to a professional publication, the visuals do not quite offer a sufficient level of sophistication or human controls.

FUTURE RESEARCH DIRECTIONS

The LLMs do not evolve in linear ways. They are trained on different data, and they are fine-tuned in different ways as well. This research work has focused on one tool, the Deep Dream Generator. Future research may take the research questions (RQs) here and apply them to a different artmaking generative AI tool.

RQ1. How does the studied generative AI apparently tailor visuals for children?
RQ2. How well does/do the synthetic image(s) convey the message that is inherent to the textual prompt?
RQ3. Are there any obvious emulative styles from known children's book artists? Is there emulation from originals, through "memorization," "data leakage," "hallucination" or other forms of repetition?
RQ4. Is there visual communicative range in the visualizations?
RQ5. What is the balance between realism and the imaginary in the synthetic images?
RQ6. Are the images "child safe"? "Child friendly"? How so or how not?
RQ7. Do the synthetic images contribute to world building in the proposed story (from the text prompts)?
RQ8. Do the synthetic images contribute to character embodiment and building?

Same or different prompts may be used to evoke image outputs. Computational means may be applied to the study for more rigor. For example, to see if such images may evoke worlds (enable worldbuilding), it may take an exporting of images at some larger scale than is available with manual extraction.

Future studies may draw from different genres of literature, not just children's literature, but subsets of adult literature, and other literary genre traditions.

The images in a children's may range from the rare and sparse all the way to the picture-only sorts of books. Such books may be read not only by children but by adults, including those with special foci in relation to such literature. The images may be read or interpreted separated from a text or sequence or overarching structure. In such cases, the images have to work in a stand-alone fashion. These same images may have to work within the complex structure of a children's story, in terms of characters, scenes, action, aesthetics, narrative, world-building, and others; they have to work within a larger macro culture that surrounds the story.

A major challenge continues to be creating consisting artworks that create a sense of theme across the trajectory of a children's book plot. It is possible to iterate from a seeding image; it is possible to "Try It" with harnessing the prompt to output a hopefully similar image. (A "Try It" with a given seeding image and text and model…may get a little closer to the original image, but the emphasis on focusing on variation makes output image consistency challenging.)

Further, if the children's book is multimodal and includes audio and video, there will be respective challenges of timing with animation and video motion visuals. Some of these concerns may be partially mitigated with digital image editing, animation editing, and video editing. However, if the A-GAI is about saving on time, effort, and work, going to outside tools will involve much higher investments.

Differing objectives (didactic or non-didactic) of the imaginary children's book for which the images are being made may also affect whether the images generated are useful or not. There are also so-called "shadow tales" related to a book. These may include biographical stories of the author, movies and films, theme parks, and other spinoffs. If visuals from the shadow tales relate to the original work and related canon, exploring spinoff imagery from A-GAI may be interesting.

A future study may enroll children to see what they find desirable in terms of visuals instead of using a researcher's sensibility. In the same way that children's books may be consumed and enjoyed by adults, drawings from children's books may also be appreciated across a wide age range and in various ways. Perhaps a future study may include a group of research participants.

It is fair to ask if the artmaking generative AI enables new ways of seeing (and illustrating) children's books. Is it able to capture seminal moments? Can it show recognizable characters across different contexts? Is it able to depict moments of conflict and emotion and denouement with different tonality?

CONCLUSION

In this study, the Deep Dream Generator offers a range of art-generating AI models that output works of varying quality for a children's book illustration context. There is a sense of child-reader sensibility to the works, in many cases. Even with serious issues, the images have something that lightens the mood. However, sometimes, critical requested elements are not included. In some cases, the visuals look to follow a particular given layout pattern that may read as repetitive.

REFERENCES

Abas, S., Bamanger, E., Gashan, A. K., & Guler, A. (2021). Navigating the land of opportunities as Muslim immigrants: A geocriticism perspective to transnationalism in multicultural children's literature. *Journal of Children's Literature*, *47*(2), 48–60.

Abrahamson, R. F., & Shannon, P. (1983). A plot structure analysis of favorite picture books. *The Reading Teacher*, *37*(1), 44–48.

Aram, D., Fine, Y., & Ziv, M. (2013). Enhancing parent–child shared book reading interactions: Promoting references to the book's plot and socio-cognitive themes. *Early Childhood Research Quarterly*, *28*(1), 111–122. doi:10.1016/j.ecresq.2012.03.005

Arizpe, E., Styles, M., Mackey, M., Bromley, H., Coulthard, K., & Noble, K. (2015). New case studies of children responding to picturebooks. In *Children Reading Picturebooks* (pp. 145–168). Routledge. doi:10.4324/9781315683911-19

Bhandari, P., & Brennan, H. M. (2023). Trustworthiness of Children Stories Generated by Large Language Models. *arXiv preprint arXiv:2308.00073*. doi:10.18653/v1/2023.inlg-main.24

Bouley, T. M., & Godfrey, P. C. (2008). Reading outside the boundaries: Children's literature as pedagogy for building empathy and understanding of social justice in the college classroom. *The Journal of Effective Teaching*, *8*(1), 33–41.

Bradford, C. (2011). Children's literature in a global age: Transnational and local identities. *Barnboken*, *34*(1), 18761. doi:10.14811/clr.v34i1.23

Cress, S. W., & Holm, D. T. (1998). *Developing empathy through children's literature*. ERIC.

Dyches, T. T., & Prater, M. A. (2005). Characterization of developmental disability in children's fiction. *Education and Training in Developmental Disabilities*, 202–216.

Dyches, T. T., Prater, M. A., & Cramer, S. F. (2001). Characterization of mental retardation and autism in children's books. *Education and Training in Mental Retardation and Developmental Disabilities*, 230–243.

Ertem, İ. (2013). Exploring the role of digital children's literature in the technology-based literacy instruction. *Okuma Yazma Eğitimi Araştırmaları*, *1*(2), 102–108.

Fang, Z. (1996). Illustrations, text, and the child reader: what are pictures in children's storybooks for? *Reading Horizons: A Journal of Literacy and Language Arts, 37*(2), 130 – 142.

Gannon, S. R. (1987). One more time: Approaches to repetition in children's literature. *Children's Literature Association Quarterly*, *12*(1), 2–5. doi:10.1353/chq.0.0202

Gardner, R. P. (2017). Discussing racial trauma using visual thinking strategies. *Language Arts*, *94*(5), 338–345. doi:10.58680/la201729058

Golden, J. M. (1984). Children's concept of story in reading and writing. *The Reading Teacher*, *37*(7), 578–584.

Halpin, H. R. (2003). *The plots of children and machines: The statistical and symbolic semantic analysis of narratives* [Unpublished master's thesis]. University of Edinburgh.

Higonnet, M. R. (1987). Narrative fractures and fragments. *Children's Literature, 15*(1), 37–54. doi:10.1353/chl.0.0617

Hudson, J., & Nelson, K. (1983). Effects of script structure on children's story recall. *Developmental Psychology, 19*(4), 625–635. doi:10.1037/0012-1649.19.4.625

Hunt, P. (1984). Narrative theory and children's literature. *Children's Literature Association Quarterly, 9*(4), 191–194. doi:10.1353/chq.0.0415

John Amos Comenius. (2023, Dec. 19). In *Wikipedia*. Retrieved Jan. 3, 2024, from https://en.wikipedia.org/wiki/John_Amos_Comenius

Kelley, L. (2018). Solution stories: A narrative study of how teachers support children's problem solving. *Early Childhood Education Journal, 46*(3), 313–322. doi:10.1007/s10643-017-0866-6

Khan, K. S., Gugiu, M. R., Justice, L. M., Bowles, R. P., Skibbe, L. E., & Piasta, S. B. (2016). Age-related progressions in story structure in young children's narratives. *Journal of Speech, Language, and Hearing Research: JSLHR, 59*(6), 1395–1408. doi:10.1044/2016_JSLHR-L-15-0275 PMID:27930767

Lancia, P. J. (1997). Literary borrowing: The effects of literature on children's writing. *The Reading Teacher, 50*(6), 470–475.

Malo, E., & Bullard, J. (2000). *Storytelling and the emergent reader. International Reading Association World Congress on Reading*. Auckland, New Zealand.

McIntyre, N., & Lapata, M. (2010, July). Plot induction and evolutionary search for story generation. In *Proceedings of the 48th Annual Meeting of the Association for Computational Linguistics* (pp. 1562-1572). Academic Press.

Monoyiou, E., & Symeonidou, S. (2016). The wonderful world of children's books? Negotiating diversity through children's literature. *International Journal of Inclusive Education, 20*(6), 588–603. doi:10.1080/13603116.2015.1102338

Morrow, L. M. (1985). Retelling stories: A strategy for improving young children's comprehension, concept of story structure, and oral language complexity. *The Elementary School Journal, 85*(5), 647–661. doi:10.1086/461427

Nicolopoulou, A. (2008). The elementary forms of narrative coherence in young children's storytelling. *Narrative Inquiry, 18*(2), 299–325.

Nicolopoulou, A., & Richner, E. S. (2007). From actors to agents to persons: The development of character representation in young children's narratives. *Child Development, 78*(2), 412–429. doi:10.1111/j.1467-8624.2007.01006.x PMID:17381781

Nikolajeva, M. (1998). Exit children's literature? *The Lion and the Unicorn, 22*(2), 221–236. doi:10.1353/uni.1998.0028

Nikolajeva, M. (2001). The changing aesthetics of character in children's fiction. *Style (Fayetteville), 35*(3), 430–453.

Nikolajeva, M. (2003). Beyond the Grammar of Story, or How Can Children's Literature Criticism Benefit from Narrative Theory? *Children's Literature Association Quarterly, 28*(1), 5–16. doi:10.1353/chq.0.1702

Norton, D. E. (1992). Engaging children in literature: Understanding plot structures. *The Reading Teacher, 46*(3), 254–258.

Pantaleo, S. (2005). "Reading" young children's visual texts. *Early Childhood Research & Practice, 7*(1), n1.

Peirce, K., & Edwards, E. D. (1988). Children's construction of fantasy stories: Gender differences in conflict resolution strategies. *Sex Roles, 18*(7-8), 393–404. doi:10.1007/BF00288391

Pelletier, J., & Wilde Astington, J. (2004). Action, consciousness and theory of mind: Children's ability to coordinate story characters' actions and thoughts. *Early Education and Development, 15*(1), 5–22. doi:10.1207/s15566935eed1501_1

Pokrivcakova, S. (2017). The digital age in literary education. *Teaching Literature for the 21st Century*, 11.

Rathmann, C., Mann, W., & Morgan, G. (2007). Narrative structure and narrative development in deaf children. *Deafness & Education International, 9*(4), 187–196. doi:10.1179/146431507790559932

Reid, S. F., & Serafini, F. (2018). More than words: An investigation of the middle-grade multimodal novel. *Journal of Children's Literature, 44*(2), 32–44.

Robertson, J., & Good, J. (2004, June). Children's narrative development through computer game authoring. In *Proceedings of the 2004 Conference on Interaction Design and Children: Building a Community* (pp. 57-64). 10.1145/1017833.1017841

Rubegni, E., Landoni, M., Malinverni, L., & Jaccheri, L. (2022). Raising awareness of stereotyping through collaborative digital storytelling: Design for change with and for children. *International Journal of Human-Computer Studies, 157*, 102727. doi:10.1016/j.ijhcs.2021.102727

Scalise Sugiyama, M. (2009). The plot thickens: What children's stories tell us about mindreading. *Journal of Consciousness Studies, 16*(6-7), 94–117.

Schulte, C. M. (2019). Plot holes in children's drawing. *Art Education, 72*(3), 15–19. doi:10.1080/00043125.2019.1577942

Serafini, F., Kachorsky, D., & Reid, S. (2018). Revisiting the multimodal nature of children's literature. *Language Arts, 95*(5), 311–321. doi:10.58680/la201829586

Shapiro, L. R., & Hudson, J. A. (1991). Tell me a make-believe story: Coherence and cohesion in young children's picture-elicited narratives. *Developmental Psychology, 27*(6), 960–974. doi:10.1037/0012-1649.27.6.960

Sinan, A. T., Demir, S., & Dogan, F. D. (2017). Teacher's views regarding the place of children's literature in first language education. *Journal of Education and Training Studies, 5*(12), 133–145. doi:10.11114/jets.v5i12.2691

Sipe, L. R. (2002). Talking back and taking over: Young children's expressive engagement during storybook read-alouds. *The Reading Teacher*, *55*(5), 476–483.

Thomas, E. E. (2016). Stories still matter: Rethinking the role of diverse children's literature today. *Language Arts*, *94*(2), 112–119. doi:10.58680/la201628803

Tschida, C. M., Ryan, C. L., & Ticknor, A. S. (2014). Building on windows and mirrors: Encouraging the disruption of "single stories" through children's literature. *Journal of Children's Literature*, *40*(1), 28–39.

Verhallen, M. J., Bus, A. G., & de Jong, M. T. (2006). The promise of multimedia stories for kindergarten children at risk. *Journal of Educational Psychology*, *98*(2), 410–419. doi:10.1037/0022-0663.98.2.410

Wiltse, L. (2015). Mirrors and windows: Teaching and research reflections on Canadian Aboriginal children's literature. *Language and Literature*, *17*(2), 22–40.

Wright, S. (2007). Graphic-narrative play: Young children's authoring through drawing and telling. *International Journal of Education & the Arts*, *8*(8), 1–28.

Yoon, B. (2022). How does children's literature portray global perspectives? *Journal of Global Education and Research*, *6*(2), 206–222. doi:10.5038/2577-509X.6.2.1090

Zapata, A., Fugit, M., & Moss, D. (2017). Awakening socially just mindsets through visual thinking strategies and diverse picturebooks. *Journal of Children's Literature*, *43*(2), 62–69.

KEY TERMS AND DEFINITIONS

Artmaking Generative AI (A-GAI): Computer models based on machine learning training from large datasets that create aesthetic or artful visuals.

Children's Literature: Fictional and nonfictional writing across various writing forms specifically written for child readers (those 16 and under).

Generative AI: Computer tools that output digital informational contents (text, imagery, audio, video, slideshows, and others).

Chapter 6
Exploratory Visual Digital Character and Visual Digital Scene Design Using Artmaking Generative AI:
Enhancing Story Problems and Other Pedagogical Narratives

Shalin Hai-Jew
https://orcid.org/0000-0002-8863-0175
Hutchinson Community College, USA

ABSTRACT

Static visual illustrations with characters and scenes play an important role in story problems and other pedagogical narratives. Such visuals may better engage learners, connect learners with the learning sequence, set the emotional tone, evoke settings, emphasize critical moments, and support the teaching and learning in other ways. With the popularization of artmaking generative AI, a practical question is how well this tool can make visual characters based on character design prompts for both animate and inanimate characters? What about the computerized drawing of scenes in which such characters may be placed, alone or in relation to each other? How difficult is it to prompt the generative AI to create consistent characters from different angles and perspectives? To create consistent scenes and backgrounds? This work explores how practically usable the AI-generated visuals are for the making of characters and scenes, with some light pre-production and post-production, as needed.

INTRODUCTION

In the past decades, in higher education, there has been a shift from "text alone" to "text with visuals and multimedia" to harness learning benefits. Visuals capture and hold learner attention. They enhance

DOI: 10.4018/979-8-3693-1950-5.ch006

memorability. They add multi-dimensionality to examples and explanations; in terms of dimensionality, think line, shapes, textures, colors, and other aspects. Visuals help make the learning—concepts, categories, processes, relationships, interrelationships, systems, and other elements—more approachable. They are used to explain data relationships. They provide insights into the natural and physical world, given what is seeable with the naked unaided eye and with technical augmentation—at micro-, meso-, and macro- scales. Core visuals used in story problems and other forms of narratives for learning may include a range of visuals, but one type includes characters (animate: humanoid, animal-ist; inanimate: robotic, plant, and others) in contexts (scenes). Much of the world is designed and communicated for human consumption. While many learning visuals are comprised of photos, many others are illustrations, re-enactments, and depictions from the human imaginary. In the current age, those latter visuals will emerge from the human-computer imaginary.

This work explores the usability of the Deep Dream Generator (originated in 2015, in v. 3 in 2024), an artmaking generative AI tool (A-GAI), in creating characters (typically in the foreground) and then the scene context (typically in the background). A-GAI tools may be designed in different ways, but many are based on deep learning models (based on various neural networks) that learn from large imagesets. The learning is based on unsupervised machine learning, and from the learning weights, the technology may be induced to output visuals based on text and / or image prompts, tags, and other inputs.

The research questions include the following:

RQ1: How usable is the Deep Dream Generator in creating static characters (animate and inanimate) for pedagogical purposes?

RQ2: How usable is the Deep Dream Generator in re-creating prior static characters (animate and inanimate) for pedagogical purposes?

RQ3: How usable is the Deep Dream Generator in creating static scenes (backgrounds) for pedagogical purposes?

RQ4: How usable is the Deep Dream Generator in re-creating prior static scenes (prior backgrounds) for pedagogical purposes?

Optimally, the visuals by the artmaking generative AI (A-GAI) would be of sufficient quality for use in learning materials. The technical tool should be flexible enough to not only create inspired characters and scenes but re-create necessary characters and scenes to enable the generation of image sequencing, reproductions in different scenarios. The characters and scenes here will be static ones, but animations may be created by setting up "joints" and "skeletons" in the characters, and then applying "walk cycles," dance sequences, and other scripted motions. Motion overlays may be applied to the respective scenes using particle effects, weather overlays, and others. Specific motion programming may be applied to both the digital characters and the scenes using various commercially available digital puppet tools, digital image editing tools, animation tools, video tools, game engines, immersive virtual world tools, and others. Similarly, voice and soundtracks may be applied to the digital puppets, animations, and videos. As a side note, given that creations by generative AIs cannot be legally copyrighted stateside, such generated visuals are usable without payment in academic and other (even commercial) contexts.

REVIEW OF THE LITERATURE

The academic literature includes research on the making of various synthetic digital characters. In some ways, the most simple are the static visual ones. The main modality of communication for a static visual digital character is its appearance, how the character is visually styled. The "silhouette, shape, proportions and pose" are some central elements of visual character design as informed by personality (Fogelström, 2013, p. 4). Other visual concepts at play include the openness and closure of shapes, the context or gestalt, color theory, cultural practice, and others. The visual representation of a virtual character stands in for perhaps deeper knowledge of the character. The physical attractiveness of a character may be appealing for a time, but looks are a "fading trait" (Nieminen, 2017, p. 6).

Human users are responsive to subtle emotional facial expressions. One empirical study asked research participants to respond to the depicted facial expressions on simple digital avatars. The study examined "the geometrical intensity of an emotional facial expression on the perceived intensity and the recognition accuracy" of that emotion (Bartneck & Reichenbach, 2005, p. 179). Some systems emulate already human-validated faces with the respective positioning of the facial features—the eyebrows, mouth, eyes, and other aspects. Another study involves empirical research with human participants to understand how they interpret static bodily postures in terms of conveyed emotions in order to support the design of synthetic characters (for use in human interactions) (Shaarani & Romano, 2007). Digital avatars are designed for how a visual communication is received by people. There are studies, too, on various types of human gesturing to communicate either without verbiage or to complement verbal (often oral) communications. Non-verbals like physical stances, gesturing, posturing, and other paralinguistic communications may be brought into play to the visual depiction. Certainly, emblematic, propositional, iconic, metaphoric, deictic, and beat gestures may be embedded into physical depictions of synthetic characters. Static characters may also be enhanced by the story problem and other narrative content around the synthetic character image.

What is undesirable is to trigger the eeriness that humans may feel in terms of the so-called "uncanny valley" effect. This effect was defined in 1970 (Mori, 1970) to describe a phenomenon the closer a robot is designed to look human but does not fully achieve the authentic look, feel, and motion. In that space prior to full representation, people may experience aversion: "Highly realistic computer-generated characters in movies, computer games, and immersive applications often evoke negative feelings—even disgust" (Schwind, Wolf, & Henze, 2018, p. 45). A mix of almost-real but not quite real to the full sense of human leads to an "uncanny valley" effect. One example in the literature is of "dead eyes" of digital avatars that do not track what is occurring in the scene or the virtual space. More recent research suggests that a more successful aim is the height of the first curve of clear synthetic nature vs. the high second curve of striving to emulate a healthy human (Mori, MacDorman, & Kageki, 2012). A "dead eyes" illustration may be seen in Figure 1. (This visual was seeded with a multimedia artwork piece by the author.)

Another work suggests that the "uncanny" response may be triggered in ways beyond character appearance. One researcher suggests that character behaviors have to match their context for likeability by the human individual interacting with the 3d animated character. People judge the computer-generated character by "how realistically (normally) it behaves" (Tharib, 2013, p. 4). Synthetic characterization is comprised of three elements: "the aesthetic, the behaviour and the contextualization" (Tharib, 2013, p. 3), and those elements have to align. Ultimately, synthetic characters have to appeal to the human viewer to be used and ultimately useful (Soikun & Ibrahim, 2018).

Figure 1. Uncanny valley and "dead eyes" in the deep dream generator

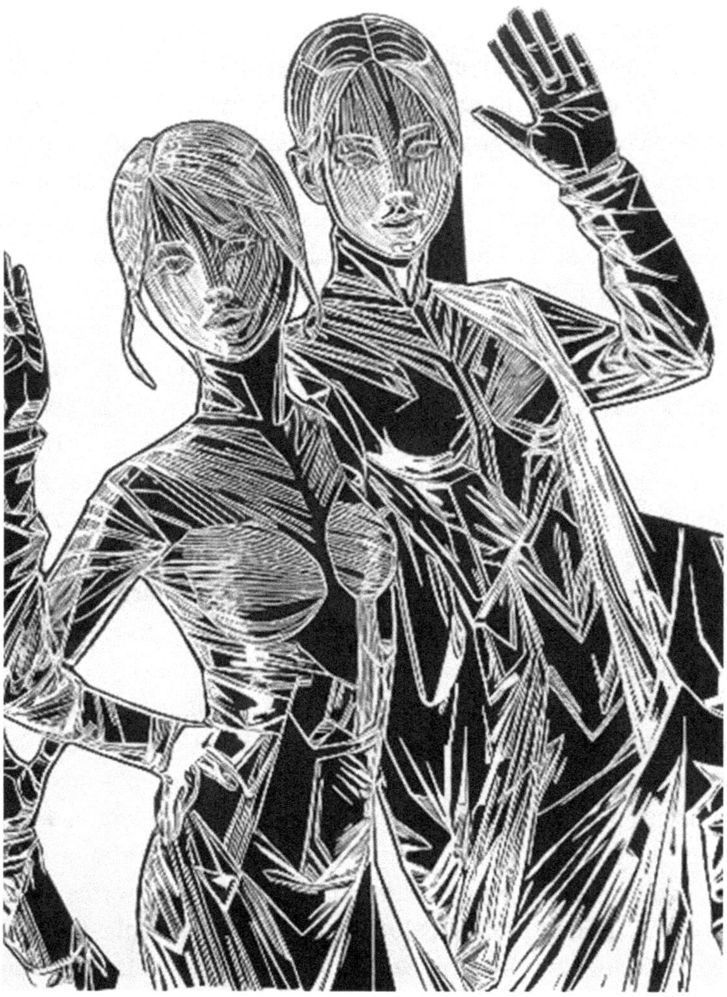

Social character design is also applied to animated agents, such as interface agents that are used to make interactions between humans and computing machines easier. A research study that found that people formed a favorable approach to agents that "previously agreed with their decisions" (Takeuchi & Katagiri, Sept. 1999, p. 53), with human-machine interactions mimicking human-human relationships in many cases. Many designers and developers encourage familiar social dynamics between people and computational agents. People form affinities with other people and with synthetic agents with whom they feel some relatedness and with whom they experience agreeable behaviors. Also, people tend towards "homophily" or the liking of those who are more similar to them. People respond empathically with synthetic characters who seem more similar to them (Hall & Woods, n.d., n.p.). One study found that similar gender is a main aspect of human identity (Hall & Woods, n.d., n.p.).

One study tested the effect of synthetic voices from digital agents to see if subtle effects might affect the human experience. The study played on issues of gender, such as whether female voices that were slightly more masculine and male voices that were slightly more feminine had an effect on the user experience.

These anthropomorphic forms of digital media, or synthetic characters, could influence people through small changes (Gulz, Ahlner, & Haake, 2007). The design is aimed at both conscious and subconscious and unconscious effects on the human user. A different and later study asked if synthetic voices altered the social responses to photorealistic characters in a virtual reality context. This study focused on trying to understand the importance of synthetic voices on human ratings of character "appeal, credibility, human-likeness and voice matching" (Zibrek, Cabral, & McDonnell, Nov. 2021, p. 229). This work did not find a close connection between synthetic voices of synthetic agents and those dependent variables.

How a digital avatar is used affects its affordances and design. For example, a digital avatar that is human-embodied offers some autonomic motions (breathing, blinking) and stance changes, but its voice, its personality, its modeled look and dress, and its locomotion depends on the human "driving" the avatar. The human user offers the partial- or full- force of human-embodied telepresence. The avatar that humans embody have different affordances of motion, action, decision-making, intercommunications, and other features. Such avatars (and player-characters) serve as the interface for the disembodied human experience of the virtual-physical and social landscape of the created world. Said another way: "...the player character is the entity to which all functionality is aimed" (Eladhari & Lindley, Nov. 2003, n.p.). Role-playing games involve both defined characters and human-embodiment of those characters (Lankoski, 2004). One model of character design includes character physiology, sociology, and psychology (Lankoski, 2004, p. 143), so including an individual but also the social context or surround for that individual.

Such avatars are a contrast to non-playable characters in both digital games and virtual worlds. These avatars are automatons programmed to play certain roles or take particular actions or engage in automated ways based on scripts. Automated agents may be designed with more complex dimensions to emulate people, such as emotions, objectives, personalities, demographic details, and other features.

Designers of synthetic characters may use rituals to express culture (Mascarenhas, Dias, Afonso, Enz, & Paiva, May 2009) and perhaps create more global senses of human identities. Cultural variability in synthetic agent design may better enable cross-cultural communication (Maldonado & Hayes-Roth, 2004). Cultural awareness in 2d and 3d animated characters may be expressed in costumes and accessories and enable people groups to engage in more shared meanings, enabled by shared cultural understandings (Khalis & Mustaffa, 2017, p. 487).

Human affect is conceptualized in different ways in terms of how to express them in synthetic agents. An affective module for one virtual reality system includes the sub-modules of "Personality, Mood and Emotion" to "characterize and influence the cognitive activities of perception, memory and decision making" of the respective digital characters (Bressane Neto & Corrêa da Silva, 2010, p. 102). The mimicry of believable affect in avatars may provide sufficient similarity to human-human dating interactions (Hoorn, Konijn, & Pontier, 2019). Believability of the digital agent is the "holy grail of character design, whether expressed through animation, acting, filmmaking, writing, or programming" (Maldonado & Hayes-Roth, 2004, n.p.). The synthetic agent should evoke a suspension of disbelief, so that users ascribe "human-like emotions to inanimate and barely animated objects" (Maldonado & Hayes-Roth, 2004, n.p.).

Digital characters that can reason about the experiences and thinking of others may "predict and manipulate the behavior of even *human* players" (Bringsjord, Shilliday, Taylor, Werner, Clark, Charpentier, & Bringsjord, 2008, n.p.). One work describes the design of a synthetic character leading people in online multi-user environments (Isbister & Hayes-Roth, Jan. 1998). Various digital social agents are designed to elicit empathy from people or "the capacity to perceive, understand and experience others' emotions" (Rodrigues, Mascarenhas, Dias, & Paiva, Sept. 2009, p. 1). Empathy smooths social relationships based on the increased mutual understanding. Historically, advents in technological capabilities have meant wider proliferation of life-like synthetic characters, such as on the Web (Andre & Rist, July 2000). Technologies have been built to enable the making of synthetic characters as communicated through multi-channel interfaces. One work describes a computer language to enable high-level controls across a range of synthetic agents and avatars. This enables developers to abstract away "from the specific communicative context in which the character is integrated" (Not, Balci, Pianesi, & Zancanaro, Oct. 2005, p. 200). Another work describes the making of directable synthetic characters, which are responsive to "direction in real-time from the narrative manager" and in alignment with the character design and social role (Assani, Mar. 2002, p. 1).

There is design work for creating multi-agent contexts in which the agents are "all interacting, collaborating or competing with each other" (Prada & Paiva, July 2005, p. 37).

Pedagogical Agentry

Digital agents have been designed for teaching and learning applications. Several works point to applications targeted to virtual learning environments for children. Synthetic characters are designed to achieve empathic engagement through affective interaction with young learners (Hall, Woods, Aylett, Newall, & Paiva, 2005, p. 731) to lessen bullying in the world. In another work, digital characters are designed for "pedagogical empathic interactions" (Paiva, Dias, Sobral, Aylett, Woods, Hall, & Zoll, 2005, p. 235).

Some designs are from-life in a sense. For example, one team used a particular storyteller design and took painstaking efforts to ensure validity and believability by striving for resemblance to a real human storyteller (Silva, Vala, Paiva, & Redol, May 2001). In simulated worlds, various animal entities are coded with the predatory behaviors as observed in mammals (Berlin, 2003). Autonomous virtual characters are also coded temporally based on biological models, so the creatures react to artificial time and various stimuli in the environment (Burke, 2001).

Humanoid characters are built to be "more adaptable to new situations, less predictable, with fast learning capabilities, memory of past situations and a variety of convincing and consistent behaviors" (Bressane Neto, & Corrêa da Silva, 2009, p. 533). Some synthetic characters are designed to learn in interactive ways based on human user inputs and behaviors (Yoon, Burke, Blumberg, & Schneider, 2000). Others synthetic agents are motivated and driven to learn based on their designed objectives (and what the characters are designed to care about) (Yoon, Blumberg, & Schneider, June 2000). Intentionality is an important aspect of synthetic personhood (Kline & Blumberg, 1999).

For years now, designers have worked to make synthetic characters seem to embody actual personalities instead of acting in deterministic ways. The more lifelike, the more compelling synthetic agents are thought to be for people.

Some designed digital characters are created to be able to traverse interfaces, such as moving between the virtual and the physical and back again (André, Dorfmüller-Ulhaas, & Rehm, 2005, p. 1). Traversable interfaces enable characters to be portable and to move from dedicated spaces in the real or the digital, with different affordances in each context.

Table 1. Strengths and weaknesses of static imagery for synthetic pedagogical characters

Strengths	Weaknesses
More consumable More accessible Less transient (and lower cognitive load / working memory to consume) Does not risk the "uncanny valley" per se	Less real world Less attention-catching than animated

EXPLORATORY VISUAL DIGITAL CHARACTER AND VISUAL DIGITAL SCENE DESIGN USING ARTMAKING GENERATIVE AI: ENHANCING STORY PROBLEMS AND OTHER PEDAGOGICAL NARRATIVES

This work is about the current capabilities of the Deep Dream Generator (an artmaking generative AI or A-GAI tool) for creating static pedagogical characters and background scenes in which to place the characters. A character needs to be recognizable whether it is an animate one (humanoid, animal, or other living creature) or an inanimate one (robotic, non-sentient, or other non-living creature). Sometimes, the physicality of the character may convey something about its capabilities, intelligence, personality, social standing, culture, and other aspects of context. Ideally, the character should be visually depicted in editable ways, with an animate-able body. It should have an expressive face to convey a range of emotions, affect, and cognition. It should be depictable from various angles but still look recognizable. It should be resizable in usage in different contexts. If a silhouette is needed, the character should be able to be created in silhouette or edited for an effective silhouette.

What is desirable in a scene? The scene should evoke locations, both indoors and outdoors and in-between. It should provide a sense of an imagined world and context. The scene should offer room in the foreground, mid-ground, and background, for the characters to exist and to interact. The background scene should enable the placement of character(s) in various situations and contexts. The background should be informative but not predominate or upstage the characters. It may contain some atmospherics. The scene should be depicted from various points-of-view, from straight-on to aerial...and various degrees of rotation. It should be reconstitute-able. Both characters and scenes should be open to both pre-production and post-production.

The review of the literature does show that synthetic pedagogical characters and other digital characters may come in various forms, with animation, decision-making, personalities, and other aspects. This work focuses on static imagery in two dimensions (2d) only. This is in part based on the capabilities of the Deep Dream Generator at present, but it is also about going with common-form visuals in the teaching and learning space. There are strengths and weaknesses in terms of static imagery for describing synthetic pedagogical characters (Table 1).

The four research questions are as follows:

RQ1: How usable is the Deep Dream Generator in creating static characters (animate and inanimate) for pedagogical purposes?

RQ2: How usable is the Deep Dream Generator in re-creating prior static characters (animate and inanimate) for pedagogical purposes?

RQ3: How usable is the Deep Dream Generator in creating static scenes (backgrounds) for pedagogical purposes?

Figure 2. "Mathematically Astute Hare" (as created in the deep dream generator with a seeding image)

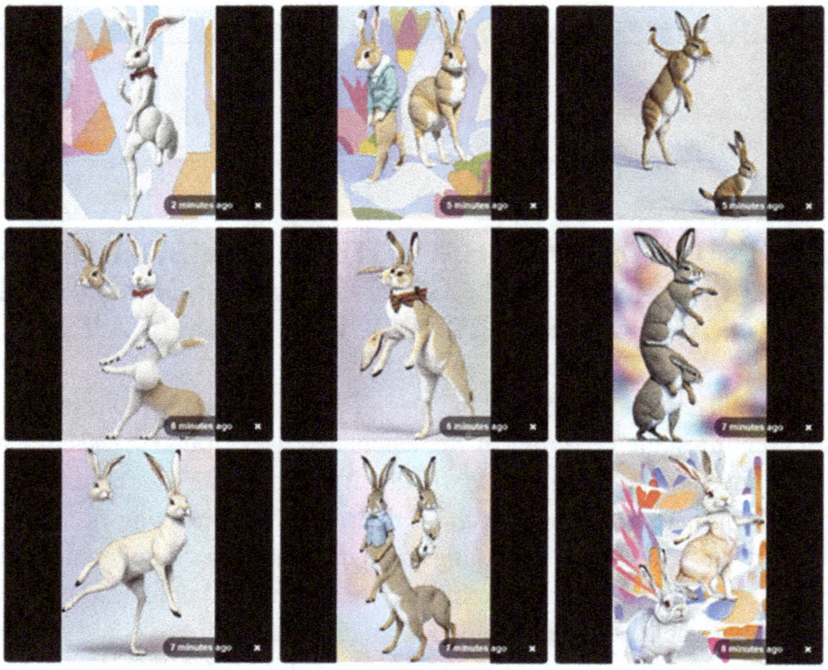

RQ4: How usable is the Deep Dream Generator in re-creating prior static scenes (prior backgrounds) for pedagogical purposes?

To answer these questions, the researcher has used the DDG for some nine months in order to test various creations of characters and scenes. Then, as this work evolved, she has created some more outputs for illustration purposes. She has used a Deep Dreamer account for many months but has not escalated to a paying professional account. There are various applications of platforms that use both virtual credit and real money as the interactions (Castronova, 2006). A paying account would mean more usage of PRO accounts, but those are accessible to non-subscribers as well but with longer wait times between usage.

Several walk-throughs were conducted for "a full body character of a mathematically astute hare in full clothing and standing on its hind legs, no background." A seeding image of a simple abstract was offered to give each of the images a basis for a look-and-feel. The influence of the text prompt was set to be 80%, to minimize the influence of the seeding image. The only style tag applied was "linocut," to give a sense of line art. The models used were all non-PRO ones for this run-through (Figure 2).

To answer the question of whether a character could be turned in different directions and still retain the identifiable characteristics of the original character, the middle image in the top row was selected as being somewhat the closest to what was imagined with the mathematically astute hare prompt. That image is not an actual working prototype though. Figure 3 shows the results.

The most flexible "math hare" was created using the AIVision model inside the DDG. This did not enable the use of a seeding image, so only the prompt above was used and the tag for "linocut." The topic is best captured here even as the image looks a little like old-school clipart with some additional details (Figure 4).

Figure 3. Selected "Mathematically Astute Hare" viewed from the left side (as created in the deep dream generator with a seeding image)

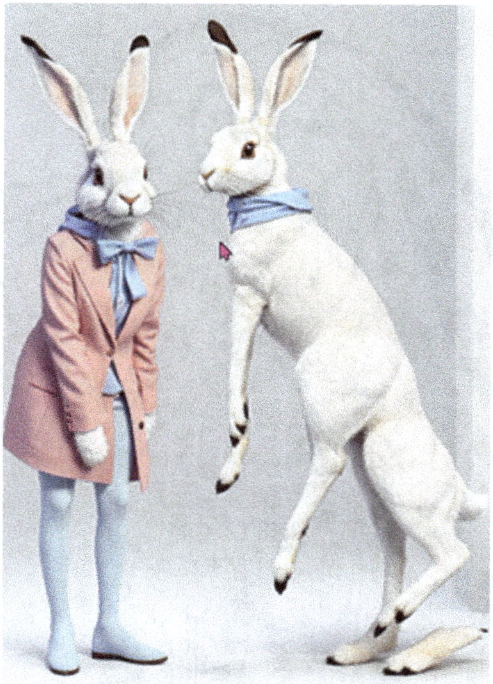

Then, some backgrounds were generated, to different visual effects. The first is an outdoor ski slope scene, and the next is an indoor scene of a room in a creaky old house. (Figure 5 and Figure 6) In the first, Figure 5, the light does come from above and to the right, given the shadow patterns. In the second, Figure 6, there is both local and global light. There are interesting textures of various surfaces, from the ceiling to the floor. The photo above the fireplace evokes something of personality in the house space. These two background images were created with one of the PRO accounts and without any seeding images. "Linocut" was the only tag used.

In Figure 7, the A-GAI was asked to create both characters and a background for an integrated scene.

This setup is an over-simplification, with the idea that characters are the main actors and the scene as the background. Certainly, elements in a scene may become the main characters, depending on what the focus of the communication is. (A common example is the idea that the weather becomes a character on its own, for example.)

To focus on the research questions in more depth, each is addressed more closely:

RQ1: How usable is the Deep Dream Generator in creating static characters (animate and inanimate) for pedagogical purposes?

The DDG does not offer sufficient levels of control yet in creating static characters with particular features.

Figure 4. "Mathematically Astute Hare" using AIVision model (as created in the deep dream generator)

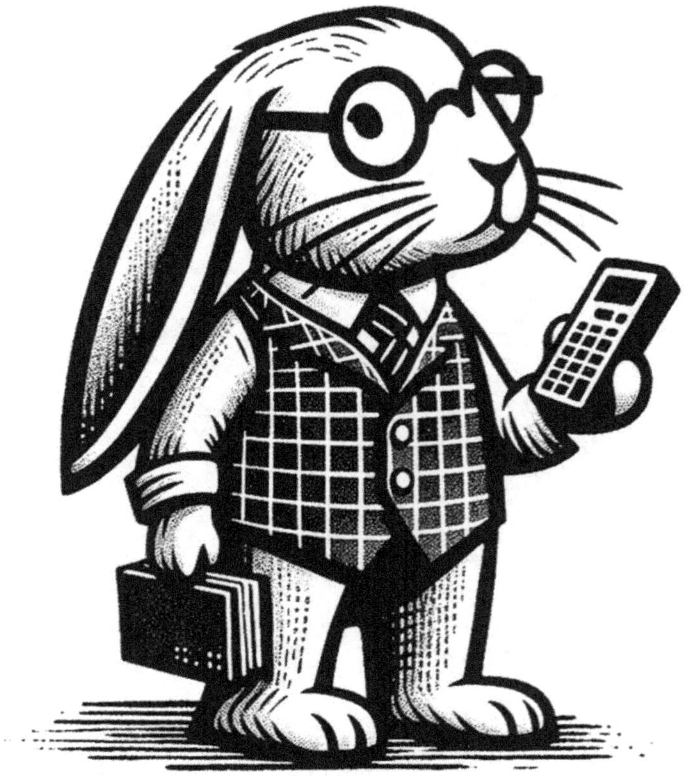

RQ2: How usable is the Deep Dream Generator in re-creating prior static characters (animate and inanimate) for pedagogical purposes?

The ability to re-create a known character also seems elusive, even if a desirable character is used as the seeding image and with no major changes to the textual prompt except for a perspective prompt.

RQ3: How usable is the Deep Dream Generator in creating static scenes (backgrounds) for pedagogical purposes?

The DDG can create evocative static scenes for backdrops.

RQ4: How usable is the Deep Dream Generator in re-creating prior static scenes (prior backgrounds) for pedagogical purposes?

The backdrops are also difficult to recreate. The tendency of the A-GAI is to offer variance and not to recreate what came before. This is not to say that the backdrop may not be used as a seeding image in a digital image editing software that has the ability to inpaint a full surround based on the original seeding image, but that will require post-production work outside of the DDG.

Figure 5. A "Ski Lift" scene background (as created by AIVision model in the deep dream generator)

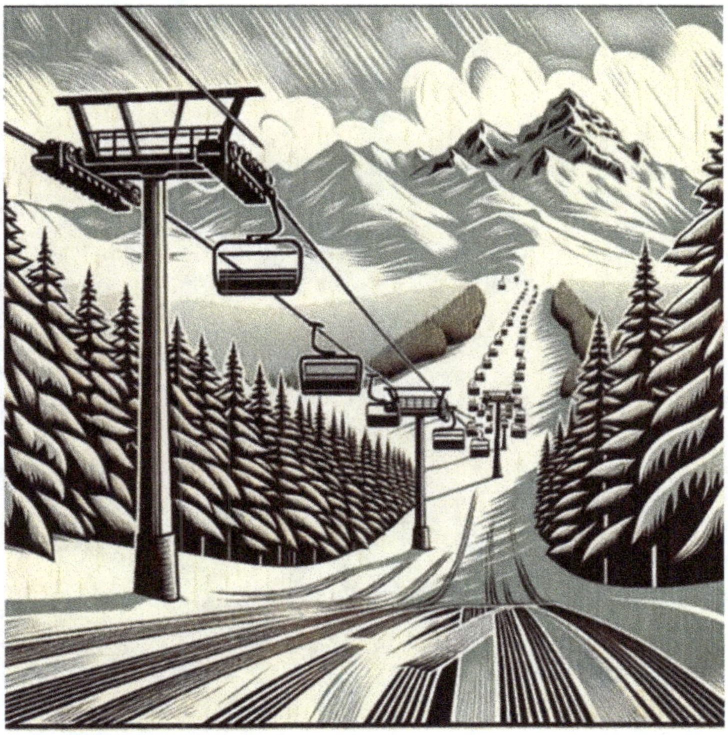

Figure 6. A "Room in a Creaky Old House" scene setting (as created by AIVision model in the deep dream generator)

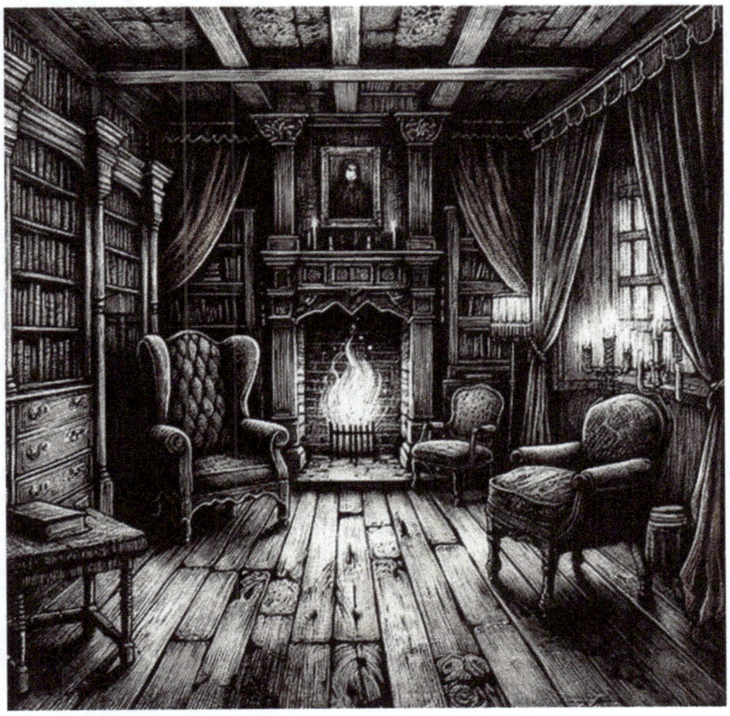

Figure 7. A "Characters and Background" (as created in the deep dream generator with a seeding image)

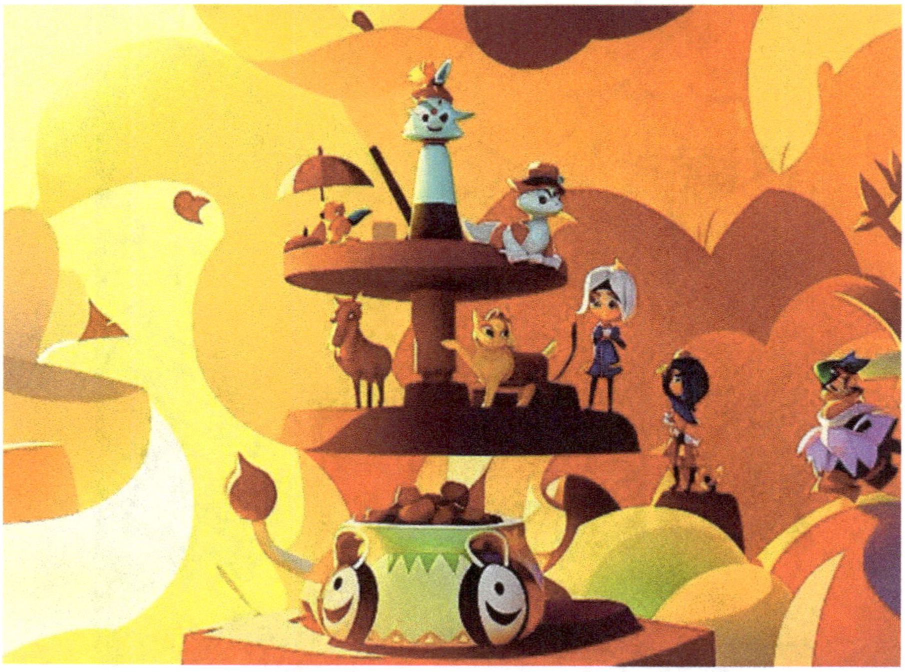

Discussion

The A-GAI tool used is one of the most cutting-edge and popular online. It has powerful capabilities, and it integrates a number of models within it. The particular use case here, though, does not highlight the tool's central strengths. It may be that there are no generative AI tools (except Adobe's commercial Firefly) that can output images with high levels of detailed specificity and then recreate the same characters again and again.

FUTURE RESEARCH DIRECTIONS

Work in this space can be ongoing, perhaps with testing of A-GAI systems, including Firefly as mentioned above. The four research questions asked here may be asked of other systems. Perhaps there can be work about pre- and post-production that may enhance the output.

There are certainly other practical use cases that may be applied to the A-GAI to see what the outcomes may be.

The work here is a limited case, but this may be informative of the affordances and constraints of the tested tool.

CONCLUSION

The advent of A-GAI tools stands to change human work and outputs. These are evolving tools and will add and remove various features over time. How the platforms are seen and used may inform how the tool's makers evolve the tool's capabilities, with different refinements.

REFERENCES

André, E., Dorfmüller-Ulhaas, K., & Rehm, M. (2005). Engaging in a conversation with synthetic characters along the virtuality continuum. *Smart Graphics: 5th International Symposium, SG 2005, Frauenwörth Cloister, Germany, August 22-24, 2005 Proceedings*, *5*, 1–12.

Andre, E., & Rist, T. (2000, July). Adding life-like synthetic characters to the web. In *International Workshop on Cooperative Information Agents* (pp. 1-13). Springer Berlin Heidelberg. 10.1007/978-3-540-45012-2_1

Assanie, M. (2002, March). Directable synthetic characters. In *Proceedings of the AAAI Spring Symposium on Artificial Intelligence and Interactive Entertainment* (pp. 1-7). AAAI.

Bartneck, C., & Reichenbach, J. (2005). Subtle emotional expressions of synthetic characters. *International Journal of Human-Computer Studies*, *62*(2), 179–192. doi:10.1016/j.ijhcs.2004.11.006

Berlin, M. R. (2003). *Predatory sequence learning for synthetic characters* [Doctoral dissertation]. Massachusetts Institute of Technology.

Bressane Neto, A. F., & Corrêa da Silva, F. S. (2009). Synthetic characters with personality and emotion. In *Intelligent Virtual Agents: 9th International Conference, IVA 2009 Amsterdam, The Netherlands, September 14-16, 2009 Proceedings 9* (pp. 533-534). Springer Berlin Heidelberg.

Bressane Neto, A. F., & Corrêa da Silva, F. S. (2010). On the construction of synthetic characters with personality and emotion. *Advances in Artificial Intelligence–SBIA 2010: 20th Brazilian Symposium on Artificial Intelligence, São Bernardo do Campo, Brazil, October 23-28, 2010 Proceedings*, *20*, 102–111.

Bringsjord, S., Shilliday, A., Taylor, J., Werner, D., Clark, M., Charpentier, E., & Bringsjord, A. (2008). Toward logic-based cognitively robust synthetic characters in digital environments. *Frontiers in Artificial Intelligence and Applications*, *171*, 87.

Burke, R. C. (2001). *It's about time: Temporal representations for synthetic characters* [Doctoral dissertation]. Massachusetts Institute of Technology.

Castronova, E. (2006). *Synthetic Worlds*. University of Chicago Press. doi:10.7208/chicago/9780226096315.001.0001

Eladhari, M., & Lindley, C. A. (2003, November). Player character design facilitating emotional depth in MMORPGs. *DIGRA Conference.*

Fogelström, E. (2013). *Investigation of shapes and colours as elements of character design.* Degree project. Game Design. Uppsala Universitet.

Gulz, A., Ahlner, F., & Haake, M. (2007). Visual femininity and masculinity in synthetic characters and patterns of affect. In *Affective Computing and Intelligent Interaction: Second International Conference, ACII 2007 Lisbon, Portugal, September 12-14, 2007 Proceedings 2* (pp. 654-665). Springer Berlin Heidelberg. 10.1007/978-3-540-74889-2_57

Hall, L., & Woods, S. (n.d.). *Empathic interaction with synthetic characters: The importance of similarity*. Academic Press.

Hall, L., Woods, S., Aylett, R., Newall, L., & Paiva, A. (2005). Achieving empathic engagement through affective interaction with synthetic characters. *Affective Computing and Intelligent Interaction: First International Conference, ACII 2005, Beijing, China, October 22-24, 2005 Proceedings*, *1*, 731–738.

Hoorn, J. F., Konijn, E. A., & Pontier, M. A. (2019). Dating a synthetic character is like dating a man. *International Journal of Social Robotics*, *11*(2), 235–253. doi:10.1007/s12369-018-0496-1

Isbister, K., & Hayes-Roth, B. (1998, January). Social implications of using synthetic characters: An examination of a role-specific intelligent agent. In *Proc. of the IJCAI-97 Workshop on Animated Interface Agents: Making them Intelligent.* Stanford University.

Khalis, F. M., & Mustaffa, N. (2017). Cultural inspirations towards Malaysian animation character design. *Malaysian Journal of Communication*, *33*(1), 487–501.

Kline, C., & Blumberg, B. (1999). The art and science of synthetic character design. *In Proceedings of the AISB 1999 Symposium on AI and Creativity in Entertainment and Visual Art* (pp. 1-6). Academic Press.

Lankoski, P. (2004). Character design fundamentals for role-playing games. *Beyond Role and Play,* 139-148.

Maldonado, H., & Hayes-Roth, B. (2004). Toward cross-cultural believability in character design. *Agent Culture: Human-Agent Interaction in a Multicultural World,* 143-175.

Mascarenhas, S., Dias, J., Afonso, N., Enz, S., & Paiva, A. (2009, May). Using rituals to express cultural differences in synthetic characters. In *Proceedings of the 8th International Conference on Autonomous Agents and Multiagent Systems-Volume 1* (pp. 305-312). Academic Press.

Mori, M. (1970). The uncanny valley: The original essay by Masahiro Mori. *IEEE Spectrum*, 6.

Mori, M., MacDorman, K. F., & Kageki, N. (2012). The uncanny valley. *IEEE Robotics & Automation Magazine*, *19*(2), 98–100. doi:10.1109/MRA.2012.2192811

Nieminen, M. (2017). *Psychology in character design: Creation of a character design tool* [Bachelor's thesis]. South-Eastern Finland University of Applied Sciences.

Not, E., Balci, K., Pianesi, F., & Zancanaro, M. (2005, October). Synthetic characters as multichannel interfaces. In *Proceedings of the 7th International Conference on Multimodal Interfaces* (pp. 200-207). Academic Press.

Paiva, A., Dias, J., Sobral, D., Aylett, R., Woods, S., Hall, L., & Zoll, C. (2005). Learning by feeling: Evoking empathy with synthetic characters. *Applied Artificial Intelligence*, *19*(3-4), 235–266. doi:10.1080/08839510590910165

Prada, R., & Paiva, A. (2005, July). Believable groups of synthetic characters. In *Proceedings of the Fourth International Joint Conference on Autonomous Agents and Multiagent Systems* (pp. 37-43). 10.1145/1082473.1082479

Rodrigues, S. H., Mascarenhas, S. F., Dias, J., & Paiva, A. (2009, September). "I can feel it too!": Emergent empathic reactions between synthetic characters. In *2009 3rd International Conference on Affective Computing and Intelligent Interaction and Workshops* (pp. 1-7). IEEE.

Schwind, V., Wolf, K., & Henze, N. (2018). Avoiding the uncanny valley in virtual character design. *Interactions (New York, N.Y.), 25*(5), 45–49. doi:10.1145/3236673

Shaarani, A. S., & Romano, D. M. (2007). Perception of emotions from static postures. In *Affective Computing and Intelligent Interaction: Second International Conference, ACII 2007 Lisbon, Portugal, September 12-14, 2007 Proceedings 2* (pp. 761-762). Springer Berlin Heidelberg.

Silva, A., Vala, M., Paiva, A., & Redol, R. A. (2001, May). The Storyteller: Building a synthetic character that tells stories. In *Proc. Workshop Multimodal Communication and Context in Embodied Agents* (pp. 53-58). Autonomous Agents 2001.

Soikun, T. M., & Ibrahim, A. A. A. (2018). Kansei engineering approach in designing appealing computer animation character. In *Proceedings of the 7th International Conference on Kansei Engineering and Emotion Research 2018: KEER 2018, 19-22 March 2018, Kuching, Sarawak, Malaysia* (pp. 470-478). Springer Singapore. 10.1007/978-981-10-8612-0_49

Takeuchi, Y., & Katagiri, Y. (1999, September). Social character design for animated agents. In *8th IEEE International Workshop on Robot and Human Interaction. RO-MAN'99 (Cat. No. 99TH8483)* (pp. 53-58). IEEE. 10.1109/ROMAN.1999.900313

Tharib, S. (2013). *An investigation into the uncanny: Character design, behaviour and context* [Doctoral dissertation]. Bournemouth University.

Yoon, S. Y., Blumberg, B. M., & Schneider, G. E. (2000, June). Motivation driven learning for interactive synthetic characters. In *Proceedings of the Fourth International Conference on Autonomous Agents* (pp. 365-372). 10.1145/336595.337537

Yoon, S. Y., Burke, R. C., Blumberg, B., & Schneider, G. E. (2000). Interactive training for synthetic characters. *AAAI/IAAI, 2000*, 249-254.

Zibrek, K., Cabral, J., & McDonnell, R. (2021, November). Does synthetic voice alter social response to a photorealistic character in virtual reality? In *Proceedings of the 14th ACM SIGGRAPH Conference on Motion, Interaction and Games* (pp. 1-6). 10.1145/3487983.3488296

KEY TERMS AND DEFINITIONS

Artmaking Generative AI: A technology that uses deep learning to train in large datasets of imagery that then can output visuals based on text and imagery singularly or in combination.

Character Design: The communication of character identity through visual and other means.

Scene Design: The communication of a location and context (and even atmospherics) based on visual means.

Chapter 7
Synthesis of Art and Technology:
Digital Expression in Jewelry Design

Metin Coşkun
Kastamonu University, Turkey

ABSTRACT

This chapter delved into the intricate intersection of artificial intelligence and the realm of jewelry art, exploring how AI catalyzes the emergence of novel forms of artistic expression within the traditional domain of jewelry art while simultaneously extending its influence on other branches of art. Moreover, it elucidated the myriad opportunities AI presents for artists, ushering in a new era of creativity and innovation. In addition to examining the symbiotic relationship between art and technology, this chapter delves into synthesizing these two seemingly disparate realms. By amalgamating the evolution of artistic expression in jewelry design with the avant-garde perspectives offered by artificial intelligence, a fertile ground for experimentation and exploration is unveiled.

INTRODUCTION

Throughout the annals of human history, art has served as a profound mirror reflecting the myriad hues of human emotion, expression, and boundless creativity. It has been the quintessential medium through which individuals across cultures and epochs have sought to articulate the complexities of human thought and the depths of our emotional landscapes. Art, in its diverse manifestations, continuously evolves, embracing new forms, techniques, and mediums. This dynamism has ensured its resonance across a myriad of disciplines and branches (Olver, 2002).

Classical disciplines such as painting, sculpture, music, theater, and literature have long been revered as bastions of artistic expression, each offering unique avenues for exploring the human experience. Yet, alongside these venerable traditions, design disciplines such as jewelry design, fashion design, performance arts, and architecture have also emerged as vital conduits of artistic expression. Despite

DOI: 10.4018/979-8-3693-1950-5.ch007

their functional aspects, these design branches transcend mere utility, delving into the realms of emotion, symbolism, and cultural discourse (Pagan, 2014).

In the intricate dance between form and function, designers infuse their creations with layers of meaning, weaving narratives that resonate with audiences on personal, cultural, and societal levels. Whether through the sculptural elegance of a piece of jewelry, the sartorial storytelling of a fashion ensemble, the immersive experience of a performance, or the spatial poetry of architectural design, artists in these disciplines engage with the fundamental aspects of the human condition (Holmes, 2016).

Indeed, the designation of these design disciplines as art branches is not merely a recognition of their aesthetic appeal but a testament to their capacity to provoke thought, evoke emotion, and catalyze change. They serve as vibrant canvases upon which the complexities of human existence are painted, inviting audiences to contemplate, engage, and find solace in the shared journey of creativity and expression. Jewelry design, interpreted as a form of artistic expression that emphasizes aesthetic value and creativity, is a multidimensional art form that is aesthetically pleasing and includes elements such as functionality, usability, material selection, and technical skill. Therefore, jewelry design can be considered both artistic expression and craftsmanship (Blauer, 2013).

Jewelry design is a captivating blend of tradition and innovation, weaving together age-old handcrafting techniques with the latest advancements in modern technology and digital design tools. This amalgamation of old and new allows artists and designers to create handmade jewelry pieces that not only exude timeless charm but also incorporate elements of contemporary flair. At the heart of jewelry design lies the artisan's mastery of traditional handcrafting methods. These time-honored techniques, passed down through generations, imbue each piece with a sense of heritage and craftsmanship. Whether it's the intricate art of metalworking, the delicate skill of stone setting, or the meticulous attention to detail in filigree work, traditional craftsmanship forms the foundation upon which all jewelry design is built (Untracht, 2011).

Yet, alongside these traditional methods, modern technology has revolutionized the landscape of jewelry design. Cutting-edge tools and equipment enable artisans to push the boundaries of creativity, exploring new forms, textures, and materials with unprecedented precision and efficiency. From computer-aided design (CAD) software to 3D printing technology, these innovations empower designers to bring their visions to life with unparalleled accuracy and speed (Tavares & Magalhaes, 2020).

In addition to modern technology, digital design tools have become indispensable resources for jewelry designers. These software programs allow artists to experiment with shapes, proportions, and compositions in a virtual environment, refining their designs before they are brought to fruition. This iterative process not only enhances the efficiency of the design process but also fosters a culture of experimentation and innovation (Adbel et al., 2018).

Through the medium of jewelry, artists and designers have a unique platform to explore and communicate personal, cultural, and social themes. Each piece serves as a canvas for storytelling, expressing narratives of identity, tradition, and belonging. Whether it's a symbolic pendant, a statement ring, or a pair of earrings adorned with cultural motifs, jewelry becomes a tangible reflection of the wearer's innermost thoughts and emotions (Satpathy, 2017).

In this way, traditional craftsmanship and artisanship remain the bedrock of jewelry design, grounding it in a rich legacy of skill and tradition. Yet, with the integration of modern technology and digital design tools, the possibilities for creative expression are endless. It is this dynamic interplay between the old and the new that fuels the evolution of jewelry design, ensuring its continued relevance and resonance in the ever-changing landscape of art and fashion (Tai, 2023).

In today's world, where technology is developing rapidly, the art of jewelry, like many other branches of art, is transforming design, production, and public offering methods in parallel with the developments. The most current and intriguing of these transformations are artificial intelligence-based applications. In this respect, jewelry design, like many other art branches, is on the verge of a new artistic revolution by meeting artificial intelligence.

Artificial intelligence is a set of intelligent systems computers create through algorithms and data analysis. It goes beyond mathematical calculations and can imitate thought processes and emotional elements. In this respect, artificial intelligence can be interpreted as a new element of transformation in the art World (Russell & Norvig, 2010).

In an evolving artistic production environment, the intersection of art and technology leads to a transformation that transcends traditional boundaries and ushers in a new era of innovation. This fusion is evident in the field of jewelry design, where digital tools and generative artificial intelligence (AI) technologies are reshaping the creative process. In this context, from the inception of an idea to the realization of a tangible product, it is crucial to examine how generative AI tools empower designers to transcend the boundaries of traditional design processes and, in the process, reveal new dimensions of creativity. In other words, through a synthesis of heuristic algorithms and human creativity, it will be revealed how jewelry designers harness the power of artificial intelligence to realize their vision by striking a harmonious balance between tradition and innovation (Ollandezou, 2022; Paul, 2020).

This chapter aims to reveal what emerges at the meeting point of traditional and modern, manual labor and digital, and how artificial intelligence contributes to the creative processes in jewelry design. In this context, it will discuss the reflections of productive artificial intelligence tools in the field of jewelry design, examine the studies in the literature, and reveal a dimension that transcends traditional paradigms. At the center of the study, it will be explained how tradition and innovation cross paths when centuries-old craftsmanship is combined with the latest digital methodologies. Through a lens combining heritage and progress, the complex tapestry of jewelry design and how technology catalyzes artistic expression will be explained. It will express how artificial intelligence interacts with art, how it shapes new forms of artistic expression in addition to jewelry among traditional art forms, and how it offers new opportunities to artists.

Jewelry Design

Jewelry design is often considered an art in terms of aesthetics and functionality. Designers in this field design creative and original pieces using different materials to increase the aesthetic value of jewelry. When we consider issues such as the aesthetic and expressive ability of jewelry design, its cultural importance, symbolism, social interactions, and its changing role throughout history, it is clear that jewelry design incorporates many elements of art. When the literature is examined, it is possible to see many anthropological and sociological studies that examine how jewelry expresses people's identities, status, and relationships (Blauer, 1991; Evans, 1989; Moreira da Silva, 2021; Pointon, 2009; Wardropper, 2000). When the elements of jewelry design are examined, the following titles are reached:

1. Aesthetic Value: Jewelry is generally designed and produced for aesthetics. Designers create unique and attractive jewelry by using different materials. Visually impressive pieces are designed by harmoniously combining colors, shapes, textures, and patterns.

2. Creativity and Expression: Jewelry design allows designers to showcase creativity and artistic expression. Each piece of jewelry reflects the designer's emotions, thoughts, and imagination. This shows that the design process is an artistic expression.
3. Material and Technical Mastery: Jewelry design requires the skillful use of various materials (gold, silver, diamonds, gemstones, glass, wood, etc.). It also requires the skillful application of various techniques such as casting, soldering, stone cutting, and wire processing. Thus, jewelry design is a discipline that requires both artistry and craftsmanship.
4. Personal Meaning and Story: Jewelry often carries meaning and represents personal stories. A piece of jewelry reflects the emotions or memories of its owner. Therefore, jewelry design produces a physical object and functions as a means of emotional connection and communication.
5. Historical and Cultural Context: Jewelry has been essential in different cultures. Jewelry reflects social status, cultural heritage, and religious beliefs. Therefore, jewelry design is considered within a cultural and historical context.

Combining these elements enables jewelry design to be recognized as an art. The aesthetic value of the design includes the mastery of technical skills and personal expression, as well as its cultural and historical significance. Therefore, jewelry design represents much more than just the physical characteristics of a piece of jewelry.

Jewelry design is a complex, integrated process chain with many stages. These stages encompass a process that guides the designer's ideas from the initial stage to the final product. In the most general terms, the stages of jewelry design are as follows:

1. Inspiration and Research: At this stage, the designer explores various sources for inspiration before starting a jewelry design project. These sources can be nature, art, culture, or personal experiences. In addition, the demands and trends of the consumer can also guide the design process on a particular theme.
2. Drafting/design: The designer develops a concept after the inspiration and research phases. The design's overall theme, shape, materials, and style are determined at this stage. The designer creates design ideas through sketches, notes, and other visual materials.
3. Material Selection: The appropriate materials are selected once the design has been determined. This process can determine the jewelry piece's style, durability, and value. The choice of material is usually made among various options, such as gold, silver, diamonds, gemstones, glass, wood, etc.
4. Technical Planning: At this stage, the technical details of the design are planned. At this stage, how the design will be produced, which techniques will be used, and the necessary labor processes will be determined. Various techniques, such as soldering, casting, stone cutting, and engraving, are evaluated at this stage.
5. Prototype Production: A design prototype is produced in this stage. This is an example of how to visualize how the design will look in actual dimensions and materials. The prototype is used to put the finishing touches on the design and to test the functionality of the design.
6. Craftsmanship and Production: After the approval of the prototype, the production process for the actual piece of jewelry begins. At this stage, craftsmanship processes are carried out according to the selected materials, creating the jewelry piece. This process is completed using master artisans or technological production equipment (Lucas et al., 2015; McGrath, 2005; Ojo et al.,2022).

These stages describe a general jewelry design process. However, each project is unique,e and the design process can vary depending on the designer's preferences, consumer demand, and the techniques used. In a design process with such detailed stages, it is essential to get technological support to use it efficiently.

Jewelry Design and Technology

Jewelry design has been the center of humanity's cultural and aesthetic expression for thousands of years. Today, however, this long-established art form is being transformed by the rapid development of technology. Alongside traditional craftsmanship, digital design tools have created an increasingly eclectic relationship between jewelry design and technology.

Jewelry design has its origins in the cultural and religious rituals of humanity. However, this ancient craft has entered a new era by integrating computer-aided design (CAD), 3D printing, and other digital technologies. Traditional craftsmanship skills have allowed artists to express their creativity on digital platforms while influencing industrial production and marketing processes (Demarco et al., 2019).

This dynamic relationship between jewelry design and technology casts a wide net that encompasses how traditional craftsmanship and digital design tools can be used together, the role of technology in jewelry design, how digital production processes are reflected in artworks, and the effects of this changing environment on designers, producers and consumers.

It is essential to re-examine the stages of jewelry design to understand where technology comes into play to expand this spectrum. Technological tools make essential contributions to many stages of the jewelry design process. Here are some of their contributions at these stages:

1. Inspiration and Research: Technological resources like the Internet and digital libraries provide designers unlimited access to inspiration and research. In this context, virtual galleries, museums and other art platforms allow designers to find visual references for inspiration.
2. Sketch/design: Computer-aided design (CAD) software helps designers quickly turn their ideas into digital prototypes. 3D modeling and rendering capabilities allow designers to visualize and examine the details of the design.
3. Material Selection: Sourcing materials online and exploring different material options helps designers compare various options and choose the most suitable material.
4. Technical Planning: CAD software speeds up and facilitates the process of planning the technical details of the design. They also allow simulating and optimizing the craftsmanship techniques to be used in the manufacturing process of the design.
5. Prototype Production: 3D printers allow designers to turn digital prototypes into physical examples. This process provides a better understanding of how the design will look in actual dimensions and materials and enables prototypes to be produced quickly.
6. Craftsmanship and Production: Besides traditional artisanal techniques, technological tools such as CNC machines and laser cutting equipment allow for the precise and repeatable production of jewelry pieces. This equipment also facilitates the production of complex shapes and details (Scarpitti, 2021; Siamptani, 2023; Ma et al, 2024; Manavis et al. 2020).

Technological tools are increasingly widely used to support and improve critical steps in the jewelry design process. These tools enable designers to work faster, more efficiently, and more innovatively.

However, as technological tools are used, artificial intelligence (AI) technologies have started to play an essential role along with technological developments in this field. Examining artificial intelligence applications in jewelry design processes is essential in this context.

Artificial Intelligence Applications in Jewelry Design

The increasing proliferation of artificial intelligence (AI) technology is causing significant changes in the design industry. In particular, generative AI systems, such as text-based and image-based models, have become widely used in design processes as they enable efficiency and quality improvements. AI models can help identify design trends, analyze user preferences and predict future trends. AI-powered design tools can provide designers with more creative and innovative ideas. For example, an AI model can analyze thousands of design examples and make unique and groundbreaking design suggestions. This allows designers to go beyond classical design patterns and create more original Works (Cautela, 2019; Jarrahi, 2018; Mariani & Dwivedi, 2024). The following figure is obtained if the themes in which AI applications are used in jewelry design processes are summarized in a diagram.

When artificial intelligence applications are examined in the jewelry design process, it is seen that they are used under different themes. When these themes were examined in detail, the following titles were reached:

Production in Jewelry Design: One of the themes that artificial intelligence affects in jewelry design is jewelry design and production processes. Artificial intelligence systems can automate certain stages of the design process. For example, an AI model can optimize the geometry of the design in 3D modeling software or make suggestions on material selection. In this way, the design process can be faster and more efficient. There are studies on the subject in the literature. According to a study by Wannarumon (2011), artificial intelligence techniques help develop algorithmic designs in the jewelry design process and the complex calculations and parameter optimizations encountered in the design and casting processes.

Analytics and Artificial Intelligence Applications: An AI-based quality control system can automatically inspect manufactured jewelry pieces and detect defects. This process can make production processes more reliable and reduce error rates. Studies examining AI systems in different types of jewelry design processes are noteworthy in the literature. For example, Gupta et al. (2018) emphasized the importance

Figure 1. Jewelry design and AI applications

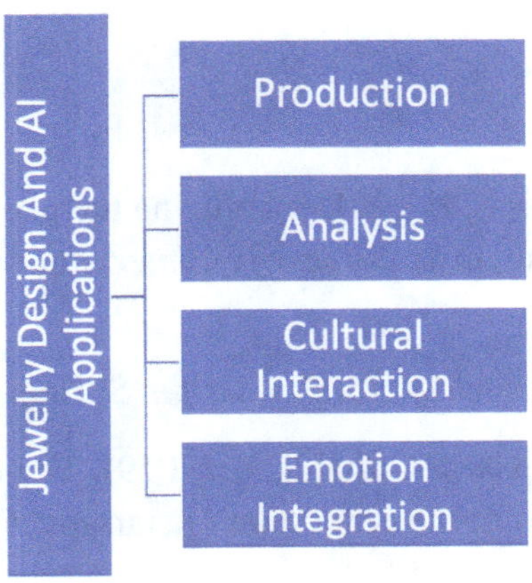

of using AI systems in analyzing, selecting,g and designing the appropriate mineral materials for jewelry design. According to the researchers, they concluded that the artificial intelligence systems used in the design process, which is formed by combining precious and semi-precious stones in various patterns, have shown that the designs produced are highly appreciated and visually attractive by removing the design of jewelry from being a time-consuming and complex task.

Cultural Interaction: Artificial intelligence (AI) technologies are used to analyze the cultural elements of jewelry products or to determine how to use a cultural element in jewelry design. For example, according to a study conducted by Lyu et al. (2023), Productive artificial intelligence (AI) profoundly impacts the idea-generation process of jewelry design. It plays an important role, especially in the technical details of the design. AI-based image generators direct designers' attention to strategic decisions related to visual appeal, cognitive engagement and emotional engagement rather than technical tasks. Therefore, AI technologies can contribute to developing culturally meaningful and emotionally expressive jewelry designs.

Emotion Integration: Another striking theme observed is the use of artificial intelligence to create or enhance emotional expression in jewelry design. In a study by Liang and Wanli (2022), an AI-powered intelligent system was used to create or enhance an emotional expression in jewelry. In this process, it was concluded that using the intelligent, emotional expression system further enhanced the impact of the jewelry design. The role of AI technology in integrating emotional expressions into jewelry design in this way opens up new possibilities for designers to create emotionally connected and meaningful jewelry products. Therefore, the use of AI-enabled systems is emerging as an essential tool with the potential to provide emotional depth and expressiveness in jewelry design.

To summarize all the themes, Artificial intelligence systems offer significant advantages to designers and manufacturers in the jewelry design process. In particular, artificial intelligence algorithms can identify design trends by learning from large data sets, analyze user preferences and create personalized jewelry designs.

AI-supported design tools enable designers to work faster and more efficiently. For example, by using AI-based 3D modeling software in the design process, tasks such as creating complex geometries or material optimization become easier. This allows designers to be more creative and innovative.

As a result, it has been determined that artificial intelligence technologies increase creativity and efficiency in the jewelry design process and contribute to creating more innovative and high-quality jewelry pieces. Therefore, designers and manufacturers are increasingly interested in integrating AI technologies into their jewelry design processes.

REFERENCES

Abdel Naby, S., Anwar, A. F., & Ali, N. H. (2018). Utilizing the integration between digital technology and interactive design to create contemporary jewelry. *International Design Journal, 8*(2), 427–437. doi:10.21608/idj.2018.86143

Blauer, E. (2013). *Contemporary American jewelry design.* Springer Science & Business Media.

Cautela, C., Mortati, M., Dell'Era, C., & Gastaldi, L. (2019). The impact of artificial intelligence on design thinking practice: Insights from the ecosystem of startups. *Strategic Design Research Journal, 12*(1), 114–134. doi:10.4013/sdrj.2019.121.08

Demarco, F., Bertacchini, F., Scuro, C., Bilotta, E., & Pantano, P. (2019). Algorithms for jewelry industry 4.0. In *International Conference on Numerical Computations: Theory and Algorithms* (pp. 425-436). Cham: Springer International Publishing.

Evans, J. (1989). *A history of jewellery*. Courier Corporation.

Gupta, K., Damani, S., & Narahari, K. N. (2018). *Using AI to Design Stone Jewelry*. arXiv preprint arXiv:1811.08759.

Holmes, E. L. (2016). *Commercial Jewellery Techniques: Innovating Selected Contemporary Manufacturing Techniques* [Doctoral dissertation]. Central University of Technology, Free State.

Jarrahi, M. H. (2018). Artificial intelligence and the future of work: Human-AI symbiosis in organizational decision making. *Business Horizons*, *61*(4), 577–586. doi:10.1016/j.bushor.2018.03.007

Liang, M., & Wanli, Z. (2022). Emotional expression in jewellery design under the background of artificial intelligence. *Expert Systems: International Journal of Knowledge Engineering and Neural Networks*, 13134. doi:10.1111/exsy.13134

Lucas, A., Chapin, M., Lin, M., & Jia, X. (2015). The Chınese Soul In Contemporary Jewelry Desıgn. *Gems & Gemology*, *51*(1), 18–30. doi:10.5741/GEMS.51.1.18

Lyu, Y., Shi, M., Zhang, Y., & Lin, R. (2023). From Image to Imagination: Exploring the Impact of Generative AI on Cultural Translation in Jewelry Design. *Sustainability (Basel)*, *16*(1), 65. doi:10.3390/su16010065

Ma, T., Ma, W., & Liu, W. (2024). The application of carving technique based on 3D printing digitalization technology in jewelry design. *International Journal on Interactive Design and Manufacturing*, 1-11.

Manavis, A., Nazlidou, I., Spahiu, T., & Kyratsis, P. (2020). Jewellery design and wearable applications: a design thinking approach. In *10th International Symposium on Graphic Engineering and Design 2020-Proceedings, GRID 2020, 12-14th November 2020, Novi Sad, Serbia* (pp. 591-596). 10.24867/GRID-2020-p67

Mariani, M., & Dwivedi, Y. K. (2024). Generative artificial intelligence in innovation management: A preview of future research developments. *Journal of Business Research*, *175*, 114542. doi:10.1016/j.jbusres.2024.114542

McGrath, J. (2005). *The jeweler's directory of decorative finishes: from enameling and engraving to inlay and granulation.* Academic Press.

Moreira da Silva, A. (2021). Jewels Design Innovation—Van Cleef & Arpels as a Case Study. In *Advances in Design, Music and Arts: 7th Meeting of Research in Music, Arts and Design, EIMAD 2020, May 14–15, 2020* (pp. 373-384). Springer International Publishing.

Ojo, E., Mears, H., & Stylianou, N. (2022). Fashioning Africa. *Creating African Fashion Histories: Politics, Museums, and Sartorial Practices*, 280.

Ollandezou, E. (2022). *New Media Art & Legal Aspects* [Master Thesis in Art, Law and Arts Management]. International Hellenic University, Thessaloniki, Greece.

Olver, E. (2002). *The Art of Jewelry Design: From Idea to Reality*. Northlight.

Pagan, S. (2014). Crafting new spatial and sensorial relationships in contemporary jewellery. *Craft+ Design Enquiry, 6*, 117.

Paul, C. (2020). Digital art now: Histories of (im) materialities. *International Journal for Digital Art History*, (5), 2–2.

Pointon, M. R. (2009). *Brilliant effects: a cultural history of gem stones and jewellery*. Paul Mellon Centre.

Russell, S. J., & Norvig, P. (2010). Artificial intelligence a modern approach. Academic Press.

Satpathy, C. (2017). *Jewelry: A Medium of Symbolic Communication*. Morehead State University.

Scarpitti, C. (2021). Post Digital Jewellery. The future scenarios of contemporary jewelry design. In *Spirit of Luxury and Design. A perspective from Contemporary Fashion and Jewellery* (pp. 274–285). ORO Editions.

Siamptani, M. (2023). Investigating the use of digital technology in Jewellery Design: A thematic analysis. In *Fashion Heritage: Narrative and Knowledge Creation* (pp. 241–261). Springer International Publishing.

Tai, L. (2023). The Application and Impact of Digital Technology in Jewelry Art. *MA Theses*. 145.

Tavares, T., & Magalhães, C. F. (2020). *New Technologies Shift in Jewelry Design: From Traditional Optimization to Contemporary Speculation. Global Fashion Conference*.

Untracht, O. (2011). *Jewelry concepts & technology*. Doubleday.

Wannarumon, S. (2011). Reviews of computer-aided technologies for jewelry design and casting. *Naresuan University Engineering Journal, 6*(1), 45–56.

Wannarumon, S., & Bohez, E. L. (2006). A new aesthetic evolutionary approach for jewelry design. *Computer-Aided Design and Applications, 3*(1-4), 385–394. doi:10.1080/16864360.2006.10738477

Wardropper, I. (2000). Between art and nature: Jewelry in the Renaissance. *Art Institute of Chicago Museum Studies, 25*(2), 7–104. doi:10.2307/4113057

Section 3

Research Potential With Synthetic AI-Generated Imagery

Chapter 8
Conducting Legitimate Research Using Various Synthetic Imagery From Artmaking Generative AIs: An Exploration

Shalin Hai-Jew
https://orcid.org/0000-0002-8863-0175
Hutchinson Community College, USA

ABSTRACT

For researchers, in-world phenomena offer many opportunities to learn in systematic ways (through various types of observation, research, and analysis). One phenomenon that can bear higher levels of insight involves artmaking generative AIs, not only in terms of how the systems work and are designed, but in terms of their output images. This work asserts that AI-generated imagery may be informative of the underlying training imageset, human culture, design, and symbolism on one level, but beyond this, offer insights about in-world phenomena. This work suggests that as artmaking generative AIs advance (and some of the more sophisticated ones now), the output imagery and imagesets may be interpreted more deeply for insights about not synthetic versions of the world but of the world itself. Precise proposals are included in this work. Both manual and computational analytics methods are proposed. And there is a proposed approach for validating/invalidating the perceived insights from the imagery.

INTRODUCTION

The popularization of artmaking generative AIs, which create visuals from text / image / mixed-modality prompts, enables researchers to tap the generated synthetic image data for learning. Certainly, the current academic literature suggests that there are insights to be had. Some researchers have used generative AI outputs to assess the capabilities of the AI tools, make predictions about the future (Haluza & Jungwirth, 2023), to form strategies, to teach, to assess learners, and other applications. They have surfaced insights about particularly effective magical combinations of text prompts for "prompt engineering." They have

DOI: 10.4018/979-8-3693-1950-5.ch008

shed light on how artificial neural networks (ANNs) of various types capture visual learning at particular nodes (among billions to trillions of them in various large language models or "LLMs"). Makers of the LLMs have released research papers about the unsupervised pre-training on image and language and code datasets and then the refinement through supervised fine-tuning, and the capture of billions to trillions of parameter weights that enable the regeneration of images and other digital contents based on text / visual / multi-modal prompts to the text-to-image models (TTI). Many such models protect against "forgetting" and "data drift" (such as the unintended changing of parameter values) but also strive to ensure diversities of outputs (protecting against overfitting to the training data and "mode collapse" or "creativity collapse" or "innovation decline").

Some works have made inferences about how the studied artmaking generative AI system functions and the quality of seeding imagery in the underlying training imageset. Some studies have involved how these technologies are used for teaching and learning, including student receptivity to such technologies and those exploring the fitness of such tools for teaching and learning. Some studies have explored how these technologies affect work sequences (work pipelines). A number have explored the implications of such technologies for various learning domains and professions. Some have explored how generative AI may be used to better communicate complex concepts and practices to the general public, such as in public health, emergency, and hard science contexts. There have been plentiful works as position papers (op eds) that take various stances on how these new technologies should or should not be used.

Various traditional research methods have been used: the gold-standard experimental design (with interventions and pre- and post- testing); action research in classrooms; lab studies including AI analytics; survey research; case studies, and others. Some of the studies have been experiential ones, reported in anecdotal ways by the lead researcher. Some follow the rigorous practices of quantitative research, with high statistical standards to reject null hypotheses.

Some computational imagesets have been used as prompts for research into perception and other applications. Synthetic imagesets have been used to improve various machine vision algorithms. There have been applications of such imagesets to train yet other models, such as those used in the healthcare diagnostics space. Synthetic data, historically, has been generated to achieve various aims, such as to supplement actual data, to test technological systems / research instruments / computational models, to enable simulations, and other applications. In many cases, the actual data may not be available yet. Or the actual data may be protected, too sensitive to use, or difficult to de-identify. The real-world data may be of poor quality and incomplete or difficult to clean. Synthetic data, in typical contexts, should be validated to actual-world data in terms of accuracy and representativeness and realism (to the world).

Where this work is pseudo-novel is in the proposition that synthetic datasets from human-machine collaborations have not been used in-depth for research and that there are many as-yet unexplored approaches. In these early days, the question is how to exploit such machine-generated image data for exploration and research. Are there ways to systematize the work and make the findings more rigorous? (Synthetic datasets are used to train LLMs, in some cases. They are also used as "filler" to test socio-technical and other systems, such as online surveys.)

There are many extant or outstanding questions in terms of trying to extract research value from the synthetic image data from human-machine collaboration via the artmaking generative AI tools. They include the following:

(Un)askable research questions with synthetic AI-generated imagery

- What are some askable questions based on human-machine generated images from artmaking generative AIs?
    - What are ways to ensure that the askable questions are relevant (and non-frivolous) and practical (and not impractical) and generalizable (and not limited to a one-off or local realia)?
- What are some effective ways to structure research questions or a series of research questions around synthetic image data?
- What are some research questions which cannot be currently answered satisfactorily but would benefit from the asking?

Generating human-machine collaborated synthetic image data

- What are various effective ways to generate the human-machine collaborated synthetic image data for research? What are methods to control for inputs to the artmaking generative AI tool?

Experiments from inputs and outputs of artmaking generative AI tools

- What are ways to set up experiments based on the inputs and outputs of artmaking generative AI tools?
- What sorts of comparative questions may be asked of respective artmaking generative AI tools, and why?
- What may be learned from visuals that are fictive (not based on facts) and based on human inputs and the machine-imaginary? The human imaginary?
- How can hypotheses about human-machine generated images be tested and validated or invalidated?
    - How can hypotheses for such research be falsifiable? Testable?
    - What may be considered somewhat confirmatory vs. somewhat dis-confirmatory?
    - Is absolute certitude possible in some cases?

Privileging human analytics

- In this space: What are ways to harness human analytics? Computational analytics? Mixes of analytics?

Exploring synthetic AI-generated image data

- What are discovery and exploratory sorts of approaches to the study of synthetic AI-generated image data that may be valid? What are methods that are considered less valid? Invalid? Why?
    - What are ways to train human eyes to observe certain dimensions in the visual outputs?
    - Ways to train machine vision to certain dimensions in visual outputs?
    - Ways to train human teams? Human-machine teams?
- What are effective ways to present AI-generated data in visually legible ways but also at scale?

The larger authorizing environment around the study of imagery and synthetic imagery

- What is the larger "authorizing" environment around the study of (synthetic and non-synthetic) imagery (single n = 1 examples, whole imagesets)? Who is in the authorizing environment? What are the professional ethics around this authorizing community?

The range of questions is well beyond the purview of this chapter to address. This is an early work built around posing the extant questions and offering some early thoughts. The power here is perhaps in the asking. [Note: It is assumed that the artmaking generative AI tools will evolve with increasing capabilities, perhaps ties to external image validation when depicting biology, history, physics, engineering, and other fields, which may broaden the types of questions asked. To control for complexity, though, local potentials will be discussed. And readers may consider the extended potentials as they emerge for use by the broader public.]

REVIEW OF THE LITERATURE

While the technologies of large language models have depended on decades of prior research, they have also required recent advances to enable the relatively smooth user experience with the beta rollouts of 2022 and 2023. Researchers have proposed important design aspects to ensure that users are not harmed by generative AI and that important technical values are upheld. One work describes seven design principles applied to generative AI systems to ensure foremost safety for users, and then "generative variability" to ensure that outputs "vary in quantity, quality, character, or other characteristics" (Weisz, Muller, He, & Houde, 2023, p. 1). Desirable outputs include "multiple outcomes & imperfection; exploration & control; and mental models & explanations" (Weisz, Muller, He, & Houde, 2023, p. 1). In terms of risks, designers and developers of generative AI systems need to design against "hazardous output, misuse, or potential for human displacement" (Weisz, Muller, He, & Houde, 2023, p. 1). Many such systems have been live in the world for years, and the research literature does not include the underlying design philosophies or scaffolds. Some research works share design principles that apply to particular applications, too, vs. a general approach. The design principles point to user objectives as critical and then suggest ways to design "for" and then design "against" various values, user experiences, and outputs / outcomes.

In the public space (and often stemming from science fiction), there have been discussions of generative AI leading to the destruction of humanity. One major worry is that people may be triggered by false information to become violent. Malicious actors can unduly affect others and foment negative actions and violence, including mass-scale violence. One work highlights the risks of distortions of historical facts, such as "mass atrocities such as war crimes and genocides" (Makhortykh, Zucker, Simon, Bultmann, & Ulloa, 2023, 3:28, n.p.). If generative AI is harnessed to distort or rewrite actual history, the lessons of the past cannot be applied to decision-making and actions in the present. For memorialization purposes, do generative AIs enforce "hegemonic narratives and practices," keep people in "information bubbles," "introduce bias in analysis and make some research practices more obscure/obsolete" by drawing attention away from "traditional qualitative practices of studying the memorialization of mass atrocities", and distort and deny history because of censorship? (Makhortykh, Zucker, Simon, Bultmann, & Ulloa, 2023, 3:28, n.p.) What if the generative AI's "non-authentic content" is harnessed as unvarnished truth? Misrepresented as actual historical artifact? Will historians and other professionals who work in the space be shunted aside by generative AI?

One study used generative AI to elicit visual senses of "place identities" by prompting for particular locations, as has been done with text-focused generative AIs (Jang, Chen, Kang, Kim, Lee, & Duarte, 2023). Even with the state of the generative AIs at present, without fact-checking, without external reviews (in most cases), the tools are used for some factuality references.

Some studies examine how humans are influenced by visual cues in subtle but patterned ways, in ways that people are conscious of in some cases, but often affecting people in subconscious and unconscious levels. One example involves the depiction of synthetic agents depicted as humanoid characters, whose voice levels can result in various forms of affect (Gulz, Ahlner, & Haake, 2007).

CONDUCTING LEGITIMATE RESEARCH USING VARIOUS SYNTHETIC IMAGERY FROM ARTMAKING GENERATIVE AIS: AN EXPLORATION

The informational value of artmaking generative AIs depends in part on how the model was created and what it was trained on and how the designers fine-tuned model performance. The research questions asked, the amount of human-machine-collaborative data created, the data cleaning, the types of data analysis, all likely affect the assertions that may be legitimately made. Generally speaking, a sequence for conducting research may look like the flowchart in Figure 1.

At present, the review standards may come from reviewer oversight and editorial oversight, but it is unclear what respective standards would be used to evaluate. Certainly, critical thinking can help. Likewise, more diverse points of view may better inform a constructive critique. There may be analyses of alignments and contradictions, consensus or dispersion, reviews of research methodologies, the framing of research, qualifications for research results, and other feedback. There may be discussions of the sizes of datasets. Perhaps various computational tools may be harnessed for at-scale analytics, with powerful reproducibility and the ability to include high-dimensionality analysis (given that visual data are high dimensional). Consider aesthetics, object depictions, atmospherics, 2d, 3d, 4d, color palettes, layout, compositing, perspective, detail, scenes, characters, and so on. The visual languages of various peoples and localities may also differ across cultures. Related tags networks may be assessed in terms of text prompts. Image analyses may be conducted on image prompts (as partial sets, as full sets).

What are some possible ways to have more structured and systematic analyses? Some questions that may be asked include the following:

- What is(are) the hypothesis(es)?
    - Is the hypothesis falsifiable or not? Why or why not?
    - How ambitious is the hypothesis?
    - Does the hypothesis generalize more broadly than the local condition?
- What is(are) the research question(s)? How are these research questions activated and actualized and operationalized?
- How was the synthetic imageset(s) created? What prompts were used? How was the generative AI system activated for the visual outputs? How were the images collected? How were they cleaned? Any pre-processing or post-processing, and what are possible implications of those steps? How were they maintained? How were they analyzed?
- How many image samples were generated? Was there enough to attain "power" based on the assertions made?

Figure 1. Conducting research from the human-machine collaboratively generated synthetic imagery from artmaking generative AI

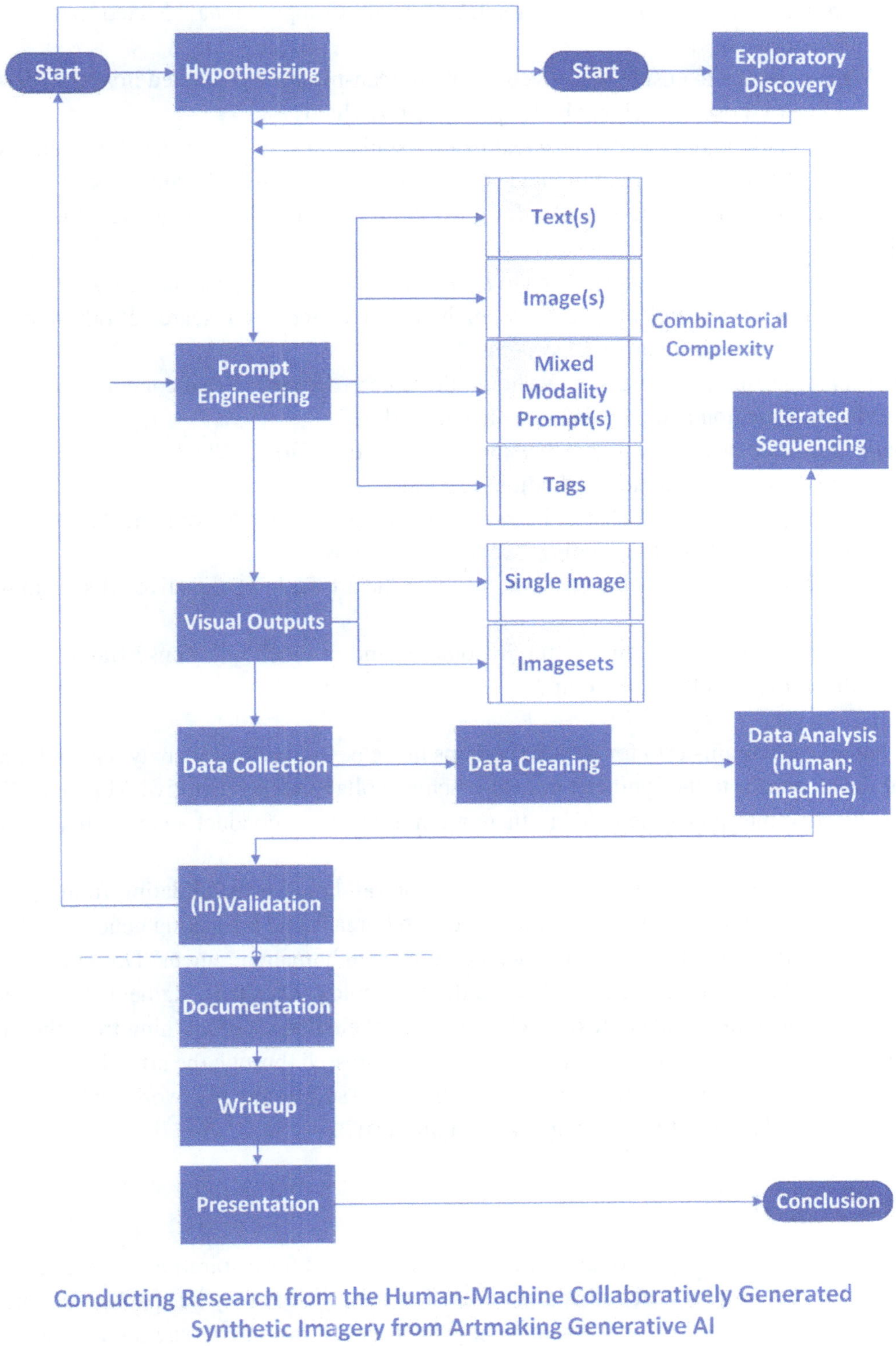

    - If n = 1, what is the justification for using just one? How was the "1" selected, and why?
    - What is being asserted from the 1 exemplar? Is it representational or not?
- How were research data observations made? Manual? Computational? Mixed manual and computational approaches?
    - What are ways to ensure that research into human-machine generated imagery (by AI) is accessible to those with sight challenges? The unsighted?
- Did the data coding get validated by a team with a statistical significance level (Cohen's Kappa) of agreement? What about computational coding to a level of statistical significance?
- If a matrix was used, was the matrix designed to be as comprehensive as possible? How was it designed?
- If a checklist was used, was it designed to be as comprehensive as possible? How was it designed?
- How well does the research approach and analytic system apply to research of different types (and uses across different generative AI systems)?
- When sharing research datasets, how should those be processed? What content should be included? What information and metadata are also needed?
- What accessories were used to enhance the data analytics? How? Why?
- Can other researchers recreate the findings?
- Do the findings align with what is known about the generative AI system? The knowns of the underlying training data? Fine-tuning? Code? Algorithms?
- Do the findings align with what is experienced by the artmaking generative AI system users writ large?
- Are there different ways to answer the hypotheses and research questions? Based on a different approach, do the hypotheses hold up?

These are an early brainstorm for ways to perhaps move beyond personal analytical and interpretive frames for the responses to the synthetic human-machine collaborated generative AI images. There is a place for subjective interpretive lenses, but there are more ways to conduct analyses that are powerful and insightful.

From these questions, are there "first principles" for validating or invalidating findings (based on data analytics of synthetic imagesets co-created between humans and artmaking generative AIs)? Does such validation or invalidation depend ultimately on informed human judgment? Does the validation or invalidation depend on statistical analysis? Particular thresholds? Do such judgments have to be generalizable? Applicable to different contexts? What are special challenges of learning from the fictive and machine-imaginary, and why? The human imaginary as expressed through the artmaking generative AI tool? How can learning from the fictive inform on relevant issues in the real world (where people live, but people also spend a lot of time in their own imaginaries)?

Discussion

At an individual level, the outputs of generative AIs may be used for inspirations, non-linear thinking, brainstorming, and other practical and applied uses. Tacit knowledge may be sparked (or surfaced) by imagery. Synthetic imagery created by artmaking generative AI may encourage research in new directions. Discrepant results in terms of image outputs may lead to "new insights for the participant" (Epstein, Schroeder, & Newman, 2022, p. 1). At the basic level of illustrations, generative AIs may ensure a more enriched sense of visuals than an impoverished one. A machine-based visual imagination may augment human abilities. The caveat is that "there are more unknowns than there are knowns" in the generative AI field (Makhortykh, Zucker, Simon, Bultmann, & Ulloa, 2023, 3:28, p. 13). Indeed, there are likely unpredictable factors in what is discoverable.

Further, such models are evolving in real time. There are ongoing experiments with connecting such systems with mathematical systems, fact checking systems, and others, which can radically change the image outputs. With added capabilities, generative AIs may output images with valuable information… that may be studied…for different insights.

To be clear, there are other lower cost ways to ask particular research questions, perhaps involving original images. But to ask questions of human-machine image collaborations created by generative AI, at the scale of training image sets, the only way currently may be to generate and extract such images and conduct various manual and computational analytics. This approach is not to "chase rabbits," but a "chasing rabbits" phase may be needed to begin to understand boundaries. And then, there will need to be efforts to push those boundaries to see if they are real or illusory.

FUTURE RESEARCH DIRECTIONS

In terms of future research, the lead-in section offers a wide range of questions that may be asked and answered about how to potentially use the images from generative AI systems for research. These ideas may be explored in more solid ways than in this preliminary work.

Present-day generative AIs may certainly be used for some image analysis for research. However, there is potential for fundamental changes in this approach as these technologies evolve. Given the trillions invested in the AI space, advances are expected very much sooner rather than later. For example, some work pipelines within models include inputting of real data vs. generated data. Others include adversarial tests for the generative AI to converge on particular desired outputs and outcomes. There are different model designs for particular outputs and optimizations. Those outputs may offer different insights for researchers than current visual-making generative AI tools.

There may be new questions that may be asked about the synthetic images as synthetic data. Perhaps a fresh approach in trying to see what is learnable would be beneficial in this space.

In Future Versions

Essentially, the question is whether artmaking generative AI models from LLMs may be used to do some of the following:

- Profile locations accurately
- Describe cuisines from particular peoples and cultures and times
- Depict climates
- Show the flora and fauna of particular natural (and other) spaces
- Capture visually the specific dress of a peoples in a particular time and place (with accuracy)
- Describe celebrations and events with accuracy
- Show defined aesthetics with accuracy
- Depict real-world physics in action

- Showcase an original choreography that is human-feasible

Can generative AI tools illustrate in ways that go beyond light representation to more heavy and accurate representation? Can it go beyond uninformed visual emulation to factuality? Can generative AIs project into the future—of a socio-political movement, a person, a cityscape, and an economy? And then can its output be used informationally? Analytically? Research-wise?

CONCLUSION

This chapter offers an initial approach to try to structure validation / invalidation of research that uses synthetic data generated from artmaking generative AIs (and could expand to general-form generative AIs that output in both text and visuals). These ideas and practices may also apply to generative AIs that generate video, digital characters, and animations…in terms of the visual space.

In a review of the literature, a scoping review, there was nothing on this particular topic in terms of direct research. One work found after the writing of the chapter was by Iain R. Edgar, who discussed various imagination-based ways to interpret imagery from across a variety of sources. (Edgar, 2004) The imaginary can be powerful, and perhaps older and newer methods may be applied to this space.

This period in human history evokes both the past with generations of research that went into the generative AI technologies and many generations more that went into the creation of the imagery that were harnessed for the training imagesets in many cases. Now is a liminal time and space that can enable humanity to move in different directions with new enablements, new thinking, and new data and information. Since the digital and generative AI emulates so much of the world (through what is harnessed for training data), what about in the other direction? How does artmaking generative AI speak into the world? Help with sense-making? How can researchers explore this space to find what may be valuable and informative? In validated ways? What may be learned from the human-machine imaginary? Nonfactuality? Counterfactuals?

REFERENCES

Edgar, I. (2004). *A guide to imagework: Imagination-based research methods.* Routledge. doi:10.4324/9780203490136

Epstein, Z., Schroeder, H., & Newman, D. (2022). When happy accidents spark creativity: Bringing collaborative speculation to life with generative AI. *arXiv preprint arXiv:2206.00533.*

Gulz, A., Ahlner, F., & Haake, M. (2007). Visual femininity and masculinity in synthetic characters and patterns of affect. In *Affective Computing and Intelligent Interaction: Second International Conference, ACII 2007 Lisbon, Portugal, September 12-14, 2007 Proceedings 2* (pp. 654-665). Springer Berlin Heidelberg. 10.1007/978-3-540-74889-2_57

Haluza, D., & Jungwirth, D. (2023). Artificial intelligence and ten societal megatrends: An exploratory study using GPT-3. *Systems, 11*(3), 1 - 18.

Jang, K. M., Chen, J., Kang, Y., Kim, J., Lee, J., & Duarte, F. (2023). Understanding place identity with Generative AI. *arXiv preprint arXiv:2306.04662.*

Makhortykh, M., Zucker, E. M., Simon, D. J., Bultmann, D., & Ulloa, R. (2023). Shall androids dream of genocides? How generative AI can change the future of memorialization of mass atrocities. *Discover Artificial Intelligence*, *3*(1), 28. doi:10.1007/s44163-023-00072-6

Weisz, J. D., Muller, M., He, J., & Houde, S. (2023). Toward general design principles for generative AI applications. *arXiv preprint arXiv:2301.05578.*

ADDITIONAL READING

Hai-Jew, S. (2024). *Generative AI in Teaching and Learning*. IGI Global.

KEY TERMS AND DEFINITIONS

Artificial Intelligence (AI): Computational systems that are designed to emulate human intelligence and capabilities.

Generative Artificial Intelligence (GAI): Computational systems that create informational contents across various modalities (text, writing, imagery, video, audio, animations, and others) through the emulation of human creativity based on human works used as training data.

Large Language Model (LLM): Various models underlying generative artificial intelligence that are trained on large datasets of human-created content (often through history) that are refined through "fine-tuning" to enable smooth outputs prompted by human users using text and / or visual prompts to elicit computational outputs as responses.

Chapter 9
Remote Virtual Sanctuary:
Exploring an Online Social Network on an Artmaking Generative AI Platform Post COVID-19

Shalin Hai-Jew
https://orcid.org/0000-0002-8863-0175
Hutchinson Community College, USA

ABSTRACT

2023 was an original year, with global humanity emerging from a deadly pandemic (COVID-19), facing the advent of artmaking generative AIs, and surviving in a time of geopolitical turmoil, economic and financial pressures, and social strife. What role does an online social network (built up around an artmaking generative AI platform) play for people in this present moment? How does the remote virtual community enable participants to seek various fulfillments? The web-facing Deep Dream Generator tool and platform has proven itself to be a powerful social space for many with rich immersions and remote social interactions. This work is a practice-led case study.

INTRODUCTION

What people might assume are common human needs after a life-threatening (and life taking) mass trauma like the COVID-19 pandemic may differ. Perhaps after so much health-based social isolation, such as "social distancing," people are more needful of human (and social pet) social connection. Perhaps their sense of empathy for others has grown. Perhaps there is a need for distractions, like "common art," aesthetic artful expression, and perhaps "show and tell" of such works. Perhaps there are all sorts of "revenge" sorts of individual and group consumption and profligate self- and mutual- entertainment. Social epidemiologist Nicholas Christakis predicted nothing less than a redux of the "roaring 20s" post-pandemic (Glenza, Dec. 21, 2020), given pent-up demands for living.

Or perhaps the social recovery will be much slower, given the years of rolling lockdowns. Perhaps people will need to get reacquainted with each other and to re-learn mutual empathy. Perhaps they will

DOI: 10.4018/979-8-3693-1950-5.ch009

engage in a slow warming up. Perhaps they have gone feral and do not want to return to domestic harness? Perhaps the extreme savings rates of the pandemic will remain, and people will not take on the role of super-consumer? Perhaps people will continue to "nest" in their respective homes and not take on traveling. Perhaps there will be signs of social disorder and lack of commitment to a rules-based order, at the micro, meso, and macro levels (based on individual, group, and nation-state behaviors). Perhaps there will be roving gangs that will engage in mass-scale retail theft and violence, resulting in some $112 billion in losses (shrinkage) by retailers. What gives?

Various crosscurrents affect the present moment. Now, in early 2024, the return to post-pandemic normalcy is perhaps less vibrant than many may have assumed. There has been a shift from material possessions to experiential ones (travel, dining out, entertainment, and others). Economies have not rebounded with any vengeance. Changes in global trade have affected economies across the range, from developing to developed. Jobs have returned to the service industries, but many others have disappeared. The past year has been a season of labor strife and strikes in the U.S. As to higher education, many learners have chosen different paths perhaps not inclusive of higher learning. To combat rising inflation, the U.S. Federal Reserve has been raising interest rates, making the cost of borrowing higher and putting a damper on personal (and non-personal) spending. Perhaps the residua from the pandemic has resulted in a variety of mixed outcomes.

A shared culture is seen to have played a core role in maintaining humanity in the time of deep isolation during COVID-19 (Department for Digital, Culture, Media and Sport, 2021:5, as cited in Lee, 2022, p. 609). That culture is both local and global, global given the interconnectivity of global social media and the Internet. People's sense of universal and shared "everyday creativity" is seen to re-humanize creativity even in a time of mass harnessing of creative computation. This creativity is part of people's everyday lived lives and part of human identity (Lee, 2022, p. 601). Artmaking is a "meta-language" for people to communicate with each other (Daniele & Song, Jan. 2019, p. 160), and to collectively face a complex future together in "emotionally experienceable" ways and to problem-solve around hard problems (Friess, 2021, p. 278). The artist has historically been inextricably linked with their art, with close ties between identity, personhood, personality; culture; language(s); historical period; learning (formal, informal, and nonformal); social influences; and other aspects.

Art has long held a vaunted respected place in human societies. It is a medium through which new ideas may emerge. Art is seen as a harmonizer:

Art is the need of artists for expression and communication. Art as a human spiritual product, its ultimate goal is to achieve the harmony between human body and mind, between people and people and between people and nature, is to actualize spiritual transcendence. Human beings are to achieve the expansion of the aesthetic mind and ultimate freedom through art. (Tao, Zou, & Ren, 2018, p. 155)

In these expectations, generative AI works are not seen to meet the standards:

...although artificial intelligence programs have been able to create works of art with unique styles, this does not mean that they are creative, because creativity is not only the uniqueness and innovation of styles, but also means that this style must be exemplary, and need creation subjects to understand the entire art history, and have independent artistic sense and problem consciousness. (Tao, Zou, & Ren, 2018, p. 155)

In terms of the outputs alone, generative AIs have been found to engage recurring patterns and visual tropes.

Images eventually seemed very repetitive, with the same mutant doggies and eyeballs appearing over and over again" perhaps because the generative AI discussed "provided relatively little opportunity for artistic control or artistic expression. (Hertzmann, 2019, p. 14)

One research team argues "the limitations of linguistic descriptions, implications of the dataset, and lastly, matters of materiality and embodiment" (McCormack, Cruz Gambardella, Rajcic, Krol, Llano, & Yang, Apr. 2023, p. 1). Text prompts have been dubbed "AI design material" since they trigger the generative AI to create a visual; text prompts are "reflective design material, facilitating exploration, iteration, and reflection in pair design" (Kulkarni, Druga, Chang, Fiannaca, Cai, & Terry, Mar. 2023, p. 1). Such systems enable "rapid exploration of a design space" but less in the way of precise controls (Kulkarni, Druga, Chang, Fiannaca, Cai, & Terry, Mar. 2023, p. 3).

Text-to-image (TTI) systems are limited:

Prompt-engineering falls short as an artistic practice for a number of reasons. Firstly, although the skill is developed through countless hours spent engaging with the medium, it is not learned in any tacit, embodied, or individualized way. Prompts can be directly shared, copied, stolen, and in an instant the entire body of knowledge and invested time is transferred. (McCormack, Cruz Gambardella, Rajcic, Krol, Llano, & Yang, Apr. 2023, p. 11)

Regardless, artistic standards are constantly evolving. In this same period of the raging pandemic and then into a gradual recovery, various artmaking generative AIs have emerged in "open" or "public beta," with web-facing interfaces that are inclusive and enable democratic access. Among the various artmaking generative AIs that have emerged in "open" or "public beta" the past few years, the Deep Dream Generator has had a longer history: it was released in 2015 by Google ("DeepDream," Sept. 24, 2023), and its main feature is an "algorithmic pareidolia," a tendency to create shapes with limited seeding imagery and / or a text prompt. It is said to algorithmically over-interpret patterns from a seeding text or image. It reifies a visual world in particulars even as the prompting text is abstract. The world has shifted from physical pigment to digital pixels. Users have become more and more practiced for asking the generative AI for "impossible things" and "nonsense prompts," with ambitious and contradictory and complex asks to see what happens and what can be created.

This is the age of post-mechanical reproduction, of what Joanna Zylinska calls "the age of machinic creation" (2020, p. 65), into the digital, the virtual, the augmented. And how artists improvise and explore may well look very different with the advent of artmaking generative AIs. [Some researchers suggest that the AI art accepted into art institutions have "not promoted new creative possibilities but have instead reinforced conservative forms" (Browne, 2022, p. 130). Perhaps new and cutting-edge generative AI art will be recognized elsewhere first.]

This work explores the use of the Deep Dream Generator (DDG) platform as a "remote virtual sanctuary," with some light sociality, as a way to recover from the social isolation of the SARS-CoV-2 / COVID-19 pandemic. Here, an artmaking generative AI platform is seen as a socio-technical system, with enablements beyond the general artmaking. This work occurred in a time when the author had already long returned to the physical workplace physically (late April 2021), after the first mRNA inoculations became available to the broad public, and after many of the social relationships she had had returned to normal, with interconnectivity. This study offers a microcosm view of what it takes for people to create a sense of a social world around themselves, even with the lightest of interaction, such as the text-prompting of visuals, the combining of visual image styles, the liking of others' work, and social commenting with others around the visuals. In this chapter, the DDG is found to be a haven, a safe place, a digital space for image making, with sustaining but fleeting and ephemeral forms of remote social engagement. The newness of artmaking generative AI gives the sense that DDG is a "happening" high-technology place that is the center of interest and perhaps some controversy. The space is informed by the values of "common art," of light novelty and mutual entertainment and social connections.

This work is a single case study. Other "remote virtual sanctuaries" exist in various ways, but this example (n = 1) is thought to be singular in its own way.

REVIEW OF THE LITERATURE

The large language models (LLMs) used to train many of the web-facing larger-scale models learn from large imagesets through deep learning methods (like neural networks), and the incremented weights (parameters) inform the visuals that are output based on text (and visual, and mixed) prompts. The training of LLMs results in "tens of millions of weights" from neural network learning (the encoding of the learned knowledge from the training data) but in ways that "are not well understood" (Ulberg, Llach, & Byrne, 2020, p. 508). These tools are not hard-coded but acquire learning based on micro details on varying neural network node weights from the training data and can recreate patterns (in a sense), albeit in ways that are non-emulative of any single visual work in the training data. The synthetic art simulates "a given distribution," described statistically (Elgammal, Liu, Elhoseiny, & Mazzone, 2017, p. 1). Certainly, small data may be used for training generative AIs as well and may enable artists to have more control over the image outputs via their curation of the seeding imagesets (Vigliensoni, Perry, & Fiebrink, 2022, p. 1).

The resulting artwork has been described as a digital and emulative "pastiche" (Choi, DiPaola, & Töyrylä, 2021, p. 020501-1) and "bricolage" bits (Browne, 2022, p. 131). Another term applied to these artmaking tools is "AI image synthesizers" (Carter & Carter, 2023, p. 2), which take elements which are combined and result in a synthetic image. "Neural network art" is another common term applied to the outputs of generative AI systems because of how these systems were trained with deep learning methods such as neural network learning. One description of neural network art is "juxtapositions of natural image cues," which are thought to result in "interesting images" (Hertzmann, 2019, p. 1). Several research studies have found that people could not distinguish between art by generative AI vs. "art generated by contemporary artists" (Elgammal, Liu, Elhoseiny, & Mazzone, 2017, p. 1).

The quality of generative AI art—that can "satisfy requirements by which creativity is currently being evaluated, validated, and valorized" such as novelty and aesthetics—will challenge the current intellectual property (IP) regimes around cultural ownership of artworks (Zeilinger, 2021, p. 1). There is growing consensus that generative AI enables the ability "to craft highly diverse and expressive works that draw on an extensive range of visual elements" (Hutson & Harper-Nichols, 2023, p. 55). They are also anticipated to challenge definitions of art, human roles in creative industries, professional work (and pay), the desirability of creative arts degrees in higher education (Bender, 2023), and a range of other aspects of modern life. Even as copyright income for most creatives is "minimal" (Lee, 2022, p. 603),

AI is seen to more greatly affect people working at the "lower end of cultural production (Lee, 2022, p. 606). The debates about how to deal with generative AI (and AI in general) are occurring in legal spaces, in legislative bodies, and on social media. There are various positions, including some polar ones—with one end as an anthropocentric consideration and a transhumanist (post-anthropocentric) one in others.

An initial response to the advent of current iterations of "creative software" (Browne, 2022, p. 9) is to lean towards "anthropocentric perspectives and analogies in attempts to frame non-human expressive agency" (Zeilinger, 2021, p. 94). Of late, many have decided that there is less need to fear:

With the democratization of art-making through these technologies, will art lose its 'aura,' its uniqueness? Of course, it won't! Art is founded on human expressivity and spirituality and its value is ultimately validated through its potential to create emotional connections between artists and audiences. While tools like machine learning models can certainly support artistic expressiveness, art transcends mere tool usage and remains a testament to human creativity. (Bourgault & E, 2023, p. 6)

The various artmaking generative AI tools that have been released to the public have varying levels of design for human usage. Some studies have been conducted to better align such technologies with how artists actually conceptualize, create, and evolve their works. The idea is to align artmaking technologies with human artists' felt needs and processes, without the technology being too intrusive (Jansen & Sklar, 2021, p. 1). Such systems may involve robot systems drawing alone, humans drawing alone, and then collaborative co-creation, which to some may be seen as the gold standard. When people collaborate with machines, they may engage simultaneously, asynchronously, in turn-taking ways, and others. They may draw ideas from the creations; they may be inspired to take works in different or new directions. They may evolve a different sense of aesthetics. After all, AI is anticipated to play a role in both "the appreciation and production of visual art" (Chatterjee, 2022, p. 01). AI-generated works have to work at a global holistic level of the image and at local levels, such as in terms of textures (Hazan, 2023, p. 77). The visual illusion has to be maintained at every level of the visual.

Users of generative AI may explore ideas and concepts and approaches that they might not otherwise. A generative AI may inspire, may jog loose an idea, may inform an artist through a "conceptual shift" (Jansen & Sklar, 2021, p. 21). Digital art may lessen "appreciation for people's daily aesthetic sensation (Mustaqim & Zahar, Nov. 2022, p. 106). Art sensibilities respond to the art that is made, which is dependent on the society from which it springs:

Art as a medium has always molded to fit the society that creates it, from cave drawings created by early humans to fine art painted with quality acrylics, to contemporary technology powered society. (Ghosh & Fossas, 2022, p. 7)

One study found that artwork is often created in solitary environments by the human artist (Jansen & Sklar, 2021, p. 10). Perhaps the work requires rumination and reworking ideas. Working with generative AIs may be quite a different experience. They "instantly serve up pleasing results, distracting me from whether that was what I was really looking for" (Merriam, Spring 2020, p. 2). An original human artist's vision may be lost in the computational process.

Researchers argue for "usage guardrails" around artmaking generative AI tools and the need to protect artist rights (Ghosh & Fossas, 2022, p. 7).

Computational Creativity

Computational creativity is not new. Algorithmic art started in the 1960s (Suryna & Serrano, 2019, p. 200). Over the decades, there have been a wide range of ways that art has been created using computational means and varying systems. One work defines some 11 types: "Ele-art, C-art, D-art, CA-art, G-art, CG-art, Evo-art, R-art, I-art, CI-art, and VR-art" (Boden & Edmonds, 2009, pp. 37 - 38). There have been artificial life ecosystems harnessed for artmaking. Some virtual ecosystems were unpredictable in terms of outputs based on various "perturbations" or irregular inputs into the system (Dorin, 2008, p. 1). Cybernetic art system enabled art from systems with automated controls. Less formal formulations of terms are revelatory:

The abundance of labels like digital art, (new) media art, information arts, artsci, etc., is already an indicator of the heterogeneity and elasticity with which contemporary artists approach and engage with new technologies. (Suryna & Serrano, 2019, p. 205)

Along the way, developers of various systems had to address a question about how AI would generate art. Would it act as a "heroic" sole generator, or would it be "collaborative AI" where "the system supports, challenges, and provokes the creative activity of humans"? (d'Inverno & McCormack, 2015, p. 1) In the present moment, the catchphrases are "collaboration" and "co-agency":

...we regard humans and AI as fundamentally entwined, receiving their agencies through intra-action (Nordström, Lundman, & Hautala, 2023, p. 1)

The stages of the creative process include "(1) coding and data, (2) learning and t raining, and (3) curating the outcome" (Nordström, Lundman, & Hautala, 2023, p. 1). The co-agency here refers to "a spatial process" (Nordström, Lundman, & Hautala, 2023, p. 1). Together, the human and machine are a "merged relation" as a cyborg (Nordström, Lundman, & Hautala, 2023, p. 3).

The role of the human artist in relation to the technology has also long been discussed. For example, human artists have taken on roles as programmer-artists, model trainers, researchers, curators, and others. [One research team observed: The "ownership of the creative process in neural media becomes a curatorial exchange at once subjective and externally mediated" (Choi, DiPaola, & Töyrylä, 2021, p. 020501-13).] The work to make the art required it. Another cited role is as a client commissioning a work of art to the generative AI: "where a client delegates much of the creative decisions to the artist" (Chung, 2023, p. 14). After all, many of the LLMs are unable to fully "preserve the artist's intentions and satisfaction in art-making, while leveraging automation and interesting surprises that AI models" (Chung, 2023, p. 1).

Some artmaking generative AI systems enable direct code editing beyond textual prompts for "creative coding" to create "*artistic* and *expressive* output" (Angert, Suzara, Han, Pondoc, & Subramonyam, 2023). One research team writes astutely:

The AI artist is placed in a technical landscape which requires a new kind of stepping away from intention to revise one's knowledge about how to proceed; stepping back now involves a fundamental reframing of embodied topologies of experience. (Choi, DiPaola, & Töyrylä, 2021, p. 020501-11)

As to the evolution of Text-to-Image (TTI) generative AI models, one researcher suggests that that came about in three main moments spread over decades, and dependent on various critical discoveries along the way. The moments include the following: "the advent of AI in the middle of the last century; the second at the 'reawakening' of a specific approach to machine learning at the turn of this century; the third that documents a rapid sequence of innovations, dubbed 'clever little tricks, that occurred just across 18 months" leading up to the summer of 2022 that enabled the practical emergences of artmaking generative AI tools (Steinfeld, 2023, p. 211). Various complex advances had to occur to enable arrival at the present moment. While the so-called "springtime" of TTI models "seemingly suddenly appeared in the summer of 2022" (Steinfeld, 2023, p. 217), that moment was technologically hard-earned and costly.

There have been a wide range of ways to arrive at the art made by computers. In some cases, inputs by humans may be only to start the process, but in other cases, humans play a much bigger role in informing the art outputs. In the current popularized iteration, artmaking generative AI is the thing, with so-called "prompt engineering" involving text and imagery and multimodal inputs to inform the visual outputs. Some work sequences may include command line inputs (Hutson & Harper-Nichols, 2023). There are practices involving iteration, which emulates the human process of artmaking:

Making art is an iterative process. One makes a mark, for example, looks at it and then makes another (or not, of course). Art-making is a continual process of conception, action and perception followed by re-conceptualization—and so on. (Boden & Edmonds, 2009, p. 26)

Decision-making at the heart of artmaking (Boden & Edmonds, 2009, p. 26). That decision-making is thought to change with the advent and popularization of generative AI artmaking, with art aesthetics and art taste evolving, too. Said another way: "machine beauty is also not the same as artistic beauty in the traditional sense" (Tao, 2022, p. 115). Given the influence of technologies, people need to use "aesthetic reason to guide AI technology" (Tao, 2022, p. 110).

Harmonizing Art and Technology

The current period has been dubbed a time involving harmonizing between art and technology. One study explored "the subjectivity and interrelationship between the artists, robots and participants in the process" of artmaking (Chen, Shidujaman, Jin, & Ahmed, 2020, p. 13). The researchers strove to consider the "cognition of human-computer symbiosis" and "collaboration among creative subjects" and other factors in proposing new generative art systems (Chen, Shidujaman, Jin, & Ahmed, 2020, p. 13) where AI is "a behind-the-scenes worker in the work of art" (p. 14). They write about the role of robots, as "other things created by humans in accordance with the ideal image in their hearts, and are an extension of human limbs and intelligence" (Chen, Shidujaman, Jin, & Ahmed, 2020, p. 22). An earlier work points to technologies as "a prosthetic extension to the human imagination" (Leach, 2019).

Technically, AI art has two methods: symbolism and connectivism" (Tao, 2022, p. 110). There are three methods of human-machine engagement: "human using machine, human guiding machine and human-machine separation" (Tao, 2022, p. 110). If art is made in a social network—as many assert—then generative AI may be considered one member of that collaborative network:

AI can be regarded as an 'agent' in art generation, and together with people constitute the 'actor network' of art. (Tao, 2022, p. 110)

Generative AI systems serve as a form of "connective memory" (Bar-Gil, Apr. 2023, p. 13). Actor-network theory is applied to art but include computers in that network (Bar-Gil, Apr. 2023, p. 1). If artmaking in the human realm is social (which is the consensus), artistic AI systems may be seen as a form of "outsider art," with an outside status that enables them to "achieve *honesty* and *inventiveness"* as compared to those of "professionally inscribed artists" (Suryna & Serrano, 2019, p. 209). Creativity is not *ex nihilo* but is more a product of deep cultural learning, life experiences, analytical depth, and other elements conveyed through socialization. Another work suggests that the human part of an artist's support network may be "unpredictable, forcing artists to minimize risk from their exposure to others" (Chung, He, & Adar, June 2022, p. 241) and perhaps turning to creative support technologies as stand-ins for more fickle humans.

With people supervising the making of artworks through computational means (Tao, 2022, p. 112), people are playing the role of a curator, an art director, a sophisticated communicator, among others, and in addition to that of being an artist. Another work suggests that the digital "is differentiated as tool, medium, mediator and partner" (Candy, 2020, p. 13), so the technology is seen as playing a role, too. While such tools may be automated (such as including a module to capture seeding terms to inform the drawing), the animating part of such tools is human. The person is the nexus, so the usability of the digital tools is critical. For example, a robot designed to co-create art with people has to take into consideration the human user's experience and feelings "to help the human to feel good" (Cooney, 2021, p. 5). Another usability angle involves improving user interfaces for large-scale text-to-image generation models (LTGMs) (Ko, Park, Jeon, Jo, Kim, & Seo, Mar. 2023, p. 919). Multimodal prompts enable users to experience more "controllability" (Ko, Park, Jeon, Jo, Kim, & Seo, Mar. 2023, p. 933). The digital is the means of creation but also the (non-analog) material. In these early days, "made with AI" is more comfortable than "made by AI" (alone).

These computing machines amplify the process of artmaking:

Digital technologies are amplifying the creative process in many ways. They can be at once a tool designed for a specific purpose, a medium that is exploited according to its particular properties, a mediator that facilitates a range of experiences or a digital partner that works together with a human. (Candy, 2020, p. 13)

The benefits of the artmaking human-machine interaction, while said to benefit both sides, generally accrue to people. Digital computers are "the most plastic medium ever to come under the hand of the artist" (Malina, 1990, p. 33), enabling much power and flexibility to express human imagination and thought and problem solving.

Another authoring team addressed algorithms as a "medium." They explore their idea:

... however, the paintbrush does not have the capacity to change, it does not make decisions based on past painting experiences, and it is not trained to learn from data. Algorithms contain all of those possibilities. Perhaps we can conceptualize AI algorithms as more than tools and closer to a medium. The word medium in the art world indicates far more than a tool, a medium includes not only the tools used (brush, oil paint, turpentine, canvas, etc.) but also the range of possibilities and limitations inherent to the conditions of creation in that area of art. Thus, the medium of painting also includes a history of painting styles, the physical and conceptual restraints of the 2-d surface, the limits of what can be rec-

ognized as a painting, a critical language that has been developed to describe and critique paintings, and so on. (Mazzone & Elgammal, Feb. 2019, p. 8)

There is work ongoing to enable different ways to engage with artmaking generative AI. If old-school artmaking was an embodied and physical process, there have been concerns that "embodied subjectivity" is displaced given the AI media ecology, with its "opaque exchange of autographic and algorithmic representation" (Choi, 2022, p. iii).

Human-Machine, Human-Machine ... Very Human Machine

Interim CIO at OpenAI, Mira Murati, has said that artificial intelligence is "an extension of the human mind" (Fung, Nov. 18, 2023). Various researchers have pointed out that artificial intelligence is a very human idea and creation:

In different modes, art and technology are both mirrors of ourselves...It is a way to make sense of the world around us as well as ourselves as a species. Similarly, technology helps us to reveal the nature of things. In fact, the same idea of AI is arguably today's highest form of 'humanized' technology, yet another way to know human nature. (Daniele & Song, 2019, p. 160)

Another observes: AI "is always intertwined with human nature despite its level of autonomy" based on reasoning from art and science (Daniele & Song, Jan. 2019, p. 155). Certainly, AI is not an object that sprung into existence *ex nihilo*. Humans are creating digital partners with whom they co-create art. Another team observes that there is an inherent bonding of people and AI given that "AI is produced (by humans)" (Nordström, Lundman, & Hautala, 2023, p. 5).

Some generative AI as purpose-made tools to achieve particular ends. One research work describes a tool made to address some human pitfalls in visual brainstorming and shape building early on in a design (Arias-Rosales, 2022, p. 30). Another strives to broaden human-artist thinking about shapes early on:

As a vital element of early shape exploration, divergence can be time-consuming and challenging, with iterative cycles where idea fixation and creative blocks must be overcome for fuzzy ideas to be fully expanded and understood. (Arias-Rosales, 2022, p. 1)

A subset of artmaking tools includes creativity support tools (CSTs) for artmaking (Chung, He, & Adar, June 2021, p. 1817). Some CSTs offer support for ideas and others actual creation through machine "labor" or "expertise" (Chung, He, & Adar, June 2021, p. 1819). Support for different steps in the artmaking process, including "aiding ideation, aiding implementation, and aiding evaluation" (Chung, He, & Adar, June 2021, p. 1817). Many designers go to exploratory freehand sketching to think about designs than technological means. They may not think to sketch with ambiguity in order to keep a broad range of possibilities open early on. Another design consideration involves the importance of chance and serendipity on historical artmaking from ancient times and working to include chance in generative AI art systems (Dorin, Mar. 2013).

One research work explored how to design future generative AI systems, while considering protections for the environment (against greenhouse gasses based on the consumption of energy), data privacy protections for people, embodiment for creativity based on human motion and gestures (in physically embodied ways), and play (to "center joy, delight and leisure in support of desirable futures" (Lin & Long, June 2023, pp. 380-381).

The closeness of AI and humanity may be a reason for the many discussions of AI perhaps attaining sentience and its own personhood in science fiction. One suggests that biological bodies are melding with technological ones in a time of the "dawning Singularity" (in sci-fi speak) (Mäki-Reinikka, 2018, p. 1). One thinker asks how human artists should take into account the dawning of Singularity as they are making art, for people and for machines or the Machine Spectator (Mäki-Reinikka, 2018, p. 1). What are machine visual experiences and aesthetics? Another more recent work touches on the idea of machine sentience as well:

At present, the most questionable aspect of AI art-making is that of self-awareness and emotion: Can AI be self-aware? Can AI have a soul? Can AI have emotions? Can AI feel pleasure or pain? Can AI have empathy or jealousy? Does AI need to have 'life experience' to create art? ... If AI had self-awareness and emotions, what would be the impact on humans? Will they turn the world upside down? (Liu, Apr. 2023, p. 6)

Another work argues that autonomy or self-determination in the world, and agency or "the ability to take action in the world and influence others" are important aspects of artmaking (DiBlasi, Castellanos, Kang, Poltronieri, & Smith, Nov. 2020, n.p.). Some build on this idea and suggest that technologies cannot make art because they lack autonomy, and they lack self-determination.

There is ongoing work to try to develop machine consciousness architectures. Researchers write:

...if the philosophical theory that consciousness arises as a flux of information in any machine is true, if we create a cognitive architecture that is able to produce as many behaviours as possible that are correlated with consciousness in humans, then, the machine may as well arise, up to some extent. Consciousness or phenomenal states. (Merchán & Molina, 2020, p. 350)

If computational machines and robots can be trained to learn and to act *as if* they were conscious, perhaps machine consciousness may be attained, seems to be the premise.

One researcher argues that AI "need not understand ideas or experience emotions to produce meaningful and evocative art" (Chatterjee, 2022, p. 01). In other words, the machine does not have to take on features of biological human life to be able to create like human artists.

The stories that people tell about the computer-created artworks matter, though. How people understand qualities of generative AI artworks, such as their "technical virtuosity" and "visual complexity" will affect how they are received and accepted or rejected (Fry, 2018, p. 81). More transparency about the technologies is seen as a net positive. Various generative AI systems are learning from human users to understand what people find compelling. How people use artmaking generative AI systems are also a concern, such as the fear of people taking credit for the work of a technology and "forging" their authorship (Piskopani, Chamberlain, & Ten Holter, July 2023, n.p.). Some researchers note, pointedly:

A philosophy within my research is that AI-generated content can only be worth as much as the total human effort put into them. Expertise and effort are what give the artifacts we venerate meaning and value. (Liu, Apr. 2023, p. 6)

Another work echoes the concept by posing questions:

How substantial must users' creative influence be for them to claim ownership? What constitutes meaningful human control in the context of generative AI, and what are the sites for increased artistic agency and meaningful human control? ... How will generative AI tools impact ideation, and the quality of outputs? (Epstein, Hertzmann, Herman, Mahari, Frank, Groh,... & Russakovsky, 2023, p. 12)

Reading learners into the complexities of generative AI art sufficiently early may be helpful. Others note that generative AI tools are already used in various tools (and social media) (Ali, DiPaola, Williams, Ravi, & Breazeal, 2023, p. 1), whether users are aware of that or not. Indeed, there is AI education for young children, in part to ensure their digital literacy and to ensure social equity, so all may harness the power of AI (Yang, 2022).

Bringing Along Learners to Adopt the Generative AI Technologies

Instructors have started engaging with their students about generative AI because of the deep sense of promise in terms of where these tools are heading. One team found that discrepant results in terms of image outputs may lead to "new insights for the participant" (Epstein, Schroeder, & Newman, 2022, p. 1), based on the power of surprise and so-called "happy accidents" (p. 1). In another classroom, instructors found that student work in user interface and user experience design benefitted from the use of generative AI, such as their "aesthetic and creative copy" and "fewer deficiencies" in their work and "better final products" (Lively, Hutson, & Melick, 2023, p. 23). Another study highlighted the "significant variations in replicating the outputs of different AI tools" (Hutson & Lang, 2023, n.p.). A course in 3d design found that generative AI tools may be integrated into artist workflows for optimal experiences and outputs (Hutson & Robertson, 2023, p. 1). Another work suggests the importance of harnessing AI at different steps of the artmaking process (Hutson & Cotroneo, 2023, p. 13).

Some visuals are not particularly rewarding as accidents, such as the problem of generative AIs creating too many or too few fingers on a hand, resulting in the sense by users that such systems "are unable to count or reproduce the desired number of objects in a particular image, even when explicitly prompted to do so" (Wasielewski, 2023, p. 71).

REMOTE VIRTUAL SANCTUARY: EXPLORING AN ONLINE SOCIAL NETWORK ON AN ARTMAKING GENERATIVE AI PLATFORM POST COVID-19

If art is a form of human truth-telling and exploration of the world, something ennobling, something that reminds humanity of history, then does generative AI art do the same? Is it capable of such high-minded uses?

Indeed, the making of visuals on a platform like Deep Dream Generator enables a broad range of explorations. The Deep Dream Generator as a tool designed to optimize "noise into images" (Yin, Molchanov, Alvarez, Li, Maliya, Hoiem, … & Kautz, 2020, p. 8717).

The platform is used by many to "dream" different dreams of characters, scenes, concepts, jokes, stories, and other elements. Depending on what features people use, the platform does require some effort to learn and to use fully. It is important to understand the technological understructures to use effectively. One writes:

There are models…that do not need the same kind of media input as the output; we call them translation models. Such a twist contributes toward creativity arousal, which manifests itself in art practice and feeds back to the developers' pipeline…AI does not create a 'push-a-button' masterpiece but requires a deep understanding of the technology behind it, and a creative and critical mindset. (Guljajeva, Sola, & Clarke, 2023, p. 1)

Generative AI tools demand capabilities from the human artist, including art understandings, to wield the technology well.

The researcher (author) started using this tool in April 2023 to sample artmaking generative AI tools more broadly. Her rationales for sampling the various tools—DallE, CrAIyon, Midjourney, Stable Diffusion, and Deep Dream Generator—were practical ones for the following reasons: learning about the new technologies, exploring the research, generating imagery for instructional design and publishing, in terms of the profession. Then, too, there were personal interests at pseudo-artful self-expression. The process of joining the platform was simple. The tool itself has a straightforward interface for making contents, with seeding verbiage and / or seeding imagery. A range of pre-built or new tags may be used to affect the style. There are style-transfer capabilities, too, with style-bearing visuals (in image icons) that may be applied to an uploaded image. Works may be published out to a user's page or left unpublished. There is a path to move from being a novice to a "deep dreamer" by making more and more images. The author stayed on the free track, but there are opportunities to buy more "energy credits" to create more works. (This is a temptation when a common artist is on a run of production.) (Figure 1)

Figure 1. Sjjalinn account on deep dream generator

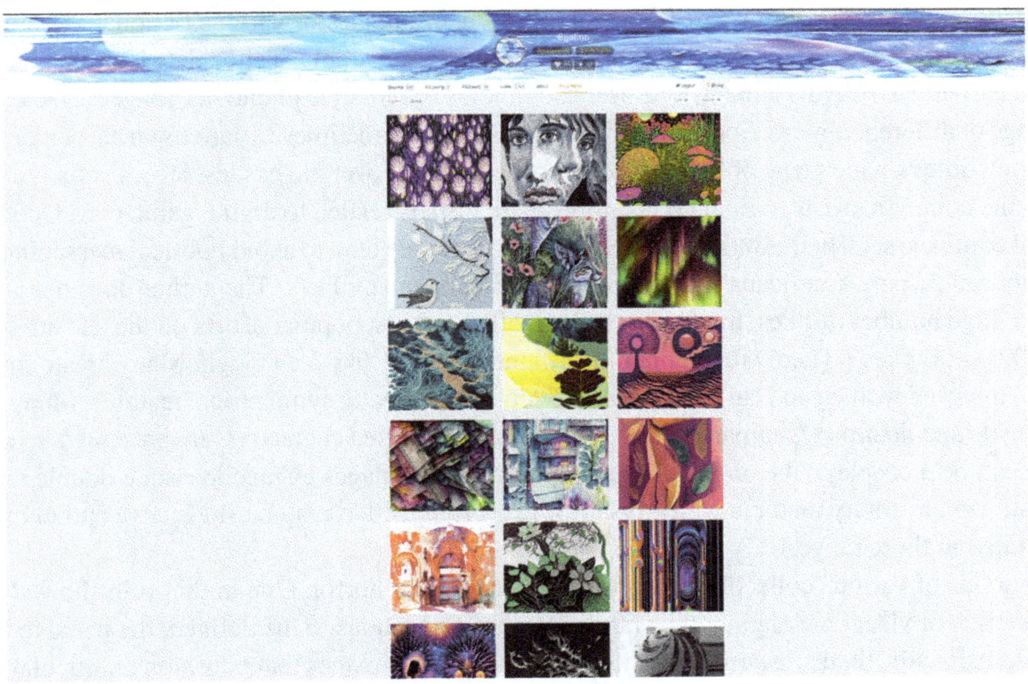

There was wide curiosity about the images that others were generating. Exploring others' artwork on their respective pages felt like being invited into other people's dreamworlds (if they and we could all illustrate). One could attain a sense of what others were thinking about, per se, in a highly curated way. The vibe was of the "cool friendly" of social media. The visual shares were to help people see differently and to look again. A funny visual effect occurs after immersing in the space for a while, where a kind of transcendence occurs, and a person's personality emerges of the common artist. It is not about the visual anymore or the sets of visuals. It is not about artfulness. Rather, there is an incandescent sense of the other person that comes through in the works based on their main visual topics, their themes, their labeling of the visuals, their commenting in the text section, their frequency of posting, their interactions with those who comment on their works, and other aspects. Their page header (with the selected visual) is another piece of important communication about the person at times. From these works and other information, some loose remote profiling of individuals may be done. Sometimes, there is a sense of human connection based on the artworks alone.

During the pandemic, the author had been dabbling in common art, by drawing and painting on various types of wood pulp paper and synthetic plastic paper. The pigment was applied via alcohol ink, pastels, watercolors, gouache, acrylics, pens, pencils, and others. The DDG was used to "salvage" some of the more formless artworks, with a sense of refinement.

Sometimes, the initial surprise of a machine-created drawing shocks the viewer with a sense of magic, which then dissipates by the time it is shared with the broader public. The sudden ability to essentially autogenerate visual artworks is not as personally satisfying as creating a work manually even as the outputs are marvelous and often eye-popping. A user's profile page may be read as a running image journal that is broadly social and publicly viewable. The platform rate-limits publications to five in a 24-hour period. Even so, sequences of images may sometimes be identified as part of a sequence of work.

A Review of User-Made Contents on the Platform

Some focus on particular object obsessions, like flowers or puppies or various fictional or public characters. Some offer visual jokes or puns and other humor. For example, a chocolate bear that has a limb mangled is "betrayed" by its human. One user uses photos of old-style phones as image seeds to create a wide range of different objects. Some share food obsessions—sometimes variations on particular types of foods, sometimes a wide menu of foods. Another page obsesses over old castles. Steam punk is a favorite style. Some common artists (casual art creators) share visuals related to digital game play. One focused on social commentary. [In the author's experience, most people tend to avoid political messaging. When the author ran a "pax Americana" visual, it did not receive many likes. The author does not generally receive a large number of likes, maybe up to about 50. The most popular artists on the site attract some 200 – 300 – 400 likes.] There are emulations of famous artists, like Van Gogh. Many create images of beautiful men and women and children with clean-cut and perfectly symmetrical features. Many characters, animate and inanimate, humanoid, robotic, animal, and mixed characters, are presented in dress-up, so there can be a cosplay vibe on the platform. Several users' pages engage in risqué double entendre. (The platform has safety features which disallow text prompts that may be suggestive and outputs that may be rated in the x-range.)

The moods of various collections may vary. Some tap into horror. One in this vein showed sinister dolls. In terms of visual messaging, they range from the ambiguous to the defined, the banal to the profound. Occasionally, there are a running short-series of several images that play along particular themes or color palettes or topical outputs. One set was made in the style of cartoons and comics. Some images evoke story, or scenes from a story.

The individual person pages give a sense of human lives invested into artmaking for a period, even as generative AI could feasibly create infinite amounts of artwork without human interventions. There are recurring motifs, recurring themes, favorite topics, and a mix of the familiar and the unfamiliar per each curated imageset by each individual. These pages provide a sense of future historiography of human-machine generated AI art. These give a sense of what creativity in the digital age looks like. The site's holdings can be explored even without the creation of any account.

In a sense, there are recurring looks-and-feels across the Deep Dream Generator based on how the artmaking generative AI is set up and what it allows and disallows. (Surprisingly, for example, images cannot be rotated in-tool. Also, there seems to be some limited color palettes if using the text prompts alone. There are limits also to style transfer based on available imagery in the online platform.)

What inspires in terms of others' visuals? The works with original looks-and-feels attract a lot of attention. In some cases, the topics depicted attract attention, such as recognizable locations (vs. the artfulness of the location depiction). The depiction of compelling characters, with powerful facial expressions, is another type of image that captures a lot of attention. Occasionally, a work of visual wit emerges. A rare work creates a new appetite for more of the same. Some larger-scale social conversations may be sparked through the enchantment of visual art, which speaks somewhat to activism, but most visuals have a short shelf life, no matter how memorable a work is. They are like fleeting public conversations that may capture attention for a few seconds, in a fast news cycle, before the human viewers move on, before they forget. They are consumed in short order and remembered or not. While the images are portable, they are subject to the "fast fires" of digital objects (vs. the "slow fires" of paper aging out as a medium that carries information). Digital contents online are consumed quickly and perhaps diminish into obscurity. (Figure 2)

Figure 2. Fast fires of digital contents online (from an alcohol ink painting processed in deep dream generator)

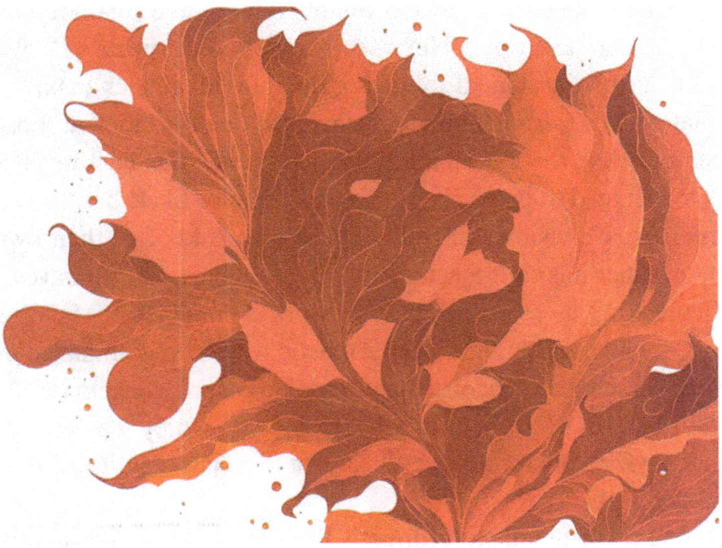

An Art-Making Generative AI Platform as a Socio-Technical Tool

The DDG platform works as a socio-technical platform. Members may upvote others' "dreams." (These votes may drive traffic to the image.) They may comment publicly on an artwork. Many of these are series of emoticons such as a face with heart-eyes. One commented, "You have such a unique imagination!" So far, the comments have been invariably kind. For those commented on, the min-max range seems to be 1 at minimum and 7 or even a few more at the maximum. They may message privately to the individual. Several examples follow to offer a sense of "color."

One participant wrote via private messaging:

Hi Sjjalinn, I was surprised not to find clowns, cats, dogs and cute animals, cloned from others, so it was a pleasure to see original and unique arts and I liked many of them! (smiley face and name)

Another wrote:

Hi! I posted a couple of dreams inspired by your dreams and credited you with it, but I'd misspelled Sjjalinn. It took me awhile to find you so I could correct it, but it is corrected now! Thank you for the inspiration! Cheers! --- (name)

Another wrote:

Love dear kitties (red heart emoticon)

There are emoticons that may be used in part of that expression.

There are "Try It" buttons that enable members to try others' text prompts (including their visual prompts if those are left on the platform). Each "Try it" usage means an accrual of some "energy credits" to the maker, which add up in an "energy battery" that may be accessed for more energy to create more visuals. Emulation is a form of flattery in the "Try it" case. The energy levels of each account replenish on their own but perhaps not at the speed that the user might prefer. There are options to follow other artists, to be notified when they upload new work. There seem to be some aspects of "follow-back," where one following another results in that individual following the individual back (as a form of reciprocation). The user base of the platform may have high variance, but if one is to look at those whose works attain the highest "likes" (heart clicks), there is an elite dominant group that captures the most attention. The social aspects of the site can lead to pandering to an audience for likes, but that seems like a distortion of an individual common artist's vision and voice. Those who kind of go their own way will find a few will follow them in their experimental trajectory. What dominates the "airwaves" on the Deep Dream Generator platform (in the 2023 slice-in-time that this work is premised on) involves works that seem to take the idea of fantasy, dreams, and nightmares seriously, with a predominance in text-based prompts. Many tap into the unconscious and subconscious to make visions conscious. Many draw on cultural images and tropes. The platform itself delimits what may be drawn by the generative AI. For example, when the author was asking for a plant colloquially known as a "pussy willow," that prompt was stopped as being untoward and not usable.

A study suggests that likes on an image "is directly linked to a physical response in the brain's reward centers, suggesting that I value my own and others' work based on a significant way on that number" (of likes) (Merriam, Spring 2020, p. 4). That social dynamic seems to be at play on the DDG site as well. The cultural practice is not to overexplain a visual…for the most part. Some will discuss their iterating a seeding image to the final one. Approaches do matter. There are experts in the hobbyist group. The most popular works can attain hundreds of likes. Some may go for days without any likes. Those may be left on the profile page, or they may be deleted by the common art maker. Visuals may be reworked with different visual effects applied. Some use comments and likes to drive attentional traffic to their own works. One lure was to like another's image and say that the person had made their own version with a URL to follow. The culture is to appreciate each other's imaginations and dreams, so people may be in each other's fantasies, in a sense.

If artmaking generative AIs are socio-technical systems, it would be important to observe whether or not social malevolence is a factor on Deep Dream Generator. After all, social media have various forms of social vitriol, gossip, accusations, erasure, and whatnot. Most sites do have automated agents heading off messaging with legal risks. In general, the researcher did not see much in the way of negativity. When people comment, it is to encourage the target individual (even as they diss others on the platform). One user had a warning on his profile that he reserved or retained copyright on everything he made. [From the author's observations, it is hard to monetize the contents made from artmaking generative AI…because much of it is available for free…and because it will take a lot of editing to get a work to be useful in a professional context. Many use generative AI to surface ideas…vs. to output a refined final work.] Another member copyrighted an image she had made that was evoked by song lyrics that she apparently found meaningful and potentially monetizable. The work, though, seemed of-a-piece with many other similar works on the Deep Dream Generator platform, a visual typical "go-to" if you will. Yet another started putting her name on images that she especially liked. She was one of the more popular individuals on the platform with instant name recognition. It was not clear if she was going to monetize her work, but she clearly wanted a watermark of her name on the work in case others downloaded her work. (Names are visible as part of the platform's display of the various works already.) In general, people "share-alike" in the spirit of receiving a free service (probably for most of the users), if they plan to share at all.

Figure 3 shows a lighthearted play on a bottom feeder fish.

The makers of the platform will occasionally reach out to users to invite participation in beta versions of their tool, apparently just prior to rollout. These opportunities do give the sense of hardy bands of users having the real privilege to immerse in large-scale experimentation of new technologies. The sense of a healthy community, with people coming and going, and of fresh work being done on the platform, are motivating.

The Social Value-Added

In many ways, it is easier to think about a tool such as Deep Dream Generator as one for eliciting digital ideas, designs, and digital resources for work like game design (Nguyen, 2023), illustration, digital character design, digital scene design, motion design, augmented reality, digital storytelling, instructional design, animations, digital posters, rotoscoping, portraiture, and other practical applications. Perhaps sub-elements, such as color palettes, may be explored and harnessed. Perhaps there are certain design look-and-feels that may be adopted. Artmaking generative AIs are considered new media (Nguyen, 2023) by many. Game design itself has already become "post-anthropocentric," with a turn to "computational creative labor" (Phillips, Smith, Cook, & Short, 2016, p. 82) to enhance gameplay and increase novelty

Figure 3. Bottom feeder (from deep dream generator and the author's alcohol ink painting)

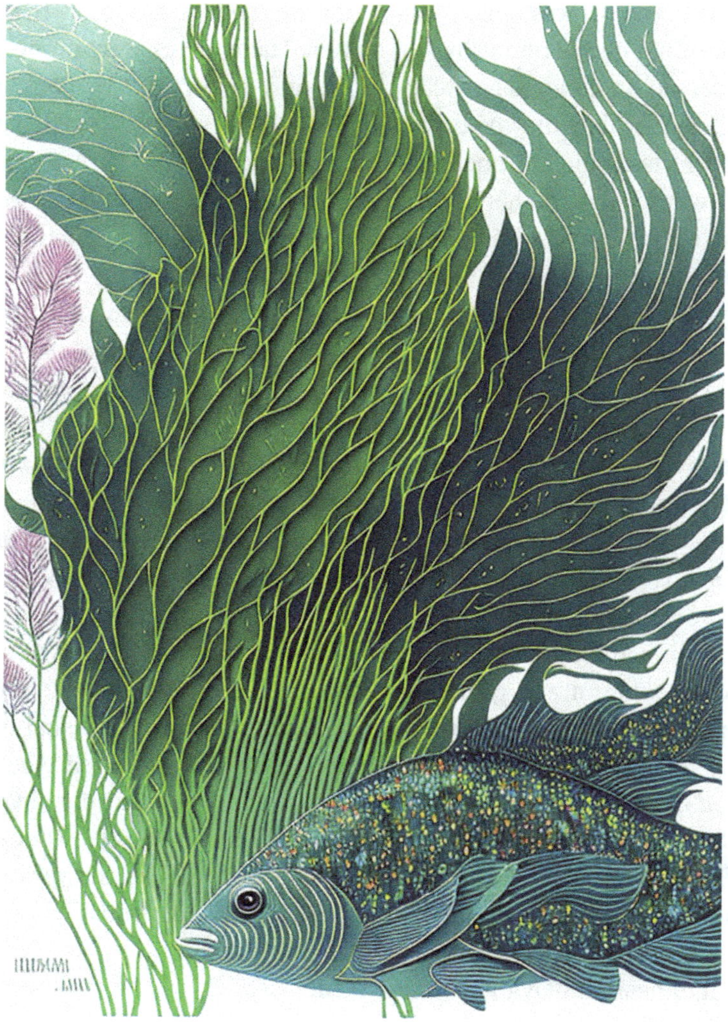

and save money. The collective judgments around art have loosened perhaps instead of the more typical anthropo-normative restrictions around art understandings. For respective artists, the platform may help impose discipline to explore artworks and to try different styles. The platform itself is evolving over time, and more user controls are being designed into the system. As a tool to see how more refined artmaking generative AI tools may be used, DDG is a fine example.

The 8-9 months of using the DDG platform provided a variety of goods for the author:

- Entertainment, pleasure, humor, surprise;
- Learning (about art, about AI, about generative art, about prompting techniques, about common artists, about themselves)
- Skill-building;
- Mutual sociality (human connection through art, through textual messaging, through social performance, through art curation and sharing);

- Affirmation of social identity building (as citizens of the world; as common artists, as humorists, as animators, as digital puppeteers, as storytellers)
- Intercommunications

A seminal observation of this work is that an artmaking generative AI, if it is built out to include a social element, may enable human interconnections.

There were messages exchanged between the author and other users of the platform. While the interactions did not go beyond art-based discussions, they were enjoyable and positive engagements and provided solace in difficult times. The potential for more solid interactions was clear.

In terms of the sociality modules, the company that runs Deep Dream Generator (run by Aifnet Limited) can benefit. The interactions may drive creativity, enthusiasms, and shared online word-of-mouth. More active members may be more creative in creating a diversity of images, showing the depth and range of the technology. The users may share insights about the tool by their behaviors and directly by emails. The release to use the system also suggested that the platform may keep records of the text prompts, which may be informative about topical foci, style interests, and others.

DISCUSSION

To presage other uses

The Deep Dream Generator tool and platform proved itself to be a powerful social space for many with rich immersions and remote social interactions. It provided solace that the author may not have realized she needed in that period, which was full of strife and stress beyond emerging from the pandemic.

The performance of the DDG tool left a strong positive impression. The visual examples do not begin to do justice to the style and expressive range available. Figure 4 shows a little boy bicycling over cobblestones. Figure 5 shows a woman wearing a coat of buttons. All the visual works generated were created based on a simple textual prompt and an alcohol ink or mixed media painting by the author.

There is a new appreciation for authentic photographs, authentic for their factuality and their quirks. There is new appreciation for an image that has perfect composition given the messiness of the world (while there is a balanced understanding of what edits may be done with a digital or digitized photo).

Artmaking Generative AI Sites That Might Emphasize the Remote Social

If owners of a generative AI platform wanted to more formalize the platform for communal connectivity, what might they do? Would they set up a social robot ('bot) that can work as an automated social director? Or multiple scripted agents serving various social roles in the space? Would they elicit information from respective users and then run that information at regular intervals to highlight personalities? Would they elicit stories behind some of the user's creations? Would they create sense of events on the platform, such as having expert individuals evaluate various works and comment on the design elements? Such as having learning events? Would they propose groupings based on AI-identified shared underlying interests and potential social clusters? Would they gamify social engagements? Would they formalize groups with opt-in members and their own names and their own designed aesthetics of their shared identity? Would they enable different rationales for the social connectedness? Would they have a "Did you know?" feature that highlights where a particular created work may be shared off-platform? (Perhaps the work is used

Figure 4. Bicycling on cobblestones (from the deep dream generator and the author's alcohol ink painting)

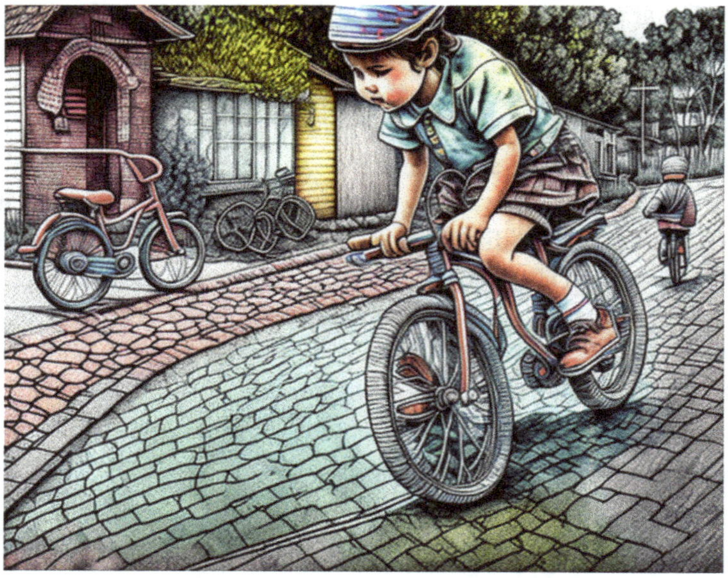

Figure 5. Coat of buttons (from the deep dream generator and the author's mixed media painting)

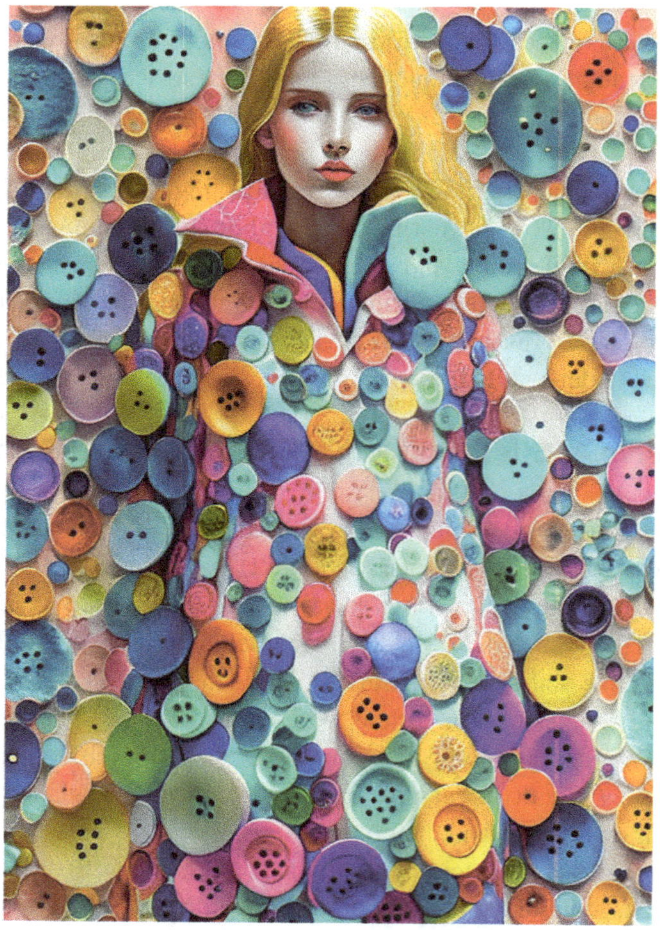

on a website, a poster, a slideshow, or other element.) Would they highlight various users—with their permission—by conducting short "bullet" interviews of them and their backgrounds and personalities and art? Would they include humanizing quotes?

Informal Online Social Networks

What about those who want to harness an artmaking generative AI site for an online community? How can they test the fitness of the site for socializing? What technologies will they explore for sociality on the site? How will they get a sense of the others on the platform and their respective willingness to engage? The most practical approach seems to be to test the waters to see who some of the others on the platform are, whether they are open to engaging, and how they may want to interact or intercommunicate. If the social communications part is not so satisfactory on the platform, perhaps any group can move to a shared social media one. Perhaps a mediated community can be right-sized for socializing and mutual support.

And those who do not want invitations to friendship or over-familiarity or relational closeness or other-knowledge, but who only want light-hearted enjoyment of machine-made art and its sharing, the technological freshness of generative AI, may choose to go along unbothered and unperturbed.

FUTURE RESEARCH DIRECTIONS

Remote virtual sanctuaries may well differ for various individuals and groups, depending on their sense of perceived needs. These may be taken up and co-created by their members as a reaction to the particular moment, which may be informed by a wide range of factors (as every human moment in a complex world means that various events are acting on the individuals). People join, participate, and leave, based on their respective felt needs. The making of such communities requires some complex learning, though, if the platform has a focus on a newer technology that enables individual and group creativity. There are social dynamics of digital performances. There is a need to acclimate to the mediated sociality. There is room for self-indulgent self-isolating along with high sociality depending on user needs. When looking at going to a generative AI tool for online social networking, after large-scale trauma, it helps to consider whether engagement in such a community makes its members better able to handle challenges and face problems, or if it is escapist and avoidant (which is negative). Inducing a generative AI to make art has major distractive value. It inspires people to engage remotely. It offers room for people to ruminate. It enables mutual entertainment. It enables speculations about how artmaking generative AI systems work. It enables visual thinking.

In terms of future research, there are a wide range of questions that may be asked:

- Are there particular artmaking generative AI platforms that have the social mechanisms that enable the building of online social networks?
  - Of these, which are the most amenable to supporting those who have experienced trauma?
  - How do people select particular online communities to join, in terms of artmaking generative AI platforms?
  - What makes such artmaking generative AI platforms inclusive? How?

- How do online social networks form on artmaking generative AI platforms? Are there events that spark such beginnings? (This is especially of interest for those platforms that do not enable the forming of dedicated groups with members who have shared interests.)
    - How do online social networks evolve over time on artmaking generative AI platforms? Are there patterns in terms of time-to-event analyses?
    - What are the typical lifespans of the usage of artmaking generative AI platforms as online social networks? Why? Are there triggering events that end user commitments to the usage of such technologies for online social network uses?
- Are there observable differences between the art profiles (and artworks, art collections) of those who engage in online social networks on an artmaking generative AI platform and those who do not?
    - Are there differences in the usage of artmaking generative AI tools between those who are more highly engaged socially than those who are not?
    - Does the heightened sociality of some members result in motivation to create more artwork, or less (on the platform)?
    - Are the artworks created by those in social networks more emotional and emotive than for those who are less social online? More cognitive? [If people are connecting via text and other messaging, are they also using their visuals to connect emotionally? Cognitively?)
- What are the relative depths of relationships built from artmaking generative AI platforms?
    - Do members interact outside of the platform?
    - Do members engage in trust acts? [Do they use pseudonyms or actual names? Do they engage with others in trustful ways, such as engaging in real space and sharing private information? How are issues of trust and security managed?]
    - Are there local face-to-face meetups? Extensions of the virtual network into physical spaces?
- Do those who use artmaking generative AI tools as online social networks experience differences in terms of the following:
    - Artmaking
    - Troubleshooting
    - Problem-solving
    - Relaxing
    - Handling stress, and others?
- For those with administrative access to such platforms (and legal releases to access the data from the users and others), what sorts of messaging is shared on private channels on artmaking generative AI platforms? Are such channels used for problem-solving? How much self-disclosure is there? Mutual support?
- Is relating on artmaking generative AIs similarly superficial as for social media platforms?
- For any population of users for an artmaking generative AI platform, what percentage turns their interactions into an online social network? What are data thresholds to use to identify an actual online social network (and its membership, both highly active and those not)?
- What makes an online social network on an artmaking generative AI platform coalesce? Act in concert? Break apart?
- In terms of subgroup members of an online social network on an artmaking generative AI platform, what are some ways to separate out or categorize the population? What unique insights are there about their respective features? Their unique needs? Their contributions? [This question is

based in part on a work which proposes the need to study human-robot co-creativity among older adults (Bossema, Allouch, Plaat, & Saunders, 2023). Focusing on particular groups may result in fresh insights.]
- Do such groups form differently on different AI content generators? Those that create contents in different modalities? If so, why? If not, why not?
- Are there opportunity costs to taking traumas to online social networks instead of in-person connections? What are ways to keep such engagements constructive?

The above is a light brainstorm of possibilities. Certainly, many other approaches would be valuable.

As to building on this direct research, what are ways for generative AI platforms that are socio-technical spaces to enhance the following for platform users in online social networks on the system?

- Entertainment, pleasure, humor, surprise;
- Learning (about art, about AI, about generative art, about prompting techniques, about common artists, about themselves) and skill-building;
- Mutual sociality (human connection through art, through textual messaging, through social performance, through art curation and sharing);
- Affirmation of social identity building (as citizens of the world; as common artists, as humorists, as animators, as digital puppeteers, as storytellers)

What are ways to increase socio-technical affordances on such sites? What rules and practices are conducive to sociality on such sites? Which are not?

What about building for mass-scale processing of shared traumas and risk? What are ways to enable thinking and rumination and discussion? For such cases, optimally more rare than common, some research would benefit people.

If such remote virtual sanctuaries are online social networks of a type, how do they function as discourse communities? How do the visual and textual lexicons intermesh? Given the prevalence of images, are the visual genres preferable to textual ones, and why? Are there shared goals? Around what do the members converge topically, and around what do they diverge?

As a commercial company, the Deep Dream Generator offers both free and paid services. Version 3 rolled out in early December 2023 [Version 1 came out in 2015, and Version 2 in 2021.] In the same way that many virtual worlds have economies that spill over into the real world and real money (Castronova, 2006), this platform's updated version offers clearer access to PRO generative AI models that cost more in points than a typical one, perhaps upselling human users, first point-wise, then dollar-wise. The lower-cost models include Artistic 2, Artistic, DreamForge, MirageMaker, and Photonic; the PRO models include EssenceOfReality, PhotoMage, DigitalDaVinci, Animatron, and AIVision. The costs for the respective models range from -4 to -40 energy points (which replenish over time for those with registered accounts). In the web platform's Terms and Conditions (aka Terms of Use), the platform restricts usage of the imagery from commercial usage unless users are paying monthly subscription fees for expanded service. ("Terms of Use," April 22, 2020) Works that users themselves create can apparently be used for non-profit application, without even a request for crediting the tool (although it seems to be a good idea to do so).

CONCLUSION

These are early days in terms of the "interdisciplinary conversations" around art and technology in the moment (Notaro, 2020, p. 322). The "true value" of humanity's "evolving (digital) semantic capital" is only just now beginning to be explored (Notaro, 2020, p. 328). As such, the viewing of artmaking generative AI platforms as socio-technical spaces for human interaction and well-being is not that unusual of a proposition. How technologies are designed and deployed can affect how people use them. After all, the design informs what people can see of themselves and others, how people can create their online "telepresence," what they can do, how their work may be stored and remembered, and other aspects. Generative AI, as a platform, does not require any paint-by-numbers approach. Further, some platforms like Deep Dream Generator, have a social element. [There is also research into uses of the artmaking generative AIs for promotion of human health, such as in fields of "mental health education, therapy, and counseling" among others (Lee, Park, & Hahn, 2023, n.p). Digital art therapy has also been described as a form of psychotherapy to apply to "anxiety disorder…, depression…, post-traumatic stress disorder…, and autism spectrum disorder" (Du, An, Leung, Li, Chapman, & Zhao, 2024, p. 1).]

Using generative AI does not necessarily result in any human loss of autonomy or creativity. It does not necessarily mean that the digital will supplant the physical, or that the machine will supplant the human. It does not mean people necessarily lose touch with the analog or physical real. Writ large. Generative AI platforms may be harnessed collaboratively for works that express the self, that illuminate the world, that connect people with others, and that leave a temporal short stay-behind digital legacy behind (with URLs for each image and URL profiles for each contributor in a web archival in a flood of information). Using particular tools does not necessarily mean a dealignment with human values and practices.

Y2023 has been a tumultuous year, geopolitically, economically, financially, and socially. The pandemic has unmoored humanity in unpredictable ways. The Deep Dream Generator, with its free generative AI creations and social tools, enables the making of social connections after mass trauma, to enable access to entertainment, learning, sociality, and affirmations of social identities. The experience is at once real and imaginary. In terms of the real, the created objects may be used for professional inspirations and development. The technology, as in other AI content generators, enables a foundational "floor" level of quality. In terms of the imaginary, the depicted world is one of abundance, safety, whimsy, humor, wit, and social commentary. It is escapist, to shallow machine dreams, and then to perhaps deeper ones. It is cold comfort. This work is a particularity of its time, with the advent of art-making generative AI in a post-global-pandemic. Human populations are in recovery, and they are looking for a salve. The users of the Deep Dream Generator, as an inter-media type for both human-machine art creation and mediated human sociality, certainly are using the tool for both intrinsic and extrinsic motivations. As in any community of practice, there are dabblers and artists, amateurs and professionals, each offering value to others. Over time, the different roles of the individual may change based on their learning and interactions. Most conjure dreams, and many end up as "deep dreamers" on the platform, with intertwining connections with others.

At a time of mass stress and fatigue, in working through the fractious COVID-19 pandemic, with many feeling feral, wild and undomesticated, perhaps not fit for social company, the Deep Dream Generator platform has proven to be a remote virtual sanctuary for many, with its web-facing tool and social enablements. Whether the digital works are passing digital ephemera that resolve to forgetting, or whether they are archived into the relative digital forever, or they land somewhere in-between, may or may not matter to the users of site. They have instigated and / or co-created works with an artmaking generative

AI, interacted with their fellow humans, engaged in visual and textual conversations, shared what was top-of-mind, and explored various forms of expressive depth. Their participation has been noted somewhere by some folks, and that may suffice as emotional solace after a multi-year global storm. While there are comforts in the human-machine artmaking and in the light social interactions, the time lost to the pandemic is irretrievable and irrecoverable, but at least, for many of the world's peoples, there are tomorrows remaining.

Delimitations. This work has emerged from some 9 months of exploration on this platform, mostly through brute force learning and contemporaneous notes. Most of the works read is visceral and perceptual but not profound per se. All social media platforms—and this Deep Dream Generator does have a core social aspect even as an artmaking generative AI tool—have natural limits in capabilities and in user bases (user populations). This work examines a use of the platform for individual well-being and is naturally constrained by the research focus.

REFERENCES

Ali, S., DiPaola, D., Williams, R., Ravi, P., & Breazeal, C. (2023). Constructing dreams using generative AI. *arXiv preprint arXiv:2305.12013.*

Angert, T., Suzara, M. I., Han, J., Pondoc, C. L., & Subramonyam, H. (2023). Spellburst: A node-based interface for exploratory creative coding with natural language prompts. *arXiv preprint arXiv:2308.03921.* doi:10.1145/3586183.3606719

Arias-Rosales, A. (2022). The perceived value of human-AI collaboration in early shape exploration: An exploratory assessment. *Plos One, 17*(9), 1 - 40.

Bar-Gil, O. (2023, Apr.). *The dance of agencies in AI art—Beyond the creator-tool Dichotomy, a netnographic analysis of Reddit forums.* Academic Press.

Bender, S. M. (2023). Coexistence and creativity: screen media education in the age of artificial intelligence content generators. *Media Practice and Education*, 1-16.

Boden, M. A., & Edmonds, E. A. (2009). What is generative art? *Digital Creativity (Exeter)*, *20*(1-2), 21–46. doi:10.1080/14626260902867915

Bossema, M., Allouch, S. B., Plaat, A., & Saunders, R. (2023). Human-robot co-creativity: A scoping review—Informing a research agenda for human-robot co-creativity with older adults. *arXiv preprint arXiv:*2309.07033. doi:10.1109/RO-MAN57019.2023.10309458

Bourgault, S., & E, J. (2023). Exploring the horizon of computation for creativity. *XRDS: Crossroads, The ACM Magazine for Students*, *29*(4), 6-9.

Browne, K. (2022). Who (or what) is an AI artist? *Leonardo*, *55*(2), 130–134. doi:10.1162/leon_a_02092

Candy, L. (2020). Creating with the digital: tool, medium, mediator, partner. *Interactivity, Game Creation, Design, Learning, and Innovation: 8th EAI International Conference, ArtsIT 2019, and 4th EAI International Conference, DLI 2019, Aalborg, Denmark, November 6–8, 2019 Proceedings*, *8*, 13–28.

Carter, R., & Carter, R. A. (2023). Machine visions: Mapping depictions of machine vision through critical image synthesis. Open Library of Humanities, 9(2).

Castronova, E. (2006). *Synthetic Worlds*. University of Chicago Press. doi:10.7208/chicago/9780226096315.001.0001

Chatterjee, A. (2022). Art in an age of artificial intelligence. *Frontiers in Psychology, 13*, 1 - 9.

Chen, W., Shidujaman, M., Jin, J., & Ahmed, S. U. (2020). A methodological approach to create interactive art in artificial intelligence. *HCI International 2020–Late Breaking Papers: Cognition, Learning and Games: 22nd HCI International Conference, HCII 2020, Copenhagen, Denmark, July 19–24, 2020 Proceedings*, *22*, 13–31.

Choi, S. K. (2022). *Losing touch: A comparative phenomenology of creative process in traditional and neural painting (Art in the age of artificial intelligence)*. Academic Press.

Choi, S. K., DiPaola, S., & Töyrylä, H. (2021). Artistic style meets artificial intelligence. *Journal of Perceptual Imaging*.

Chung, J. J. Y. (2023). Designing AI-Powered Art-Making Tools. *XRDS: Crossroads. The ACM Magazine for Students*, *29*(4), 14–19.

Chung, J. J. Y., He, S., & Adar, E. (2021, June). The intersection of users, roles, interactions, and technologies in creativity support tools. In *Designing Interactive Systems Conference 2021* (pp. 1817-1833). 10.1145/3461778.3462050

Chung, J. J. Y., He, S., & Adar, E. (2022, June). Artist support networks: Implications for future creativity support tools. In *Designing Interactive Systems Conference* (pp. 232-246). 10.1145/3532106.3533505

Cooney, M. (2021). Robot art, in the eye of the beholder? Personalized metaphors facilitate communication of emotions and creativity. *Frontiers in Robotics and AI*, *8*, 1 - 19.

d'Inverno, M., & McCormack, J. (2015). *Heroic versus collaborative AI for the arts*. Academic Press.

Daniele, A., & Song, Y. Z. (2019, January). Ai+ art= human. In *Proceedings of the 2019 AAAI/ACM Conference on AI, Ethics, and Society* (pp. 155-161). 10.1145/3306618.3314233

DeepDream. (2023, Sept. 24). In *Wikipedia*. Retrieve3d Nov. 8, 2023, from https://en.wikipedia.org/wiki/DeepDream

DiBlasi, J., Castellanos, C., Kang, E., Poltronieri, F., & Smith, L. (2020, November). Agency & autonomy: Intersections of artificial intelligence and creative practice. In *International Symposium on Electronic Art* (*Vol. 7*). Academic Press.

Dorin, A. (2008). A survey of virtual ecosystems in generative electronic art. In *The Art of Artificial Evolution: A Handbook on Evolutionary Art and Music* (pp. 289–309). Springer Berlin Heidelberg. doi:10.1007/978-3-540-72877-1_14

Dorin, A. (2013, March). Chance and complexity: stochastic and generative processes in art and creativity. In *Proceedings of the Virtual Reality International Conference: Laval Virtual* (pp. 1-8). 10.1145/2466816.2466837

Du, X., An, P., Leung, J., Li, A., Chapman, L. E., & Zhao, J. (2024). DeepThInk: Designing and probing human-AI co-creation in digital art therapy. *International Journal of Human-Computer Studies, 181*(103139), 1–17. doi:10.1016/j.ijhcs.2023.103139

Elgammal, A., Liu, B., Elhoseiny, M., & Mazzone, M. (2017). CAN: Creative Adversarial Networks, generating" art" by learning about styles and deviating from style norms. *arXiv preprint arXiv*:1706.07068.

Epstein, Z., Hertzmann, A., Herman, L., Mahari, R., Frank, M. R., Groh, M., . . . Russakovsky, O. (2023). Art and the science of generative AI: A deeper dive. *arXiv preprint arXiv:2306.04141.*

Epstein, Z., Schroeder, H., & Newman, D. (2022). When happy accidents spark creativity: Bringing collaborative speculation to life with generative AI. *arXiv preprint arXiv:2206.00533.*

Friess, P. (2021). Existence Beyond transhumanism–Context-based research-creation for critical art making. *Proceedings of Politics of the Machines-Rogue Research, 2021*(3), 278–284. doi:10.14236/ewic/POM2021.36

Fry, C. (2018). Enchanting algorithms: How the reception of generative artworks is shaped by the audience's understanding of the experience. In *XXI Generative Art Conference Proceedings.* Available at: http://www. generativeart. com/GA2018_paper s/GA2018_Christopher% 20Fry. pdf

Fung, B. (2023, Nov. 18). *OpenAI. Why Sam Altman was fired and what's next after the shocking shakeup.* CNN. Retrieved Nov. 18, 2023, from https://www.cnn.com/2023/11/18/tech/openai-sam-altman-shakeup-what-happened/index.html

Ghosh, A., & Fossas, G. (2022). Can there be art without an artist? *arXiv preprint arXiv:*2209.07667. 1 - 8.

Glenza, J. (2020, Dec. 21). Coronavirus: Epidemiologist looks to the past to predict second post-pandemic 'roaring 20s'. *The Guardian.* Retrieved Nov. 8, 2023, from https://www.theguardian.com/world/2020/dec/21/epidemiologist-1918-flu-pandemic-roaring-20s-post-covid

Guljajeva, V., Sola, M. C., & Clarke, I. J. (2023). Artistic strategies to guide neural networks. *arXiv preprint arXiv:2307.07521.*

Hazan, S. (2023, July). The dance of the doppelgängers: AI and the cultural heritage community. *Proceedings of EVA London, 2023*, 77–84. doi:10.14236/ewic/EVA2023.13

Hertzmann, A. (2019). Aesthetics of neural network art. *arXiv preprint arXiv:1903.05696.*

Hutson, J., & Cotroneo, P. (2023). Generative AI tools in art education: Exploring prompt engineering and iterative processes for enhanced creativity. *Metaverse, 4*(1), 1–13.

Hutson, J., & Harper-Nichols, M. (2023). Generative AI and algorithmic art: Disrupting the framing of meaning and rethinking the subject-object dilemma. *Global Journal of Computer Science and Technology: D, 23*(1).

Hutson, J., & Lang, M. (2023). Content creation or interpolation: AI generative digital art in the classroom. *Metaverse, 4*(1), 1–14. doi:10.54517/m.v4i1.2158

Hutson, J., & Robertson, B. (2023). Exploring the educational potential of AI generative art in 3D design fundamentals: A case study on prompt engineering and creative workflows. *Global Journal of Human-Social Science: A Arts & Humanities-Psychology, 23*(2), 1 - 11.

Jansen, C., & Sklar, E. (2021). Exploring co-creative drawing workflows. *Frontiers in Robotics and AI, 8*(577770), 1–26. PMID:34055899

Ko, H. K., Park, G., Jeon, H., Jo, J., Kim, J., & Seo, J. (2023, March). Large-scale text-to-image generation models for visual artists' creative works. In *Proceedings of the 28th International Conference on Intelligent User Interfaces* (pp. 919-933). 10.1145/3581641.3584078

Kulkarni, C., Druga, S., Chang, M., Fiannaca, A., Cai, C., & Terry, M. (2023). A word is worth a thousand pictures: Prompts as AI design material. *arXiv preprint arXiv:2303.12647.*

Leach, N. (2019). Do robots dream of digital sheep? *Proceedings of ACADIA 19: Ubiquity and Autonomy.* 10.52842/conf.acadia.2019.298

Lee, H. K. (2022). Rethinking creativity: Creative industries, AI and everyday creativity. *Media Culture & Society, 44*(3), 601–612. doi:10.1177/01634437221077009

Lee, Y. K., Park, Y. H., & Hahn, S. (2023). A portrait of emotion: Empowering self-expression through AI-generated art. *arXiv preprint arXiv:2304.13324.*

Lin, L., & Long, D. (2023, June). Generative AI futures: A speculative design exploration. In *Proceedings of the 15th Conference on Creativity and Cognition* (pp. 380-383). 10.1145/3591196.3596616

Liu, B. (2023, Apr.) Arguments for the rise of artificial intelligence art: Does AI art have creativity, motivation, self-awareness and emotion? *Arte,* 1 - 12.

Liu, V. (2023, April). Beyond text-to-image: Multimodal prompts to explore generative AI. In *Extended Abstracts of the 2023 CHI Conference on Human Factors in Computing Systems* (pp. 1-6). ACM.

Lively, J., Hutson, J., & Melick, E. (2023). Integrating AI-generative tools in web design Education: Enhancing student aesthetic and creative copy capabilities using image and text-based AI generators. *Journal of Artificial Intelligence and Robotics, 1*(1), 23–33.

Mäki-Reinikka, K. (2018). Cave paintings for the AI: Art in the age of singularity. *Politics of the Machines-Art and After, 7*, 1–7. doi:10.14236/ewic/EVAC18.13

Malina, R. F. (1990). Digital image: Digital cinema: The work of art in the age of post-mechanical reproduction. *Leonardo*, 33-38.

Mazzone, M., & Elgammal, A. (2019, February). Art, creativity, and the potential of artificial intelligence. In Arts (Vol. 8, No. 1, p. 26). MDPI. doi:10.3390/arts8010026

McCormack, J., Cruz Gambardella, C., Rajcic, N., Krol, S. J., Llano, M. T., & Yang, M. (2023, April). Is writing prompts really making art? In *International Conference on Computational Intelligence in Music, Sound, Art and Design (Part of EvoStar)* (pp. 196-211). Cham: Springer Nature Switzerland.

Merchán, E. C. G., & Molina, M. (2020). A machine consciousness architecture based on deep learning and Gaussian processes. *Hybrid Artificial Intelligent Systems: 15th International Conference, HAIS 2020, Gijón, Spain, November 11-13, 2020 Proceedings, 15*, 350–361.

Merriam, P. (2020, Spring). Grappling with technology: The post digital printmaker. *IMPACT Printmaking Journal,* 1-10.

Mustaqim, K., & Zahar, I. (2022, November). The presence of digital art: Towards the oblivion of aesthetics sense and beyond. In *IICACS: International and Interdisciplinary Conference on Arts Creation and Studies* (*Vol. 4*, pp. 106-114). Academic Press.

Nguyen, D. (2023). The effects of AI on digital artist. Bachelor's thesis. Haaga-Helia University of Applied Sciences. *Business Information Technology,* 1 - 66.

Nordström, P., Lundman, R., & Hautala, J. (2023). Evolving coagency between artists and AI in the spatial cocreative process of artmaking. *Annals of the Association of American Geographers*, 1–16.

Notaro, A. (2020). State-of-the-art: AI through the (artificial) artist's eye. *EVA London 2020: Electronic Visualisation and the Arts*, 322-328.

Piskopani, A. M., Chamberlain, A., & Ten Holter, C. (2023, July). Responsible AI and the arts: The ethical and legal implications of AI in the arts and creative industries. In *Proceedings of the First International Symposium on Trustworthy Autonomous Systems* (pp. 1-5). 10.1145/3597512.3597528

Steinfeld, K. (2023). Clever little tricks: A socio-technical history of text-to-image generative models. *International Journal of Architectural Computing, 21*(2), 211–241. doi:10.1177/14780771231168230

Suryna, K., & Serrano, R.G. (2019). Agents without agency: Artificial Intelligence as artistic medium. *Taboo Transgression Transcendence,* 200 - .209.

Tao, F. (2022). A new harmonisation of art and technology: Philosophic interpretations of artificial intelligence art. *Critical Arts, 36*(1-2), 110–125. doi:10.1080/02560046.2022.2112725

Tao, F., Zou, X., & Ren, D. (2018). The art of human intelligence and the technology of artificial intelligence: artificial intelligence visual art research. In *Intelligence Science II: Third IFIP TC 12 International Conference, ICIS 2018, Beijing, China, November 2-5, 2018, Proceedings 2* (pp. 146-155). Springer International Publishing.

Ulberg, E., Llach, D. C., & Byrne, D. (2020). Hand-crafting neural networks for art-making. In ICCC (pp. 508-511). Academic Press.

Vigliensoni, G., Perry, P., & Fiebrink, R. (2022). A small-data mindset for generative AI creative work. Association for Computing Machinery.

Wasielewski, A. (2023). "Midjourney can't count": Questions of representation and meaning for text-to-image generators. *The Interdisciplinary Journal of Image Sciences, 37*(1), 71–82.

Yang, W. (2022). Artificial Intelligence education for young children: Why, what, and how in curriculum design and implementation. *Computers and Education: Artificial Intelligence, 3*, 100061. doi:10.1016/j.caeai.2022.100061

Yin, H., Molchanov, P., Alvarez, J. M., Li, Z., Mallya, A., Hoiem, D., ... Kautz, J. (2020). Dreaming to distill: Data-free knowledge transfer via deepinversion. In *Proceedings of the IEEE/CVF Conference on Computer Vision and Pattern Recognition* (pp. 8715-8724). 10.1109/CVPR42600.2020.00874

Zeilinger, M. (2021). Generative adversarial copy machines. *Culture Machine*, *20*, 1–23.

Zeilinger, M. (2021). *Tactical entanglements: AI art, creative agency, and the limits of intellectual property*. Meson Press.

Zylinska, J. (2020). *AI art: machine visions and warped dreams*. Open Humanities Press.

ADDITIONAL READING

Hai-Jew, S. (2024). *Generative AI in Teaching and Learning*. IGI Global.

Chapter 10

Generative AI Methodology for Producing Assisted Art:
Representation of the Historical-Cultural Identity of Southern Brazil

William Alberto Cruz Castañeda
https://orcid.org/0000-0002-9803-1387
Alana AI Research, Brazil

Marcellus Amadeus
https://orcid.org/0009-0002-7777-2562
Alana AI Research, Brazil

André Felipe Zanella
Alana AI Research, Brazil

Felipe Rodrigues Perche Mahlow
Alana AI Research, Brazil

ABSTRACT

Generative artificial intelligence is an emerging technology that has impacted society recently and with productivity gains in the coming years. This technology learns from existing data to generate high-quality content such as text, images, music, speech, videos, and code. As part of the creative industries, collaboration between generative algorithms and human creativity brings challenges due to producing content and artistic images in response to natural language requests. Thus, this chapter establishes a methodology based on text-to-image generative artificial intelligence for producing assisted art in contextualized cultural content to generate unique and diverse images of the historical-cultural identity of southern Brazil. The steps of the methodology that can portray elements of Brazil's biome, cultural, and historical events are dataset assembling, model training and fine-tuning, and content enhancement and post-processing. In addition, the methodology allows an immersed experience with people being transported in period clothing and within a historical or cultural setting.

DOI: 10.4018/979-8-3693-1950-5.ch010

INTRODUCTION

Generative Artificial Intelligence (GenAI) is one of the top 10 emerging technologies reported by the World Economic Forum that impact society in the next three to five years (World Economic Forum, 2023). GenAI is a type of deep-learning model that doesn't require knowledge or entering code but can learn from existing data to generate a variety of high-quality realistic content such as text, images, music, speech, videos, software code, or others. A GenAI model differs from a predictive machine learning model, which performs a discrimination behavior, solving classification or regression problems. Thus, GenAI models use techniques that produce or create information on the transformed data rather than simply analyzing or acting on the data they trained on.

GenAI has the potential to disrupt several industries. Healthcare applies as a tool for accelerating drug discovery, supporting clinicians to transcribe patient consultations, generating drug molecules (Anstine & Isayev, 2023), and analyzing brain activity data to produce drawings of the objects that human participants are holding in mind (Takagi & Nishimoto, 2023). Environmental science predicts weather patterns and simulates the effects of climate change. Education integrates into teaching practices or training students (Baidoo-Anu & Owusu Ansah, 2023) to develop customized learning materials that cater to students' learning styles. Finance analyzes market patterns, anticipates stock market trends, and assists financial analysts. In advertising, creates new advertisements based on existing ones, making it easier for companies to reach new audiences. Art and design help artists and designers create new works by generating new ideas and concepts. Entertainment creates new video games, movies, and TV shows, making it easier for content creators to reach new audiences (World Economic Forum, 2023). In the workplace, increase productivity and quality, restructuring human tasks towards idea generation and editing (Shakked & Whitney, 2023).

In 2018, the professional art world was upended when the renowned Christie's auction house sold an AI-augmented work, "Portrait of Edmond Belamy" for the unexpected sum of $435,000. That sale, which came with the tacit imprimatur of the established art community, generated much gnashing of teeth and hand-wringing in the arts sector over what artificial intelligence means for the creative industry (Stanford University Human-Centered Artificial Intelligence, 2023). A 2022 McKinsey survey shows that AI adoption has more than doubled over the past five years, and investment in AI is increasing quickly. Generative AI tools, like ChatGPT and DALL-E, improve jobs and have the potential to achieve this (McKinsey Global Publishing, 2023).

In the context of the creative industries, a collaboration between intelligent algorithms and human creativity brings challenges. Creativeness defines the ability to produce original and unusual ideas or to make something new or imaginative. Creative tasks generally require some degree of original thinking, extensive experience, and an audience understanding. Today, GenAI associates human creativity and artistic practice relevant to the creative industry due to producing content and artistic images in response to natural language requests. Research conducted by Adobe to understand the role technology plays in their creative process revealed that three-quarters of artists in the US, UK, Germany, and Japan would consider using AI tools as assistants in areas such as image search, editing, and other non-creative tasks (Pfeiffer Consulting, 2018). Creative professionals participating in this research feel that AI is a technology transformation, but they don't know how it will change their work. Over 60% of respondents said these developments will impact quite a lot, and only 5% think they will have no impact. The number of interviewees interested in having a head-start in AI is even higher, at 73%. Respondents in Japan, in particular, showed great enthusiasm and receptivity for developments based on AI.

The report of (Amato, et al., 2019) presents how media and creative industries use AI. Helps to understand the emergent challenges in research and development. Researchers in the field of music, audio, image, videos, media, and design have contributed to this report by summarizing the state of the art in their own field and collecting the outstanding challenges that remain to be solved to fully design innovative tools, knowledge, and products in this sector. The report identifies the primary creative application areas where AI catalyzes new research and development directions within the media and creative industries, encompassing creation, production, and consumption/diffusion. It also delves into AI tools currently in use or with potential for application in these areas. Furthermore, it addresses the principal scientific, technological, and societal challenges to fully harness the potential of AI in the media and creative industries.

(Davies, Klinger, Mateos-Garcia, & Stathoulopoulos, 2020) revealed that the growth rate of research publications on AI exceeds 500% in countries like Germany, China, South Korea, Poland, Japan, and Sweden. Taiwan's rate is 1490% related to image-based data, followed by text-based and sound-based. Analysis of research publications indicates that AI is used in virtual reality/augmented reality (about 150 publications), advertising (about 110 publications), artistic activity (about 105 publications), computer games (about 70 publications), and museums (about 20 publications).

Applications of GenAI in the creative industries have increased in the last five years. Horizon Worlds game allows you to wander into the virtual world related to content consumption and creation. In Horizon, users have more control over how they want to tailor their online experience to meet their needs (Meta, 2024). The game Traveler concentrates on generating gorgeous scenarios to present users with visual impact and immersive soundscapes to embark on a journey through a diverse world where each scene is unique, and the content can range from dark forests to bustling cities (STEAM, 2024).

As reported by (Shah, Engineer, Bhagat, Chauhan, & Shah, 2020), GenAI has transformed the advertising industry by enabling advertisers to create highly personalized and engaging content at scale while saving time and resources. A creative advertising system generates and tests advertising ideas, which helps aspiring and mature creators understand that creativity is a systematic process assisted by data and computation (Vakratsas & Wang, 2021). Vinci is another intelligent system that supports the automatic generation of advertising posters. By inputting product images and slogans specified by users, Vinci uses deep-generation models to generate beautiful posters (Guo, et al., 2021).

The artwork created by MidJourney under the title 'Space Opera Theatre' earned first place in the Colorado State Fair Art Competition, demonstrating the capability of AI painting tools to produce excellent pieces of art (DelSignore, 2022). The creation of various art forms, such as abstract painting generation (Li, Lv, Wang, & Sang, 2020), Chinese shanshui painting (Zhou, Wang, Huang, & Lo, 2019), and Chinese ink paintings (Chung & Huang, 2023), undoubtedly promotes the advancement of painting. Moreover, GenAI can assist in conservation and restoration (Yu, et al., 2022), (Hu, 2022). In this sense, a GenAI is a tool to generate genuine artistic content, not to replace humans, but to enhance the content to attend as an inspiration for professionals. Nonetheless, current intelligent design focuses on AI to replace repetitive work, ignoring the changes in thinking and methodology to provide assistance and support in making art and into a creative process envisioned by human creators.

Thus, this chapter aims to guide researchers or professionals to understand the development process for producing assisted art with GenAI. The chapter describes a methodology based on a text-to-image GenAI for producing assisted art in contextualized cultural content to generate unique and diverse images of the historical-cultural identity of southern Brazil. Its look first, Section II describes current scientific-related works to understand the process of producing assisted art. Section III describes a methodology organized into three steps: dataset assembling, model training/fine-tuning, and content enhancement. Section IV describes the outcomes of the methodology application to produce unique and diverse images along with an interactive experience of the historical-cultural identity of southern Brazil. Section V presents the conclusion, as well as challenges.

SCIENTIFIC RELATED WORKS

The study in (Vakratsas & Wang, 2021) proposes a conceptual framework for advertising creativity founded on the principles of computational creativity. A basic tenet of computational creativity is that creative ideas or artifacts can represent objects in a conceptual space defined by a set of rules *R*. Thus, the framework improves the current thinking into a process for generating creative advertising. New ideas can be generated by either exploring (traversing) a conceptual space using a set of rules *T*, or by transforming an existing space equivalent to utilizing a new set of traversal rules *T'*. One way to visualize the conceptual space is to think about styles or genres. Outcome evaluation uses a set of evaluative rules *E* (the value function) in combination with *R*, as one would also wish to test whether a newly generated idea conforms (or does not conform) to a style or genre.

The research of (Chung N., 2021) conceptualizes existing and future human-in-the-loop (HITL) approaches for creative applications and to develop an expressive, nuanced, and multimodal models. The proposed HITL helps algorithms to learn creative processes that are harder to codify or quantify. (Turchi, Carta, Ambrosini, & Malizia, 2023) investigate how the interaction with large-scale Text-to-image Generative Models (LTGMs) impacts creativity by analyzing the feedback provided by groups of design students developing an architectural project with the help of LTGMs tools. (Demirel, Goldstein, Li, & Sha, 2023) formulate a human-centered generative design framework that injects human factors into the design for concept creation and evaluation. The results show that the framework enhances human factors representation within the generative design workflow.

(Jovanović & Campbell, 2022) propose a deployment workflow as a closed system with a feedback loop. The workflow has two phases: offline/test and online/production. In the offline/test phase are proposed three stages: (re)train, mitigate, and verify. The online/production phase proposes three stages: deploy, observe, and evaluate. This workflow provides benefits beyond GenAI because synthetic data creation increases the dataset size for a particular model and becomes part of the model's iterative and incremental development cycle to improve performance continually.

(Weisz, Muller, He, & Houde, 2023) propose design principles to aid the designers of generative AI systems. The principles are grounded in an environment of generative variability. In this environment, six principles focus on designing for characteristics of GenAI: multiple outcomes, imperfection, exploration, control, mental models, and explanations. In addition, against potential harm proposes to verify the generative model's hazardous output, misuse, or human displacement.

A systematic literature review conducted by (Hughes, Zhu, & Bednar, 2021) brings evidence of the AI-augmented creative design cycle of (Zeng, Sun, & Liao, 2019), which expands new methods and design forms to improve the quality of designs. The AI-augmented creative design cycle consists of the following phases: inspiration, creation, reflection, re-creation, and re-reflection. In a narrow sense, creativity results in a continuous interaction between creation and reflection. An external design problem will motivate the designer to create an intrinsic idea (inspiration). Designers will link and react to the design works representing internal creativity with the external design problems and past design experience (creation). Similarly, reflection will stimulate new design ideas and start a new round of creation and reflection (reflection, re-creation, and re-reflection).

Yousif & Vermisso (2022) investigate new AI-assisted workflows for architectural design to enhance the designer's capacity to explore options within an expanded space. The workflow integrates AI with other computational tools to provide a different design exploration than other methods. Three components develop the workflow: generating mechanisms, testing mechanisms, and a control approach. Within generating mechanisms, methods of discrete assembly, in particular, the wave function collapse (WFC) method, agent-based modeling (ABM), and generative adversarial networks (GANs) evaluate possible scenarios of those methods.

Revealing the measurable impacts on creative production, Zhou & Lee (2023) investigates how the adoption of GenAI impacts the creative evaluation of artifacts and how humans' prior creative abilities correspond to artwork quality. The authors define the following measures: creative productivity, creative value, content novelty, and visual novelty. Creative productivity is the log of posted artifacts by the user in a month. Creative value measures artifact aspects of utility, performance, and attractiveness, subject to temporal and cultural contexts. A content novelty is the adopters' ideas becoming more similar over time. Visual novelty suggests that users prefer a visual style from which they diverge little.

This scientific literature indicates a general acceptance of GenAI as a tool across the community that reflects a general awareness of the state of the art since GenAI technologies have developed to assist and support humans rather than replace them. Better collaboration between humans and AI technologies can thus maximize the benefits of synergy.

METHODOLOGY

The methodology organizes the development process to produce assisted art based on a text-to-image GenAI model and establishes a pipeline to generate unique and diverse images. Figure 1 shows the methodological pipeline divided into three steps: dataset assembling, model training/fine-tuning, and content enhancement.

Figure 1. Methodological three-step pipeline to produce assisted art based on a text-to-image GenAI model

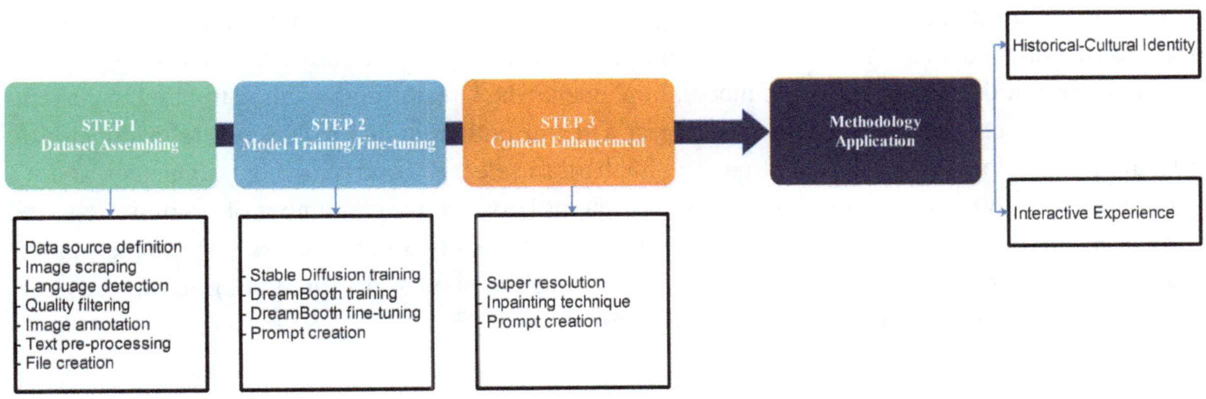

Dataset Assembling

This step compiles information to establish the dataset used in a text-to-image GenAI model. Involve the tasks of data source definition, image scraping, language detection, quality filtering, image annotation, text pre-processing, and file creation.

Data source definition is the tasks that provide data in the desired language and define the specific domain or topic to collect images. Domain expert collaboration defines the target topic and understands its characteristics and requirements (resolution, format, color space, size, etc.). Each data directory should contain images and captions. Captions are saved in a text file to retrieve into the model training/fine-tuning step. Also, JSON files containing stats collected during downloading (URL, caption, status, error_message, width, height, original_width, original_height). If existing datasets don't fully meet the requirements, an image scraping task collects domain-specific images. Scraping tools or libraries (e.g., Beautiful Soup, Scrapy) allow the extraction of images from relevant websites. Text data scraping complements image scraping by collecting textual descriptions, captions, or metadata associated with the image. At this point, ensure compliance with legal and ethical guidelines while scraping is required. When the labeled samples from the raw metadata file have different language captions, the LINGUA library performs a language detection task that detects the source language of the captions (Lingua, 2022) because they can affect the results.

In some cases, datasets have pre-computed quality filtering in their metadata (as datasets from LAION) and may be necessary to carry out in other data sources. A quality filtering task applies CLIP Similarity or CLIPScore, Aesthetic Predictor, and Watermark Detector filter images to ensure the metadata (Hessel et al., 2021; LAION, 2022; LAION-AI, 2021). An optional task is the image annotation with BLIP-2s to perform auto-captioning and give a preliminary understanding of the images (Huggingface, 2023; Li et al., 2023). However, these automated captions need refinement to match the specific scenarios accurately if the concept is unknown to the model to conduct manual captions annotation. Finally, to enable data preprocessing, the metadata file is transformed into a parquet file for efficient retrieval, with at least the following columns: URL, caption, height, and width. This task is specific to each dataset and required for LAION datasets.

Model Training/Fine-Tuning

This step iteratively trains the data to the model and adjusts its parameters to minimize the difference between the generated and the appropriate output. Implements the Stable Diffusion as a latent text-to-image diffusion model capable of generating photo-realistic images given any text input (Huggingface, 2022). As part of the Stable Diffusion model, implements the DreamBooth method training to customize the model given just a few images of a subject. DreamBooth training involves several parameters to determine its performance and output quality. It's hard to select the correct set of parameters, and it's easy to overfit. To obtain quality images, an ideal point between a high number of training steps and a low learning rate until the results are satisfactory. Fine-tuning these parameters impacts the training process, influencing the quality and efficiency of the resulting model. All fine-tuning scripts are open-source and available in the Diffusers library (Huggingface, 2023).

Content Enhancement

Include the super-resolution and Inpainting techniques to fit the original content for the target audience. Super-resolution enables the image upsampling for resolution increase of a low-resolution image. On the other hand, Inpainting estimates lost or damaged parts of an image and the exhibited occluded background by using a mask (Wang et al., 2019). Additionally, covering an interactive experience, the photo background of a person is replaced with one of the generated images together with the person dressed in traditional clothing.

METHODOLOGY APPLICATION: HISTORICAL-CULTURAL IDENTITY OF SOUTHERN BRAZIL CASE STUDY

According to the methodology, the process defines the three steps for assisted art. Dataset Assembling to structure a dataset to encapsulate relevant cultural and historical regional concepts. Model Training and Fine-Tuning to carry out DreamBooth concept training and model parameters fine-tuning. Content Enhancement to apply super-resolution and Inpainting techniques to improve content.

Step 1: Dataset Assembling

The encapsulated cultural and historical regional concepts in the dataset are related to the following four categories: regional biome, historical events and personalities, cultural customs, and traditional attire. For the regional biome category, the selected concepts include the "Araucária" a distinctive tree native to the southern region, as well as the "Gato do mato pequeno" and "Sapinho admirável de Barriga vermelha" which are distinctive regional animals. For the historical events and personality category, the "Farroupilha Revolution" concept with portrayals of battles and the proclamation of the Rio Grandense Republic is a significant historical event in the southern Brazilian state of Rio Grande do Sul (RS) that influenced Brazilian history. For the representation of the historical personalities concept of this conflict: "Giuseppe Garibaldi", "Anita Garibaldi", and "Bento Gonçalves", are milestone personage in the revolution as well as the importance of the female figure during the conflict. Regarding the cultural customs category, the "Chimarrão", a typical beverage of the southern region, and, finally, the traditional attire category highlights the RS people. Table 1 shows the final number of images in the dataset to use in the training step.

Step 2: Model Training/Fine-Tuning

Model training uses Stable Diffusion checkpoints, versions 1.5 and 1.4, and DreamBooth non-LoRA implementation. In this step a prompt with a specific token in each concept is produced. Those tokens are cuiaBombaChimarrao, indumentariaGaucha, araucaria, pampa, gatoDoMato, sapinhoBarrigaVermelha, bentoGonçalves, giuseppeGaribaldi, aniGaribaldi, and batalhafarroupilha.

On the other hand, in the training process of the DreamBooth algorithm, parameters are set up to determine its performance and quality outcomes. Important parameters used are resolution, batch size, learning rate, and number of training steps. Fine-tuning these parameters needs to represent a balance, as they directly influence the training process, impacting the quality and efficiency of the resulting model.

Table 1. Images number used for training each concept

Concept	Number of Images
Cuia e Bomba de Chimarrão	28
Indumentária Gaúcha	84
Araucárias	97
Pampas	46
Gato-do-mato-pequeno	41
Sapinho-admirável-de-barriga-vermelha	31
Anita Garibaldi	14
Bento Gonçalves	12
Giuseppe Garibaldi	22
Batalha Farroupilha	49

The selection of these parameters achieves the expected outcomes for image generation and concept representation. Model training with the default resolution of 512×512 with a batch size of *1*, different learning rate values ranging from 3×10^{-6} to 5×10^{-7}, and training steps range of *1.000 to 10.000.*

Fine-tuning accomplishes each concept that the model expects to learn. Fine-tuning enables the model to adapt to specific nuances and characteristics associated with individual concepts. One of the most critical aspects of the fine-tuning process is the set of training images. These training images played a pivotal role in enhancing the model's ability to comprehend and accurately recognize the target concept due to the foundation upon which the model is constructed and refined. Captions in the training process are unused due to the distinctive nature of DreamBooth training.

Some of the prompts used were structured as follows:

SPECIFIC_TOKEN = [cuiaBombaChimarrao, indumentariaGaucha, araucaria, pampa, gatoDoMato, sapinhoBarrigaVermelha, bentoGonçalves, giuseppeGaribaldi, aniGaribaldi, batalhafarroupilha]

CONTEXT = ["leonardo da vinci style","tarsila do amaral style", "inside of an storm", "with birds flying around", "anita malfatti style", "horror style", "ismael nery style", "on outer space, with stars and planets around", "claude monet style", "romero britto style", "salvador dali style", "van gogh style", "close to a cat", "kid's drawing style", "with a dragon surrounding", "halloween style", "with golden coins all around", "pontillism style", "impressionism style", "modernism style"]

Above is the list of specific tokens and contexts used in the generation prompt. The prompt for training was

PROMPT= A painting of + SPECIFIC_TOKEN

For inference, they follow the rule of "A painting of" + specific token + context, being the prompt indicated as follows:

PROMPT= A painting of + SPECIFIC_TOKEN + CONTEXT

Figure 2. Images generated by DreamBooth to represent the tea and clothing culture of Rio Grande do Sul, Brazil. The prompts adopted were (a) a painting of cuiaBombaChimarrao, (b) a painting of cuiaBombaChimarrao, (c) a painting of indumentariaGaucha, Claude Monet Style, (d) a painting of indumentariaGaucha, impressionism style.

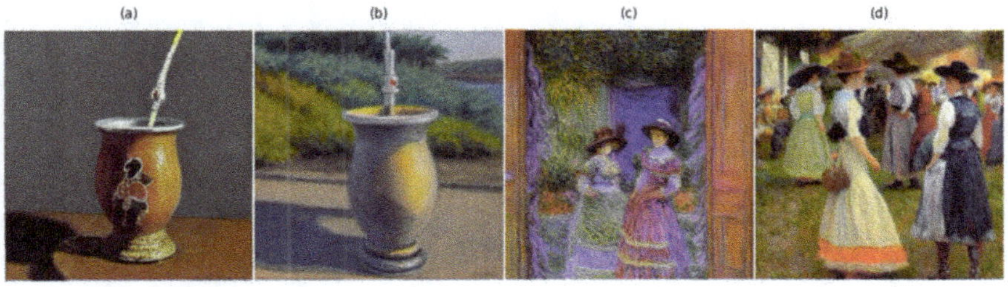

The journey through these visual narratives showcases the ability of the methodology to portray elements of biome, cultural, and historical events. First, the focus is on cultural customs and traditional attire that explore the representation of the "Cuia e Bomba de Chimarrão" and the "Indumentária Gaúcha" as essential elements of the mate tea culture and the traditional gaucho costume. Second, it is explored the representation of the regional biome with emphasis on the "Pampas" landscape, "Araucárias" trees, and endangered endemic animals, such as the red-bellied frog ("Sapinho-admirável-de-barriga-vermelha") and the "Gato-do-mato-pequeno" cat. Third, the visual narrative of historical events and personalities through the Farroupilha Revolution delves deeper into historical and significant battles.

Cultural Customs, and Traditional Attire

The cultural aspects have generated images of paintings capable of representing some of the customs of RS. Figure 2 (a) shows a "Cuia de Chimarrão" while Figure 2 (b) portrays a "Cuia de Chimarrão" painting without a specified artistic style, demonstrating the versatility in creating unique visual representations for a concept. Despite the high-quality images, a significant challenge arose because several samples featured logos, demanding a curatorship to remove these unwanted samples from the training dataset. The fact that most photos were close-up shots also caused difficulties, with the model interpreting the mate gourd larger than its actual size or mistaking it for a cup instead of being used with a straw. Additionally, the model sometimes added flowers inside the mate gourd, mistaking it for a plant pot. Figure 2 (c, d) characterizes the traditional attire, or "Indumentária Gaúcha" in the Claude Monet and Impressionism styles. These visual representations are biased when generating multiple individuals in the frame because the training data has image samples with more than one individual. Additionally, traditional clothing often became intertwined, blending with more contemporary adapted pieces, and source definition and image scraping are applied to mitigate them.

Regional Biome

Regarding the regional biome, this topic represents threatened natural flora and fauna. Figure 3 (a) represents the flora, specifically the "Araucárias", a group of conifers trees native to South Brazil. In this case, the challenge was curating the dataset to exclude other tree species, avoiding bias. Single tree-centered images skewed the model preferences, leading to less success with denser vegetation. Overall,

Figure 3. Images generated by DreamBooth to represent the fauna and flora of Rio Grande do Sul, Brazil. The prompts adopted were (a) a painting of Araucaria, in outer space with planets and stars behind, (b) a painting of Pampa landscape, impressionism style, (c) a painting of gatoDoMato, impressionism style, (d) a painting of sapinhoBarrigaVermelha, Halloween style.

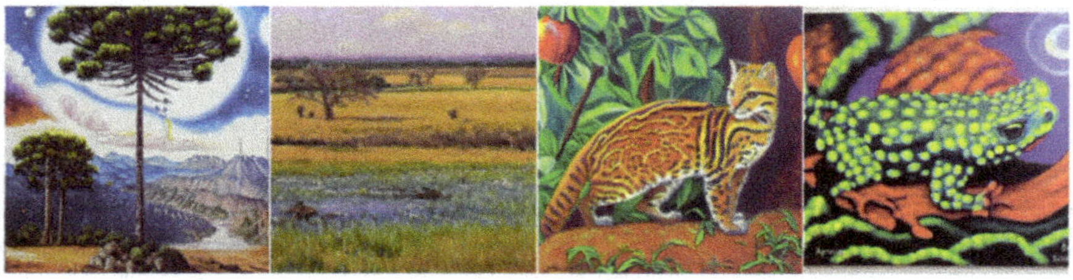

this concept showed an easy learning process and greater flexibility in our study. Figure 3 (b) represents the painting of the "pampas" landscape, a natural biome of RS. Figure 3 (c, d) depicts the endangered animals "gato-do-mato-pequeno" and the "sapinho-admirável-de-barriga-vermelha". Generating images of this nature can be challenging, as in the case of the "sapinho-admirável-de-barriga-vermelha" there are few high-quality images available, and those found are close-up shots, which may cause the model to lose the sense of scale. In this case, the model shows red legs and faces difficulties with limb and toe representation, making this concept challenging to illustrate. However, such artifacts contribute to enriching the visual representation of the species.

Historical Events: Farroupilha Revolution

The Farroupilha Revolution (1835-1845) happened in RS Brazil's southern state, and aimed for significant reforms and regional autonomy. Iconic leaders like Anita Garibaldi, Bento Gonçalves, and Giuseppe Garibaldi left a lasting impact beyond the region's borders. Figure 4 depicts these leading historical figures. Each historical figure has a limited collection of images in terms of variety. For example, the samples of Anita Garibaldi (a, b) collected through web scraping represent her from a similar perspective. The fine-tunings capture and represent this perspective. The same factor occurs with Bento Gonçalves (c) and Giuseppe Garibaldi (d) samples. Even with the trained models biased towards generating from these perspectives, we obtained satisfactory samples that capture the essence of such personalities and represent them creatively and artistically.

Just like the concepts of historical personalities (Figure 4), the visual documentation collected through our web-scraping process comprises images of paintings. Battle images typically depict numerous combatants on horseback, contrasting with other presented concepts where the subject was central in the image, resulting in generations with this bias (Figure 5 (b,c,d)). The scarcity of high-quality samples (DPI and resolution) was a difficulty. However, despite the mentioned challenges, generated images represent the period with fidelity. A notable detail was the model's intrinsic generative ability to incorporate the typical colors of RS, as seen in Figure 5 (b, d) without the specification in the prompt. It explored the models' ability to incorporate other contexts into the desired concept, such as the presence of women in battle, as depicted in Figure 5 (a). However, this task proved particularly challenging, generating few images of satisfactory quality. Figure 5 (a) acknowledges the often-overlooked role of women in the Farroupilha Revolution. They served as nurses, managed logistics, acted as couriers, and supported troops in various

Figure 4. DreamBooth generated images to represent the Farroupilha revolution. The prompts used were (a) a painting of aniGaribaldi, happy on a farm, (b) a painting of aniGaribaldi, with a big sun behind her, (c) a painting of bentoGonçalves, (d) a painting of giuseppeGaribaldi, captain of a ship.

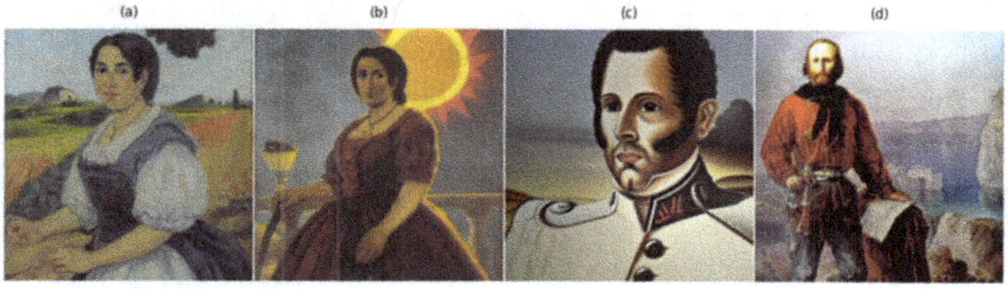

Figure 5. DreamBooth generated images to represent historical battles from the Farroupilha revolution. The prompts used were (a) a painting of batalhaFarroupilha, a woman in the center of the frame, Van Gogh style, (b) a painting of batalhaFarroupilha, (c) a painting of batalhaFarroupilha, horror style, (d) a painting of batalhaFarroupilha.

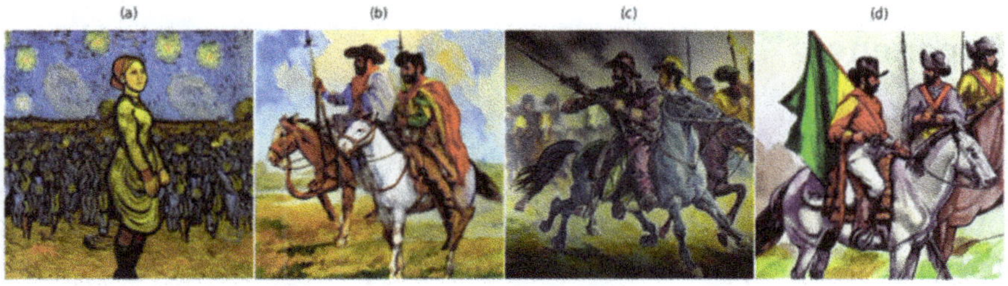

ways, including preparing meals and burying fallen soldiers. Figure 5 shows the model's versatility in combining unique concepts with artistic styles.

Step 3: Content Enhancement

Finally, Inpainting results allow an immersive visual experience with people being transported in period clothing and within a historical or cultural setting. For this purpose, the sequence of content enhancement actions is as follows: Mask, Inpainting, Face-extraction, and Background work together effectively. Mask action detects and isolates individuals within an image. It harnesses the power of a pre-trained face detection classifier to identify the positions of faces. Following this detection, it performs a crucial dual task: create a mask that turns the green screen background black and simultaneously places a black circle over the person's face, effectively rendering the person's body with a white silhouette. In that way, is established a clear distinction between the altered elements (the white silhouettes) and those that should remain intact (the black regions). The Inpainting action, triggered by a provided prompt, transforms only the clothing while preserving the individual's appearance. The Inpainting algorithm reproduces traditional Gaúcho attire using a process and similar parameters to DreamBooth but with the Inpainting pipeline. This training involved leveraging a dataset specifically curated for traditional Gaúcho clothing. The prompt used was:

A person wearing Indumentária Gaúcha, 4k high resolution.

Face-extraction action removes a person's face from the original image and replaces it in the image post-execution of the Inpainting action. It was a way to ensure high quality on the face and maintain its resolution. The Background action replaces the background of a person's image with a new background, using the created mask to isolate the person from the original background.

The interactive experience covers changing the person's photo background with one of the generated images plus dressing the person in traditional Gaúcho clothing. The sequence of post-processing actions involved are Noise-extraction, Increase-resolution, and Image-enrichment. The Noise-extraction action applies a Gaussian blur filter to remove any residual noise in the image to enhance visual quality and make the image smoother. The Increase-resolution action augments the resolution of an image by proportionally enlarging its size based on a provided factor. The Image-enrichment action improves the visual quality of an image in various ways, resulting in a visually pleasing and sharp image. Check if an image is black by evaluating the average pixel value of the image. This append if the Inpainting filter detects any not-safe-for-work (NSFW) content. Creates a rounded rectangle-shaped background image used to round the corners of the image created, and finally pastes a generated image into a frame.

Interactive Experience

To exemplify the interactive experience described above, Figure 6 illustrates how one individual (one author of this work) has been inserted into a pampa landscape wearing traditional Gaúcho attire. The creation of the mask is a fundamental aspect of recognizing between the altered elements and those to preserve, enabling the selective application of the Inpainting process to the clothing while maintaining the individual's appearance. Poor lighting in the original image and remnants of the green background appeared in the image after the pipeline, and improvement requires better lighting; however, we present it here as a use case under realistic and possibly adverse conditions.

Figure 6. Generated image for the interactive experience: a) Image before passing through the pipeline, b) after the pipeline application; the prompt used: a pampa landscape background and traditional Gaúho attire

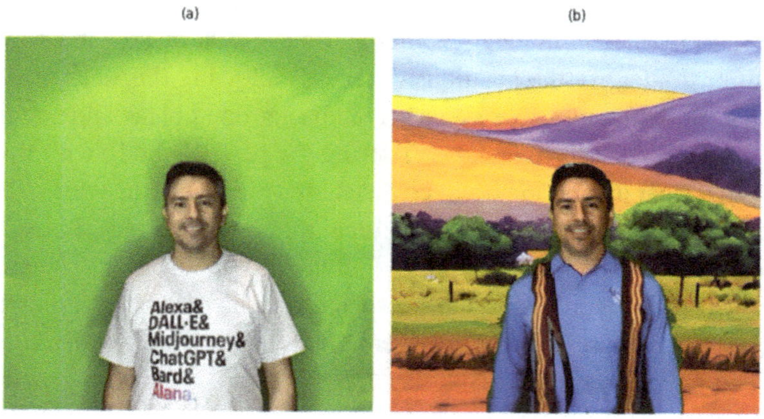

The Inpainting technique was crucial in replacing the person's clothing based on the provided prompt, resulting in a representation of Gaúcho attire. For this process, a trained DreamBooth Inpainting model (scripts available at Diffusers (Huggingface, 2024; 2024a) with the Indumentária Gaúcha dataset ensures the accuracy and fidelity in reproducing traditional clothing. Regarding post-processing, contribute to improving the visual quality of the generated image. The result is a visually pleasing image, preserving the integrity of the content and adding a vintage touch. In summary, the results demonstrate the feasibility and effectiveness of the proposed method for generating interactive images where individuals are inserted into specific environments, dressed in traditional attire such as Gaúcho clothing, with satisfactory visual quality and aesthetics.

CONCLUSION AND FURTHER RESEARCH DIRECTIONS

This chapter proposes a methodology for creating artistic images using GenAI models based on specific concepts. As a proof of concept, a case study follows the methodological steps to generate unique and diverse images representing the historical-cultural identity of southern Brazil. Besides serving as a guide for assisted art generation tools, and due to the generative capacity with limited data of GenAI models like DreamBooth, the methodology emphasizes that creating such models can aid in the preservation and enrichment of the historical-cultural heritage of communities or events with scarce representation in web data. Additionally, there is potential for blending various styles from historical art movements, further enriching the creative output.

With the correct controls in place, GenAI can provide more time for creativity, demonstrate the boundaries of knowledge, and act as a sparring partner to challenge conventional thinking. The intention is that the GenAI model offers the potential to create assistive intelligent tools that improve both the quality and custom content produced. With the support of the methodology, the obtained GenAI tool can generate unique cultural aspects of southern Brazil into the narrative of the Farroupilha Revolution, reflecting the region's singular characteristics and demands. Centered on the province of São Pedro do Rio Grande do Sul, there are scarce images of the Farroupilha Revolution as a movement that sought substantial reforms with historically relevant events between 1835 and 1845, including the quest for autonomy. The GenAI tool delves deeper into historical iconic figures and battles to transcend the boundaries of southern Brazil, leaving an indelible mark on the country's history. It also examines the representation of the fundamental cultural elements, the clothing, and capturing the essence of traditional fashion.

As a result, the proposed methodology establishes an assisted art process through the GenAI tool that enables the creation of new digital imagery or trained art forms based on customized datasets. The development of these tools has the purpose of early adoption as collaborative assistants to support and augment human creativity. Moreover, the support of the methodology represented customized cultural applications, where the elements provided are not inherently valuable as stand-alone works but are illustrative examples of how were harnessed to depict crucial concepts for various cultural communities. The historical context has faded into the past, with very few accessible images in public archives. In this context, the methodology to develop GenAI tools can play a vital role in creating more visual content related to such events for educational purposes or other potential applications. The methodology underscores how to generate representative art for historic local contexts, allowing preservation and revitalization of cultural and historical significance. The ethical questions relating to the creative capacity and ideas where the GenAI tool is included usually focus on the fundamental difference between humans and machines.

The GenAI tool cannot offer broad context, emotion, or social relationships. However, it can affect modern human life culturally and societally. In contrast, the development process for assisting in creating art does not have pre-defined outcomes classified as good or bad. Although many may follow contemporary trends or be in some way derivative, based on known audience preferences, there is no obvious way of measuring the quality of the result in advance. Creativity almost always involves combining ideas, often in an abstract yet coherent way, from different domains or multiple experiences, driven by curiosity and experimentation. Hence, data labeling for these applications is not straightforward or even possible in many cases.

For creative applications, technological developments will, for some time yet, remain human-centric, designed to augment, rather than replace, human creativity. As GenAI tools begin to spread through the creative sector, developers and deployers must continue to build trust; technological advances must go hand-in-hand with a greater understanding of ethical issues, data bias, and social impact. Producing novel work increases diversity and context when training the GenAI tool. The quality of the solution in such cases is difficult to define and will inevitably depend on audience preferences. To generate a new artwork, low-level features from semantics are a one-to-many relationship, leading to inconsistencies between outputs.

Various limitations of Stable Diffusion are seen in the literature and corroborated by our experiments. The notion of diversity for image creation from prompts needs more attention. Though we have focused on some of it, there are still open avenues. Biome, cultural, and the Farroupilha revolution diversity in text-to-image generation calls for further research. Furthermore, ten diverse datasets tune the model, and more heterogeneous data can be considered. Also, it was observed overfitting in the original images when the prompt is similar to the original setting. There is also variability in the subject fidelity in some generated images that might contain hallucinated features, like the hands when exposed, more than two, or deformed are generated by the model.

As opportunities for improvement, fine-tuning configurations and the hyperparameters selection for a concept depend on the training dataset. Furthermore, the creative image generation capability also varies with training. Prompt diversification and practicing prompt engineering (such as adopting negative prompts) can improve results in the inference stage. As much as the model, attention to creating image datasets is crucial for achieving good results; hence, variety, quantity, and quality to ensure they embrace the concept is a central point to consider.

ACKNOWLEDGMENT

We acknowledge the support of the National Council for Scientific and Technological Development (CNPq). This research is supported by the National Council for Scientific and Technological Development, Ministry of Science, Technology and Innovation (CNPq/MCTI/SEMPI Number 424359/2021-9 RHAE).

REFERENCES

Amato, G., Behrmann, M., Bimbot, F., Caramiaux, B., Falchi, F., Garcia, A., . . . Vincent, E. (2019). AI in the media and creative industries. *Arxiv*, 34. doi:https://doi.org//arXiv.1905.04175 doi:10.48550

Anstine, D., & Isayev, O. (2023). Generative Models as an Emerging Paradigm in the Chemical Sciences. *Journal of the American Chemical Society, 145*(16), 8736–8750. doi:10.1021/jacs.2c13467 PMID:37052978

Baidoo-Anu, D., & Owusu Ansah, L. (2023). Education in the Era of Generative Artificial Intelligence (AI): Understanding the Potential Benefits of ChatGPT in Promoting Teaching and Learning. *SSRN, 11*. Advance online publication. doi:10.2139/ssrn.4337484

Chung, C., & Huang, S. (2023). Interactively transforming chinese ink paintings into realistic images using a border enhance generative adversarial network. *Multimedia Tools and Applications, 82*(8), 11663–11696. doi:10.1007/s11042-022-13684-4

Chung, N. (2021). Human in the Loop for Machine Creativity. *Arxiv*, 4. doi:https://doi.org//arXiv.2110.03569 doi:10.48550

Davies, J., Klinger, J., Mateos-Garcia, J., & Stathoulopoulos, K. (2020). *AI and the Creative Industries: The art in the artificial.* London: Creative Industries Policy and Evidence Centre and Nesta. Retrieved from https://pec.ac.uk/research-reports/the-art-in-the-artificial

DelSignore, P. (2022). *Medium.* Retrieved 02 12, 2024, from AI Art Wins Competition And Sparks Controversy: https://medium.com/mlearning-ai/ai-art-wins-fine-arts-competition-and-sparks-controversy-882f9b4df98c

Demirel, H., Goldstein, M., Li, X., & Sha, Z. (2023). Human-Centered Generative Design Framework: An Early Design Framework to Support Concept Creation and Evaluation. *International Journal of Human-Computer Interaction, 40*(4), 933–944. doi:10.1080/10447318.2023.2171489

Guo, S., Jin, Z., Sun, F., Li, J., Li, Z., Shi, Y., & Cao, N. (2021). Vinci: An Intelligent Graphic Design System for Generating Advertising Posters. In *Conference on Human Factors in Computing Systems* (p. 17). Yokohama: ACM. 10.1145/3411764.3445117

Hessel, J., Holtzman, A., Forbes, M., Le Bras, R., & Choi, Y. (2021). CLIPScore: A Reference-free Evaluation Metric for Image Captioning. *Association for Computational Linguistics*, 7514-7528. doi:10.18653/v1/2021.emnlp-main.595

Hu, Z. (2022). Analysis of the Impact of Artificial Intelligence Technology-Assisted Environmental Protection on the Integrity of Chinese Painting. *Journal of Environmental and Public Health, 8*, 1–8. Advance online publication. doi:10.1155/2022/3245947 PMID:36065168

Huggingface. (2022). *Stable Diffusion with Diffusers.* Retrieved 02 12, 2024, from Stable Diffusion with Diffusers: https://huggingface.co/blog/stable_diffusion

Huggingface. (2023a). *DreamBooth training example.* Retrieved 02 12, 2024, from DreamBooth training example: https://github.com/huggingface/diffusers/tree/main/examples/dreambooth

Huggingface. (2023b). *BLIP-2.* Retrieved 02 12, 2024, from BLIP-2: https://huggingface.co/docs/transformers/model_doc/blip-2

Huggingface. (2024a). *Stable-diffusion-inpainting.* Retrieved from stable-diffusion-inpainting: https://huggingface.co/runwayml/stable-diffusion-inpainting

Huggingface. (2024b). *huggingface diffusers*. Retrieved from huggingface diffusers: https://github.com/huggingface/diffusers/tree/main/examples/research_projects/dreambooth_inpaint

Hughes, R., Zhu, L., & Bednar, T. (2021). Generative Adversarial Networks–Enabled Human–Artificial Intelligence Collaborative Applications for Creative and Design Industries: A Systematic Review of Current Approaches and Trends. *Frontiers in Artificial Intelligence*, *17*, 604234. Advance online publication. doi:10.3389/frai.2021.604234 PMID:33997773

Jovanović, M., & Campbell, M. (2022). Generative Artificial Intelligence: Trends and Prospects. *Computer*, 107-112. https://doi.ieeecomputersociety.org/10.1109/MC.2022.3192720

LAION. (2022). *LAION-Aesthetics_Predictor V1*. Retrieved 02 12, 2024, from LAION-Aesthetics_Predictor V1: https://github.com/LAION-AI/aesthetic-predictor

LAION-AI. (2021). *Watermark-detection*. Retrieved 02 12, 2024, from watermark-detection: https://github.com/LAION-AI/watermark-detection

Li, J., Li, D., Savarese, S., & Hoi, S. (2023). *BLIP-2: Bootstrapping Language-Image Pre-training with Frozen Image Encoders and Large Language Models. In International Conference on Machine Learning*. ACM. https://dl.acm.org/doi/10.5555/3618408.3619222

Li, M., Lv, J., Wang, J., & Sang, Y. (2020). An Abstract Painting Generation Method Based on Deep Generative Model. *Neural Processing Letters*, *52*(2), 949–960. doi:10.1007/s11063-019-10063-3

Lingua. (2022). *The most accurate natural language detection library*. Retrieved 02 12, 2024, from The most accurate natural language detection library: https://github.com/pemistahl/lingua

McKinsey Global Publishing. (2023). *What is generative AI?* McKinsey Global Publishing. Retrieved from https://www.mckinsey.com/~/media/mckinsey/featured%20insights/mckinsey%20explainers/what%20is%20generative%20ai/what%20is%20generative%20ai.pdf

Meta. (2024). *Meta Horizon*. Retrieved from Meta Horizon Worlds: https://horizon.meta.com

Pfeiffer Consulting. (2018). *Creativity and technology in the age of AI*. Pfeiffer Consulting. Retrieved from https://www.pfeifferreport.com/wp-content/uploads/2018/11/Creativity_and_AI_Report_INT.pdf

Shah, N., Engineer, S., Bhagat, N., Chauhan, H., & Shah, M. (2020). Research Trends on the Usage of Machine Learning and Artificial Intelligence in Advertising. *Augmented Human Research*, *5*(1), 19. doi:10.1007/s41133-020-00038-8

Shakked, N., & Whitney, Z. (2023). Experimental Evidence on the Productivity Effects of Generative Artificial Intelligence. *SSRN*, *15*. Advance online publication. doi:10.2139/ssrn.4375283

Stanford University Human-Centered Artificial Intelligence. (2023). *Generative AI: Perspectives from Stanford HAI*. Stanford University. Retrieved from https://hai.stanford.edu/sites/default/files/2023-03/Generative_AI_HAI_Perspectives.pdf

STEAM. (2024). *Traveler - The AI Story*. Retrieved from Traveler - The AI Story: https://store.steampowered.com/app/2216270/Traveler__The_AI_Story/

Takagi, Y., & Nishimoto, S. (2023). High-Resolution Image Reconstruction With Latent Diffusion Models From Human Brain Activity. In *Conference on Computer Vision and Pattern Recognition* (pp. 14453-14463). IEEE. 10.1109/CVPR52729.2023.01389

Turchi, T., Carta, S., Ambrosini, L., & Malizia, A. (2023). Human-AI Co-creation: Evaluating the Impact of Large-Scale Text-to-Image Generative Models on the Creative Process. In *International Symposium on End User Development* (pp. 35–51). Springer. 10.1007/978-3-031-34433-6_3

Vakratsas, D., & Wang, X. (2021). Artificial Intelligence in Advertising Creativity. *Journal of Advertising, 50*(1), 39–51. doi:10.1080/00913367.2020.1843090

Wang, X., Yu, K., Wu, S., Gu, J., Liu, Y., Dong, C., & Loy, C. (2019). *ESRGAN: Enhanced Super-Resolution Generative Adversarial Networks. In Computer Vision – ECCV Workshops*. ACM. doi:10.1007/978-3-030-11021-5_5

Weisz, J., Muller, M., He, J., & Houde, S. (2023). Toward General Design Principles for Generative AI Applications. *Arxiv*, 16. doi:https://doi.org//arXiv.2301.05578 doi:10.48550

World Economic Forum. (2023). *Top 10 Emerging Technologies of 2023*. World Economic Forum. Retrieved from https://www3.weforum.org/docs/WEF_Top_10_Emerging_Technologies_of_2023.pdf

Yousif, S., & Vermisso, E. (2022). *Towards AI-assisted design workflows for an expanded design space. In International Conference of the Association for Computer-Aided Architectural Design Research in Asia*. CAADRIA. Retrieved from https://papers.cumincad.org/data/works/att/caadria2022_503.pdf

Yu, T., Lin, C., Zhang, S., Wang, C., An, H., Liu, X., ... Zhang, J. (2022). Artificial Intelligence for Dunhuang Cultural Heritage Protection: The Project and the Dataset. *International Journal of Computer Vision, 130*(11), 2646–2673. doi:10.1007/s11263-022-01665-x

Zeng, Z., Sun, X., & Liao, X. (2019). Artificial Intelligence Augments Design Creativity: A Typeface Family Design Experiment. In *International Conference on Human-Computer Interaction* (pp. 400–411). Springer. 10.1007/978-3-030-23541-3_29

Zhou, E., & Lee, D. (2023). Generative AI, Human Creativity, and Art. *SSRN, 50*. Advance online publication. doi:10.2139/ssrn.4594824

Zhou, L., Wang, Q., Huang, K., & Lo, C. (2019). An Interactive and Generative Approach for Chinese Shanshui Painting Document. In *International Conference on Document Analysis and Recognition* (pp. 819-824). IEEE. 10.1109/ICDAR.2019.00136

KEY TERMS AND DEFINITIONS

Deep Generative Models: Neural networks with many hidden layers trained to approximate complicated, high-dimensional probability distributions. The goal is to learn an unknown or intractable probability distribution from a typically small number of independent and identically distributed samples.

DreamBooth: Is a training methodology used in text-to-image generation model that updates the entire Diffusion model by training on just a few images of a subject or style. It works by associating a special word in the prompt with the example images.

Fine-Tuning: Approach to transfer learning in which the weights of a pre-trained model are trained on new data. Is done on the entire neural network, or on only a subset of its layers, in which case the layers that are not being fine-tuned are frozen.

Generative Artificial Intelligence: Artificial intelligence capable of producing novel and realistic content across a broad spectrum (texts, images, audio, video, code) for various domains based on basic user prompts.

Inpainting: Task of reconstructing regions in an image. It is an important problem in computer vision and an essential functionality in many imaging and graphics applications, e.g. object removal, image restoration, manipulation, re-targeting, compositing, and image-based rendering.

Latent Diffusion Model: Also known as diffusion probabilistic models or score-based generative models, are a class of latent variable generative models. Consists of three major components: the forward process, the reverse process, and the sampling procedure. The goal of Diffusion models is to learn a diffusion process that generates the probability distribution of a given dataset. They learn the latent structure of a dataset by modeling the way in which data points diffuse through their latent space.

Text-to-Image: Generation systems based on deep generative models for creating digital images and artworks. Given an input prompt in natural language, these generative systems are able to synthesize digital images of high aesthetic quality.

Section 4
Human–Computer Collaboration and Intellectual Property

Chapter 11

Artistic Expressions, Generative AI, and Legal Tapestry:

Exploring the Dynamics of Copyright Laws in the Confluence of AI and Artistic Creation

Anuttama Ghose
https://orcid.org/0000-0002-7210-4074
Dr. Vishwanath Karad MIT-World Peace University, India

S. M. Aamir Ali
https://orcid.org/0000-0002-8686-0217
Symbiosis Law School, Symbiosis International University (Deemed), Pune, India

Aayush Mayank Mishra
Dr. Vishwanath Karad MIT-World Peace University, India

ABSTRACT

This study delves into the transformative impact of generative artificial intelligence (AI) on creative production, exploring the collaborative efforts of artists and cutting-edge technology. The convergence of human ingenuity and AI in artistic expression expands creative boundaries but introduces complex intellectual property (IP) challenges. Examining beyond visual art, the study reveals the intricate engagement between humans and advanced algorithms, offering a unique perspective on the creative process. The intersection of AI and creativity raises critical copyright concerns, challenging traditional concepts of authorship and infringement. Addressing the global scope of AI-generated art, the study advocates for a unified framework to navigate legal complexities and ensure ethical considerations in the evolving landscape of creative technology.

DOI: 10.4018/979-8-3693-1950-5.ch011

1. INTRODUCTION

A revolutionary change is taking place in the dynamic field of creative production as artists work together with cutting-edge technology, most notably via the use of generative artificial intelligence (AI) tools for the creation of art. The convergence of human inventiveness and artificial intelligence not only broadens the scope of creative representation but also presents complex issues pertaining to intellectual property (IP) entitlements. As artists explore the domain of generative artificial intelligence (AI), the scope of creative expression extends beyond conventional artistic materials, incorporating the intangible worlds of algorithms and pixels (Somaya & Varshney, 2020). This study examines beyond the simple act of creating visual art as it goes into the complexities of human engagement with sophisticated algorithms (Dollens, 2014). It provides a unique perspective from which to understand and interpret the process of creativity. Artistic collaborations with the very structure of artificial intelligence produce everything from awe-inspiring visual compositions generated spontaneously to algorithms that are intentionally manipulated to elicit particular emotions (Jackson, 2017). The research methodology utilized in this work is distinguished by its comprehensive nature, as it will integrate legal analysis, case studies, and an exhaustive literature review. The legal analysis component entails a comprehensive scrutiny of domestic and international intellectual property legislation presently in effect with respect to art generated by artificial intelligence. This research further conducts an examination of copyright regulations, fair use doctrines, and the legal structures that regulate proprietorship and authorship in artificial intelligence-related creative works. Furthermore, this chapter will incorporate case studies to illustrate and offer insights into the practical difficulties encountered by legal practitioners, artists, and AI developers as they navigate the complex relationship between artificial intelligence and artistic expression.

This study is highly relevant and significant in today's society for a variety of reasons. As AI technology continues to progress, it is becoming more and more involved in the production of original artworks. This presents a unique challenge to the traditional concepts of authorship and ownership. This study offers valuable insights into the intricate legal aspects surrounding AI-generated art. It delves into crucial inquiries concerning copyright protection, attribution, and the rights of both creators and users. Furthermore, in a time characterized by swift technological advancements and the shift towards digitalization, it is crucial for policymakers, legal experts, artists, and individuals involved in the creative sectors to grasp the significance of AI's impact on intellectual property laws. This study provides valuable guidance for navigating the evolving landscape of copyright in the digital age, fostering informed decision-making and ensuring the fair and equitable treatment of creators and consumers alike. It examines the intersection of AI and artistic creation, offering insights from a legal perspective. In the end, the study's findings help us gain a deeper understanding of the complex connection between technology, creativity, and the law. This has significant implications for the future of artistic expression, innovation, and the enforcement of intellectual property rights.

The main objectives of this chapter are based on a thorough comprehension of the intellectual property (IP) environment related to the combination of creative expression and generative artificial intelligence (AI). Moreover, the need to update regulatory and legislative measures becomes evident when considering the adjustment of legal frameworks to effectively incorporate the swift advancements in AI technology. As we embark on an examination of creative expressions, generative AI, and the complex legal landscape, the subtleties of intellectual property assume a prominent role, influencing the discourse around the obstacles and possibilities inherent in this transformational convergence of creativity and technology. The chapter aims to explore the complexities of this growing artistic domain, with a specific focus on the contemporary methodologies used by persons who utilize AI to enhance and intensify their creative endeavors. A crucial element of this investigation is the scrutiny of ethical entitlements, with a particular emphasis on allocating contributions from human and machine collaborators. This research also examines the international aspects of AI-generated art from a critical perspective, aiming to comprehend and suggest remedies for the discrepancies in intellectual property rules across different countries.

2. BACKGROUND OF THE LITERATURE

The convergence of Artificial Intelligence with creative expression gives birth to an intricate terrain where several Intellectual Property issues emerge and need meticulous examination. This chapter examines the legal and theoretical basis for establishing property rights over works created by artificial intelligence and if copyright ownership should be assigned to the creators of the AI system. The study explores the utilitarian ethical theory, highlighting the significance of providing incentives to writers for producing works that contribute to the betterment of society. The text explores the role of copyright as a utilitarian tool that promotes creativity in artistic and practical products. The topic is substantiated by the writings of *Buccafusco*, elucidating the four fundamental principles of utilitarianism and its function in safeguarding intellectual property (Buccafusco, 2016). Furthermore, it references *Tasioulas* to emphasize the notion that AI systems have the capability to produce artwork without any external impetus (Tasioulas, 2022). The paper examines the assignment of copyright to AI systems, raising doubts about the suitability of natural rights concepts as a basis for justifying copyright ownership by AI. This examines the involvement of human developers in the creation of AI-generated works and the degree to which their contributions can be attributed to the end result. The discourse relies on the research conducted by *Barfield & Pagallo* to assert that natural rights principles are intrinsically relevant to human beings but not algorithms (Barfield & Pagallo, 2021). . The debate utilizes the research of *Barbosa* to examine the notion of natural rights theory and its consequences for intellectual property rights, specifically in relation to copyright protection for works created by artificial intelligence (Barbosa, 2009)

Additionally, the chapter cites *Hristov's* work to propose that property rights may not be necessary for AI-generated output if it significantly deviates from human input (Hristov, 2017). The conversation alludes to the research conducted by *Menninghaus* in order to investigate the essence of aesthetic feelings and their consequences for art produced by artificial intelligence (Menninghaus, 2019). It emphasizes the capacity of AI to transform our comprehension of art and creativity. The traditional notion of authorship is being challenged as a result of the significant participation of artificial intelligence in the creative process, hence prompting concerns about legal ownership. *Caldwell* elucidates philosophical views of authorship in his paper entitled "*What Is a 'Author'? Copyright Authorship of AI Art Through a Philosophical Lens*". The chapter explores the concept of inherent rights and its specific relevance to the safeguarding of copyright for works generated by artificial intelligence. The text examines the suitability of the notion of natural rights as a justification for granting copyright protection to works created by artificial intelligence. The debate cites *Choudhary & Ali's* works to analyze the issues of copyright infringement and fair use in AI art (Choudhary & Ali, 2023). It highlights the need of understanding how existing legal concepts tackle the specific challenges posed by AI-generated content. *Watiktinnakorn* and other researchers emphasize the potential infringement of existing copyrights as a major concern. This is particularly relevant when AI systems utilize large datasets that may contain copyrighted material, as discussed in their publication "*Blurring the lines: how AI is redefining artistic ownership and copyright*"

(Watiktinnakorn et al., 2023). The discussion further draws on the works of Salah, to explore the presence of systematic biases in AI systems and their impact on the output of AI-generated art, emphasizing the need for ethical considerations and measures to address bias in creative AI applications (Salah, 2021).

Cotter, in his article titled "*Transformative Use and Cognizable Harm,*" delves deeper into the intricate matter of distinguishing between transformative usage and copyright infringement. He explores the complexities surrounding the monetization of AI-generated art and the need to establish appropriate compensation frameworks for all parties involved (Cotter, 2010). Miernicki and Irene emphasize that acknowledging moral rights, such as the requirement for proper attribution, is essential for comprehending the various elements encompassed in the creative process, involving both human and machine collaborators, as discussed in their article "*Artificial intelligence and moral rights*" (Miernicki & Ng, 2021). The conversation references Dollens research to provide insights into the intricacies of human interaction with advanced algorithms in the creative process, emphasizing the profound influence of AI on artistic creativity (Dollen 2014). The global reach of art generated by AI presents a difficulty due to the variations in Intellectual Property laws among different nations. advocates for international alignment of intellectual property regulations to ensure uniformity and transparency for artists, developers, and stakeholders across different countries. This necessitates the development of a unified framework to ensure a logical and consistent approach. Ahuja highlights this need in his article titled "*Artificial Intelligence and Copyright: Issues and Challenges*" (Ahuja, 2020).

3. JURISPRUDENTIAL FOUNDATIONS OF INTELLECTUAL PROPERTY IN THE NEXUS OF AI AND ARTISTIC CREATION

3.1 Conceptual Understanding of Generative AI and its Legalities

The phrase "Artificial Intelligence" is not conducive to our public conversation. Artificial Intelligence lacks true intelligence. The phrase is very broad, without a clear definition, and hence cannot be debated with precision. But it is important for policy-makers to understand what they are encouraging or prohibiting. Passing a law to "restrict artificial intelligence" is a dangerous exercise under current definitions. Different functions of artificial intelligence create different problems for law and society. Generative AI creates not only new text, code, audio or video, but problems with deepfakes, plagiarism and falsehoods presented as convincing facts. AI that predicts whether a prisoner is likely to commit future crimes raises issues of bias, fairness and transparency. AI operating multi-ton vehicles on the road creates physical risks to human bodies. AI that masters the game the chess may not raise any societal issues at all. So why would politicians and courts treat them the same? Thus, in this study, the author attempts to categorically understand Generative AI through its functional ability in order to examine its accountability (Atlantic Council, 2023).

Generative AI utilizes predictive algorithms to generate outputs based on a given set of prompts. These AI tools may create very realistic imitations of human-like works, whether it be in the form of text or visual content, by meticulously reproducing each word or pixel. This may result in the creation of operational software code and functional websites, artistic works in the style of Jan van Eyck, scholarly articles on the use of symbols in The Scarlett Letter, or legal arguments in a contract dispute. These tools give rise to concerns around intellectual property and plagiarism, since they may be taught using unlawfully acquired content (Margetts, 2022). This technology has the capability to generate deep-fakes that are almost impossible to differentiate from concrete evidence. When it functions inadequately, it has the potential to produce utter gibberish portrayed as factual information. Generative artificial intelligence, including sophisticated language models like ChatGPT and image-generation software like Stable Diffusion, provide potent resources for people and enterprises. Additionally, they provoke significant and innovative inquiries about the utilization of data in AI models and the legal implications surrounding the outcomes of such models, such as a textual passage or a computer-generated picture (Zittrain, 2006).

3.2. Theoretical Framework Regarding Intellectual Property Rights Issues of Artificial Intelligence Creations

Generative artificial intelligence (AI) systems exhibit the capacity to autonomously generate textual content, visual imagery, and various other forms of creative material, thereby introducing intricate considerations within the realm of intellectual property rights and copyright protection. A captivating and dynamic topic of discussion in legal scholarship pertains to the jurisprudential underpinnings of intellectual property as it intersects with artistic creation and Artificial Intelligence (AI). The fundamental legal principles that regulate intellectual property must be thoroughly scrutinized as AI progressively emerges as a catalyst for innovation in the domain of artistic expression.

Jeremy Bentham and John Stuart Mill proposed the utilitarian theory of ethics in the 18th and 19th centuries. According to utilitarianism, one should consider the outcomes of an action while making a moral judgment. Utilitarianism holds that, ideally, we should aim to maximize the improvement of everyone's well-being. The four pillars of utilitarianism are aggregationism, impartiality, welfarism, and consequentialism (Buccafusco, 2016). The Utilitarian theory is commonly recognized as the fundamental basis for protecting intellectual property. To foster the creation of artistic or practical works that enhance society, these theories view copyright as a utilitarian mechanism. The promotion of artistic or utilitarian works involves fostering innovation that is inherent in utilitarian theory. According to scholarly research, without a catalyst for innovation, authors may be less motivated to invest the necessary resources, such as time, effort, and financial investment, to create literary works (Buccafusco, 2016). Others easily and affordably duplicate them, which reduces the authors' ability to gain advantages from their works. The utilization of utilitarian theory in analyzing artistic works created by artificial intelligence (AI) is mainly based on the belief that AI systems can generate artwork without the need for external motivation (Tasioulas, 2022). Artificial intelligence (AI) systems are not affected by short-term memory loss, information overload, sleep deprivation, or distractions, unlike humans. This allows them to function without the need for external support to mitigate these issues. Thus, when considering the incorporation of AI into the realm of copyright protection, the argument based on motivation presented by the utilitarian theory becomes unnecessary. Nevertheless, it is crucial to acknowledge that even when an artificial intelligence (AI) system is employed, human participation remains indispensable in the production of work. At first, AI systems are created by individuals, usually working together in teams. Furthermore, the active participation of individuals is crucial in the production of results by the existing artificial intelligence system. As an individual, you have the choice to either provide input data or, at the very least, start the AI system to begin generating work.

Further supporting the establishment of copyright protection for works produced by artificial intelligence is the theory of inherent rights. The natural rights theory, at its core, concerns the notion of intrinsically inviolable fundamental rights. John Locke, a philosopher, recognizes property as an intrinsic and fundamental natural right, asserting that people are entitled to both the results of their own labor and the merchandise of their efforts (Barbosa, 2009). It is imperative to take into account the contextual development of this theory, given that it originated in an era prior to the establishment of intellectual property legislation. Solely tangible property is applicable to the theory under a strict interpretation (Barbosa, 2009). Notwithstanding the conceptual nature of intellectual property, researchers have consistently utilized the structural framework of natural rights theory in the examination and discourse surrounding intellectual property. Since then, some individuals have begun to argue that intellectual property rights, particularly copyright, ought to be treated similarly to property rights associated with different types of assets. Therefore, one could contend that copyright protection is an intrinsic entitlement of authors, given that it ensures the security of the intellectual works that are the consequence of their scrupulous endeavors. Can the application of the principle of natural rights serve as a rationale for bestowing copyright protection upon works produced by artificial intelligence (AI) systems? The intricacy of the circumstance exceeds initial assessments, as demonstrated through the implementation of incentive theory (Barfield & Pagallo, 2021). The application of natural rights principles to justify the attribution of copyright to AI systems is unfounded, given that these principles are inherently applicable to human beings and not algorithms. It is crucial to contemplate the extent to which contributors to works produced by artificial intelligence have the ability to assert property rights over those works due to their efforts. However, can the effort put forth by human beings on a consistent basis be considered satisfactory and adequately linked to the final product, allowing them to claim dominion over the innovations produced by artificial intelligence?

When specific circumstances arise, human developers of artificial intelligence may consider the possible performance consequences that could be generated by the AI system. Regarding the Meandering River, it is probable that the programmers of the artificial intelligence (AI) system tasked with integrating and collecting satellite images for a real-time application had a comprehensive knowledge of the expected results that AI would produce. Under the condition that programmers had a thorough comprehension of the resultant output, it would be rational to attribute copyright ownership of the artwork produced by artificial intelligence to the original developers of the AI system. In a similar vein, certain judicial systems have recognized the unique safeguards afforded to the graphical user interface (GUI) in contrast to the software it operates on (Onformative, n.d.). It can be deduced from the foregoing discourse that there are circumstances in which the granting of exclusive rights to works generated by artificial intelligence may be considered suitable. This is especially true in cases where the individual has made a significant contribution to the development of the work, and that contribution is closely tied to the ultimate product. In the event that the output produced by the AI system substantially differs from the input given by human individuals, the theory of natural rights would not require property rights to be allocated for that output (Hristov, 2017). After that, this specific type of labor would be classified as belonging to the public domain and could therefore be put to use.

4. DELVING INTO COPYRIGHT INFRINGEMENT AND FAIR USE QUANDARIES IN AI ART

The changing environment requires a reassessment of traditional ideas such as authorship and ownership. The integration of AI technology poses a challenge to the conventional concept of creative authority, leading researchers and legal professionals to reassess ideas of personal authorship and shared ownership in relation to AI-assisted artistic production (Ghose & Ali, 2023). An essential aspect of this investigation is examining copyright infringement and fair use concerns (Choudhary & Ali, 2023). When trained on extensive datasets that may include copyrighted items, AI systems raise complex issues about originality and the allocation of intellectual property rights. An in-depth analysis of these matters requires a sophisticated comprehension of how current legal principles address, or potentially fail to address, the distinct difficulties presented by AI-generated material.

4.1 Articulating the Role of AI in Creative Genesis

Exploring the role of Artificial Intelligence (AI) in creative genesis constitutes a pivotal exploration within the context of intellectual property jurisprudence. This scholarly inquiry delves into the transformative influence of AI on the creative process, drawing insights from pertinent case studies that exemplify the intricate dynamics at the confluence of technology and artistic expression.

An exemplary instance is the production and ensuing legal ramifications around the AI-generated artwork, "Portrait of Edmond de Belamy," produced by the art team Obvious. The use of a generative adversarial network (GAN) to create a portrait that is completely created by an algorithm has prompted significant inquiries over the attribution and ownership of the artwork. This case highlights the need for legal frameworks to address the cooperative aspect of AI-human creative collaborations, which poses a challenge to conventional ideas of individual authorship. Similarly, "The Machine Hallucination" is an immersive art piece created by media artist Refik Anadol, using AI technology (Hencz, 2022). Refik Anadol utilizes a unique combination of AI algorithms and machine learning approaches to analyze enormous quantities of data pertaining to New York City. The collection comprises a wide range of sources, such as architectural plans, historical images, and modern photography. The AI system utilizes deep neural networks to acquire the ability to comprehend and produce visual content using extensive data collection. "The Machine Hallucination" poses thought-provoking inquiries on copyright and authorship from a legal perspective. The creativity process is characterized by collaboration among the artist, the AI system, and several sources of varied datasets. The legal discussion may examine the scope of copyright protection for images created by artificial intelligence and how intellectual property laws address the unique dynamics of cooperation between humans and AI in the arts (Artechouse, n.d.).

Further, we have also witnessed "The Next Rembrandt", an innovative artwork created using artificial intelligence in 2016. It was a joint effort by J. Walter Thompson Amsterdam, a Dutch advertising agency, Microsoft, and TU Delft, a Dutch art study and reproduction organization (Guadamuz, 2017). The research used machine learning techniques to examine Rembrandt's whole artistic collection, investigating his utilization of color, composition, and subject matter. The algorithms detected certain patterns and traits exclusive to Rembrandt's artistic style, allowing the AI system to produce an entirely original artwork that imitated the legendary artist's technique. The artwork titled "The Next Rembrandt" has sparked thought-provoking legal inquiries pertaining to the identification of the creator, the ownership of the artwork, and the protection of intellectual property rights. The AI system independently created the artwork by using acquired patterns from Rembrandt's body of work. This phenomenon blurred the boundaries of conventional authorship since the AI system functioned as a tool, but human designers were involved in its programming and guidance. The project highlighted the need for legal frameworks to adjust to the involvement of AI in the creative process, leading to debates on whether the AI system or its human designers should be recognized as the "author" of the artwork (Guadamuz, 2017).

The capacity of AI to evaluate extensive information and produce original, unexpected material creates a situation in which the line between human and machine-generated creativity becomes indistinct.

This raises significant inquiries about the originality and individuality often linked to works created by humans, requiring a thorough examination from a legal perspective. Furthermore, comprehending the function of AI in the creation of new ideas is crucial for defining intellectual property rights. As artificial intelligence (AI) plays a role in producing creative output, concerns emerge around the ownership and safeguarding of these works. The conventional framework of exclusive authorship privileges, deeply rooted in intellectual property principles, has to evolve in order to include the collaborative aspect of AI-human collaborations in the creative domain.

4.2 Deconstructing Traditional Notion of Artistic Authorship

The World Intellectual Property Office issued a study in 2020 named "Revised Issues Paper on Intellectual Property Policy and Artificial Intelligence" (WIPO, 2020). This publication provides a clear differentiation between "AI-assisted" and "AI-generated" outputs. The phrases "AI-generated output" and "AI-assisted output" both denote creations that are crafted with a certain level of human involvement and/or supervision. It is crucial to define the precise demarcation between outputs generated solely by AI and those facilitated by AI. The existence of a range of human interventions may complicate this differentiation. Typically, algorithms rely on human assistance to undergo "training," but if the system reaches a particular degree of maturity, the extent of human engagement may become insignificant. The level of assistance varies as the notion of autonomy evolves throughout time (Barfield & Pagallo, 2021).

Nevertheless, while considering copyright, it is crucial to see independence from a distinct perspective. The ability of the person using an AI system to anticipate the final outcome is a reliable determinant of whether the result was created solely by AI or assisted by AI. Hence, it is necessary to credit the algorithm for any instances of creativity that cannot be directly attributed to a human (Pokhariyal et al., 2020). Consequently, it is possible that the autonomy of an AI system starts exactly at the point when a human's intellectual output concludes. In such circumstances, the occurrence of "un-foreseeability" severs the connection between the outcome of the process and the one who launched it. The AI cannot be credited for providing inspiration if it is only utilized to bring to life an idea that has already been conceived. Hence, it ought to be regarded as AI-facilitated manufacturing. Thus, any output generated by an AI system without substantial and foreseeable creative contribution from a human author would be considered the result of an independent AI system. An AI is considered autonomous unless it is being guided by a human in a manner that enables it to exceed the limit of intellectual advancement achievable by humans. In general, copyright law does not provide protection for ideas. While the instructor is responsible for choosing the readings, determining the topic, and providing writing skills, they cannot be held accountable for the student's ultimate outcome (Gaon, 2021 pp 112-13). Within this document, AI-assisted output is explicitly characterized as creations that faithfully depict the author's initial intellectual creation, with the AI system functioning just as a tool (WIPO, 2020). Similar to how a camera serves as a device for capturing images and a computer is used for writing books, this instrument is also designed to accomplish a certain purpose.

4.3 Categorizing AI's Artistically Creative Capacity

When discussing AI's ability to be artistically creative, we can identify three different types of creativity that can help us understand the value of AI art: combinatory, transformational, and explanatory creativity.

4.3.1 *Combinatory Creativity*

Combinatory creativity within the realm of artificial intelligence manifests as the capacity to engender novel and innovative artistic expressions by adeptly amalgamating disparate elements or concepts gleaned from extensive datasets. In the context of AI's artistic prowess, this phenomenon entails the synthesis, fusion, or recombination of diverse artistic styles, patterns, or features to produce outputs that transcend conventional paradigms (Sawyer, 2014). This sophisticated ability enables AI systems to contribute meaningfully to the creative process by generating compositions or visual artworks that exhibit a level of originality extending beyond the confines of predefined templates. Thus, combinatorial creativity emerges as a transformative facet of AI, facilitating the generation of artistic expressions that are not only inspired by existing conventions but also imbued with a capacity to transcend and redefine established boundaries in the realm of artistic innovation (Sawyer, 2014).

4.3.2 Explanatory Creativity

Explanatory creativity in the domain of artificial intelligence pertains to the system's capacity to elucidate and rationalize the creative decisions or outputs it generates, thereby providing insight into the underlying processes. In the context of AI's artistic creativity, explanatory creativity involves the ability to articulate the reasoning behind the selection, synthesis, or adaptation of specific elements within a generated work. This facet of creativity enhances the interpretability and transparency of AI-generated art, fostering a deeper understanding of the machine's creative mechanisms (Boden, 2004). Through explanatory creativity, AI systems can articulate the conceptual frameworks, stylistic influences, or thematic considerations that inform their creative outputs, thereby contributing to a more profound comprehension of the collaborative interplay between algorithmic processes and artistic intuition. In essence, explanatory creativity bridges the gap between machine-generated art and human interpretation, enriching the discourse surrounding AI's role in the creative landscape (Boden, 2004).

4.3.3 *Transformational Creativity*

Transformational creativity in the context of artificial intelligence refers to the system's ability to bring about significant and profound changes in the creative process, resulting in the emergence of entirely new paradigms and artistic possibilities. Unlike incremental innovations, transformational creativity involves a radical departure from existing norms, introducing groundbreaking concepts and pushing the boundaries of artistic expression. In the realm of AI-generated art, transformational creativity may manifest as the generation of works that challenge conventional aesthetics, redefine established genres, or pioneer entirely novel modes of artistic representation (Boden, 2004). This facet of creativity within AI has the power to revolutionize the artistic landscape, inspiring not only awe and admiration but also sparking dialogue and reflection on the potential intersections between technology and human creativity. Through its transformative impact, AI's transformational creativity contributes to the ongoing evolution of artistic discourse, prompting new avenues of exploration and expanding the horizons of creative expression (Sawyer, 2014).

5. EXAMINING THE SIGNIFICANCE OF ARTISTIC INTENT AND PURPOSE IN HUMAN-CREATED AND AI-GENERATED ART

Art, at its most potent, has the ability to completely change the way someone sees the world and themselves, stirring profound emotions and fostering fresh insights. The convergence of art and artificial intelligence (AI) brings about a significant transformation in the dynamics of artistic creation, leading to a reassessment of the conventional principles that dictate the importance of artistic intent and purpose. The world of human-created art has always been seen as a powerful means of conveying the artist's intentions and giving voice to their emotions, ideas, and perspectives. The artist's deliberate choices, guided by personal encounters, cultural backgrounds, and societal stories, shape the intended message within a piece. From the brushstrokes of a painting to the composition of a photograph, or the arrangement of musical notes, the artist carefully selects each element to convey a story, evoke feelings, or provoke thoughts (Menninghaus et al., 2019). In a contrasting manner, the emergence of AI in art brings about a new perspective where the artist is no longer a conventional human creator but rather a sophisticated algorithm that has been trained on extensive datasets. The significance of AI-generated art resides in the fusion of various patterns, styles, and data embedded within the machine learning models. Although lacking personal experiences or conscious intentions, AI algorithms have the ability to mimic and combine elements from various sources to create unique and captivating artworks (Elam, 2022).

But will there be a purpose for AI art? AI has the potential to be, at the absolute least, a very useful tool for artists, much as a smart camera may be for fine art photographers. In such instances, the goal of the work is still determined by a human artist. When employing AI art-producing algorithms, an individual's education, personal history, and cultural background influence their decisions and changes to the first "drafts" of pictures created by the generator. In the event that AI becomes sentient, concerns about the intent behind AI art and its cultural setting—assuming any such work is created at all—will surface and complicate our relationship with it.

Understanding the purpose behind art, whether it is created by humans or generated by AI, can be quite difficult. In the realm of human-created art, the artist's subjective experiences and nuanced emotions may not always be readily apparent to the viewer. Likewise, art created by AI does not have a conscious creator, which makes it difficult to ascribe traditional ideas of intention to the artwork. This prompts philosophical inquiries regarding the essence of intention and whether it requires conscious agency to be considered valid (Jung, 2020). The intersection of human-created and AI-generated art signifies a significant moment in the development of artistic intent. The interaction between the artist and the artwork takes on a complex dynamic of deliberate decisions, subconscious influences, and algorithmic factors. The importance of intention goes far beyond the contrast between humans and machines, encouraging a more comprehensive examination of the purpose that arises from working together, enhancing abilities, and the harmonious relationship between creativity and technology. The complex relationship between human agency, deterministic algorithms, and the ever-evolving capabilities of technology calls for a detailed examination of intention and objective. As the world of art progresses, researchers, creators, and viewers are faced with the challenge of understanding the complexities that shape the intentional manifestation of imagination, surpassing the limits of the natural and the man-made (Ginsburg & Budiardjo, 2019).

6. OVERVIEW OF LEGAL PROTECTION AVAILABLE TO THE ARTWORK CREATED BY AI UNDER THE COPYRIGHT REGIME

Original ideas from the "author" play a crucial role in obtaining copyright for a work. Looking at the situation from a broader perspective, it is worth noting that Article 2.6 of the Berne Convention acknowledges the importance of copyright protection in favor of the creator (UN WIPO, 1886). However, it is worth mentioning that the convention does not provide a specific definition for the term "author." Within the copyright law of the European Union (EU), the concept of "author" remains undefined. However, a significant ruling by the European Union Court of Justice in the case of *Eva-Maria Painer v Standard Verlags GmbH 1* (2011) established that only creations made by humans would be protected. This idea is reflected in the legal systems of civil law countries like Spain (The Intellectual Property Act, 2012), France (Intellectual Property Code, 2022), and Germany (Copyright Act, 2017), where it is necessary for works to bear the unique mark of the author's personality (Ramalho, 2022). However, AI systems are unable to achieve authorship as they lack the ability to infuse their creations with a distinct personality. In countries such as Australia, New Zealand, the United Kingdom, Canada, and others, copyright law is founded on the idea of promoting social well-being (Vezina & Moran, n.d.). It recognizes that in order to encourage the creation of works, it is important to provide rewards and incentives while also ensuring public access. From this perspective, the importance of personality in relation to authorship is diminished, suggesting that non-human authors could potentially be considered. In the United States, the Macaque selfie case of 2016 reached the conclusion that photographs taken by a monkey cannot be granted copyright (*Naruto et al v. David Slater*, 2018). This decision was based on the fact that the photographs were taken without any human intervention. In line with the perspective of the US Copyright Office, it is believed that works created by animals are not eligible for registration (Sarmiento, 2014). Works generated by computer programs are granted copyright in countries like Ireland, New Zealand, the United Kingdom, and India.

In the Indian Copyright legislation, according to "Section 2(d) of the Indian Copyright Act, 1957", the term "author," "*in the case of a literary or dramatic work, the author; in the case of a musical piece, the composer; in the case of a computer-generated literary, dramatic, musical, or artistic work, the person who causes the work to be made*", while specified, in concerns involving autonomously generated computer labor, it is left somewhat open-ended. This is evident from the mentioned section and is emphasized in various parts that discuss the author's family, life, and passing (Copyright Act, 1957). The application of the law is unquestionable when it comes to AI software created by humans. This is because it aligns with the Copyright law's idea that a person is the original author/creator. However, as AI evolves and becomes more capable of generating unique creations and independent products, its status as a mere assistant to humans becomes less significant. This poses a challenge to the Copyright law's definition of a person as the original author/creator (Barfield, 2006). It is important to highlight that according to sub-clause (vi) of the Act, the individual who creates the computer-generated work is considered the author. The provision seems to overlook the possibility of computers being capable of human-like behavior. Instead, it only takes into account computers that are operated by humans (Rehan, n.d.).

There is a gap in the law regarding whether an AI can possess autonomous creativity and be entitled to separate ownership rights due to the assumption that computers can only assist human creativity. It is important to mention that the purpose of the Act was to restrict copyright law to individuals. As stated in section 22, any work created during the author's lifetime is only legally protected for a period of 60 years, starting from the first day of the calendar year following the year of the author's death (Copyright Act, 1957). In this case, the author's personality has a significant impact. However, it is important to highlight a significant gap in the Indian Copyright Act. The definition of "author" does not explicitly include the requirement of being a "human" or consider the author's legal personality (Kulkarni, 2016). Just recently, the copyright office in India recognized the artistic contribution of an AI tool called "Raghav" (Sarkar, 2021). This painting app has been granted copyright protection, acknowledging its role as a co-author of artistic work. Given the absence of a specific requirement stating that the author must be a "natural person," it is possible to consider AI as a co-author, at the very least (Lath, 2022). At present, possessing human-like intellectual abilities and expertise in a particular field, such as writing novels or creating paintings, is not sufficient to grant AI legal personality status. Thus, despite the potential of AI to become a prominent figure in ownership, complications arise due to the unclear definition of "author" in copyright law.

Protecting artists and encouraging them to create more creative works is the main goal of copyright laws. But AI doesn't need that kind of incentive to crank out additional material. Because of this, it is also considered impossible to divide up ownership of the public domain. Every possible solution has its own set of limitations, and there is no one certain way to fix this problem.

7. CHALLENGES AND CONCERNS INHERENT IN AI-GENERATED ART: A FUTURIST STUDY

Technology has the potential to be abused. An inherent drawback of deep learning is that biases present in training data sets might be concretely manifested. AI "predictions" include systematic biases present in the legal system, employment procedures, and loan procurement while creating a sense of impartiality (Salah, 2021). The current output of Dall-E reinforces and perpetuates preconceptions related to race and gender. While individuals may generally have no difficulty recognizing a dog, their ability to discern outstanding art might greatly differ. Male European masters may still get more praise than women or underrepresented minority artists, as well as those who have yet to gain recognition (Walsh et al., 2021).

Conversely, the present custodians of art, whether its prestigious galleries, museums, or biennales, already exhibit a predisposition towards certain artists and artworks. In the future, the accessibility of AI-generated art may increase, allowing for more participation and involvement. Art institutions throughout are converting their collections into digital formats. The art market in the 21st Century encompasses regions outside Europe and the United States. Significant exhibitions as a component of art's globalization now extend beyond Venice, Basel, and Miami to include prominent events in Sao Paulo, Dakar, Istanbul, Sharjah, Singapore, and Shanghai (Chatterjee, 2022). In addition to prominent exhibitions, smaller art galleries are digitizing and promoting their collections. With the inclusion of a greater variety of pictures, including artwork from Asia, Africa, and South America, as well as unconventional art forms like street art or textile art, the definition of what is considered excellent or great art may become more comprehensive and inclusive.

Is it possible for art to devolve into a competition based on popularity? In order to maintain public interest, museums might use artificial intelligence (AI) to forecast the kind of art that will attract the largest number of spectators. Utilizing AI in this manner might limit the variety of artworks that are shown. Likewise, some artists may choose to create art using conventional methods but adapt their production to align with AI-generated predictions of market demand. Over time, art may gradually diminish in its originality, its ability to challenge societal norms and its wide range of forms. The disposition of the artist may also undergo transformation if the aptitudes required for creating art undergo alteration. An artist working in collaboration with AI may use machine learning outputs at the first part of their creative process and include their own input, along with more AI assessments, in the later stages of evaluating and making art (Taylor, 2022).

A notable concern revolves around the utilization of AI in the advancement of deepfake technologies. Deepfakes utilize advanced algorithms to produce incredibly realistic fabricated videos or images, frequently portraying individuals engaging in actions or making statements they never actually did (Chesney & Citron, 2019). This technology has the potential to be used in a harmful manner, as it can deceive and manipulate viewers by presenting fake content as real. This raises important ethical concerns regarding misinformation and the potential harm that can be caused by manipulated visuals. Furthermore, there is a larger issue surrounding the creation of deceptive information using AI. With the increasing proficiency of artificial intelligence in generating lifelike images and videos, there is a concern that some may misuse this ability to create misleading or deceitful content. This could involve producing counterfeit artworks, altering historical footage, or manufacturing evidence in legal or political situations. The result poses a threat to the credibility of information as it becomes more and more challenging to differentiate between genuine and altered visuals (Chesney & Citron, 2019). The potential impact of AI in manipulating visual narratives is highlighted, highlighting the concerns it raises in relation to societal norms surrounding trust and authenticity. In a world where digital content plays a significant role in shaping perceptions and narratives, the use of AI to generate realistic but misleading visuals raises concerns about the trustworthiness of visual information. This disrupts traditional beliefs in trust, as people may grow more doubtful of the credibility of images and videos they come across in different situations, such as news, social media, and other means of communication (Schick, 2023).

In addition, there is a debate going on about the aesthetic characteristics of art that is produced by artificial intelligence. Some people believe that it does not have the genuine emotional depth and conscious intentionality that is present in art that is created by humans. The authenticity of creative expression emerges as a significant point of contention, with sceptics questioning whether artificial intelligence is capable of really capturing the essence of human creativity and passion. The need for creative services may decrease. AI has the potential to replace artists who work as illustrators for books, technical manuals, and other media, including ads, by creating visuals. The absence of these lucrative positions may provide a challenge for some artists in their pursuit of fine art aspirations, particularly if they lack a dependable means of financial support.

8. CONCLUSION

In conclusion, our investigation into the intersection of creative manifestation, generative artificial intelligence (AI), and the corresponding realm of intellectual property (IP) exposes a multifaceted and swiftly evolving domain. The advent of AI technologies in artistic collaborations has presented significant challenges to the conventional paradigms of authorship, ownership, and copyright. The research has emphasized the complex dynamics that revolve around art created by artificial intelligence (AI), providing insights into matters like identifying the creator, managing the potential for copyright violations, and dealing with the concept of transformative usage within the framework of current legal systems. The research has also highlighted the worldwide scope of AI art, advocating for the need to establish international alignment of intellectual property (IP) regulations in order to guarantee uniformity and transparency for artists, developers, and interested parties across different countries. Furthermore, the study has emphasized the urgent want for flexible legal frameworks that can proficiently tackle the difficulties presented by the ever-changing development of artificial intelligence technology. This research aims to enhance our complete knowledge of the complex difficulties and potential possibilities surrounding AI-generated art and intellectual property (IP) by including legal analysis, case studies, literature evaluation, and stakeholder viewpoints.

The notion that creative pursuits are an invincible stronghold of humanity is unsustainable. AI is already being utilized as a formidable tool and even as a collaborator for some artists. The continuous advancement of machines with a keen sense of aesthetics will push the boundaries of our perception of beauty and creativity and potentially reshape our comprehension of art. In the current juncture when technological advancement and artistic manifestation converge, the outcomes of this research endorse the adoption of a cooperative and progressive mindset. Ongoing communication among policymakers, legal practitioners, artists, and AI developers is crucial in order to establish a legislative framework that fosters innovation while ensuring the protection of the rights of all relevant stakeholders. By implementing this approach, it is possible to cultivate a setting in which the collaboration between human ingenuity and artificial intelligence flourishes while also guaranteeing ethical, legal, and fair results for the continuously increasing domain of AI-generated art.

REFERENCES

Ahuja, V. K. (2020, Winter). Artificial Intelligence and Copyright: Issues and Challenges. *ILI Law Review*, 270-285. https://ili.ac.in/pdf/vka.pdf

Artechouse. (n.d.). Artechouse announces the return of the ground breaking exhibition machine hallucinations: NYC with refik anadol for a special limited-duration run in New York City. *Artechouse.* https://www.artechouse.com/news/artechouse-announces-return-of-machine-hallucination-nyc/

Atlantic Council. (2023). Annex 6: Learning from Cybersecurity, Preparing for Generative AI. In *Scaling Trust The On Web* (pp. 1–12). Atlantic Council. https://www.jstor.org/stable/resrep51651.26

Barbosa, R. G. (2009). The Philosophical Approaches to Intellectual Property and Legal Transplants - The Mexican Supreme Court and NAFTA Article 1705. *Houston Journal of International Law*, *31*(3), 515–564.

Barfield, W. (2006). Intellectual Property Rights in Virtual Environments: Considering the Rights of Owners, Programmers and Virtual Avatars. *Akron Law Review*, *39*(3), 649–700.

Barfield, W., & Pagallo, U. (2021). *Advanced Introduction to Law and Artificial Intelligence*. Edward Elgar Publishing Ltd.

Boden, M. A. (2004). *The Creative Mind: Myths and Mechanisms*. Psychology Press. doi:10.4324/9780203508527

Buccafusco, C. (2016). A theory of copyright authorship. *Virginia Law Review*, *102*(5), 1229–1295. https://www.jstor.org/stable/43923336

Caldwell, M. (2023). What is an “author”? -Copyright authorship of ai art through a philosophical lens. *Houston Law Review*, *61*(2), 411–442. https://houstonlawreview.org/article/92132-what-is-an-author-copyright-authorship-of-ai-art-through-a-philosophical-lens

Chatterjee, A. (2022). Art in an age of artificial intelligence. *Frontiers in Psychology*, *13*, 1024449. doi:10.3389/fpsyg.2022.1024449 PMID:36533018

Chesney, B., & Citron, D. (2019). Deep fakes: A looming challenge for privacy, democracy, and national security. *California Law Review*, *107*(6), 1753–1820. https://www.jstor.org/stable/26891938

Choudhary, V. & Ali, A. S. M. (2023). ChatGPT and Copyright Concerns. *Economic and Political Weekly*, *58*(16), 4–5.

Copyright, D., & Act, P. United Kingdom (1988). https://www.legislation.gov.uk/ukpga/1988/48/contents

Cotter, T. (2010). Transformative use and cognizable harm. *Vanderbilt Journal of Entertainment and Technology Law*, *12*(4), 701–753. https://scholarship.law.vanderbilt.edu/jetlaw/vol12/iss4/3

Dollens, D. (2014). Alan Turing’s Drawings, Autopoiesis and Can Buildings Think? *Leonardo*, *47*(3), 249–253. doi:10.1162/LEON_a_00766

Elam, M. (2022). Signs taken for wonders: Ai, art & the matter of race. *Daedalus*, *151*(2), 198–217. doi:10.1162/daed_a_01910

Eva-Maria Painer v Standard Verlags GmbH 1[2011] ECR I-2533

Gaon, A. H. (2021). *The Future of Copyright in the Age of Artificial Intelligence*. Edward Elgar Publishing Ltd. doi:10.4337/9781839103155

Ghose, A. & Ali, A. S. M. (2023). Amplifying Music with Artificial Intelligence. *Economic and Political Weekly*, *58*(17), 4–6.

Ginsburg, J. C., & Budiardjo, L. A. (2019). Authors and machines. *Berkeley Technology Law Journal*, *34*(2), 343–448. https://www.jstor.org/stable/26954389

Guadamuz, A. (2017). Artificial intelligence and copyright. *WIPO Magazine*. https://www.wipo.int/wipo_magazine/en/2017/05/article_0003.html

Hencz, A. (2022, August 19). Digitized memories and machine hallucinations. *Artland Magazine*. https://magazine.artland.com/refik-anadol/

Hristov, K. (2017). Artificial Intelligence and the Copyright Dilemma. *IDEA: The Journal of the Franklin Pierce Center for Intellectual Property*, *57*(3), 431–454.

Jackson, T. E. (2017). Imitative Identity, Imitative Art, and “AI: Artificial Intelligence.” *Mosaic: An Interdisciplinary Critical Journal, 50*(2), 47–63. https://www.jstor.org/stable/45158927

Jung, G. (2020). Do androids dream of copyright?: Examining ai copyright ownership. *Berkeley Technology Law Journal*, *35*(4), 1151–1178. https://www.jstor.org/stable/27121773

Kulkarni, R. M. (2016, December 16). *Of Artificial Intelligence and Authorship*. Spicy IP. https://spicyip.com/2016/12/of-artificial-intelligence-and-authorship.html

Lath, A. (2022, October 10). *AI Art and Indian Copyright Registration.* Spicy IP. https://spicyip.com/2022/10/ai-art-and-indian-copyright-registration.html

Margetts, H. (2022). Rethinking AI for Good Governance. *Daedalus, 151*(2), 360–371. https://www.jstor.org/stable/48662048. doi:10.1162/daed_a_01922

Menninghaus, W., Wagner, V., Wassiliwizky, E., Schindler, I., Hanich, J., Jacobsen, T., & Koelsch, S. (2019). What are aesthetic emotions? *Psychological Review, 126*(2), 171–195. doi:10.1037/rev0000135 PMID:30802122

Miernicki, M., & Ng, I. (2021). Artificial intelligence and moral rights. *AI & Society, 36*(1), 319–329. doi:10.1007/s00146-020-01027-6

Ministerio de Justicia, Spain. (2012). *The Intellectual Property Act.* https://www.wipo.int/edocs/lexdocs/laws/en/es/es177en.pdf

Naruto et al v. David Slater (2018) WL 1902414.

Onformative. (n.d.). *Meandering river.* https://onformative.com/work/meandering-river

Pokhariyal, P., Kashyap, A. K., & Prasad, A. B. (2020). *Artificial Intelligence: Law And Policy Implications.* Eastern Book Company.

Ramalho, A. (2022). *Intellectual Property Protection for AI-generated Creations Europe, United States, Australia and Japan.* Routledge, Taylor & Francis Group.

Rehan. (n.d.). *Who owns computer generated works.* Learn and Digest. https://learndigest.blogspot.com/2014/06/who-owns-computer-generated-works.html

Salah, A. A. A. (2021). AI bugs and failures: How and why to render AI-algorithms more human? In P. Verdegem (Ed.), *AI for Everyone?* (pp. 161–180). University of Westminster Press. https://www.jstor.org/stable/j.ctv26qjjhj.12

Sarkar, S. (2021, August 5). *India recognises AI as co-author of copyrighted artwork.* Managing IP, https://www.managingip.com/article/2a5czmpwixyj23wyqct1c/exclusive-india-recognises-ai-as-co-author-of-copyrighted-artwork

Sarmiento, S. M. (2014, August 22). *Us copyright office says animal authors aren't protected by copyright.* Hyperallergic. https://hyperallergic.com/145217/us-copyright-office-says-animals-authors-arent-protected-by-copyright/

Sawyer, R. K. (2014). *Explaining Creativity: The Science of Human Innovation.* Oxford University Press.

Schick, N. (2023). Faking It: Navigating the new era of generative AI may be the most critical challenge to democracy yet. *RSA Journal, 169*(2), 40–43. https://www.jstor.org/stable/48737215

Somaya, D., & Varshney, L. R. (2020). Ownership Dilemmas in an Age of Creative Machines. *Issues in Science and Technology, 36*(2), 79–85. https://www.jstor.org/stable/26949112

Tasioulas, J. (2022). Artificial intelligence, humanistic ethics. *Daedalus, 151*(2), 232–243. doi:10.1162/daed_a_01912

Taylor, J. (2022, July 28). No Quick Fix: How OpenAI's DALL-E 2 illustrated the challenges of bias in AI. *NBC News*. https://www.nbcnews.com/tech/tech-news/no-quick-fix-openais-dalle-2-illustrated-challenges-bias-ai-rcna39918

The Copyright Act, 1957 (Act 14 of 1957), India. s. 2(d). https://copyright.gov.in/documents/copyright-rules1957.pdf

UN WIPO. (1886, September 9). *Berne Convention for the Protection of Literary and Artistic Works,* No. 11850.

Vezina, B., & Moran, B. (n.d.). *Artificial Intelligence and Creativity: Why We're Against Copyright Protection for AI-Generated Output*. Creative Commons. https://creativecommons.org/2020/08/10/no-copyright-protection-for-ai-generated-output/

Walsh, K. R., Mahesh, S., & Trumbach, C. C. (2021). Autonomy in ai systems: Rationalizing the fears. *The Journal of Technology Studies*, *47*(1), 38–47. https://www.jstor.org/stable/48657934

Watiktinnakorn, C., Seesai, J., & Kerdvibulvech, C. (2023). Blurring the lines: How AI is redefining artistic ownership and copyright. *Discover Artificial Intelligence*, *3*(1), 37. doi:10.1007/s44163-023-00088-y

WIPO. Germany. Copyright Act, 2017. https://www.wipo.int/wipolex/en/legislation/details/17676

WIPO. (2020, May 21). *Conversation on Intellectual Property (IP) and Artificial Intelligence (AI)*, Second Session, Revised Issues Paper on Intellectual Property Policy and Artificial Intelligence, WIPO. https://www.wipo.int/edocs/mdocs/mdocs/en/wipo_ip_ai_2_ge_20/wipo_ip_ai_2_ge_20_1_rev.pdf

WIPO. France. Intellectual Property Code, 2022. https://www.wipo.int/wipolex/en/legislation/details/19865

Zittrain, J. L. (2006). The Generative Internet. *Harvard Law Review*, *119*(7), 1974–2040. https://www.jstor.org/stable/4093608

KEY TERMS AND DEFINITIONS

AI Art: AI art, also known as generative art or computational creativity, refers to artworks that are created with the assistance of artificial intelligence (AI) algorithms and machine learning techniques.

Algorithm Bias: Algorithmic bias refers to repeated mistakes in a computer system that unfairly favor one user group over another.

Artificial Intelligence: The theory and development of computer systems that can execute human activities, including visual perception, voice recognition, decision-making, and language translation.

Generative AI: Generative AI is an artificial intelligence that can generate text, pictures, audio, and synthetic data.

Chapter 12
Artificial Intelligence in Architecture: Innovations, Challenges, and Ethical Considerations

Ilker Karadag
https://orcid.org/0000-0001-7534-2839
Faculty of Fine Arts, Design, and Architecture, Manisa Celal Bayar University, Turkey

Aslı Yıldız
Faculty of Engineering and Architecture, Nevşehir Hacı Bektaş Veli University, Turkey

ABSTRACT

The advent of artificial intelligence (AI) has significantly impacted many disciplines, including architecture. AI started redefining design boundaries and possibilities by opening up new realms of creativity. Within this scope, this chapter investigates the integration of AI in architectural design by exploring the potential of these advanced technologies. Moreover, ethical considerations regarding the role of AI in architectural design, which is an area of increasing importance and complexity, will also be investigated. The chapter will also engage with concerns about the potential loss of human touch in the design process, a critical aspect considering the intrinsic value of personal creativity and intuition in architecture. By addressing these concerns and presenting a detailed view, the chapter aims to foster a comprehensive understanding of AI's role in architecture, proposing an informed approach to integrate AI tools in the architectural design process.

1. INTRODUCTION

In the past, architectural creations were a direct result of human creativity. Materials were shaped by man's innate ability to make. Even though human creativity has been partially interrupted by developing technologies throughout history, human cognitive nature has never been interrupted. Human creative power

DOI: 10.4018/979-8-3693-1950-5.ch012

Figure 1. The modernist architect Le Corbusier and AI architects

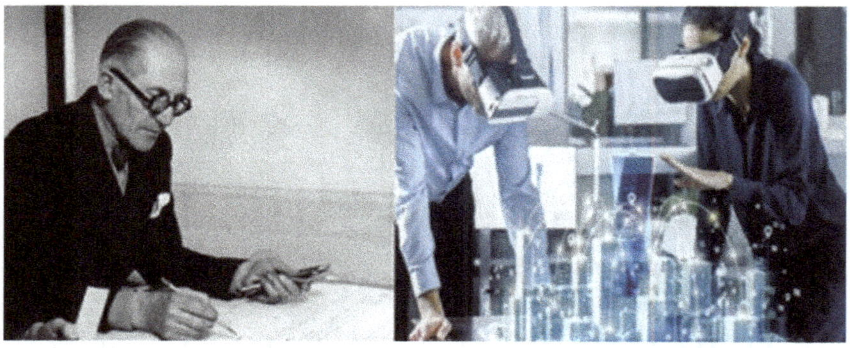

has always maintained its importance until the modern age. In the modern era, architectural creations are inextricably linked to technology and the advances made in this field. Human creativity is undergoing a severe transformation, especially in the age of artificial intelligence. New materials, new technologies and new aesthetic approaches are shaped by the unlimited possibilities offered by artificial intelligence.

With artificial intelligence, a multifaceted technological revolution occurs in all sectors. As in every field, architecture is also taking its share of this development, and the possibilities of using artificial intelligence in this field are increasing. According to the American Institute of Architects (AIA), it is predicted that approximately 90% of architectural firms will either start using artificial intelligence or increase their use in the next three years. According to Lane (2023), artificial intelligence has the potential to automate up to 37% of the tasks performed by architects and engineers. However, this automation is likely to target routine and less creative tasks, allowing professionals to focus more on the strategic and creative aspects of their work. Similar to how Building Information modeling (BIM) software and 3D design software did not replace architects but transformed their workflows, the same principle applies to artificial intelligence tools, as well (Figure 1).

In parallel with the increasing importance of artificial intelligence, it is noticed that artificial intelligence studies are gaining popularity in the related literature. The relationship of artificial intelligence with architecture and creativity is an area that has recently been more recognized and questioned. Therefore, there is a limited number of studies on the subject. One of these studies is conducted by Zhang et al. (2023), where the designs of the famous architect Antoni Gaudi were produced through an artificial intelligence system. These designs were evaluated based on originality, appeal, creativity, harmony, and preferability parameters. The study concluded that designs produced by artificial intelligence exhibited competitive results in the categories of appeal and creativity. Moreover, AI-Sayed et al. (2021) investigated spatial features and patterns associated with creativity that could be used to distinguish between creativity and efficiency in design. The drawing activities of a group of 12 architects were recorded. An experienced group of architects then evaluated these designs by considering creativity and efficiency. In addition, Hanafy (2023) conducted a study that explored the effectiveness of artificial intelligence tools, specifically DALL-E2, Midjourney, and Stable Diffusion, in generating typical examples for use in architectural design. A total of 2.6 million contents serving architectural purposes were identified in an artificial intelligence system with a database of approximately 40 million. Thus, Hanafy's study reveals the diversity and comprehensiveness of the databases of artificial intelligence systems in terms of architecture. Similarly, Mrosla et al. (2019) discussed the extent to which artificial intelligence, based on different concepts and examples, has shaped the profession of architecture through its contemporary potential applications and underlying algorithms. In the study by Qian et al. (2023), a method is presented where architectural sketches are reproduced with AI according to concepts of form preference and architectural fusion. Sketches incorporating artistic style and local cultural elements based on user preferences were produced. A study by Mirra and Pugnale (2021) revealed that design outputs produced by artificial intelligence possessed greater diversity compared to those produced by human hands. Li and Xu (2022) used the CycleGAN algorithm to generate building images from sketches. Chen et al. (2023) developed a method based on artificial intelligence tools to help ordinary designers improve their design quality.

In the following sections, the state-of-the-art studies on the use of artificial intelligence in architecture and design have been examined. Assessing the relationship of artificial intelligence with architecture and creativity in a theoretical framework is an area that is still up to date. The fact that AI is in its developmental stage and limited use in architecture makes it difficult to understand how these systems create a paradigm shift in architecture. Therefore, discussing the relationship of AI with architecture and creativity within the framework of relevant studies in literature and architectural projects will be helpful for architects and designers. Using a qualitative research method, the study questions how AI affects architectural creativity and the possibilities, limitations, and legal aspects of its use in architecture. As a result of the evaluations made, the opportunities provided by AI in architectural creativity are summarized in a detailed table. The study also includes examples of architectural projects that produce creative solutions using AI. Three architectural projects utilizing AI designed by renowned architects Zaha Hadid, BIG Architects, and Foster+Partners are analyzed.

2. TRANSFORMATIVE POTENTIALS AND APPLICATIONS OF ARTIFICIAL INTELLIGENCE IN ARCHITECTURE

Artificial intelligence, broadly defined, is a multidisciplinary approach that combines various aspects of computer science, psychology, and mathematics to create systems capable of thinking, perceiving, problem-solving, and understanding like humans (Russell & Norvig, 1995). Applying this approach to architecture has led to a paradigm shift in how architects plan, design, optimize, and manage their projects. Artificial intelligence is becoming increasingly influential in architecture and offers the potential to be influential in many ways. Primarily, design now involves expressing architectural concepts in words and transforming these into commands and scripts. By providing only words as input to the system, it is possible to obtain an unlimited number of design outputs. Even seemingly unrelated concepts can lead to impressive design outcomes due to AI (Matoso, 2023).

AI enables rapid development in architectural form and mass studies. Various scenarios and parameters can be tested in real time. AI tools can extract urban information from open-access databases and allow for mass studies considering environmental data, climate, wind, daylight, and land conditions. Thus, AI facilitates a more efficient and sustainable design process. Also, AI shortens the time between intention and implementation, providing designers with a new perspective and the ability to explore more design possibilities (Magsamen & Ivy, 2023).

Another potential impact of AI in architecture is the fundamental transformation in the field of visualization. Traditional architectural visualization techniques begin with three-dimensional modeling in solid modeling programs, followed by rendering and post-production processes. These processes are iterative and can be time-consuming. AI-assisted visualization tools, however, offer significant time sav-

Figure 2. Machine hallucinations by Refik Anadol

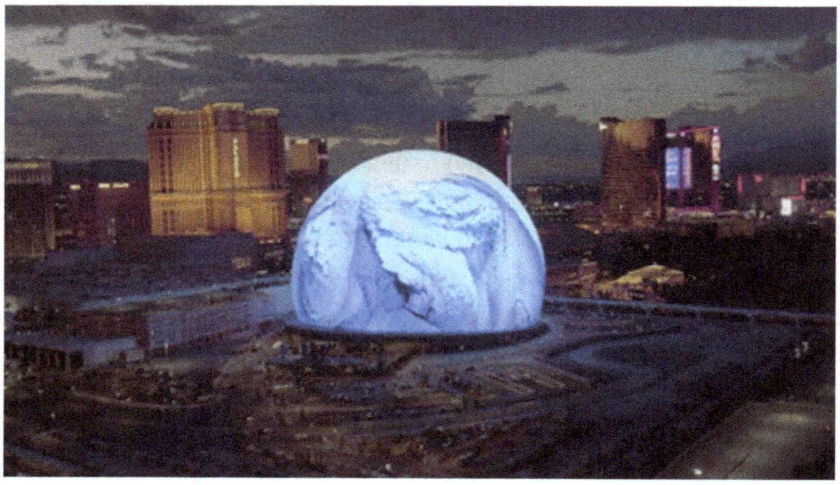

ings compared to traditional techniques. Architecture, encompassing various processes from the initial idea to implementation, is a multidimensional process. In this process, visualization plays a crucial role in pre-presenting the imagined design. Visualization is currently the most prominent area of AI use in architecture. According to Tovar (2023), visualization is valuable for expressing design ideas and interpreting and discussing aesthetic elements. Therefore, AI surpasses traditional methods in visualization, offering fast, easy, and creative solutions. Additionally, AI extends beyond 2D visualization, enhancing virtual interaction with buildings through virtual and augmented reality, allowing for a more detailed and real-time decision-making process regarding the building's design and layout (Figure 2) (Tovar, 2023).

Another opportunity provided by the use of AI in architecture is that it redefines existing workflows. The automation provided by AI both improves the way of working and creates a profound transformation in the industry. Thanks to AI systems, large amounts of data can be easily processed. It provides significant savings in business processes and reshapes the balance in work sharing. While laborious tasks that require automation can be easily handled with artificial intelligence, it offers more time and opportunity for tasks that require creativity and originality, which constitute architects' main focus and interest. According to Kåre Stokholm Poulsgaard of 3XN Architects, in the future, architects are expected to coordinate criteria such as budget, spatial needs, and sustainability goals with AI to produce optimal goals in their workflow (Figure 3). Moreover, thanks to AI's pattern recognition capabilities, it will be possible to identify and analyze architectural drawings, technical data, and extensive data from past projects.

Michael Maggio, director of Ralph Appelbaum Associates, describes the change and transformation that artificial intelligence will create in business processes as follows: *"AI's influence on architecture has emerged as a pivotal force, optimizing how architects analyze, design, and construct buildings."* AI can assist architects in designing energy-efficient and sustainable buildings. AI algorithms can analyze factors such as climate data, building orientation, and material and energy consumption patterns and suggest design modifications that improve energy use and reduce environmental impact. AI can be used in the fast and effective analysis of comprehensive and detailed data. It aids in scanning information from books, reports, regulations, and standards, quickly identifying and summarizing key details.

Figure 3. Artificial intelligence taxonomy by 3XN architects

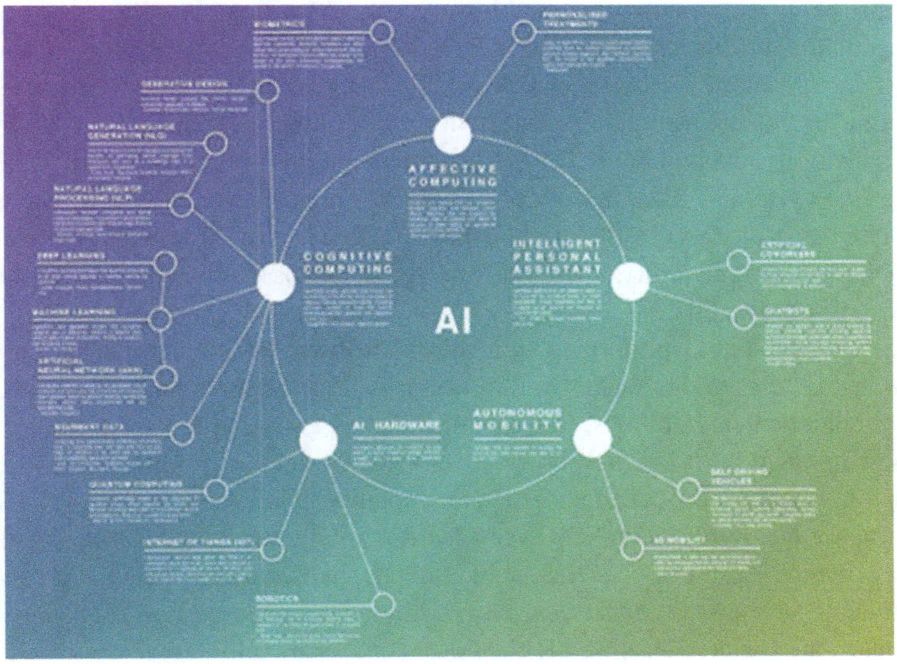

Another advantage of AI in architecture is that it provides new opportunities in building/project management, cost analysis, and material selection. AI tools can identify weak points in building facades and roads for infrastructure damage assessments. They can analyze Building Information Model (BIM) data, identify potential conflicts and overlaps, optimize schedules, and assist project management activities. This improves coordination from design to implementation and minimizes errors in the construction process. AI algorithms can also provide accurate cost estimates and material recommendations by analyzing cost data, building material properties, and market trends.

Artificial intelligence systems are currently used in architecture in a limited way due to their developmental stage and limitations in terms of access, cost, and legislation. On the other hand, since AI technologies are advancing very rapidly, it is expected to become a tool that provides a great deal of convenience in almost all areas of architecture in the very near future.

3. ARTIFICIAL INTELLIGENCE VERSUS ARCHITECTURAL CREATIVITY

While AI offers many opportunities and potential in the architectural field, concerns have been raised since the beginning of its development about limiting and replacing architects' creativity. According to a recent study conducted at Oxford University, concerns about AI are largely unfounded, and AI is expected to facilitate the routine work of architects. According to the research data, the probability of AI replacing architects is only 1.8%, which is relatively low (Frey & Osborne, 2013).

According to Magsamen and Ivy, human memory is superior to machine memory (Magsamen & Ivy, 2023). This is because a genius or a craftsman selects or saves only the best of what he or she saves in his or her memory for later use. Even if AI makes the design process more efficient, it cannot replace the creative aspects and unique design skills of human memory. AI is limited by the data it is trained on and the ability of algorithms to analyze and learn from it. AI will produce different results as data is renewed/changed or algorithms are improved. On the other hand, the databases on which AI is trained may not contain architecturally valuable and useful information. In fact, there is very little digital data on modernism and its pioneering buildings, one of the turning points of architecture. The digitally stored examples are usually clichéd buildings. The works of contemporary star architects such as Rem Koolhaas, Norman Foster, Bernard Tschumi, Zaha Hadid, and Frank Gehry are widely available digitally. However, despite being pioneers in their fields, these designs are not always appropriate examples in terms of budget, function, and utility. Therefore, any digital database is only as good as the examples it contains (Magsamen & Ivy, 2023).

Moreover, most of the tasks performed by architects involve multidimensional work based on human decisions, which technology cannot yet replicate, such as creative, analytical thinking, original perspectives, problem-solving abilities, and social skills. AI tools can automate the routine tasks of architects, allowing them to focus more on creative work. However, AI only knows what it is taught or programmed to understand. AI cannot generate a solution if it encounters an obstacle outside its programmed knowledge. Furthermore, not every decision in the timeline of an architectural project is predictable or efficient. Aesthetic concerns, market trends, marketing campaigns, and the interests of stakeholders (clients, investors, architects, and administrations) are also parts of the equation. Therefore, as long as humans are the ones making the final decisions, artificial intelligence will also be subject to these decisions. According to Labatut (2023), "*if artificial intelligence were capable of thinking, it would have blind spots. If it succeeds in being creative, there will be limits. This is because boundaries are efficient, and if they can mimic our reasoning ability, they might also need our capacity for madness. If it lacks understanding, does not care about the beauty and horror it can create, then entrusting ourselves to it would be foolish*" (Labatut, 2023).

To summarize, the scope and capabilities of artificial intelligence tools are not clearly known as they are still in the development stage. It will only be possible to fully understand the architectural capabilities and potential of artificial intelligence and determine its positive and negative aspects when these tools become widespread and are tested by architects. Therefore, the results of the competition of artificial intelligence against human creativity will be clearly understood over time.

4. NAVIGATING INTELLECTUAL PROPERTY RIGHTS IN THE ERA OF AI AND CREATIVE TECHNOLOGIES

Intellectual property rights undoubtedly come to mind when discussing artificial intelligence and architectural creativity. Artificial intelligence systems are based on the processing of digital data. Digital data is obtained from existing databases. At this point, whether the digital data is open access or restricted is essential. Since 2022, when artificial intelligence first emerged, many people have gained access to artificial intelligence tools and started producing content with them. Because this process developed so rapidly and uncontrollably, measures against property violations caused by artificial intelligence only came to the agenda in July 2023. The rapid development of artificial intelligence has begun to cause concern among experts, various organizations, and governments. In particular, it was realized that AI could pose significant risks to society and humanity in many areas, from job losses due to automation to disruptions in democratic processes and the automation of weapons. At this point, Google, Microsoft, and OpenAI established the Frontier Model Forum in July 2023 to regulate the development of artificial intelligence. In November of the same year, 28 countries signed the Bletchley Declaration (AI Safety Summit 2023), the first international manifesto recognizing the catastrophic risk of AI to humanity. Thus, the relationship between artificial intelligence and intellectual property rights has begun to be discussed in the relevant literature as an essential topic of debate (Guzik & Sitek, 2023).

Artificial intelligence and intellectual property violations are significant problems in architecture, as in all disciplines. As artificial intelligence systems begin to generate unique architectural images by humans entering keywords, the protection of creative works and copyright issues in architects' works have come to the fore. The GNU General Public License and Creative Commons (CC) are networks that make publicly available content based on data collected from public content repositories. In these networks, images can be adapted under different copyright licenses (Chen et al., 2023).

Artificial intelligence systems used to generate architectural content, such as DALL-E and Midjourney, use an intelligence system trained on publicly available datasets. Midjourney provides a 'Noncommercial Asset License' under the Attribution Noncommercial 4.0 framework for non-paid items, allowing their use as long as they are non-commercial and attributed to Midjourney. For paid members, the owner of the image is the creator of the image, even if it is an imitation of someone else's work, meaning that others can use the image as a base for their own experiments. On DALL-E, users have full usage rights for all media they create, including reprint, sale, and merchandising rights. However, it remains unclear whether the images used to train the platform's algorithms are properly published and legally authorized for such use. Thus, the legal frameworks for the rights to use both the data used to train the algorithms and the images produced by the algorithms remain unclear.

As seen from the different application methods in artificial intelligence systems, there is not yet a valid and reliable practice on intellectual property rights. It remains unclear how the data is obtained. Therefore, establishing a clear framework for intellectual property rights in creativity and original design development is a priority issue to be addressed by AI tools.

5. EXAMPLES OF CREATIVE PROJECTS USING ARTIFICIAL INTELLIGENCE IN ARCHITECTURE

This section of the study exemplifies how star architects use artificial intelligence in their work in a creative and innovative way. Star architects and other practitioners in architecture are increasingly using AI to improve their projects and design processes. One of the primary uses of AI in architecture is to produce complex and innovative forms.

In 2019, Zaha Hadid Architects used artificial intelligence algorithms in the Beijing Daxing International Airport design. Parameters such as passenger flows, aircraft circulation, and energy efficiency were optimized with artificial intelligence tools to shape the building's most appropriate form of design. Thus, form design, functionality, and structural efficiency have been improved with a mathematical and systematic approach (Figure 4).

In another example, Foster+Partners utilized artificial intelligence's communication and information flow capabilities. The Applied R&D team is developing tools and systems to aid design collaboration. These innovations include Extended Reality design systems and real-time design data exchange solutions. The team has created innovative systems to transform physical models and hand drawings into digital models that can be analyzed in design software. The Hermes project (2021) effectively uses artificial

Figure 4. Beijing Daxing Int. airport interior design

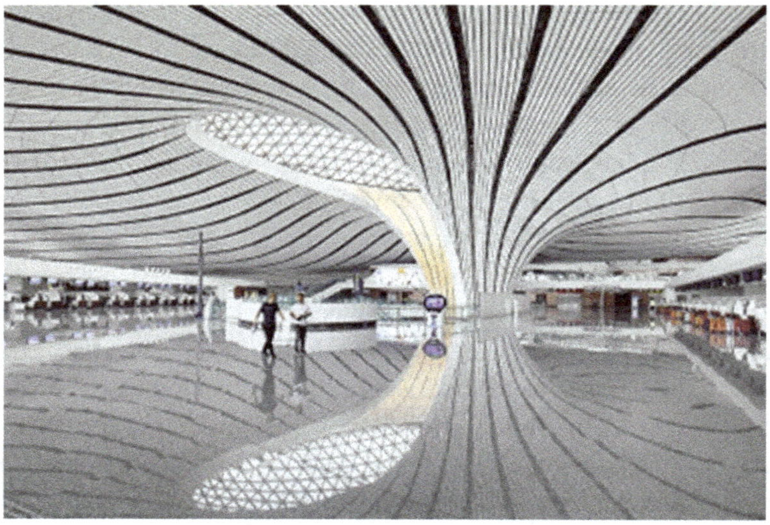

intelligence to exchange design data between different software applications, computers, design disciplines, and locations worldwide in real-time. Hermes is a web application with client plug-ins for CAD, BIM, interactive, and business applications, enabling seamless collaboration. This enhances multidisciplinary, integrated design coordination and accelerates design and analysis (Figure 5).

Another example of AI being used in a creative and innovative way is the Amager Bakke Waste-to-Energy Plant in Copenhagen, designed by Bjarke Ingels Group (BIG) in 2017. Amager Bakke is the first waste-to-energy plant in Denmark equipped with a catalyst to remove oxides of nitrogen (NOx). In addition to the power plant, the project includes a recreational area (the dry ski run, hiking trail, and climbing wall) that dominates the city skyline. The architects used artificial intelligence in their project to improve decision-making processes, analyze design options, and optimize the building form to generate maximum energy (Figure 6).

Figure 5. Hermes project by Foster+Partners

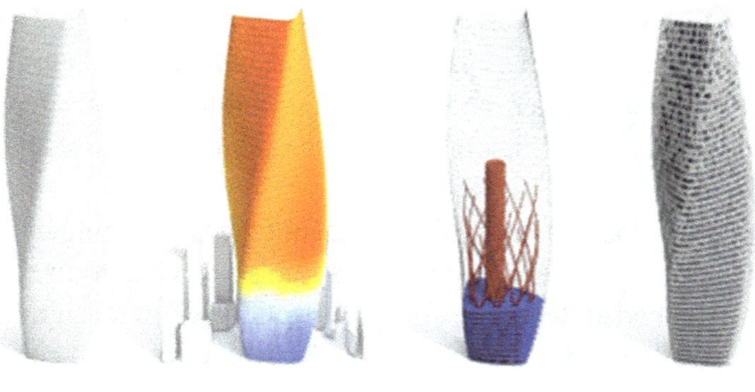

Figure 6. Amager Bakke by BIG architects

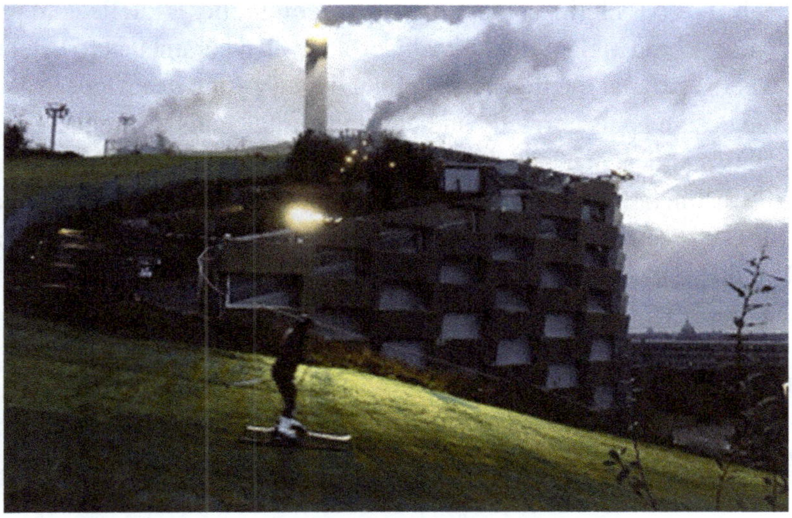

6. DISCUSSION

Artificial intelligence has made rapid progress since 2022 and has started to be effective in all sectors. The discipline of architecture has also taken its share from this rapid rise of AI. The use of AI in all processes of architectural project design, such as design, implementation, management, and optimization,

Table 1. Creative benefits of AI in architecture

Feature	Descriptions	
Innovation	**Provides the Ability to Design With Abstract Concepts/Keywords**	**Provides Unlimited Design Options by Matching Different Content and Themes**
Automated Design Generation/ Feedback	Automatically generate hundreds of design solutions based on specific parameters.	Provides real-time feedback on design choices
Efficiency	Increases the efficiency of the design and project design process. Shortens the time between design and the final product	Analyzes a large number of numerical data. Analyzes also visual, technical, and drawing data
Sustainability/ Building Performance	Facilitates the design of energy-efficient and sustainable buildings	Optimizes energy and resource use
Visualization	Integrates 3d visualization with augmented reality, virtual reality, and metaverse	Simplifies and accelerates 3d visualization
Generative Design	Supports an unlimited number of design possibilities	Analyzes details such as structural integrity, temperature control, light direction, and even traffic flow around the building
Material Selection	Enables innovative and optimal material selection	
Structural Analysis	Optimizes structure analysis and simulation	
Risk Assessment	Provides upfront analysis of potential risks in various processes from design to implementation	
Project Management	Facilitates project management through communication, coordination, and predictability	Reshapes workflows. Separates automation from creative works

offers different possibilities. Table 1 briefly summarizes the possibilities and creative aspects of AI in architecture. Although AI's possibilities in architecture seem limitless, intellectual property rights and design principles that are compatible with the real world are also parameters to be considered.

In this process, where artificial intelligence is gradually increasing its influence and dominance, it is essential to define the design goals correctly and develop digital skills to use these systems efficiently. At this point, architects and designers need to improve their skills in text commands and scripting. In addition, AI blurs the distinction between imitation and innovation in the field of creativity. The question of whether it produces something completely new or presents a collection of architectural history remains unclear. For this reason, the ethical use of artificial intelligence and the development of the system by respecting intellectual property rights are among the most critical issues.

In conclusion, this study discusses the relationship between artificial intelligence, architecture, and creativity within the framework of studies in literature. The study presents the potential of artificial intelligence in architecture, its usage areas, legal procedures, and how star architects use artificial intelligence in their projects. This study is intended to be a guide for future studies on the subject.

REFERENCES

AI Safety Summit. (2023). *The Bletchley Declaration*, https://www.gov.uk/government/publications/ai-safety-summit-2023-the-bletchley-declaration

Al-Sayed, K., Cheng, P. C. H., & Penn, A. (2021). An Investigation into the Cognitive, Metacognitive, and Spatial Markers of Creativity and Efficiency in Architectural Design, Al Edam-. *Artificial Intelligence for Engineering Design, Analysis and Manufacturing*, *35*(4), 423–437. doi:10.1017/S0890060421000251

Bao, Y., Gong, W., & Yang, K. (2023). A Literature Review of Human–AI Synergy in Decision Making: From the Perspective of Affordance Actualization Theory. *Systems*, *11*(9), 442. doi:10.3390/systems11090442

Chen, J., Yoshida, N., & Takada, H. (2023). An investigation of licensing of datasets for machine learning based on the GQM model. *arXiv - CS - Machine Learning*. DOI:arxiv-2303.13735

Chen, J.M., Wang, D.L., Shao, Z.C., Zhang, X., Ruan, M.C., Li, H.T., & Li, J.Q. (2023). Using Artificial Intelligence to Generate Master Quality Architectural Designs from Text Descriptions. *Buildings, 13*(9).

Epstein, Z., Hertzmann, A., Herman, L., Mahari, R., Frank, M. R., Groh, M., . . . Russakovsky, O. (2023). *Art and the science of generative AI: A deeper dive*. arXiv preprint arXiv:2306.04141.

Frey, C. B., & Osborne, M. A. (2013). The Future of Employment: How Susceptible are Jobs to Computerisation? *Technological Forecasting and Social Change*, *114*, 254–280. doi:10.1016/j.techfore.2016.08.019

Guzik, T. J., & Sitek, A. (2023). Global accord on the integration of artificial intelligence in medical science publishing: Implications of the Bletchley Declaration. *Cardiovascular Research*, *119*(17), 2681–2682. doi:10.1093/cvr/cvad170 PMID:37995330

Hanafy, N. O. (2023). Artificial Intelligence's Effects on Design Process Creativity: A Study on Used A.I. Text-to-Image in Architecture. *Journal of Building Engineering*, *80*, 107999. doi:10.1016/j.jobe.2023.107999

Labatut, B. (2023). *The Maniac*. Pushkin Press.

Lane, T. (2023). *What Does Artificial Intelligence Mean for Construction?* Building Magazine.

Li, Y. Q., & Xu, W. G. (2022). Using CycleGAN to Achieve the Sketch Recognition Process of Sketch-Based Modeling. *3rd International Conference on Computational Design and Robotic Fabrication*, 26-34. 10.1007/978-981-16-5983-6_3

Magsamen, S., & Ivy, R. (2023). *Your Brain on Art: How the Arts Transform Us*. Canongate Books.

Manovich, L. (2018). *Ai aesthetics*. Strelka Press.

Matoso, M. (2023). *Will Artificial Intelligence Replace Architects?* Archdaily.

Mrosla, L., Koch, V., & von Both, P. (2019). Quo vadis AI in Architecture? Survey of the Current Possibilities of AI in the Architectural Practice. *37th Conference on Education and Research in Computer Aided Architectural Design in Europe*, 45-54.

Qian, W. L., Yang, F., Mei, H. Y., & Li, H. (2023). Artificial Intelligence-designer for high-rise Building Sketches with User Preferences. *Engineering Structures*, *275*, 115171. doi:10.1016/j.engstruct.2022.115171

Raza, S., Venaik, A., & Khalil, S. N. (2023). Unveiling the Impact of AI and ChatGPT on Architectural and Interior Design Studies: A Comprehensive Exploration. *Tuijin Jishu/Journal of Propulsion Technology, 44*(3), 580-591.

Russell, S. J., & Norvig, P. (1995). *Artificial Intelligence a Modern Approach*. Pearson Education, Inc.

Tovar, E. (2023). *Prompting Creativity: The Role of AI in Visualization and Design Tools for Architects*. ArchDaily. Accessed 20 Dec 2023. https://www.archdaily.com/1010426/prompting-creativity-the-role-of-ai-in-visualization-and-design-tools-for-architects

Zhang, Z. H., Fort, J. M., & Mateu, L. G. (2023). Exploring the Potential of Artificial Intelligence as a Tool for Architectural Design: A Perception Study Using Gaudi's Work. *Buildings*, *13*(7), 1–18. doi:10.3390/buildings13071863

Chapter 13
Ethical Dilemmas of AI Perspectives Towards Common Digital Art and Digital Crafting:
AI Artistic View on Morality

Huong-Tra Le-Nguyen
https://orcid.org/0000-0003-4718-8920
Hanoi University, Vietnam

ABSTRACT

The integration of artificial intelligence (AI) into common digital art and digital crafting has ushered in a new era of creative possibilities, but it has also brought forth a myriad of ethical dilemmas that require careful consideration. This chapter explores the ethical complexities and challenges arising from AI perspectives in the realm of digital art and crafting, shedding light on the nuanced interplay between technology, creativity, and ethical values. At the heart of the discussion lies the concept of ethical dilemmas, which emerge at the intersection of AI and digital creativity. These dilemmas encompass a range of issues, including bias in AI algorithms, ownership and authorship disputes, environmental impact, exploitative uses of AI-generated content, fairness, sustainability, intellectual property rights, creative rights, and responsible practices.

INTRODUCTION

1. Introduction to the integration of AI in common digital art and digital crafting

The integration of artificial intelligence (AI) into common digital art and digital crafting represents a profound shift in the creative landscape, with implications that extend far beyond mere technical innovation. As artists embrace AI algorithms to augment their creative processes, they confront a myriad of ethical dilemmas that challenge traditional notions of authorship, originality, and moral responsibility. This intersection of technology and artistry raises questions about the ethical implications of relying on

DOI: 10.4018/979-8-3693-1950-5.ch013

AI-generated content, particularly in terms of authenticity and the commodification of creativity. Artists grapple with the tension between harnessing AI as a tool for experimentation and expression while also preserving the human element in their work. Moreover, the democratization of AI tools introduces concerns about accessibility and equity within the digital art community, as not all artists have equal access to advanced technology or the resources to navigate its complexities. Additionally, the use of AI in digital crafting raises concerns about cultural appropriation and the exploitation of marginalized communities, as algorithms may perpetuate biases inherent in their training data. From a broader perspective, the integration of AI challenges society to reassess the value and meaning of art in an increasingly technologically mediated world, prompting reflections on the role of human creativity and empathy in the face of automation (Calo et al., 2020). Ultimately, addressing the ethical dilemmas inherent in the integration of AI in common digital art and crafting requires a nuanced understanding of the complex interplay between technology, creativity, and morality, inviting artists and stakeholders to engage in critical dialogue and ethical reflection to navigate this evolving landscape responsibly.

2. Statement of purpose: exploring ethical dilemmas

Bias in AI algorithms poses significant challenges to the integrity and fairness of digital art and crafting. The inherent biases present in training data can lead to the perpetuation of stereotypes and marginalization of certain groups, raising ethical concerns about the authenticity and inclusivity of AI-generated artworks. Addressing bias requires a multifaceted approach that prioritizes transparency, accountability, and diversity in AI development and deployment (Buolamwini & Gebru, 2018).

Ownership and authorship disputes further complicate the ethical landscape of AI in digital creativity. As AI algorithms contribute to the creative process, questions arise about who holds the rights to AI-generated artworks and how to attribute creative contributions fairly (Calo et al., 2020). Ethical frameworks are needed to navigate these complexities and ensure that the rights of artists, AI developers, and other stakeholders are respected in the digital ecosystem.

The environmental impact of AI in digital art and crafting is another pressing ethical concern. The computational resources required for training AI models contribute to carbon emissions and ecological degradation, highlighting the need for sustainable practices and responsible use of technology (Yu, 2016). Efforts to minimize the environmental footprint of AI in digital creativity are essential to mitigate its negative impact on the planet.

Exploitative uses of AI-generated content raise ethical questions about privacy, consent, and societal harm. From deepfakes to misinformation campaigns, the misuse of AI technology poses significant risks to individuals and communities. Ethical guidelines and responsible practices are necessary to prevent exploitation and uphold ethical standards in the digital landscape (Yusa & Aditama, 2020).

3. Significance of understanding and addressing ethical challenges in AI-enhanced creativity

In navigating these ethical dilemmas, stakeholders in the digital art and crafting communities must prioritize ethical considerations and adopt a proactive approach to ethical decision-making (Mikalonytė & Kneer, 2021). Collaboration between artists, AI developers, policymakers, ethicists, and other stakeholders is essential to develop ethical frameworks that promote fairness, integrity, and social responsibility in AI-enhanced creativity.

Ultimately, the ethical integration of AI into common digital art and digital crafting requires a holistic understanding of the ethical implications and a commitment to ethical principles. By embracing transparency, accountability, and responsible practices, we can harness the transformative potential of

AI while safeguarding against its unintended consequences and ensuring that digital creativity thrives in an ethical and inclusive manner.

OBJECTIVES AND SCOPE

1. Identification of primary research objectives

In delineating the objectives for research on the ethical dilemmas surrounding the integration of AI in common digital art and digital crafting, several primary goals emerge. Firstly, it is imperative to explore the ethical frameworks that guide artistic practice and how they intersect with emerging technologies, particularly AI. Understanding the values and principles that underpin the creative process will inform discussions on morality and responsibility in the context of AI-generated content. Secondly, there is a need to examine the specific ethical challenges that arise from the use of AI in digital art and crafting, such as questions of authorship, authenticity, and cultural appropriation. Investigating these dilemmas will help elucidate the ethical implications of AI integration and provide insights into potential mitigating strategies. Additionally, research aims to assess the societal impacts of AI-driven creativity, including its effects on artistic communities, cultural diversity, and accessibility. By examining these broader implications, stakeholders can better anticipate the ethical considerations inherent in the widespread adoption of AI in the arts (Mondal, 2020). Furthermore, research seeks to identify best practices and ethical guidelines for artists, technologists, and policymakers to navigate the ethical terrain of AI integration responsibly. By establishing ethical frameworks and guidelines, stakeholders can promote ethical decision-making and foster a more inclusive and equitable creative ecosystem. Ultimately, the primary research objectives aim to advance our understanding of the ethical dilemmas surrounding AI in digital art and crafting and to provide actionable insights for ethical practice and policy development in this rapidly evolving field.

2. Delimitation of the scope to ethical dilemmas

In delimiting the scope to ethical dilemmas within the context of integrating AI in common digital art and digital crafting, the primary objective is to provide a focused examination of the moral complexities inherent in this intersection of technology and creativity (Buolamwini & Gebru, 2018). By narrowing the scope to ethical considerations, the research aims to delve deeply into the nuanced ethical challenges faced by artists, technologists, and stakeholders as they navigate the landscape of AI-driven artistic expression. This approach allows for a comprehensive analysis of issues such as accountability, transparency, bias, and cultural sensitivity within the specific context of AI-generated content in digital art and crafting. By concentrating on ethical dilemmas, the research seeks to provide actionable insights and practical recommendations for addressing these challenges, thereby facilitating informed decision-making and responsible innovation in the field. Moreover, focusing on ethical considerations fosters a critical dialogue around the moral implications of AI integration, encouraging reflection on the values and principles that should guide the development and use of AI technologies in creative practices. By delineating the scope to ethical dilemmas, the research aims to contribute to a deeper understanding of the ethical dimensions of AI in digital art and crafting and to stimulate further inquiry into the ethical implications of emerging technologies in the arts (Yusa & Putra, 2016).

3. Explanation of the research's relevance to artists, AI developers, policymakers, and ethicists

The research on ethical dilemmas in the integration of AI in common digital art and digital crafting holds significant relevance for a diverse array of stakeholders, including artists, AI developers, policymakers, and ethicists. For artists, the findings offer critical insights into navigating the ethical complexities of incorporating AI technologies into their creative processes, enabling them to make informed decisions that align with their artistic principles and values (Yusa et al., 2017). AI developers benefit from understanding the ethical considerations unique to the field of digital art and crafting, guiding the development of AI tools and algorithms that prioritize ethical standards such as transparency, fairness, and cultural sensitivity. Policymakers gain valuable perspectives on the regulatory frameworks needed to address ethical challenges in AI-driven creativity, informing the development of policies that promote innovation while safeguarding against potential harms. Ethicists find the research relevant in advancing theoretical discussions on the ethical implications of AI integration in the arts, contributing to the broader discourse on technology, morality, and society. By elucidating the ethical dilemmas inherent in the intersection of AI and digital art, the research serves as a catalyst for interdisciplinary dialogue and collaboration, fostering a more nuanced understanding of the moral dimensions of technological innovation in the creative domain (Yusa et al., 2021). Ultimately, the research's relevance extends beyond disciplinary boundaries, offering actionable insights and ethical guidelines that empower stakeholders to navigate the ethical landscape of AI integration responsibly and ethically.

LITERATURE REVIEW

1. Review of existing literature on AI ethics, digital art, and technological impacts

There are various methodologies for using AI in art, each with their own unique aesthetic, technical, and social dimensions (Calo et al., 2020). Here are some of the main methodologies:

Style Transfer: Style transfer is a technique where the style of one image is transferred to another image using machine learning algorithms. This technique has been used to generate new artworks in the style of famous artists such as Van Gogh and Picasso.

1. **Aesthetic dimension**: Style transfer allows for the creation of new artworks that blend the styles of different artists, resulting in unique and visually striking compositions.
2. **Technical dimension**: The technical process of style transfer involves training a neural network to recognize the style of a given artwork and applying that style to another image.
3. **Social dimension:** Style transfer has raised questions around authorship and originality, as the resulting artwork is created through the use of pre-existing images.

Generative Adversarial Networks (GANs): GANs are a type of machine learning algorithm that can generate new images based on a given set of parameters. In the context of art, GANs can be used to create entirely new artworks or to modify existing ones.

1. **Aesthetic dimension**: GANs can create highly realistic and detailed images, resulting in new artworks that are difficult to distinguish from those created by humans.
2. **Technical dimension**: GANs require a large amount of data to train the neural network, and the output can be unpredictable.
3. **Social dimension**: The use of GANs in art has raised concerns around the potential for the technology to be used for unethical purposes, such as generating deepfakes or perpetuating stereotypes.

Interactive Systems: Interactive systems allow for real-time collaboration between humans and machines, enabling artists to create new artworks that respond to user input.

1. **Aesthetic dimension**: Interactive systems can result in dynamic and responsive artworks that engage the viewer in new and unique ways.
2. **Technical dimension**: Interactive systems require sophisticated software and hardware to facilitate real-time collaboration between humans and machines.
3. **Social dimension**: The use of interactive systems raises questions around the role of the artist, as the resulting artwork is created through a collaborative process with the machine.

Overall, the different methodologies for using AI in art each offer unique aesthetic, technical, and social dimensions, and have contributed to a range of debates and discussions around the role of technology in the creative process. The aesthetic, technical, and social dimensions of AI-generated art are complex and multifaceted.

On the aesthetic front, AI-generated art can be evaluated based on its formal qualities such as color, composition, texture, and shape. AI-generated art can exhibit a range of styles, from mimicking the work of past artists to creating entirely new and unique styles. Evaluating the aesthetic quality of AI-generated art can be a subjective task, as what may be considered beautiful or aesthetically pleasing can vary greatly among individuals (Yusa & Aditama, 2020). From a technical perspective, AI-generated art involves the use of algorithms to create new artworks. The quality of the algorithms and the accuracy of the data used to train them can have a significant impact on the resulting artwork. The use of advanced technologies such as machine learning, computer vision, and natural language processing can also enhance the technical quality of the artworks generated by AI. The social dimensions of AI-generated art are perhaps the most significant. The use of AI in art can raise questions about the role of technology in creative expression, as well as issues related to ownership, authenticity, and authorship. Additionally, the use of AI can perpetuate biases present in the data used to train the algorithms, leading to works that reinforce existing social and cultural norms. On the other hand, AI-generated art has the potential to democratize the art world by allowing more people to create and participate in artistic expression (Mikalonytė & Kneer, 2021). In summary, the aesthetic, technical, and social dimensions of AI-generated art are complex and intertwined. Evaluating AI-generated art requires considering these dimensions and recognizing the potential implications of this emerging technology on the art world and beyond.

2. Exploration of discussions on biases in AI algorithms, ownership disputes, environmental concerns, and societal implications

The integration of artificial intelligence (AI) into common digital art and digital crafting presents a myriad of ethical dilemmas that demand critical examination. Within the scope of literature review for ethical dilemmas in this domain, discussions on biases in AI algorithms emerge as a central theme. Scholars have extensively examined how biases inherent in training data can perpetuate social inequalities and reinforce existing power structures. For instance, Joy Buolamwini's research has highlighted the racial and gender biases embedded in facial recognition algorithms, underscoring the urgent need for algorithmic transparency and accountability in AI-driven creative processes.

Ownership disputes constitute another significant area of concern within the literature. As AI systems generate content autonomously or through collaboration with human artists, questions arise regarding the rightful ownership of the resulting artworks. The absence of clear legal frameworks and established norms complicates matters further, leading to potential conflicts between artists, AI developers, and other stakeholders. Some scholars advocate for the recognition of AI as co-creators, while others argue for stricter regulations to protect the intellectual property rights of human artists (Lyu et al., 2021).

Environmental concerns also feature prominently in discussions surrounding the integration of AI in digital art and crafting. The energy-intensive nature of training large-scale AI models and the proliferation of computationally intensive creative processes raise apprehensions about the environmental impact of AI-driven creativity (Kadish et al., 2021). Researchers emphasize the importance of adopting sustainable practices and optimizing algorithms to minimize energy consumption without compromising artistic quality. Furthermore, the ethical implications of digital waste generated by obsolete AI models and hardware contribute to ongoing debates about the environmental sustainability of AI-driven art production.

Societal implications constitute a broader category encompassing various ethical considerations arising from the widespread adoption of AI in the creative domain. These implications include concerns about job displacement, economic inequality, cultural homogenization, and the erosion of human creativity and agency. Scholars argue that while AI has the potential to democratize access to artistic tools and platforms, it also risks exacerbating existing disparities and marginalizing certain artistic communities. Moreover, the commodification of AI-generated content raises questions about the value and authenticity of art in a digital age, prompting reflections on the role of human intentionality and emotional resonance in artistic expression (Pitt et al., 2020).

3. Identification of gaps in the literature for the proposed research to address

In the burgeoning field of ethical dilemmas surrounding the integration of AI in common digital art and digital crafting, there exist several notable gaps in the existing literature that warrant further investigation (Wang et al., 2020). This part aims to identify these gaps and highlight the significance of addressing them in the proposed research.

One significant gap pertains to the lack of comprehensive ethical frameworks tailored specifically to AI-driven creativity. While scholars have explored ethical considerations in AI development and deployment, there remains a dearth of guidelines and best practices specifically geared towards the ethical use of AI in the arts. Addressing this gap is essential for providing artists, AI developers, policymakers, and ethicists with actionable insights and tools to navigate the ethical complexities of AI integration in the creative domain (Kang et al., 2019).

Another notable gap lies in the limited understanding of the socio-cultural implications of AI-driven art and crafting. While some studies have touched upon issues such as cultural appropriation and representation in AI-generated content, there is a need for more nuanced analyses that consider the diverse cultural contexts within which AI-based creative practices operate (Chung et al., 2022). By exploring how AI intersects with cultural identity, heritage, and expression, researchers can contribute to a more inclusive and culturally sensitive approach to AI-driven creativity.

Furthermore, the literature currently lacks a comprehensive examination of the environmental sustainability of AI-driven art production. While scholars have acknowledged the energy-intensive nature of AI algorithms and computational processes, there is a paucity of research on strategies for mitigating the environmental impact of AI in the arts. Exploring alternative approaches to AI training and optimization, as well as assessing the carbon footprint of AI-generated content, are crucial steps towards promoting environmentally sustainable practices in digital art and crafting (Chung et al., 2022).

Additionally, there is a notable gap in research focusing on the ethical implications of AI collaboration and co-creation in the artistic process. As AI systems increasingly collaborate with human artists or generate content autonomously, questions arise regarding the ethical responsibilities of both humans and machines in the creative process. By examining issues such as authorship, agency, and accountability in AI-driven collaboration, researchers can contribute to a deeper understanding of the ethical dimensions of human-AI interaction in the arts (Chen et al., 2020).

In conclusion, the identification of gaps in the literature for ethical dilemmas in the integration of AI in common digital art and digital crafting underscores the need for interdisciplinary research that addresses these gaps comprehensively. By filling these gaps, the proposed research can contribute to a more nuanced understanding of the ethical challenges and opportunities posed by AI integration in the creative domain, ultimately guiding ethical practice and policy development in this rapidly evolving field.

ETHICAL DILEMMAS AND CONCERNS

1.Biases in AI Algorithms

a. Definition and Examples of Biases

Biases in AI algorithms represent a critical ethical concern within the realm of integrating AI into common digital art and digital crafting. These biases refer to systematic errors or distortions in AI decision-making processes that result in unfair or discriminatory outcomes. They can manifest in various forms, including but not limited to, racial, gender, socio-economic, and cultural biases. Understanding biases in AI algorithms is essential for artists, AI developers, policymakers, and ethicists to mitigate their negative impacts and promote ethical AI integration in creative practices (Microsoft, 2016).

One prominent example of biases in AI algorithms is racial bias in facial recognition systems. Studies have shown that many facial recognition algorithms exhibit higher error rates when identifying individuals with darker skin tones, particularly women and people of color (Mondal, 2020). This bias stems from imbalances in the training data used to develop the algorithms, which often overrepresent lighter-skinned individuals. Consequently, these biased algorithms can lead to unjust outcomes, such as misidentification and wrongful arrests, disproportionately affecting marginalized communities.

Gender bias is another prevalent form of bias in AI algorithms, particularly in natural language processing (NLP) systems (Mezei, 2020). Research has demonstrated that NLP models trained on large datasets tend to replicate and reinforce gender stereotypes present in the data. For example, language models may associate certain occupations or roles with specific genders, leading to biased language generation and reinforcement of gender-based stereotypes (Clayton, 2005). This bias can perpetuate gender inequality and limit opportunities for individuals whose identities deviate from societal norms.

Socio-economic biases in AI algorithms can also have profound implications for digital art and crafting. For instance, recommendation algorithms used in online art platforms may favor content produced by artists from privileged backgrounds or well-funded institutions, thereby perpetuating existing disparities in visibility and recognition within the art community. Similarly, pricing algorithms in digital art marketplaces may undervalue the work of emerging or independent artists, favoring established artists or commercially successful artworks (Sovhyra, 2021).

Cultural biases in AI algorithms pose additional challenges in the integration of AI into digital art and crafting. These biases can manifest in various ways, such as favoring certain artistic styles, themes, or cultural references over others. For example, image recognition algorithms trained on Western-centric datasets may struggle to accurately identify or interpret artworks influenced by non-Western cultures, leading to misclassification or misrepresentation of cultural identities and artistic expressions (Nast, 2022).

b. Impact on Artistic Expression and Societal Values

The integration of AI into common digital art and digital crafting has brought about significant changes in artistic expression and societal values (Calo et al., 2020). However, the presence of biases in AI algorithms poses a substantial ethical dilemma, impacting both artistic expression and societal values. Understanding these impacts is crucial for addressing the ethical considerations inherent in the intersection of AI and creativity.

One significant impact of biases in AI algorithms on artistic expression is the reinforcement of dominant cultural narratives and stereotypes. AI systems trained on biased datasets may perpetuate existing biases present in society, leading to the replication of stereotypes in AI-generated content. For example, biased image recognition algorithms may prioritize certain artistic styles or themes over others, limiting the diversity of artistic expression and marginalizing underrepresented voices. This narrowing of artistic expression not only hinders creativity but also reinforces societal inequalities and cultural homogenization (Cohn, 2021).

Furthermore, biases in AI algorithms can influence societal values by shaping perceptions and attitudes towards different groups and identities. AI-generated content that perpetuates stereotypes or discriminatory narratives can contribute to the normalization of prejudice and discrimination, thereby undermining efforts towards social justice and inclusivity. For instance, biased language models may generate text that reinforces harmful stereotypes about marginalized communities, leading to the perpetuation of prejudice and discrimination in society (Poole & Mackworth, 2017).

Moreover, biases in AI algorithms can have profound implications for the representation and visibility of diverse voices in the digital art and crafting communities. Biased recommendation algorithms in online art platforms may prioritize content produced by artists from privileged backgrounds, thereby limiting opportunities for emerging or underrepresented artists to gain recognition and exposure. This lack of diversity not only stifles artistic innovation but also perpetuates systemic inequalities within the art community (Buolamwini & Gebru, 2018).

On a broader societal level, the presence of biases in AI algorithms can erode trust in AI technology and undermine its potential to benefit society. Public distrust in biased AI systems can lead to reluctance in adopting AI-driven solutions in various domains, including healthcare, finance, and criminal justice (Winner, 2010). Additionally, the normalization of biased AI-generated content in digital art and crafting may desensitize individuals to the harmful impacts of bias, further perpetuating inequality and discrimination in society.

In response to these challenges, artists, AI developers, policymakers, and ethicists must work collaboratively to address biases in AI algorithms and promote ethical AI integration in the creative domain. This requires a concerted effort to diversify training data, develop bias detection and mitigation techniques, and implement transparent and accountable AI systems (O'Neil, 2016). Moreover, fostering critical engagement with AI technology and promoting awareness of its ethical implications are essential for empowering individuals to challenge biased representations and advocate for fairness and inclusivity in AI-driven creative practices.

c. Strategies for Identifying and Mitigating Biases

Identifying and mitigating biases in AI algorithms is crucial for promoting ethical AI integration in common digital art and digital crafting. By implementing strategies to address biases, artists, AI developers, policymakers, and ethicists can foster fairness, inclusivity, and diversity in AI-driven creative practices. This essay explores key strategies for identifying and mitigating biases in AI algorithms within the context of ethical dilemmas in the integration of AI in digital art and crafting (Zuboff, 2019).

One effective strategy for identifying biases in AI algorithms is conducting comprehensive bias audits and evaluations. This involves systematically assessing AI systems for potential biases across various stages of development, including data collection, model training, and deployment. By analyzing training data and model outputs, researchers can identify patterns of bias and discrimination, allowing for targeted interventions to address these issues. Additionally, employing diverse and representative datasets can help mitigate biases by ensuring that AI systems are trained on a wide range of perspectives and experiences (Dutton et al., 2009).

Another strategy for mitigating biases in AI algorithms is implementing bias detection and mitigation techniques during the development and deployment phases. This includes utilizing techniques such as adversarial training, which involves training AI models to recognize and counteract biases present in training data (Wallach et al., 2011). Additionally, employing fairness-aware machine learning algorithms can help mitigate biases by optimizing model performance while minimizing unfair outcomes across different demographic groups. Moreover, developing interpretable and transparent AI systems can facilitate the identification and mitigation of biases by allowing stakeholders to understand how decisions are made and identify potential sources of bias.

Furthermore, promoting diversity and inclusion in AI development teams can help mitigate biases by bringing diverse perspectives and expertise to the development process. By fostering interdisciplinary collaboration and inclusive decision-making processes, developers can identify and address biases more effectively. Additionally, involving artists and representatives from diverse communities in the design and development of AI-driven creative tools can help ensure that AI systems are sensitive to a wide range of cultural contexts and artistic practices (Marcus, 2019).

Moreover, promoting accountability and transparency in AI development and deployment is essential for mitigating biases and promoting ethical AI integration (Rubinstein et al., 2021). This includes establishing clear guidelines and standards for ethical AI development and deployment, as well as implementing mechanisms for monitoring and auditing AI systems for bias and discrimination. Additionally, promoting open access to AI algorithms and data can facilitate independent scrutiny and evaluation, enabling stakeholders to identify and address biases more effectively.

In conclusion, identifying and mitigating biases in AI algorithms is essential for promoting ethical AI integration in common digital art and digital crafting. By implementing strategies such as bias audits, bias detection and mitigation techniques, promoting diversity and inclusion, and promoting accountability and transparency, stakeholders can foster fairness, inclusivity, and diversity in AI-driven creative practices. These strategies are essential for addressing the ethical dilemmas posed by biases in AI algorithms and promoting ethical AI integration in the artistic domain.

2. Ownership and Authorship Disputes

a. Ambiguity in Authorship Determination

The integration of AI into common digital art and digital crafting has sparked complex debates surrounding ownership and authorship, leading to numerous ethical dilemmas. As AI algorithms play an increasingly active role in the creative process, the determination of authorship becomes ambiguous. Unlike traditional artistic collaborations between human creators, the contributions of AI systems to artworks often lack clear delineation, raising questions about who should be credited as the author (O'Neil, 2018). This ambiguity in authorship determination can lead to conflicts over intellectual property rights, as stakeholders seek to assert ownership over AI-generated content.

One of the key ethical dilemmas in the integration of AI in digital art and crafting is the ambiguity surrounding authorship determination. Unlike human creators whose contributions to artworks are typically discernible, the role of AI algorithms in generating artistic content blurs the lines of authorship. AI systems can autonomously generate, manipulate, and combine elements to produce artworks, making it challenging to attribute authorship to a single individual or entity. This ambiguity complicates legal and ethical frameworks surrounding intellectual property rights and ownership, as traditional notions of authorship may not apply in the context of AI-generated content (Dennett, 2019).

The integration of artificial intelligence (AI) into common digital art and digital crafting has introduced a myriad of ethical dilemmas, particularly regarding the ambiguity in authorship determination (Wisnioski & Hendler, 2020). Unlike traditional artistic collaborations where the roles of human creators are well-defined, the involvement of AI algorithms in generating artistic content complicates the attribution of authorship. This ambiguity arises from the unique capabilities of AI systems to autonomously generate, manipulate, and combine elements to produce artworks, blurring the lines between human and machine contributions (Schumann et al., 2021).

One of the primary challenges in determining authorship in AI-generated art lies in the nature of the creative process itself. AI algorithms can analyze vast amounts of data, learn patterns, and generate novel outputs based on their training. As such, the creative decisions made by AI systems may not always be explicitly guided or controlled by human creators. This raises questions about the extent to which human intervention influences the final artwork and whether AI systems can be considered autonomous creators in their own right (Mondal, 2020).

Furthermore, the lack of discernible human agency in AI-generated art complicates traditional notions of authorship, which often rely on the intentionality and expression of individual creators (Wisnioski & Hendler, 2020). While human artists may provide input, select parameters, or curate outputs generated by AI algorithms, the degree of creative control exerted by humans varies widely across different artistic collaborations. As a result, determining the relative contributions of humans and AI systems to the artistic process becomes inherently ambiguous.

The ambiguity in authorship determination gives rise to various ethical implications, particularly concerning the recognition and attribution of creative labor. In cases where AI algorithms play a significant role in generating artworks, questions arise about whether and how human creators should be credited as authors. Additionally, the lack of clear authorship attribution can impact the economic interests of artists, as ownership of AI-generated artworks may influence their commercial value, copyright status, and licensing opportunities (Rubinstein et al., 2021).

Addressing the ambiguity in authorship determination requires a nuanced understanding of the roles and responsibilities of human creators and AI systems in the artistic process. Ethical frameworks should consider factors such as the level of human input, the degree of creative autonomy afforded to AI algorithms, and the transparency of collaborative practices. Moreover, promoting transparency and accountability in AI-driven creative processes is essential for fostering trust and ensuring that authorship attribution reflects the contributions of all stakeholders involved.

b. Conflicts Over Intellectual Property Rights

The ambiguity in authorship determination gives rise to conflicts over intellectual property rights, as stakeholders vie for control and recognition of AI-generated artworks. Artists, AI developers, and other stakeholders may assert ownership over AI-generated content, leading to disputes over copyright, licensing, and commercial (Bailey et al., 2019; Lips-Wiersma & Morris, 2009; Martela & Riekki, 2018). Furthermore, existing legal frameworks may be ill-equipped to address the complexities of ownership and authorship in the context of AI-driven creativity, exacerbating tensions and uncertainties surrounding intellectual property rights.

One of the primary sources of conflict over intellectual property rights in AI-generated art is the ambiguity surrounding authorship attribution. Unlike traditional artistic collaborations where human creators retain clear authorial control over their works, the involvement of AI algorithms complicates the determination of ownership. As a result, disputes may arise between human creators, AI developers, and other parties seeking to assert ownership or control over AI-generated content, leading to legal battles, commercial negotiations, and ethical dilemmas (Acemoglu & Restrepo, 2020).

Furthermore, the lack of established legal frameworks and precedents for addressing intellectual property rights in AI-generated art exacerbates conflicts and uncertainties surrounding ownership. Traditional copyright laws may not adequately address the unique challenges posed by AI-driven creativity, such as determining authorship, assigning ownership, and regulating commercial exploitation (Lips-Wiersma & Morris, 2009). As a result, stakeholders may resort to litigation or alternative dispute resolution mechanisms to protect their interests, further complicating the ethical dimensions of ownership and authorship disputes.

Moreover, the commercialization of AI-generated art introduces additional complexities into conflicts over intellectual property rights. As AI-driven creativity becomes increasingly commodified, questions arise about the ownership of AI-generated artworks, the licensing of AI algorithms, and the distribution of revenue generated from AI-driven creative processes (Rubinstein et al., 2021). Stakeholders may seek to maximize their profits or gain competitive advantages through exclusive ownership or control over AI-generated content, leading to tensions and conflicts within the digital art and crafting communities.

Addressing conflicts over intellectual property rights in the integration of AI in digital art and crafting requires the development of clear guidelines and ethical frameworks that promote fairness, transparency, and accountability (Schumann et al., 2021). These frameworks should consider the contributions of all stakeholders involved in the creative process, including human creators, AI developers, and users of AI-generated content. Moreover, promoting collaboration, dialogue, and negotiation among stakeholders can help mitigate conflicts and foster mutually beneficial outcomes (Nast, 2022).

Additionally, promoting transparency and ethical conduct in AI-driven creative practices is essential for upholding principles of integrity and fairness in the digital art and crafting communities. By establishing clear attribution mechanisms, licensing agreements, and revenue-sharing models, stakeholders can ensure that intellectual property rights are respected and that the economic benefits of AI-driven creativity are distributed equitably among all parties involved.

c. Need for Clear Guidelines and Ethical Frameworks

Addressing ownership and authorship disputes in the integration of AI in digital art and crafting requires the establishment of clear guidelines and ethical frameworks. These frameworks should delineate the respective contributions of human creators and AI systems to artworks, providing clarity on authorship determination and intellectual property rights (Wisnioski & Hendler, 2020). Moreover, ethical considerations such as transparency, accountability, and fairness should inform the development of these guidelines, ensuring that they One of the primary reasons for the need for clear guidelines and ethical frameworks is the ambiguity surrounding authorship determination in AI-generated art. Traditional notions of authorship, which rely on human intentionality and expression, may not apply in the context of AI-driven creativity. As a result, stakeholders require clear guidelines to determine how credit should be attributed to human creators, AI algorithms, or collaborative entities involved in the artistic process. Establishing transparent attribution mechanisms can help mitigate conflicts and ensure that all contributors receive appropriate recognition for their creative contributions (Nast, 2022).

Moreover, clear guidelines and ethical frameworks are essential for addressing conflicts over intellectual property rights in AI-generated art. Traditional copyright laws may not adequately address the unique challenges posed by AI-driven creativity, such as determining ownership, licensing, and commercial exploitation (Schumann et al., 2021). As a result, stakeholders require ethical frameworks that provide guidance on how to navigate these legal and ethical complexities while upholding principles of fairness and integrity. By establishing clear guidelines for ownership, licensing, and revenue-sharing, stakeholders can mitigate conflicts and promote equitable outcomes in the digital art and crafting communities.

Furthermore, clear guidelines and ethical frameworks are essential for promoting transparency and accountability in AI-driven creative practices. Transparency is critical for ensuring that stakeholders understand how decisions are made, who owns the rights to AI-generated content, and how revenue generated from AI-driven creativity is distributed. Additionally, accountability mechanisms can help hold stakeholders responsible for their actions and decisions, promoting ethical conduct and fostering trust within the digital art and crafting communities (Wisnioski & Hendler, 2020).

Addressing the need for clear guidelines and ethical frameworks requires collaboration and dialogue among stakeholders, including artists, AI developers, policymakers, and ethicists. By engaging in interdisciplinary discussions, stakeholders can identify key ethical considerations, develop consensus on ethical principles, and establish guidelines that reflect the values and interests of the digital art and crafting communities. Moreover, involving diverse perspectives and expertise can help ensure that guidelines and frameworks are comprehensive, inclusive, and responsive to the evolving nature of AI-driven creativity. uphold ethical principles and promote equitable outcomes for all stakeholders.

3. Environmental Impact

a. Environmental Consequences of AI Training

The integration of artificial intelligence (AI) into common digital art and digital crafting has brought about remarkable advancements in creativity and innovation. However, the environmental consequences of AI training present a significant ethical dilemma that cannot be ignored. AI training, the process by which AI algorithms learn from data to perform specific tasks, requires extensive computational resources and energy consumption. This leads to several environmental impacts, including increased carbon emissions, resource depletion, and electronic waste generation. The energy-intensive nature of AI training, coupled with the use of hardware such as graphics processing units (GPUs) and data centers, contributes to the environmental footprint of AI technology (Nast, 2022).

One of the primary environmental consequences of AI training is the substantial energy consumption associated with running large-scale computational processes. Training AI models involves processing vast amounts of data through complex algorithms, which requires extensive computational power. This, in turn, leads to high energy consumption, contributing to increased carbon emissions and environmental degradation. The environmental footprint of AI training is further exacerbated by the use of energy-intensive hardware such as graphics processing units (GPUs) and data centers, which consume large amounts of electricity and produce heat as a byproduct (Formosa, 2021).

Moreover, the environmental impact of AI training extends beyond energy consumption to include resource depletion and electronic waste generation. The production and disposal of hardware components used in AI training, such as GPUs and servers, require significant amounts of raw materials and contribute to resource depletion and pollution. Additionally, the rapid pace of technological advancement in AI research and development leads to frequent hardware upgrades and replacements, resulting in the generation of electronic waste that poses environmental hazards if not properly managed and recycled. On top of that, the environmental consequences of AI training are compounded by the lack of sustainable practices and ethical considerations in the development and deployment of AI systems. While AI researchers and practitioners focus on optimizing algorithms for performance and accuracy, environmental sustainability is often overlooked as a secondary concern. This prioritization of technical goals over environmental considerations perpetuates unsustainable practices and exacerbates the environmental impact of AI training (Pritchett, 2021).

Addressing the environmental consequences of AI training requires a multifaceted approach that integrates environmental sustainability into AI research and development processes. One strategy is to optimize AI algorithms and training processes to minimize energy consumption and resource usage. This can be achieved through techniques such as algorithmic efficiency improvements, model compression, and distributed computing, which reduce the computational resources required for AI training while maintaining performance and accuracy. Furthermore, promoting the use of renewable energy sources for AI training can help mitigate the environmental impact of energy consumption (Rubinstein et al., 2021). By powering AI training processes with renewable energy sources such as solar, wind, and hydroelectric power, stakeholders can reduce carbon emissions and lessen the environmental footprint of AI training. Additionally, implementing energy-efficient hardware designs and adopting sustainable practices in data center operations can further reduce the environmental impact of AI training.

Incorporating environmental considerations into ethical frameworks and guidelines for AI development and deployment is essential for promoting responsible and sustainable AI integration. Ethical guidelines should prioritize environmental sustainability as a core principle and encourage stakeholders to consider the environmental consequences of AI training in decision-making processes. By promoting transparency, accountability, and ethical conduct in AI research and development, stakeholders can address the environmental consequences of AI training and foster a more sustainable approach to AI integration in digital art and crafting.

b. Ethical Responsibility to Address Ecological Footprint

In light of the environmental consequences of AI training, there exists an ethical responsibility to address the ecological footprint of AI integration in digital art and crafting. As creators and consumers of AI-driven creative content, artists, AI developers, and other stakeholders have a duty to minimize the environmental impact of AI technology. This ethical responsibility extends beyond individual actions to include systemic changes in AI research, development, and deployment practices. By prioritizing environmental sustainability and adopting responsible practices, stakeholders can mitigate the ecological footprint of AI training and promote a more sustainable approach to AI integration in the artistic domain (Michaelson et al., 2014).

One of the key ethical considerations in addressing the ecological footprint of AI integration is the recognition of the interconnectedness between AI technology and the natural environment. AI training, which involves processing vast amounts of data through energy-intensive computational processes, contributes to increased carbon emissions, resource depletion, and electronic waste generation. As such, the environmental impact of AI technology extends beyond the digital realm to have tangible consequences for ecosystems, biodiversity, and climate stability. Recognizing the ethical responsibility to address the ecological footprint of AI integration requires a commitment to environmental stewardship and sustainability. This entails minimizing energy consumption, reducing resource usage, and mitigating environmental harm throughout the lifecycle of AI technology. By prioritizing environmental sustainability in AI research, development, and deployment, stakeholders can mitigate the ecological footprint of AI integration and promote a more sustainable approach to creativity and innovation (Acemoglu & Restrepo, 2020).

Moreover, addressing the ecological footprint of AI integration is essential for upholding ethical principles of justice, equity, and accountability. Environmental degradation disproportionately affects marginalized communities and vulnerable populations, exacerbating social inequalities and exacerbating environmental injustices. As such, addressing the ecological footprint of AI technology is not only a matter of environmental ethics but also a question of social justice and human rights. Furthermore, promoting environmental sustainability in the integration of AI into digital art and crafting practices can foster ethical and responsible innovation (Pritchett, 2021). By adopting sustainable practices, such as optimizing AI algorithms for energy efficiency, promoting the use of renewable energy sources, and minimizing electronic waste generation, stakeholders can reduce the environmental impact of AI technology while fostering creativity and innovation in the artistic domain.

c. Exploration of Sustainable Practices in Digital Art

Exploring sustainable practices in digital art and crafting is essential for addressing the environmental impact of AI training and promoting ethical AI integration. Sustainable practices encompass a wide range of strategies aimed at reducing energy consumption, minimizing resource usage, and mitigating environmental harm. For example, optimizing AI algorithms and training processes to minimize energy consumption and resource usage can help reduce the environmental footprint of AI technology. Additionally, promoting the use of renewable energy sources for AI training, such as solar and wind power, can further reduce carbon emissions and lessen the environmental impact of AI integration (Winner, 2010).

Furthermore, incorporating principles of sustainability into digital art and crafting practices can foster creativity and innovation while minimizing environmental harm. For instance, adopting eco-friendly materials and production methods in digital art can reduce waste and pollution, leading to more sustainable artistic practices (Pritchett, 2021). Moreover, promoting awareness of environmental issues and encouraging collaboration among artists, AI developers, and environmental experts can help drive systemic change and promote a culture of sustainability in the artistic community.

In conclusion, the ethical responsibility to address the ecological footprint of AI integration is paramount in the integration of AI into common digital art and digital crafting. By prioritizing environmental sustainability, adopting responsible practices, and promoting systemic changes in AI research and development, stakeholders can mitigate the environmental impact of AI technology and promote a more sustainable and ethical approach to creativity and innovation. Moreover, addressing the ecological footprint of AI integration is essential for upholding principles of justice, equity, and accountability and ensuring a more just and sustainable future for all.

4. Exploitative Uses of AI-Generated Content

a. Potential for Misuse and Malicious Applications

The integration of artificial intelligence (AI) into common digital art and digital crafting has opened up new possibilities for creativity and expression. However, alongside these advancements come significant ethical concerns regarding the potential for misuse and malicious applications of AI-generated content. AI algorithms can be trained to generate highly realistic images, videos, and audio clips, which can be manipulated and used for deceptive purposes (Piotrovsky et al., 2019). For example, deepfake technology allows individuals to create convincing yet entirely fabricated videos of real people saying or doing things they never actually did. This technology has the potential to be used for various malicious purposes, including spreading misinformation, defaming individuals, and manipulating public opinion. Additionally, AI-generated content can be exploited for fraudulent activities such as identity theft, financial scams, and cyberattacks, posing significant risks to individuals and society as a whole.

One of the most alarming aspects of AI-generated content is the emergence of deepfake technology. Deepfakes utilize AI algorithms to create convincing yet entirely fabricated videos of real people saying or doing things they never actually did (Michaelson et al., 2014). These videos are often indistinguishable from genuine footage, making them highly deceptive and potentially damaging. The potential for misuse of deepfakes is vast, ranging from spreading misinformation and propaganda to defaming individuals, manipulating public opinion, and even disrupting democratic processes .

Moreover, the rise of deepfakes exacerbates existing ethical concerns surrounding consent and privacy. Victims whose faces or voices are used in deepfake videos may have their likeness exploited without their knowledge or consent, leading to violations of their privacy and dignity. Deepfakes can be used to create non-consensual pornography, harass individuals, and tarnish reputations, causing significant harm to victims and perpetuating online abuse and harassment (Allan et al., 2019).

Furthermore, the widespread dissemination of deepfakes poses a threat to trust, credibility, and the integrity of information in the digital age. With the ability to create convincing yet entirely fabricated videos, deepfakes undermine the authenticity and reliability of media and information sources. This erosion of trust can have far-reaching consequences, leading to increased skepticism, polarization, and societal unrest. Beyond deepfakes, AI-generated content also has the potential to be exploited for fraudulent activities such as identity theft, financial scams, and cyberattacks. For example, AI algorithms can be used to create synthetic identities or manipulate digital documents for fraudulent purposes. Additionally, AI-generated content can be used to deceive individuals into revealing sensitive information or engaging in harmful behaviors, posing significant risks to cybersecurity and personal safety (Floridi et al., 2018).

Addressing the potential for misuse and malicious applications of AI-generated content requires a comprehensive and collaborative approach. Artists, developers, policymakers, and civil society organizations must work together to establish ethical guidelines and regulations governing the creation, distribution, and use of AI technology in digital art and crafting. This includes implementing safeguards to detect and prevent the spread of malicious content, promoting awareness and education about the risks of AI-driven manipulation and deception, and advocating for the protection of individuals' rights and dignity in the digital realm (Winner, 2010).

b. Ethical Concerns About Deepfakes and Other Exploitative Uses

The rise of deepfakes and other exploitative uses of AI-generated content raises profound ethical concerns about the manipulation of truth, consent, and privacy. Deepfakes blur the lines between reality and fiction, making it increasingly difficult to discern authentic content from manipulated or fabricated ones. This has serious implications for trust, credibility, and the integrity of information in the digital age. Moreover, deepfakes can be used to create non-consensual pornography, harass individuals, and tarnish reputations, violating the rights and dignity of those targeted (Michaelson et al., 2014). Furthermore, the widespread dissemination of deepfakes can undermine public trust in media, institutions, and democratic processes, leading to social unrest and erosion of societal values (Dutton et al., 2009).

Deepfakes, which utilize AI algorithms to create highly realistic yet entirely fabricated videos of real individuals, pose significant ethical concerns due to their potential for abuse and manipulation. These videos can be used to depict individuals saying or doing things they never actually did, blurring the lines between truth and fiction and undermining the authenticity and credibility of digital content. This raises concerns about the manipulation of truth, consent, and privacy, as well as the potential for harm to individuals' reputations and well-being.

One of the primary ethical concerns surrounding deepfakes is the violation of individuals' privacy and consent. Victims whose faces or voices are used in deepfake videos may have their likeness exploited without their knowledge or consent, leading to significant violations of their privacy and dignity. Deepfakes can be used to create non-consensual pornography, harass individuals, and damage reputations, causing profound harm to victims and perpetuating online abuse and harassment.

Moreover, the widespread dissemination of deepfakes undermines trust, credibility, and the integrity of information in the digital age. With the ability to create convincing yet entirely fabricated videos, deepfakes can deceive viewers and manipulate public opinion, leading to misinformation, confusion, and social unrest. This erosion of trust poses serious risks to democratic processes, media integrity, and societal cohesion, highlighting the urgent need to address the ethical implications of deepfake technology (Piotrovsky et al., 2019).

Furthermore, deepfakes raise concerns about the manipulation of truth and the potential for malicious actors to exploit AI technology for deceptive purposes. Deepfake videos can be used to spread false information, defame individuals, and manipulate public discourse, undermining the reliability and authenticity of digital content. This poses significant ethical challenges for media literacy, critical thinking, and digital citizenship, as individuals must navigate an increasingly complex landscape of digital manipulation and deception.

Addressing the ethical concerns surrounding deepfakes and other exploitative uses of AI-generated content requires a multifaceted approach that involves collaboration among artists, developers, policymakers, and civil society organizations. Artists and developers have a responsibility to uphold ethical standards and promote responsible use of AI technology in digital art and crafting. This includes refraining from creating or disseminating deepfakes or other deceptive content and implementing safeguards to detect and prevent the spread of malicious content (Allan et al., 2019).

c. Responsibilities of Artists and Developers to Prevent Exploitation

In light of the ethical concerns surrounding exploitative uses of AI-generated content, artists, developers, and other stakeholders have a responsibility to prevent exploitation and promote ethical AI integration in digital art and crafting. Artists play a crucial role in setting ethical standards and norms within the creative community. By adhering to ethical principles such as authenticity, transparency, and respect for human rights, artists can contribute to the responsible use of AI technology and mitigate the risks of exploitation. Moreover, artists should be vigilant in verifying the authenticity of AI-generated content and refrain from creating or disseminating deepfakes or other deceptive materials.

Similarly, developers have a responsibility to design and deploy AI systems in a manner that minimizes the potential for misuse and exploitation. This includes implementing safeguards such as authentication mechanisms, watermarking techniques, and content moderation algorithms to detect and prevent the spread of malicious content. Additionally, developers should prioritize user privacy and data security in the design of AI systems, ensuring that individuals' rights and autonomy are protected. Moreover, developers should collaborate with policymakers, ethicists, and civil society organizations to establish clear guidelines and regulations governing the ethical use of AI technology in digital art and crafting.

EXPECTED OUTCOMES

1. Anticipated Contributions of the Research

The research on the ethical dilemmas in the integration of AI in common digital art and digital crafting is expected to make several significant contributions to both academia and practice. Firstly, it will deepen our understanding of the ethical implications of AI technology in creative processes, shedding light on the potential risks and challenges associated with AI-generated content. By exploring the intersection of ethics, technology, and art, the research will contribute to a more nuanced understanding of the ethical dilemmas faced by artists, developers, and other stakeholders in the digital art and crafting communities. Secondly, the research is expected to generate insights into the ethical frameworks and guidelines needed to promote responsible AI integration in digital art and crafting (Piotrovsky et al., 2019). By identifying best practices and ethical principles, the research will provide practical guidance for artists, developers, policymakers, and other stakeholders seeking to navigate the ethical complexities of AI technology. This will help foster a culture of responsibility, transparency, and accountability in the integration of AI into creative processes, ultimately benefiting both creators and consumers of digital art.

The research on ethical dilemmas in the integration of AI in common digital art and digital crafting is poised to make significant contributions across various dimensions, encompassing both theoretical advancements and practical applications. These anticipated contributions are expected to enrich our understanding of the complex interplay between technology, creativity, and morality while offering actionable insights for stakeholders involved in digital art and crafting (Dutton et al., 2009).

Firstly, the research is expected to deepen our understanding of the ethical implications inherent in the integration of AI technology into artistic processes. By examining the ethical dilemmas arising from the use of AI-generated content, such as bias in algorithms, ownership disputes, and societal implications, the research will shed light on previously unexplored facets of AI ethics. This deeper understanding will not only contribute to scholarly discourse but also inform practical decision-making processes among artists, developers, and policymakers (Kaplan, 2021). Secondly, the research is anticipated to generate new knowledge and insights that can be translated into ethical guidelines and responsible practices for the integration of AI in digital art and crafting. By identifying best practices and ethical principles, the research will provide a roadmap for navigating the ethical complexities inherent in AI-driven creative processes. These guidelines will serve as a valuable resource for stakeholders seeking to uphold ethical standards, promote transparency, and mitigate the risks of exploitation and harm associated with AI technology.

Moreover, the research is expected to foster collaboration and dialogue among diverse stakeholders in the digital art and crafting communities. By bringing together artists, developers, ethicists, policymakers, and other relevant actors, the research will create opportunities for interdisciplinary exchange and collective problem-solving. This collaborative approach will help build consensus around ethical norms and standards, promote mutual understanding, and foster a culture of responsibility and accountability in the integration of AI technology (Formosa, 2021). Furthermore, the research has the potential to raise awareness of the societal implications of AI technology in creative processes. By highlighting the ethical dilemmas and broader social implications associated with AI-generated content, the research will stimulate public discourse and engagement on these issues. This increased awareness will not only empower individuals to make informed decisions but also catalyze broader societal discussions on the ethical, cultural, and philosophical dimensions of AI integration in digital art and crafting.

In conclusion, the anticipated contributions of the research on ethical dilemmas in the integration of AI in common digital art and digital crafting are multifaceted and far-reaching. From deepening our theoretical understanding of AI ethics to informing practical decision-making and fostering collaborative dialogue, the research is poised to make significant contributions to both academia and practice. By addressing these anticipated outcomes, the research will help shape a more ethical, responsible, and sustainable approach to AI integration in the artistic domain.

2. Development of Ethical Guidelines and Responsible Practices

The development of ethical guidelines and responsible practices is a crucial expected outcome of research on ethical dilemmas in the integration of AI in common digital art and digital crafting. These guidelines and practices serve as essential tools for navigating the complex ethical terrain of AI-driven creative processes while promoting integrity, transparency, and respect for human dignity.

One of the key outcomes of the research will be the development of ethical guidelines and responsible practices for the integration of AI in common digital art and digital crafting. Drawing on insights from ethical theory, stakeholder consultations, and case studies, these guidelines will provide practical recommendations for addressing ethical dilemmas such as bias, exploitation, and privacy in the use of AI-generated content. By promoting ethical conduct and responsible use of AI technology, these guidelines will help mitigate the risks of misuse and exploitation while promoting trust, integrity, and respect for human rights in the artistic domain. Moreover, the development of ethical guidelines and responsible practices will help bridge the gap between ethical theory and practical application in the integration of AI in digital art and crafting. By translating ethical principles into actionable recommendations, the research will empower artists, developers, and other stakeholders to make informed decisions and navigate ethical challenges in their creative processes. This will contribute to the development of a more ethical and sustainable approach to AI integration, ensuring that AI technology is used in a manner that promotes the well-being and dignity of all individuals involved (Kaplan, 2021).

Firstly, the research is expected to contribute to the establishment of ethical guidelines that outline the principles and standards governing the ethical use of AI technology in digital art and crafting. These guidelines will draw upon insights from ethical theory, stakeholder consultations, and case studies to provide clear and actionable recommendations for artists, developers, policymakers, and other stakeholders. By articulating ethical norms and values, these guidelines will help guide decision-making and promote responsible conduct in the integration of AI technology. Moreover, the research will contribute to the development of responsible practices that translate ethical principles into actionable strategies for ethical AI integration. These practices may include measures such as transparency in the use of AI-generated content, accountability mechanisms for addressing ethical concerns, and safeguards for protecting user privacy and autonomy (Tubaro et al., 2020). By implementing these practices, stakeholders can mitigate the risks of exploitation, bias, and harm associated with AI technology while promoting trust and confidence in the integrity of digital art and crafting processes.

Additionally, the development of ethical guidelines and responsible practices will help bridge the gap between ethical theory and practical application in the integration of AI in digital art and crafting. By providing concrete guidance and recommendations, these resources will empower artists, developers, and other stakeholders to make informed decisions and navigate ethical challenges in their creative processes. This will help ensure that AI technology is used in a manner that upholds ethical standards and promotes the well-being and dignity of all individuals involved. Furthermore, the development of ethical guidelines and responsible practices will foster a culture of responsibility, transparency, and accountability in the digital art and crafting communities. By promoting awareness of ethical issues and encouraging adherence to ethical standards, these resources will help build trust and confidence among creators and consumers of digital art. This will ultimately contribute to the long-term sustainability and integrity of the artistic domain, ensuring that AI technology is used in a manner that respects ethical principles and values.

3. Awareness of Societal Implications of AI in Creative Processes

Finally, the research is expected to raise awareness of the societal implications of AI in creative processes and foster dialogue on the ethical, social, and cultural dimensions of AI technology. By engaging with stakeholders from diverse backgrounds and disciplines, the research will facilitate discussions on the ethical dilemmas, opportunities, and risks associated with AI-generated content in digital art and crafting. This will help promote a broader understanding of the societal implications of AI technology and encourage collaboration among artists, technologists, policymakers, and ethicists to address these issues collaboratively.

Firstly, the research is expected to raise awareness of the ethical dilemmas and challenges inherent in the integration of AI technology into creative processes. By examining the ethical implications of AI-generated content, such as bias in algorithms, ownership disputes, and societal implications, the research will shed light on the complex ethical considerations at play in AI-driven artistic practices. This increased awareness will help stakeholders recognize the potential risks and pitfalls associated with AI technology, enabling them to make more informed decisions and navigate ethical challenges more effectively (Kaplan, 2021). Moreover, the research is expected to raise awareness of the broader societal implications of AI integration in creative processes. By exploring the social, cultural, and political dimensions of AI technology, the research will highlight the ways in which AI-driven creative practices intersect with broader societal trends and issues. This will help stakeholders understand how AI technology can both reflect and shape social norms, values, and power dynamics, leading to more nuanced discussions and debates about the role of AI in shaping our collective future.

Additionally, the research is expected to foster awareness of the potential impact of AI technology on various stakeholders, including artists, audiences, and society as a whole. By examining the ways in which AI-generated content can influence perceptions, behaviors, and interactions, the research will help stakeholders anticipate and address potential risks and challenges associated with AI integration in digital art and crafting. This will enable stakeholders to develop strategies for promoting responsible use of AI technology and mitigating the negative consequences of AI-driven creative practices. Furthermore, the research is expected to raise awareness of the ethical, cultural, and philosophical implications of AI technology in creative processes. By engaging with diverse perspectives and disciplinary approaches, the research will stimulate dialogue and debate on the ethical and societal dimensions of AI integration in the artistic domain. This will contribute to a more holistic understanding of the implications of AI technology, fostering a more informed and engaged public discourse on these important issues (Winner, 2010).

Overall, the anticipated contributions of the research include deepening our understanding of the ethical dilemmas in the integration of AI in digital art and crafting, developing ethical guidelines and responsible practices, and raising awareness of the societal implications of AI technology. By fostering a culture of responsibility, transparency, and accountability, the research will contribute to the development of a more ethical and sustainable approach to AI integration in creative processes, ultimately benefiting both creators and consumers of digital art.

SIGNIFICANCE OF THE STUDY

1. Implications for Various Stakeholders

The study on ethical dilemmas in the integration of AI in common digital art and digital crafting holds significant implications for various stakeholders involved in the creative process. For artists, the research provides valuable insights into the ethical challenges and considerations associated with AI-driven artistic practices (Lozano-Hemmer, 2019b). By raising awareness of these issues, artists can make more informed decisions and navigate ethical dilemmas more effectively, ensuring that their creative endeavors uphold ethical standards and respect human dignity.

For artists, the study offers valuable insights into the ethical challenges and considerations associated with AI-driven artistic practices. It provides a framework for understanding the potential risks and ethical dilemmas involved in using AI technology in creative processes (Allan et al., 2019). By raising awareness of these issues, artists can make more informed decisions and navigate ethical dilemmas more effectively. This enables them to uphold ethical standards and ensure that their creative endeavors respect human dignity and promote societal values.

Similarly, for developers and technologists, the study provides critical insights into the ethical implications of AI technology in digital art and crafting. It highlights the need to design and deploy AI systems in a manner that promotes responsible use and minimizes the risk of harm. Developers can use these insights to implement safeguards for detecting and preventing bias, exploitation, and other ethical concerns. By prioritizing user privacy and autonomy in the design of AI-driven creative tools, developers can contribute to the development of ethical and responsible technology (Lozano-Hemmer, 2019a).

Moreover, the study has implications for policymakers and regulators responsible for governing the use of AI technology in the artistic domain. It underscores the importance of enacting regulations and guidelines that promote ethical conduct and protect individuals' rights and well-being. Policymakers can use the findings of the study to develop laws and regulations governing the creation, distribution, and use of AI-generated content (Lozano-Hemmer, 2006). By promoting awareness and education about the ethical implications of AI technology in digital art and crafting, policymakers can foster a culture of ethical reflection and dialogue within the creative community.

Furthermore, the study has broader implications for society as a whole. By addressing ethical dilemmas in AI-driven creative processes, the study contributes to the development of a more ethical and responsible approach to technology integration. This helps build trust and confidence among consumers and the public, ensuring that AI-enhanced creativity is guided by ethical principles and values. Ultimately, by promoting ethical considerations in AI integration, the study contributes to the well-being and dignity of all individuals involved in the creative process, while also fostering a more ethical and sustainable digital art and crafting ecosystem (Yu et al., 2020).

2. Contributions to AI Ethics, Digital Art, and Responsible Technology Development

The study on ethical dilemmas in the integration of AI in digital art and crafting makes significant contributions to the fields of AI ethics, digital art, and responsible technology development. By examining the ethical challenges and considerations associated with AI-driven creative practices, the research contributes to the growing body of literature on AI ethics and responsible technology development (Yu et al., 2020). This includes advancing our understanding of the ethical principles and frameworks needed to ensure that AI technology is used in a manner that promotes human well-being and respects ethical norms and values.

Firstly, the study contributes to the field of AI ethics by exploring the ethical challenges and considerations associated with AI-driven artistic practices. By examining issues such as bias in algorithms, ownership disputes, and societal implications, the research advances our understanding of the ethical dimensions of AI technology. This contributes to the development of ethical principles and frameworks needed to ensure that AI technology is used in a manner that promotes human well-being and respects ethical norms and values (Tubaro et al., 2020).

Moreover, the study contributes to the field of digital art by providing insights into the ethical implications of AI integration in creative processes. By examining the intersection of technology, creativity, and morality, the research enriches our understanding of the ethical dimensions of digital art and crafting. This contributes to the development of more ethical and responsible approaches to artistic expression in the digital age (Yu et al., 2020). Additionally, the study contributes to responsible technology development by highlighting the need to design and deploy AI systems in a manner that promotes responsible use and minimizes the risk of harm. By identifying best practices and ethical guidelines for the integration of AI in digital art and crafting, the research provides practical recommendations for developers, policymakers, and other stakeholders. This promotes the development of ethical and responsible technology that upholds human dignity and promotes societal values.

Furthermore, the study contributes to the field of digital art by providing insights into the ethical implications of AI integration in creative processes. By exploring the intersection of technology, creativity, and morality, the research enriches our understanding of the ethical dimensions of digital art and crafting, paving the way for more ethical and responsible approaches to artistic expression in the digital age. These contributions are crucial for advancing our understanding of the ethical implications of AI technology and promoting ethical conduct in creative processes.

3. Call to Action for Ethical Considerations in AI-Enhanced Creativity

Overall, the study serves as a call to action for ethical considerations in AI-enhanced creativity. By highlighting the ethical dilemmas and challenges associated with AI integration in digital art and crafting, the research underscores the importance of promoting ethical conduct and responsible use of AI technology in the artistic domain. This includes advocating for transparency, accountability, and fairness in the development and deployment of AI systems, as well as fostering a culture of ethical reflection and dialogue among artists, developers, policymakers, and other stakeholders (Tubaro et al., 2020). Ultimately, the study calls for a collaborative effort to ensure that AI-enhanced creativity is guided by ethical principles and values, promoting the well-being and dignity of all individuals involved. As AI technology continues to play an increasingly prominent role in the creative process, it is imperative that ethical principles and values guide its integration to ensure the well-being and dignity of all individuals involved.

Firstly, the study calls for a heightened awareness of the ethical challenges and considerations associated with AI-driven artistic practices (Formosa, 2021). By highlighting issues such as bias in algorithms, ownership disputes, and societal implications, the research underscores the importance of recognizing and addressing these ethical dilemmas. This awareness serves as a foundation for promoting ethical conduct and responsible decision-making in AI-enhanced creativity.

Moreover, the study calls for the development of ethical guidelines and responsible practices for the integration of AI in digital art and crafting. These guidelines should provide clear and actionable recommendations for artists, developers, policymakers, and other stakeholders, outlining ethical principles and standards that promote integrity, transparency, and respect for human dignity. By implementing these guidelines, stakeholders can ensure that AI technology is used in a manner that upholds ethical standards and promotes the well-being of individuals involved in the creative process (Yu et al., 2020).

Additionally, the study calls for collaboration and dialogue among diverse stakeholders in the digital art and crafting communities. By bringing together artists, developers, ethicists, policymakers, and other relevant actors, the research fosters a culture of ethical reflection and engagement. This collaboration enables stakeholders to share insights, exchange perspectives, and work together to address ethical challenges and promote responsible AI integration in creative processes (O'Neil, 2016).

Furthermore, the study calls for a commitment to ongoing education and awareness-raising efforts on the ethical implications of AI technology. By promoting awareness and understanding of these issues among creators, consumers, and the general public, the research empowers individuals to make informed decisions and engage in ethical dialogue. This fosters a more ethical and responsible approach to AI-enhanced creativity, ensuring that AI technology is used in a manner that promotes human well-being and respects ethical principles and values.

ETHICAL CONSIDERATIONS

1. Commitment to Ethical Research Practices

In the realm of ethical dilemmas in the integration of AI in common digital art and digital crafting, a commitment to ethical research practices is paramount. Researchers must adhere to ethical principles such as integrity, honesty, and transparency throughout the research process. This includes conducting research with the highest standards of scientific rigor and accuracy, ensuring that all data collection and analysis methods are ethical and transparent. Moreover, researchers should strive to minimize any potential harm or discomfort to participants and ensure that their rights and well-being are protected at all times.

Additionally, researchers must maintain impartiality and avoid conflicts of interest that could compromise the integrity of the research. This involves disclosing any potential conflicts of interest and taking steps to mitigate their impact on the research findings. By upholding these ethical standards, researchers can ensure the credibility and reliability of their research, thereby contributing to the advancement of knowledge and understanding in the field of AI ethics and digital art.

In the exploration of ethical considerations surrounding the integration of AI in common digital art and crafting, a fundamental aspect is the commitment to ethical research practices. Ethical research practices are essential for upholding integrity, respecting the rights of participants, and ensuring the validity and reliability of research findings (Lyu et al., 2021).

Firstly, a commitment to ethical research practices involves obtaining informed consent from all participants involved in the study. This ensures that individuals understand the purpose of the research, the potential risks and benefits, and their rights as participants. Informed consent is crucial for respecting autonomy and ensuring that participants willingly and voluntarily participate in the research process. Moreover, ethical research practices entail maintaining confidentiality and privacy of participants' data. Researchers must take measures to protect sensitive information and ensure that data is anonymized or de-identified whenever possible. This helps to prevent potential harm or stigmatization to participants and maintains trust between researchers and participants (Allan et al., 2019).

Additionally, ethical research practices include conducting research with honesty, transparency, and integrity. Researchers should accurately report their methods, procedures, and findings, avoiding any form of deception or manipulation. Transparency in research practices fosters trust within the scientific community and ensures that research findings are credible and reliable. Furthermore, a commitment to ethical research practices involves ensuring the well-being and safety of participants throughout the research process. Researchers should prioritize the physical, emotional, and psychological safety of participants, providing support and resources as needed. This may include offering counseling services or referrals to support organizations for participants who may experience distress or discomfort during the research (Sovhyra, 2021). In the context of ethical dilemmas in the integration of AI in digital art and crafting, ethical research practices are particularly crucial. As AI technology becomes increasingly integrated into creative processes, it is essential to conduct research that explores the ethical implications of this integration in a responsible and ethical manner. Researchers must be mindful of the potential risks and consequences of their research, taking steps to minimize harm and ensure that their work contributes positively to the understanding of ethical issues surrounding AI technology in the artistic domain.

In conclusion, a commitment to ethical research practices is essential for conducting research on ethical dilemmas in the integration of AI in common digital art and crafting. By obtaining informed consent, maintaining confidentiality and privacy, conducting research with honesty and transparency, and prioritizing the well-being of participants, researchers can uphold integrity, respect participants' rights, and ensure the validity and reliability of their research findings. This commitment to ethical research practices is crucial for advancing our understanding of the ethical implications of AI technology in digital art and crafting in a responsible and ethical manner.

2. Ensuring Participant Consent, Data Privacy, and Responsible Dissemination

Another crucial ethical consideration in the integration of AI in digital art and crafting is ensuring participant consent, data privacy, and responsible dissemination of research findings. Researchers must obtain informed consent from all participants involved in the research, ensuring that they fully understand the nature of the study, their rights as participants, and how their data will be used. This involves providing clear and comprehensive information about the research objectives, procedures, and potential risks and benefits, and allowing participants to make voluntary and informed decisions about their participation (Chen et al., 2020).

Furthermore, researchers must prioritize data privacy and confidentiality, ensuring that all participant data is handled securely and in accordance with applicable laws and regulations. This includes taking measures to protect the anonymity and confidentiality of participants, securely storing and transmitting data, and obtaining necessary permissions for data sharing and dissemination. Researchers should also be transparent about their data management practices and inform participants about how their data will be used and shared (Lips-Wiersma & Morris, 2009).

In terms of dissemination, researchers must ensure that their findings are disseminated responsibly and ethically, taking into account the potential impact on participants, stakeholders, and the broader community. This involves presenting research findings accurately and objectively, avoiding sensationalism or misrepresentation, and acknowledging any limitations or uncertainties in the research. Researchers should also consider the potential implications of their findings for policy, practice, and public discourse, and take steps to ensure that their research contributes positively to the advancement of knowledge and understanding in the field (Lyu et al., 2021). In the realm of ethical considerations for exploring the integration of AI in common digital art and crafting, ensuring participant consent, data privacy, and responsible dissemination are paramount. These principles safeguard the rights and well-being of individuals involved in research endeavors while promoting transparency and integrity in the dissemination of findings.

Firstly, ensuring participant consent is essential for upholding ethical standards in research. Researchers must obtain informed consent from all participants, ensuring they fully understand the purpose of the study, potential risks and benefits, and their rights as participants. This process involves providing clear and comprehensible information to participants and obtaining their voluntary agreement to participate without coercion or undue influence. By securing informed consent, researchers respect participants' autonomy and ensure that they are fully aware of their involvement in the research. Moreover, safeguarding data privacy is crucial for protecting participants' confidentiality and personal information. Researchers must implement measures to securely store and handle data, ensuring that it is only accessible to authorized individuals and used for the intended research purposes. This includes anonymizing or de-identifying data whenever possible to minimize the risk of re-identification and unauthorized access. By prioritizing data privacy, researchers uphold participants' trust and confidence in the research process and mitigate the risk of potential harm or misuse of their data (O'Neil, 2016).

Furthermore, responsible dissemination of research findings is essential for promoting transparency and accountability. Researchers have a responsibility to accurately report their methods, procedures, and findings, avoiding any form of distortion or misrepresentation. They must also consider the potential implications of their research on various stakeholders and ensure that findings are communicated in a manner that is accessible, understandable, and respectful. Additionally, researchers should adhere to ethical guidelines and standards for authorship and citation, acknowledging the contributions of all individuals involved in the research process. In the context of ethical dilemmas in the integration of AI in digital art and crafting, ensuring participant consent, data privacy, and responsible dissemination are particularly crucial. As AI technology becomes increasingly integrated into creative processes, researchers must be diligent in upholding ethical principles and standards throughout the research process. This includes obtaining informed consent from participants involved in studies exploring AI-driven artistic practices, protecting their data privacy, and disseminating research findings responsibly and ethically (Kadish et al., 2021).

In conclusion, ensuring participant consent, data privacy, and responsible dissemination are foundational principles in ethical considerations for research on the integration of AI in common digital art and crafting. By upholding these principles, researchers promote integrity, transparency, and accountability in the research process and contribute to the advancement of knowledge in an ethical and responsible manner. This commitment to ethical conduct is essential for building trust and confidence among participants, stakeholders, and the wider community involved in AI-driven creative endeavors.

3. Acknowledgment of Potential Sensitivities and Diverse Perspectives

Finally, ethical considerations in the integration of AI in digital art and crafting require researchers to acknowledge and respect the potential sensitivities and diverse perspectives of participants and stakeholders. This includes recognizing the cultural, social, and ethical implications of AI technology and digital art practices, and being mindful of how these may vary across different communities and contexts (Winner, 2010). Researchers should strive to engage with participants and stakeholders in a respectful and culturally sensitive manner, listening to their perspectives and incorporating their input into the research process where appropriate. In the exploration of ethical considerations surrounding the integration of AI in common digital art and digital crafting, it is imperative to acknowledge potential sensitivities and diverse perspectives. This acknowledgment fosters inclusivity, respects individual identities, and ensures that ethical dilemmas are approached with sensitivity and cultural awareness.

Firstly, acknowledging potential sensitivities involves recognizing the diverse backgrounds, experiences, and identities of individuals involved in research and creative processes. Researchers must be mindful of the potential impact of their work on different communities and consider how their research may intersect with issues of race, gender, sexuality, religion, and other aspects of identity. By acknowledging and respecting diverse perspectives, researchers can promote inclusivity and ensure that their work is culturally sensitive and respectful. Moreover, acknowledging potential sensitivities requires researchers to be vigilant in identifying and addressing any potential harm or discomfort that may arise from their research. This includes conducting thorough risk assessments and taking proactive measures to minimize harm and mitigate potential risks to participants and stakeholders. Researchers must also be prepared to respond to any concerns or grievances raised by participants, ensuring that their voices are heard and their rights are respected throughout the research process (O'Neil, 2016).

Furthermore, acknowledging potential sensitivities involves engaging in meaningful dialogue and collaboration with diverse stakeholders throughout the research process. This includes consulting with community members, advocacy groups, and other relevant stakeholders to ensure that research objectives, methods, and outcomes are culturally appropriate and respectful. By incorporating diverse perspectives into the research process, researchers can promote greater understanding, empathy, and inclusivity in their work (Sovhyra, 2021). In the context of ethical dilemmas in the integration of AI in digital art and crafting, acknowledging potential sensitivities and diverse perspectives is particularly crucial. As AI technology becomes increasingly integrated into creative processes, researchers must be mindful of the potential impact of their work on different communities and cultures. This requires researchers to approach ethical dilemmas with humility, openness, and cultural awareness, acknowledging the complexity of the issues at hand and the diverse perspectives that exist within the artistic community.

In conclusion, acknowledging potential sensitivities and diverse perspectives is essential for addressing ethical considerations in the integration of AI in common digital art and digital crafting. By recognizing the diverse backgrounds, experiences, and identities of individuals involved in research and creative processes, researchers can promote inclusivity, respect, and cultural sensitivity in their work. This acknowledgment fosters greater understanding, empathy, and collaboration within the artistic community, ensuring that ethical dilemmas are approached with sensitivity and cultural awareness.

CONCLUSION

1. Recapitulation of the Proposal's Key Components

Throughout this discourse, we have examined several key components of the proposal, including the identification of primary research objectives, the delineation of the scope to ethical dilemmas, the review of existing literature on AI ethics and digital art, and the analysis of potential impacts on artistic expression and societal values. These components collectively provide a comprehensive framework for understanding and addressing the ethical challenges inherent in the integration of AI in digital art and crafting (Kadish et al., 2021). Recapitulation of the proposal's key components involves revisiting and summarizing the main elements and objectives outlined in the research proposal. This recap serves as a reminder of the fundamental aspects of the proposed study, providing clarity and coherence to the overall research framework.

Firstly, the proposal outlines the overarching theme of exploring ethical dilemmas in the integration of AI in common digital art and digital crafting. It emphasizes the need to examine the ethical implications of AI technology in creative processes, highlighting the potential risks and challenges associated with AI-driven artistic practices. Secondly, the proposal identifies the specific areas of focus within the scope of ethical dilemmas. This may include issues such as bias in AI algorithms, ownership disputes, environmental impacts, and exploitative uses of AI-generated content. Each of these areas represents a distinct ethical challenge that requires careful consideration and analysis. Furthermore, the proposal outlines the research objectives and scope, providing a roadmap for the study. This includes identifying the primary research questions, objectives, and methodologies to be employed. By clearly defining the scope of the research, the proposal establishes the boundaries and parameters within which the study will be conducted (Kadish et al., 2021).

Additionally, the proposal highlights the significance of the research in addressing broader ethical, social, and cultural concerns. It emphasizes the importance of promoting ethical conduct and responsible use of AI technology in the artistic domain, ultimately aiming to contribute to the development of a more ethical and sustainable digital art and crafting ecosystem. Moreover, the proposal discusses the expected outcomes and contributions of the research. This may include anticipated advancements in AI ethics, digital art, and responsible technology development, as well as greater awareness of societal implications and ethical considerations in AI-enhanced creativity.

Overall, the recapitulation of the proposal's key components provides a comprehensive overview of the research framework, objectives, and significance. It serves to reinforce the rationale and purpose of the proposed study, ensuring that stakeholders have a clear understanding of its aims and objectives. By revisiting the key components of the proposal, researchers can reaffirm their commitment to addressing ethical dilemmas in AI integration and advancing ethical considerations in digital art and crafting.

2. Emphasis on the Importance of Addressing Ethical Dilemmas in AI Integration

It is evident that addressing ethical dilemmas in AI integration is of paramount importance. As AI technology becomes increasingly prevalent in creative processes, it is essential to consider the ethical implications of its use. From biases in algorithms to ownership disputes and exploitative uses of AI-generated content, ethical considerations play a crucial role in shaping the ethical landscape of AI-enhanced creativity (Chen et al., 2020). By addressing these dilemmas head-on, we can ensure that AI technology is used in a manner that upholds ethical principles and respects human dignity.

Emphasizing the importance of addressing ethical dilemmas in AI integration entails delving into the profound implications and consequences of neglecting ethical considerations in the development and deployment of AI technology. This emphasis underscores the critical need for ethical awareness, responsibility, and accountability in the rapidly evolving landscape of AI-driven innovation (O'Neil, 2016).

Firstly, addressing ethical dilemmas in AI integration is essential for safeguarding fundamental human values and rights. As AI technology becomes increasingly pervasive in various aspects of daily life, including digital art and crafting, it has the potential to significantly impact individual autonomy, privacy, and dignity. Without ethical oversight, there is a risk of AI systems perpetuating biases, discrimination, and harm against vulnerable populations, exacerbating existing inequalities and injustices. Furthermore, addressing ethical dilemmas in AI integration is crucial for maintaining public trust and confidence in technology. Trust is essential for widespread adoption and acceptance of AI-driven solutions, and ethical lapses can erode trust and undermine the legitimacy of AI systems. By prioritizing ethical considerations, developers and policymakers can build transparency, accountability, and integrity into AI systems, fostering trust and confidence among users and stakeholders (Winner, 2010).

Moreover, addressing ethical dilemmas in AI integration is vital for promoting fairness and justice in society. AI algorithms have the potential to influence decision-making processes in areas such as employment, healthcare, and criminal justice, with far-reaching implications for individuals' lives and well-being. Ethical oversight is necessary to ensure that AI systems are designed and deployed in a manner that upholds principles of fairness, non-discrimination, and social justice, mitigating the risk of algorithmic bias and inequitable outcomes (Lyu et al., 2021). Additionally, addressing ethical dilemmas in AI integration is essential for fostering innovation that aligns with societal values and aspirations. Ethical considerations can guide the development of AI technology towards outcomes that prioritize human well-being, environmental sustainability, and the common good. By integrating ethical principles into the design and implementation of AI systems, researchers and developers can promote innovation that benefits individuals, communities, and society as a whole.

In conclusion, emphasizing the importance of addressing ethical dilemmas in AI integration is crucial for ensuring the responsible and ethical development and deployment of AI technology. By safeguarding fundamental human values and rights, maintaining public trust and confidence, promoting fairness and justice, and fostering innovation that aligns with societal values, ethical considerations play a central role in shaping the future of AI-driven innovation. As AI technology continues to evolve and permeate various aspects of human life, it is imperative that ethical considerations remain at the forefront of AI development and deployment efforts, guiding the responsible use and impact of AI technology for the betterment of society.

3. Forward-Looking Perspective on the Potential Impacts and Ethical Advancements in AI-Enhanced Creativity

Looking ahead, there is tremendous potential for both positive impacts and ethical advancements in AI-enhanced creativity. As AI technology continues to evolve, it has the power to democratize access to artistic tools and foster new forms of expression. However, to realize these benefits, it is essential to address ethical considerations and ensure that AI-enhanced creativity is guided by ethical principles and values. By fostering a culture of ethical reflection, promoting responsible technology development, and prioritizing the well-being of individuals involved in the creative process, we can harness the potential of AI technology to create a more inclusive, diverse, and ethically sound artistic landscape. A forward-looking perspective on the potential impacts and ethical advancements in AI-enhanced creativity involves envisioning the future trajectory of AI technology and its implications for artistic expression, innovation, and ethical considerations. This perspective explores how advancements in AI technology may shape the future of creative processes and the ethical frameworks that guide them.

Firstly, looking forward, AI-enhanced creativity has the potential to revolutionize artistic practices and unlock new possibilities for expression and innovation. AI algorithms can generate and manipulate digital content in ways that were previously unimaginable, enabling artists to explore new forms, styles, and techniques. From generating original artworks to assisting in the creative process, AI technology offers a wealth of opportunities for artists to push the boundaries of creativity and experiment with novel approaches to artistic expression. Moreover, a forward-looking perspective acknowledges the ethical challenges and dilemmas that may arise from the integration of AI in creative processes. As AI technology becomes more sophisticated and autonomous, ethical considerations surrounding issues such as bias, privacy, ownership, and accountability become increasingly complex. It is essential to anticipate and address these challenges proactively, developing ethical frameworks and guidelines that promote responsible use and mitigate potential risks and harms (Sovhyra, 2021).

Additionally, looking forward, ethical advancements in AI-enhanced creativity may involve the development of innovative solutions and approaches to ethical dilemmas. This may include the integration of ethical principles into the design and implementation of AI systems, the adoption of transparency and accountability measures, and the promotion of diversity and inclusion in AI-driven creative practices. By fostering collaboration and dialogue among stakeholders, researchers, and policymakers, ethical advancements can help ensure that AI technology is used in a manner that upholds ethical standards and promotes the well-being of individuals and communities. Furthermore, a forward-looking perspective acknowledges the potential societal impacts of AI-enhanced creativity and the importance of ethical considerations in shaping these impacts (Zuboff, 2019).. AI technology has the power to democratize access to artistic tools and resources, empower marginalized communities, and foster cultural exchange and understanding. However, it also poses risks such as job displacement, loss of cultural authenticity, and erosion of privacy and autonomy. Ethical advancements in AI-enhanced creativity are essential for navigating these complexities and ensuring that the benefits of AI technology are equitably distributed and aligned with societal values and aspirations.

In conclusion, a forward-looking perspective on the potential impacts and ethical advancements in AI-enhanced creativity offers insights into the future of artistic expression, innovation, and ethical considerations. By envisioning a future where AI technology is integrated responsibly and ethically into creative processes, we can harness the transformative potential of AI technology while safeguarding human values, rights, and well-being. This forward-looking perspective underscores the importance of ongoing dialogue, collaboration, and ethical reflection in shaping the future of AI-enhanced creativity for the betterment of society.

REFERENCES

Acemoglu, D., & Restrepo, P. (2020). The wrong kind of AI? Artificial intelligence and the future of labour demand. *Cambridge Journal of Regions, Economy and Society, 13*(1), 25–35. doi:10.1093/cjres/rsz022

Allan, B. A., Batz-Barbarich, C., Sterling, H. M., & Tay, L. (2019). Outcomes of meaningful work: A meta-analysis. *Journal of Management Studies, 56*(3), 500–528. doi:10.1111/joms.12406

Bailey, C., Yeoman, R., Madden, A., Thompson, M., & Kerridge, G. (2019). A review of the empirical literature on meaningful work: Progress and research agenda. *Human Resource Development Review, 18*(1), 83–113. doi:10.1177/1534484318804653

Buolamwini, J., & Gebru, T. (2018). *Bias in AI and Machine Learning: An Overview*. Stanford University.

Calo, R. (Ed.). (2020). AI Ethics. Academic Press.

Chen, W., Shidujaman, M., Jin, J., & Ahmed, S. U. (2020). A methodological approach to create interactive art in artificial intelligence. *HCI International 2020—Late Breaking Papers: Cognition, Learning and Games: 22nd HCI International Conference, HCII 2020, Copenhagen, Denmark, July 19–24, 2020 Proceedings, 22*, 13–31.

Chung, J. J. Y., He, S., & Adar, E. (2022). Artist support networks: Implications for future creativity support tools. In *Designing Interactive Systems Conference* (pp. 232–246). 10.1145/3532106.3533505

Clayton, R. (2005). Rafael Lozano-Hemmer's interactive installations, using light and shadows, are designed to engage the public intimately. *Design Week, Journal of Aesthetics, Design, and Art Management*, 167.

Cohn, J. (2021). 'The Scientist of the Holy Ghost': Sunspring and Reading Nonsense. *JCMS J. Cine. Media Stud.*, *60*(5), 1–21. doi:10.1353/cj.2021.0017

Dennett, D. C. (2019). AI and Art: A Love Story. *Philosophy & Technology*.

Dutton, W. H. (2009). *Moral Machines: Teaching Robots Right from Wrong*. Academic Press.

Floridi, L., Cowls, J., Beltrametti, M., Chatila, R., Chazerand, P., Dignum, V., Luetge, C., Madelin, R., Pagallo, U., Rossi, F., Schafer, B., Valcke, P., & Vayena, E. (2018). AI4People - An ethical framework for a good AI society. *Minds and Machines*, *28*(4), 689–707. doi:10.1007/s11023-018-9482-5 PMID:30930541

Formosa, P. (2021). Robot autonomy vs human autonomy: Social robots, artificial intelligence (AI), and the nature of autonomy. *Minds and Machines*, *31*(4), 595–616. doi:10.1007/s11023-021-09579-2

Kadish, D., Risi, S., & Løvlie, A. S. (2021). Improving object detection in art images using only style transfer. In *2021 International Joint Conference on Neural Networks (IJCNN)* (pp. 1–8). 10.1109/IJCNN52387.2021.9534264

Kang, Y., Gao, S., & Roth, R. E. (2019). Transferring multiscale map styles using generative adversarial networks. *International Journal of Cartography*, *5*(2–3), 115–141. doi:10.1080/23729333.2019.1615729

Kaplan, H. G. (2021). Border Tuner and Teeter-Totter Wall: Two works of participatory public pedagogy. *Visual Inquiry Learning & Teaching Art*, *10*(1), 31–48. doi:10.1386/vi_00024_1

Lips-Wiersma, M., & Wright, S. (2012). Measuring the meaning of meaningful work: Development and validation of the comprehensive meaningful work scale. *Group & Organization Management*, *37*(5), 655–685. doi:10.1177/1059601112461578

Lozano-HemmerR. (2006). *Pulse Room*. Retrieved from https://www.lozano-hemmer.com/pulse_room.php

Lozano-Hemmer, R. (2019). *Atmospheric Memory*. Manchester International Festival.

Lozano-Hemmer, R. (2019). *Border Tuner / Sintonizador Fronterizo*. Retrieved from https://www.lozano-hemmer.com/border_tuner__sintonizador_fronterizo.php

Lysova, E. I., Allan, B. A., Dik, B. J., Duffy, R. D., & Steger, M. F. (2019). Fostering meaningful work in organizations: A multi-level review and integration. *Journal of Vocational Behavior*, *110*, 374–389. doi:10.1016/j.jvb.2018.07.004

Lyu, Y., Lin, C.-L., Lin, P.-H., & Lin, R. (2021). The cognition of audience to artistic style transfer. *Applied Sciences (Basel, Switzerland)*, *11*(7), 3290. doi:10.3390/app11073290

Marcus, M. (2019). *The Creativity Code: Art and Innovation in the Age of AI*. Academic Press.

Martela, F., & Riekki, T. J. J. (2018). Autonomy, competence, relatedness, and beneficence: A multicultural comparison of the four pathways to meaningful work. *Frontiers in Psychology*, *9*, 1157. doi:10.3389/fpsyg.2018.01157 PMID:30042710

Mezei, P. (2020). *From Leonardo to the Next Rembrandt--the need for AI-Pessimism in the age of algorithms*. Academic Press.

Michaelson, C., Pratt, M. G., Grant, A. M., & Dunn, C. P. (2014). Meaningful work: Connecting business ethics and organization studies. *Journal of Business Ethics*, *121*(1), 77–90. doi:10.1007/s10551-013-1675-5

Microsoft. (2016). *The Next Rembrandt: Blurring The Lines Between Art, Technology And Emotion.* Microsoft News. Retrieved from https://news.microsoft.com/europe/features/next-rembrandt/

Mikalonytė, E., & Kneer, M. (2021). Can artificial intelligence make art? *arXiv Prepr. arXiv2104.07598.*

Mondal, B. (2020). Artificial intelligence: state of the art. In *Recent Trends Adv* (pp. 389–425). Artif. Intell. Internet Things.

Nast, C. (2022). *Sunspring | A Sci-Fi Short Film Starring Thomas Middleditch. Ars Technica.* Retrieved from https://arstechnica.com/video/watch/sunspring-sci-fi-short-film

O'Neil, C. (2016). *Weapons of Math Destruction: How Big Data Increases Inequality and Threatens Democracy*. Academic Press.

O'Neil, M. (2018). *Artificial Unintelligence: How Computers Misunderstand the World.* Academic Press.

Piotrovsky, K. D. M., Kondrashova, V., & Ozerkov, D. (2019). *Artificial Intelligence and Intercultural Dialogue: Playing With Shadow*. The Hermitage Museum XXI Century Foundation.

Pitt, C. S., Bal, A. S., & Plangger, K. (2020). New approaches to psychographic consumer segmentation: Exploring fine art collectors using artificial intelligence, automated text analysis and correspondence analysis. *European Journal of Marketing*. Advance online publication. doi:10.1108/EJM-01-2019-0083

Poole, D. L., & Mackworth, A. K. (2017). *Artificial Intelligence: Foundations of Computational Agents*. Academic Press.

Pritchett, G. (2021). *Pulse Topology: A Conversation with Artist Rafael Lozano-Hemmer*. MIKCexplore. Retrieved from https://mikcexplore.com/home/2021/11/8/pulse-topology-a-conversation-with-artist-rafael-lozano-hemmer

Rubinstein, R. Z. (2021). *Machine Learning and Human Values*. Academic Press.

Schumann, E. (2021). Artificial Intelligence in the Arts: An Overview of AI-Generated Art and Its Ethical Implications. *Frontiers in Robotics and AI.*

Sovhyra, T. (2021). Artificial Intelligence and Issue of Authorship and Uniqueness for Works of Art (Technological Research of the Next Rembrandt). *Kult. i mystetstvo u suchasnomu sviti, 22*, 156–163. . doi:10.31866/2410-1915.22.2021.235903

Tubaro, P., Casilli, A. A., & Coville, M. (2020). The trainer, the verifier, the imitator: Three ways in which human platform workers support artificial intelligence. *Big Data & Society*, *7*(1). Advance online publication. doi:10.1177/2053951720919776

Wallach, W. (Ed.). (2011). Artificial Intelligence and Ethics: An Open Letter. Academic Press.

Wang, L., Chen, W., Yang, W., Bi, F., & Yu, F. R. (2020). A state-of-the-art review on image synthesis with generative adversarial networks. *IEEE Access : Practical Innovations, Open Solutions*, *8*, 63514–63537. doi:10.1109/ACCESS.2020.2982224

Winner, S. S. G. (2010). *The Ethics of Invention: Technology and the Human Future*. Academic Press.

Wisnioski, T. P., & Hendler, J. A. (2020). Ethical Considerations for AI in the Creative Industries. *AI Magazine*.

Yu, Y. (2016). Research on digital art creation based on artificial intelligence. Rev. Ibérica Sist. e Tecnol. *Informação*, (18B), 116.

Yu, Y., Binghong, Z., Fei, G., & Jiaxin, T. (2020). Research on artificial intelligence in the field of art design under the background of convergence media. *IOP Conference Series. Materials Science and Engineering*, *825*(1), 12027. doi:10.1088/1757-899X/825/1/012027

Yusa, I. M. M., & Aditama, P. W. (2020). Expression of spirituality concept through augmented reality technique in digital painting works entitled Sarvaprani Hitankara. *Proceedings of the 4th International Symposium of Arts, Crafts & Design in South East Asia (ARCADESA).* 10.2139/ssrn.3807700

Yusa, I. M. M., Pandawana, I., Putra, I., & Herawan, T. (2021). Manik angkeran storytelling based on android mobile tap gameplay. *Journal of Physics: Conference Series*, *1810*(1), 12034. doi:10.1088/1742-6596/1810/1/012034

Yusa, I. M. M., & Putra, I. N. A. S. (2016). *Literasi visual tokoh Hanoman Bali dengan pendekatan augmented reality.* An1mage.

Yusa, I. M. M., Putra, P. S. U., & Putra, I. N. A. S. (2017). Sinergy of art and animation technology in multimedia performance art creation entitled sad ripu. In *2017 4th International Conference on New Media Studies (CONMEDIA)* (pp. 174–181). 10.1109/CONMEDIA.2017.8266052

Zuboff, S. (2019). *The Age of Surveillance Capitalism: The Fight for a Human Future at the New Frontier of Power*. Academic Press.

Conclusion

Over time, the initial fears and some concerns have worn off about generative AI tools. Those initial concerns have been replaced by other questions.

If drawing were no object, what would people imagine? What would their raw imagination speak? What would they visualize to share with others? What images would they curate to share with peers? If people could imagine and express separate from years spent in embodied learning (drawing from the head and the heart and the whole body), what would they share? What would entrance humanity visually, and why?

Follow-On Research

Certainly, there are continuing questions:

- What are optimal ways to set up particular text, visual, and mixed-modal prompts for the generative AI tools for particular outcomes?
- What are the desirable aesthetics from the human-machine collaborations around generative AI tools?
- How are the large language model-based generative AIs evolving? Other types? What are the various methods around fine-tuning such models? The approaches for the training sets?
    - What about the customized small-scale A-GAIs? The small language models?
- What sorts of human-machine collaborations are most effective? What sequences of work are the most effective?
- What are the thresholds for artistic originality in terms of the art-generating generative AI (A-GAI) tools based on human-machine collaborations? Why?
- Are there benefits to research based on AI-generated synthetic imagery?
- Who are the foremost and celebrated human artists in this space, and why?
- What sorts of pre-production are helpful for the making of seeding imagery for use as prompts in A-GAIs? Post-production?
- How can the outputs of A-GAIs be processed for refinement?
- What are methods to take some of the edges off of the output from A-GAI tools? Why? How can computational machine repetitions be offset? Mitigated?
- What are unique sequences of production for particular outputs?
- What are some of the curated collections of works by A-GAIs? Topical sets? Sequential series? What may be learned from them?

- How about photo-realistic sets? Artful ones? Others?
- What are optimized ways to make seeding visuals for A-GAIs? Why?

There are many additional questions that may be explored through further research than the ones above.

It's an AI World Now

AI tools have been in development for generations. This is a moment of the AI world, with AI extending human capabilities across all fronts. Some of the changes are incremental, with changes at the margins; some of the changes are at the core of human endeavors. The AI tools may offer suggestions; they may offer new choices altogether. In the art-making generative AI space, the changes are somewhere in the middle, with new meshes, new creations, and new collegial human collaborations, each strengthening the other. AI tools have traction, and the challenges involve how to harness these constructively and how to continue to evolve them for value.

Wrap-Up

Making Art With Generative AI Tools works as an exploratory of ideas, some whimsical, most practical. The contents of this book introduce a broad range of thinking and practice in the space. How people choose to carry forward the work will depend on various on-ground realities and human ambitions.

Thank you to the readers and dreamers who will define next iterations.

Shalin Hai-Jew
Hutchinson Community College, USA
March 2024

Compilation of References

Abas, S., Bamanger, E., Gashan, A. K., & Guler, A. (2021). Navigating the land of opportunities as Muslim immigrants: A geocriticism perspective to transnationalism in multicultural children's literature. *Journal of Children's Literature, 47*(2), 48–60.

Abdel Naby, S., Anwar, A. F., & Ali, N. H. (2018). Utilizing the integration between digital technology and interactive design to create contemporary jewelry. *International Design Journal, 8*(2), 427–437. doi:10.21608/idj.2018.86143

Abrahamson, R. F., & Shannon, P. (1983). A plot structure analysis of favorite picture books. *The Reading Teacher, 37*(1), 44–48.

Acemoglu, D., & Restrepo, P. (2020). The wrong kind of AI? Artificial intelligence and the future of labour demand. *Cambridge Journal of Regions, Economy and Society, 13*(1), 25–35. doi:10.1093/cjres/rsz022

Ahuja, V. K. (2020, Winter). Artificial Intelligence and Copyright: Issues and Challenges. *ILI Law Review*, 270-285. https://ili.ac.in/pdf/vka.pdf

AI Safety Summit. (2023). *The Bletchley Declaration*, https://www.gov.uk/government/publications/ai-safety-summit-2023-the-bletchley-declaration

AI. (n.d.). https://ai.plainenglish.io/the-complete-timeline-of-text-to-image-evolution-b63298234ed6

Ali, S., DiPaola, D., Williams, R., Ravi, P., & Breazeal, C. (2023). Constructing dreams using generative AI. *arXiv preprint arXiv:2305.12013.*

Ali, O., Murray, P., Momin, M., & Al-Anzi, F. S. (2023). The knowledge and innovation challenges of ChatGPT: A scoping review. *Technology in Society, 75*, C7–C102402. doi:10.1016/j.techsoc.2023.102402

Allan, B. A., Batz-Barbarich, C., Sterling, H. M., & Tay, L. (2019). Outcomes of meaningful work: A meta-analysis. *Journal of Management Studies, 56*(3), 500–528. doi:10.1111/joms.12406

Al-Sayed, K., Cheng, P. C. H., & Penn, A. (2021). An Investigation into the Cognitive, Metacognitive, and Spatial Markers of Creativity and Efficiency in Architectural Design, Al Edam-. *Artificial Intelligence for Engineering Design, Analysis and Manufacturing, 35*(4), 423–437. doi:10.1017/S0890060421000251

Amabile, T. M. (1983). The social psychology of creativity: A componential conceptualization. *Journal of Personality and Social Psychology, 45*(2), 357–376. doi:10.1037/0022-3514.45.2.357

Amabile, T. M. (1996). *Creativity in context: Update to the social psychology of creativity.* Westview Press.

Amershi, S., Weld, D., Vorvoreanu, M., Fourney, A., Nushi, B., Collisson, P., . . . Horvitz, E. (2019). Guidelines for human-AI interaction. In *Proceedings of the 2019 CHI Conference on Human Factors in Computing Systems* (pp. 1-13). Available at: https://www.microsoft.com/en-us/research/uploads/prod/2019/01/Guidelines-for-Human-AI-Interaction-camera-ready.pdf

Anantrasirichai, N., & Bull, D. (2022). Artificial intelligence in the creative industries: A review. *Artificial Intelligence Review*, *55*(1), 589–656. doi:10.1007/s10462-021-10039-7

Andre, E., & Rist, T. (2000, July). Adding life-like synthetic characters to the web. In *International Workshop on Cooperative Information Agents* (pp. 1-13). Springer Berlin Heidelberg. 10.1007/978-3-540-45012-2_1

André, E., Dorfmüller-Ulhaas, K., & Rehm, M. (2005). Engaging in a conversation with synthetic characters along the virtuality continuum. *Smart Graphics: 5th International Symposium, SG 2005, Frauenwörth Cloister, Germany, August 22-24, 2005 Proceedings*, *5*, 1–12.

Angert, T., Suzara, M. I., Han, J., Pondoc, C. L., & Subramonyam, H. (2023). Spellburst: A node-based interface for exploratory creative coding with natural language prompts. *arXiv preprint arXiv:2308.03921*. doi:10.1145/3586183.3606719

Anstine, D., & Isayev, O. (2023). Generative Models as an Emerging Paradigm in the Chemical Sciences. *Journal of the American Chemical Society*, *145*(16), 8736–8750. doi:10.1021/jacs.2c13467 PMID:37052978

Aram, D., Fine, Y., & Ziv, M. (2013). Enhancing parent–child shared book reading interactions: Promoting references to the book's plot and socio-cognitive themes. *Early Childhood Research Quarterly*, *28*(1), 111–122. doi:10.1016/j.ecresq.2012.03.005

Arias-Rosales, A. (2022). The perceived value of human-AI collaboration in early shape exploration: An exploratory assessment. *Plos One, 17*(9), 1 - 40.

Arizpe, E., Styles, M., Mackey, M., Bromley, H., Coulthard, K., & Noble, K. (2015). New case studies of children responding to picturebooks. In *Children Reading Picturebooks* (pp. 145–168). Routledge. doi:10.4324/9781315683911-19

Artechouse. (n.d.). Artechouse announces the return of the ground breaking exhibition machine hallucinations: NYC with refik anadol for a special limited-duration run in New York City. *Artechouse.* https://www.artechouse.com/news/artechouse-announces-return-of-machine-hallucination-nyc/

Ashktorab, Z., Liao, Q., Dugan, C., Johnson, J., Pan, Q., Zhang, W., Kumaravel, S., & Campbell, M. (2020). Human-AI Collaboration in a Cooperative Game Setting. *Proceedings of the ACM on Human-Computer Interaction*, *4*(CSCW2), 1–20. doi:10.1145/3415167

Assanie, M. (2002, March). Directable synthetic characters. In *Proceedings of the AAAI Spring Symposium on Artificial Intelligence and Interactive Entertainment* (pp. 1-7). AAAI.

Atlantic Council. (2023). Annex 6: Learning from Cybersecurity, Preparing for Generative AI. In *Scaling Trust The On Web* (pp. 1–12). Atlantic Council. https://www.jstor.org/stable/resrep51651.26

Avrahami, O., Lischinski, D., & Fried, O. (2021). *Blended diffusion for text-driven editing of natural images.* arXiv:2111.14818v2 [cs.CV]

Aydın, N., & Erdem, O. A. (2022, December). A Research on the New Generation Artificial Intelligence Technology Generative Pretraining Transformer 3. In *2022 3rd International Informatics and Software Engineering Conference (IISEC)* (pp. 1-6). IEEE. http://dx.doi.org/10.1109/IISEC56263.2022.9998298

Baidoo-Anu, D., & Owusu Ansah, L. (2023). Education in the Era of Generative Artificial Intelligence (AI): Understanding the Potential Benefits of ChatGPT in Promoting Teaching and Learning. *SSRN, 11*. Advance online publication. doi:10.2139/ssrn.4337484

Bailey, C., Yeoman, R., Madden, A., Thompson, M., & Kerridge, G. (2019). A review of the empirical literature on meaningful work: Progress and research agenda. *Human Resource Development Review, 18*(1), 83–113. doi:10.1177/1534484318804653

Banafa, A. (2023). *Transformative AI: Responsible, Transparent, and Trustworthy AI Systems*. River Publishers.

Bandi, A., Adapa, P. V. S. R., & Kuchi, Y. E. V. P. K. (2023). The power of generative ai: A review of requirements, models, input–output formats, evaluation metrics, and challenges. *Future Internet, 15*(8), 260. doi:10.3390/fi15080260

Bao, Y., Gong, W., & Yang, K. (2023). A Literature Review of Human–AI Synergy in Decision Making: From the Perspective of Affordance Actualization Theory. *Systems, 11*(9), 442. doi:10.3390/systems11090442

Barbosa, R. G. (2009). The Philosophical Approaches to Intellectual Property and Legal Transplants - The Mexican Supreme Court and NAFTA Article 1705. *Houston Journal of International Law, 31*(3), 515–564.

Barfield, W. (2006). Intellectual Property Rights in Virtual Environments: Considering the Rights of Owners, Programmers and Virtual Avatars. *Akron Law Review, 39*(3), 649–700.

Barfield, W., & Pagallo, U. (2021). *Advanced Introduction to Law and Artificial Intelligence*. Edward Elgar Publishing Ltd.

Bar-Gil, O. (2023, Apr.). *The dance of agencies in AI art—Beyond the creator-tool Dichotomy, a netnographic analysis of Reddit forums*. Academic Press.

Barratt, S., & Sharma, R. (2018). A Note on the Inception Score. *arXiv [stat.ML]*. arXiv. http://arxiv.org/abs/1801.01973

Bartneck, C., & Reichenbach, J. (2005). Subtle emotional expressions of synthetic characters. *International Journal of Human-Computer Studies, 62*(2), 179–192. doi:10.1016/j.ijhcs.2004.11.006

Bender, S. M. (2023). Coexistence and creativity: screen media education in the age of artificial intelligence content generators. *Media Practice and Education*, 1-16.

Berlin, M. R. (2003). *Predatory sequence learning for synthetic characters* [Doctoral dissertation]. Massachusetts Institute of Technology.

Bhambri, P., & Hans, S. (2010). Evaluation of Integrated Development Environments for Embedded System Design. *Apeejay Journal of Management and Technology, 5*(2), 138–146.

Bhandari, P., & Brennan, H. M. (2023). Trustworthiness of Children Stories Generated by Large Language Models. *arXiv preprint arXiv:2308.00073*. doi:10.18653/v1/2023.inlg-main.24

BieF.YangY.ZhouZ.GhanemA.ZhangM.YaoZ.WuX. (2023). RenAIssance: A Survey into AI Text-to-Image Generation in the Era of Large Model. *arXiv [cs.CV]*. https://arxiv.org/abs/2309.00810

Bigham, J. P., Jayant, C., Ji, H., Little, G., Miller, A., Miller, R. C., ... White, B. (2010). VizWiz: nearly real-time answers to visual questions. *UIST '10: Proceedings of the 23nd annual ACM symposium on User interface software and technology*, 333-342. 10.1145/1866029.1866080

Bishop, C. M. (2006). *Pattern Recognition and Machine Learning*. Springer.

Blauer, E. (2013). *Contemporary American jewelry design*. Springer Science & Business Media.

Boden, M. A. (1977). *Artificial Intelligence and Natural Man*. Harvester Press.

Boden, M. A. (1998). Creativity and artificial intelligence. *Artificial Intelligence, 103*(1-2), 347–356. doi:10.1016/S0004-3702(98)00055-1

Boden, M. A. (2004). *The Creative Mind: Myths and Mechanisms*. Routledge. doi:10.4324/9780203508527

Boden, M. A., & Edmonds, E. A. (2009). What is generative art? *Digital Creativity (Exeter), 20*(1-2), 21–46. doi:10.1080/14626260902867915

Bossema, M., Allouch, S. B., Plaat, A., & Saunders, R. (2023). Human-robot co-creativity: A scoping review—Informing a research agenda for human-robot co-creativity with older adults. *arXiv preprint arXiv:*2309.07033. doi:10.1109/RO-MAN57019.2023.10309458

Bouley, T. M., & Godfrey, P. C. (2008). Reading outside the boundaries: Children's literature as pedagogy for building empathy and understanding of social justice in the college classroom. *The Journal of Effective Teaching*, *8*(1), 33–41.

Bourgault, S., & E, J. (2023). Exploring the horizon of computation for creativity. *XRDS: Crossroads, The ACM Magazine for Students*, *29*(4), 6-9.

Bradford, C. (2011). Children's literature in a global age: Transnational and local identities. *Barnboken*, *34*(1), 18761. doi:10.14811/clr.v34i1.23

Bressane Neto, A. F., & Corrêa da Silva, F. S. (2009). Synthetic characters with personality and emotion. In *Intelligent Virtual Agents: 9th International Conference, IVA 2009 Amsterdam, The Netherlands, September 14-16, 2009 Proceedings 9* (pp. 533-534). Springer Berlin Heidelberg.

Bressane Neto, A. F., & Corrêa da Silva, F. S. (2010). On the construction of synthetic characters with personality and emotion. *Advances in Artificial Intelligence–SBIA 2010: 20th Brazilian Symposium on Artificial Intelligence, São Bernardo do Campo, Brazil, October 23-28, 2010 Proceedings*, *20*, 102–111.

Bringsjord, S., Shilliday, A., Taylor, J., Werner, D., Clark, M., Charpentier, E., & Bringsjord, A. (2008). Toward logic-based cognitively robust synthetic characters in digital environments. *Frontiers in Artificial Intelligence and Applications*, *171*, 87.

Browne, K. (2022). Who (or what) is an AI artist? *Leonardo*, *55*(2), 130–134. doi:10.1162/leon_a_02092

Brynjolfsson, E., Li, D., & Raymond, L. R. (2023). *Generative AI at work* (No. w31161). National Bureau of Economic Research. https://www.nber.org/system/files/working_papers/w31161/w31161.pdf

Buccafusco, C. (2016). A theory of copyright authorship. *Virginia Law Review*, *102*(5), 1229–1295. https://www.jstor.org/stable/43923336

Buckley, A. (2023). Generative AI: A master or servant of market research analysis? *Applied Marketing Analytics*, *9*(2), 145–152.

Budhwar, P., Chowdhury, S., Wood, G., Aguinis, H., Bamber, G. J., Beltran, J. R., Boselie, P., Lee Cooke, F., Decker, S., DeNisi, A., Dey, P. K., Guest, D., Knoblich, A. J., Malik, A., Paauwe, J., Papagiannidis, S., Patel, C., Pereira, V., Ren, S., ... Varma, A. (2023). Human resource management in the age of generative artificial intelligence: Perspectives and research directions on ChatGPT. *Human Resource Management Journal*, *33*(3), 606–659. doi:10.1111/1748-8583.12524

Buolamwini, J., & Gebru, T. (2018). *Bias in AI and Machine Learning: An Overview*. Stanford University.

Burke, R. C. (2001). *It's about time: Temporal representations for synthetic characters* [Doctoral dissertation]. Massachusetts Institute of Technology.

Caldwell, M. (2023). What is an “author”? -Copyright authorship of ai art through a philosophical lens. *Houston Law Review, 61*(2), 411–442. https://houstonlawreview.org/article/92132-what-is-an-author-copyright-authorship-of-ai-art-through-a-philosophical-lens

Calo, R. (Ed.). (2020). AI Ethics. Academic Press.

Cambridge Dictionary. (2024). *Creativity*. Available at: https://dictionary.cambridge.org/dictionary/english/creativity

Candy, L. (2020). Creating with the digital: tool, medium, mediator, partner. *Interactivity, Game Creation, Design, Learning, and Innovation: 8th EAI International Conference, ArtsIT 2019, and 4th EAI International Conference, DLI 2019, Aalborg, Denmark, November 6–8, 2019 Proceedings, 8*, 13–28.

Cao, Y., Li, S., Liu, Y., Yan, Z., Dai, Y., Yu, P. S., & Sun, L. (2023). A Comprehensive Survey of AI-Generated Content (AIGC): A History of Generative AI from GAN to ChatGPT. *arXiv [cs.AI]*. arXiv. http://arxiv.org/abs/2303.04226

Caporusso, N. (2023). Generative Artificial Intelligence and the Emergence of Creative Displacement Anxiety [Review]. *Research Directs in Psychology and Behavior., 3*(1). Advance online publication. doi:10.53520/rdpb2023.10795

Carter, R., & Carter, R. A. (2023). Machine visions: Mapping depictions of machine vision through critical image synthesis. Open Library of Humanities, 9(2).

Castronova, E. (2006). *Synthetic Worlds*. University of Chicago Press. doi:10.7208/chicago/9780226096315.001.0001

Caulfield, H. J. (1995). The computer subconscious. *Kybernetes, 24*(4), 46–52. doi:10.1108/03684929510089349

Cautela, C., Mortati, M., Dell’Era, C., & Gastaldi, L. (2019). The impact of artificial intelligence on design thinking practice: Insights from the ecosystem of startups. *Strategic Design Research Journal, 12*(1), 114–134. doi:10.4013/sdrj.2019.121.08

Chan, E. R., Lin, C. Z., Chan, M. A., Nagano, K., Pan, B., De Mello, S., & Gallo, O. (2021). Efficient Geometry-Aware 3D Generative Adversarial Networks. *arXiv [cs.CV]*. arXiv. http://arxiv.org/abs/2112.07945

Chan, C. K. Y., & Hu, W. (2023). Students’ voices on generative AI: Perceptions, benefits, and challenges in higher education. *International Journal of Educational Technology in Higher Education, 20*(43), 1–18. doi:10.1186/s41239-023-00411-8

Chandramouli, P., & Gandikota, K. V. (2022). LDEdit: Towards Generalized Text Guided Image Manipulation via Latent Diffusion Models. *arXiv [cs.CV]*. arXiv. http://arxiv.org/abs/2210.02249

Chatterjee, A. (2022). Art in an age of artificial intelligence. *Frontiers in Psychology, 13*, 1 - 9.

Chatterjee, A. (2022). Art in an age of artificial intelligence. *Frontiers in Psychology, 13*, 1024449. doi:10.3389/fpsyg.2022.1024449 PMID:36533018

Chen, J., Yoshida, N., & Takada, H. (2023). An investigation of licensing of datasets for machine learning based on the GQM model. *arXiv - CS - Machine Learning*. DOI:arxiv-2303.13735

Chen, J.M., Wang, D.L., Shao, Z.C., Zhang, X., Ruan, M.C., Li, H.T., & Li, J.Q. (2023). Using Artificial Intelligence to Generate Master Quality Architectural Designs from Text Descriptions. *Buildings, 13*(9).

Chen, W., Hu, H., Saharia, C., & Cohen, W. W. (2022). Re-Imagen: Retrieval-Augmented Text-to-Image Generator. *arXiv [cs.CV]*. arXiv. http://arxiv.org/abs/2209.14491

Chen, M., Jiang, Y., Cao, Y., & Zomaya, A. (2019). CreativeBioMan: A Brain- and Body-Wearable, Computing-Based, Creative Gaming System. *IEEE Systems, Man, and Cybernetics Magazine, 6*(1), 14–22. doi:10.1109/MSMC.2019.2929312

Chen, W., Shidujaman, M., Jin, J., & Ahmed, S. U. (2020). A methodological approach to create interactive art in artificial intelligence. *HCI International 2020–Late Breaking Papers: Cognition, Learning and Games: 22nd HCI International Conference, HCII 2020, Copenhagen, Denmark, July 19–24, 2020 Proceedings, 22*, 13–31.

Chen, W., Shidujaman, M., Jin, J., & Ahmed, S. U. (2020). A methodological approach to create interactive art in artificial intelligence. *HCI International 2020—Late Breaking Papers: Cognition, Learning and Games: 22nd HCI International Conference, HCII 2020, Copenhagen, Denmark, July 19–24, 2020 Proceedings, 22*, 13–31.

Chesney, B., & Citron, D. (2019). Deep fakes: A looming challenge for privacy, democracy, and national security. *California Law Review, 107*(6), 1753–1820. https://www.jstor.org/stable/26891938

Cheung, K. S. (2023). Real Estate Insights Unleashing the potential of ChatGPT in property valuation reports: The "Red Book" compliance Chain-of-thought (CoT) prompt engineering. *Journal of Property Investment & Finance*. Advance online publication. doi:10.1108/JPIF-06-2023-0053

Choi, J., Choi, Y., Kim, Y., Kim, J., & Yoon, S. (2023). Custom-Edit: Text-Guided Image Editing with Customized Diffusion Models. *arXiv [cs.CV]*. arXiv. http://arxiv.org/abs/2305.15779

Choi, S. K. (2022). *Losing touch: A comparative phenomenology of creative process in traditional and neural painting (Art in the age of artificial intelligence)*. Academic Press.

Choi, S. K., DiPaola, S., & Töyrylä, H. (2021). Artistic style meets artificial intelligence. *Journal of Perceptual Imaging*.

Chollet, F. (2018). *Deep Learning with Python*. Manning Publications.

Choudhary, V. & Ali, A. S. M. (2023). ChatGPT and Copyright Concerns. *Economic and Political Weekly, 58*(16), 4–5.

Chung, C., & Huang, S. (2023). Interactively transforming chinese ink paintings into realistic images using a border enhance generative adversarial network. *Multimedia Tools and Applications, 82*(8), 11663–11696. doi:10.1007/s11042-022-13684-4

Chung, J. J. Y. (2023). Designing AI-Powered Art-Making Tools. *XRDS: Crossroads. The ACM Magazine for Students, 29*(4), 14–19.

Chung, J. J. Y., He, S., & Adar, E. (2021, June). The intersection of users, roles, interactions, and technologies in creativity support tools. In *Designing Interactive Systems Conference 2021* (pp. 1817-1833). 10.1145/3461778.3462050

Chung, J. J. Y., He, S., & Adar, E. (2022, June). Artist support networks: Implications for future creativity support tools. In *Designing Interactive Systems Conference* (pp. 232-246). 10.1145/3532106.3533505

Çiçek, Ö., Abdulkadir, A., Lienkamp, S. S., Brox, T., & Ronneberger, O. (2016). 3D U-Net: Learning Dense Volumetric Segmentation from Sparse Annotation. *ArXiv*. /abs/1606.06650

Clayton, R. (2005). Rafael Lozano-Hemmer's interactive installations, using light and shadows, are designed to engage the public intimately. *Design Week, Journal of Aesthetics, Design, and Art Management*, 167.

Cohn, J. (2021). 'The Scientist of the Holy Ghost': Sunspring and Reading Nonsense. *JCMS J. Cine. Media Stud., 60*(5), 1–21. doi:10.1353/cj.2021.0017

Collins English Dictionary. (2024). *Creativity*. Available at: https://www.collinsdictionary.com/dictionary/english/creative

Colton, S., & Wiggins, G. A. (2012). Computational creativity: The final frontier? *Proceedings of 20th European Conference on Artificial Intelligence*, 21-26. 10.3233/978-1-61499-098-7-21

Cooney, M. (2021). Robot art, in the eye of the beholder? Personalized metaphors facilitate communication of emotions and creativity. *Frontiers in Robotics and AI, 8*, 1 - 19.

Copyright, D., & Act, P. United Kingdom (1988). https://www.legislation.gov.uk/ukpga/1988/48/contents

Cotter, T. (2010). Transformative use and cognizable harm. *Vanderbilt Journal of Entertainment and Technology Law, 12*(4), 701–753. https://scholarship.law.vanderbilt.edu/jetlaw/vol12/iss4/3

Couairon, G., Verbeek, J., Schwenk, H., & Cord, M. (2022). DiffEdit: Diffusion-Based Semantic Image Editing with Mask Guidance. *arXiv [cs.CV]*. arXiv. http://arxiv.org/abs/2210.11427

Cress, S. W., & Holm, D. T. (1998). *Developing empathy through children's literature*. ERIC.

Cropley, A. (2020). Creativity-focused Technology Education in the Age of Industry 4.0. *Creativity Research Journal, 32*(2), 184–191. doi:10.1080/10400419.2020.1751546

Csikszentmihalyi, M. (1997). *Creativity: Flow and the Psychology of Discovery and Invention*. Harper Perennial.

Dalalah, D., & Dalalah, O. M. A. (2023). The false positives and false negatives of generative AI detection tools in education and academic research: The case of ChatGPT. *International Journal of Management Education, 21*(2). doi:10.1016/j.ijme.2023.100822

Daniele, A., & Song, Y. Z. (2019, January). Ai+ art= human. In *Proceedings of the 2019 AAAI/ACM Conference on AI, Ethics, and Society* (pp. 155-161). 10.1145/3306618.3314233

Das, P., & Varshney, L. R. (2022). Explaining Artificial Intelligence Generation and Creativity: Human interpretability for novel ideas and artifacts. *IEEE Signal Processing Magazine, 39*(4), 85–95. doi:10.1109/MSP.2022.3141365

Daun, M., & Brings, J. (2023). How ChatGPT Will Change Software Engineering. *Education. Annual Conference on Innovation and Technology in Computer Science Education, ITiCSE.*

Davies, J., Klinger, J., Mateos-Garcia, J., & Stathoulopoulos, K. (2020). *AI and the Creative Industries: The art in the artificial.* London: Creative Industries Policy and Evidence Centre and Nesta. Retrieved from https://pec.ac.uk/research-reports/the-art-in-the-artificial

DCMS. (1998). *Mapping the Creative Industries*. Available at: http://www.culture.gov.uk/creative/creative_industries.html

DeepDream. (2023, Sept. 24). In *Wikipedia*. Retrieve3d Nov. 8, 2023, from https://en.wikipedia.org/wiki/DeepDream

Dekel, R. (2023). *A.I. And Human Originality and Creativity Will humanity run out of original, innovative ideas?* Available at: https://www.inc.com/inc-masters/ai-and-human-originality-and-creativity.html

DelSignore, P. (2022). *Medium*. Retrieved 02 12, 2024, from AI Art Wins Competition And Sparks Controversy: https://medium.com/mlearning-ai/ai-art-wins-fine-arts-competition-and-sparks-controversy-882f9b4df98c

Demarco, F., Bertacchini, F., Scuro, C., Bilotta, E., & Pantano, P. (2019). Algorithms for jewelry industry 4.0. In *International Conference on Numerical Computations: Theory and Algorithms* (pp. 425-436). Cham: Springer International Publishing.

Demirel, H., Goldstein, M., Li, X., & Sha, Z. (2023). Human-Centered Generative Design Framework: An Early Design Framework to Support Concept Creation and Evaluation. *International Journal of Human-Computer Interaction, 40*(4), 933–944. doi:10.1080/10447318.2023.2171489

Dennett, D. C. (2019). AI and Art: A Love Story. *Philosophy & Technology.*

DiBlasi, J., Castellanos, C., Kang, E., Poltronieri, F., & Smith, L. (2020, November). Agency & autonomy: Intersections of artificial intelligence and creative practice. In *International Symposium on Electronic Art* (*Vol. 7*). Academic Press.

Ding, M., Yang, Z., Hong, W., Zheng, W., Zhou, C., & Da Yin, J. L. (2021). CogView: Mastering Text-to-Image Generation via Transformers. *arXiv [cs.CV]*. arXiv. http://arxiv.org/abs/2105.13290

d'Inverno, M., & McCormack, J. (2015). *Heroic versus collaborative AI for the arts*. Academic Press.

Dollens, D. (2014). Alan Turing's Drawings, Autopoiesis and Can Buildings Think? *Leonardo*, *47*(3), 249–253. doi:10.1162/LEON_a_00766

Domingos, P. (2015). *The Master Algorithm: How the Quest for the Ultimate Learning Machine Will Remake Our World*. Basic Books.

Dorin, A. (2008). A survey of virtual ecosystems in generative electronic art. In *The Art of Artificial Evolution: A Handbook on Evolutionary Art and Music* (pp. 289–309). Springer Berlin Heidelberg. doi:10.1007/978-3-540-72877-1_14

Dorin, A. (2013, March). Chance and complexity: stochastic and generative processes in art and creativity. In *Proceedings of the Virtual Reality International Conference: Laval Virtual* (pp. 1-8). 10.1145/2466816.2466837

Dutton, W. H. (2009). *Moral Machines: Teaching Robots Right from Wrong*. Academic Press.

Du, X., An, P., Leung, J., Li, A., Chapman, L. E., & Zhao, J. (2024). DeepThInk: Designing and probing human-AI co-creation in digital art therapy. *International Journal of Human-Computer Studies*, *181*(103139), 1–17. doi:10.1016/j.ijhcs.2023.103139

Dwivedi, Y. K., Hughes, L., Bhadeshia, H. K. D. H., Ananiadou, S., Cohn, A. G., Cole, J. M., . . . Wang, X. (2023). Artificial intelligence (AI) futures: India-UK collaborations emerging from the 4th Royal Society Yusuf Hamied workshop. *International Journal of Information Management*. 10.1016/j.ijinfomgt.2023.102725

Dwivedi, Y. K., Kshetri, N., Hughes, L., Slade, E. L., Jeyaraj, A., Kar, A. K., Baabdullah, A. M., Koohang, A., Raghavan, V., Ahuja, M., Albanna, H., Albashrawi, M. A., Al-Busaidi, A. S., Balakrishnan, J., Barlette, Y., Basu, S., Bose, I., Brooks, L., Buhalis, D., ... Wright, R. (2023). "So what if ChatGPT wrote it?" Multidisciplinary perspectives on opportunities, challenges and implications of generative conversational AI for research, practice and policy. *International Journal of Information Management*, *71*, C7–C102642. doi:10.1016/j.ijinfomgt.2023.102642

Dwivedi, Y. K., Pandey, N., Currie, W., & Micu, A. (2023). Leveraging ChatGPT and other generative artificial intelligence (AI)-based applications in the hospitality and tourism industry: Practices, challenges and research agenda. *International Journal of Contemporary Hospitality Management*. Advance online publication. doi:10.1108/IJCHM-05-2023-0686

Dyches, T. T., & Prater, M. A. (2005). Characterization of developmental disability in children's fiction. *Education and Training in Developmental Disabilities*, 202–216.

Dyches, T. T., Prater, M. A., & Cramer, S. F. (2001). Characterization of mental retardation and autism in children's books. *Education and Training in Mental Retardation and Developmental Disabilities*, 230–243.

Eapen, T. T., Finkenstadt, D. J., Folk, J., & Venkataswamy, L. (2023). How generative AI can augment human creativity. *Harvard Business Review*. Available at: https://hbr.org/2023/07/how-generative-ai-can-augment-human-creativity

Earley, S. (2023). What executives need to know about knowledge management, large language models and generative AI. *Applied Marketing Analytics*, *9*(3), 215–229.

Edgar, I. (2004). *A guide to imagework: Imagination-based research methods*. Routledge. doi:10.4324/9780203490136

Eladhari, M., & Lindley, C. A. (2003, November). Player character design facilitating emotional depth in MMORPGs. *DIGRA Conference.*

Elam, M. (2022). Signs taken for wonders: Ai, art & the matter of race. *Daedalus, 151*(2), 198–217. doi:10.1162/daed_a_01910

Elasri , M., Elharrouss , O., Al-ma'adeed , S., & Tairi , H. (2022). Image Generation: A Review. *Neural Processing Letters, 54.* Advance online publication. doi:10.1007/s11063-022-10777-x

Elgammal, A., Liu, B., Elhoseiny, M., & Mazzone, M. (2017). CAN: Creative Adversarial Networks, generating" art" by learning about styles and deviating from style norms. *arXiv preprint arXiv*:1706.07068.

Elgammal, A., Liu, B., Elhoseiny, M., & Marey, M. (2017). To hide or not to hide: A transparent 3D model of deep neural networks. *Proceedings of the IEEE Conference on Computer Vision and Pattern Recognition (CVPR).*

Epstein, Z., Hertzmann, A., Herman, L., Mahari, R., Frank, M. R., Groh, M., . . . Russakovsky, O. (2023). Art and the science of generative AI: A deeper dive. *arXiv preprint arXiv:2306.04141.*

Epstein, Z., Schroeder, H., & Newman, D. (2022). When happy accidents spark creativity: Bringing collaborative speculation to life with generative AI. *arXiv preprint arXiv:2206.00533.*

Ertem, İ. (2013). Exploring the role of digital children's literature in the technology-based literacy instruction. *Okuma Yazma Eğitimi Araştırmaları, 1*(2), 102–108.

Eshraghian, J. (2020). Human ownership of artificial creativity. *Nature Machine Intelligence, 2*(3), 157–160. doi:10.1038/s42256-020-0161-x

Esling, P., & Devis, N. (2020). Creativity in the era of artificial intelligence. *arXiv:2008.05959.* https://doi.org//arXiv.2008.05959 doi:10.48550

Esser, P., Rombach, R., & Ommer, B. (2021). Taming transformers for high-resolution image synthesis. *Proceedings of the IEEE/CVF Conference on Computer Vision and Pattern Recognition*, 12873–12883.

Eva-Maria Painer v Standard Verlags GmbH 1[2011] ECR I-2533

Evans, J. (1989). *A history of jewellery*. Courier Corporation.

Fang, Z. (1996). Illustrations, text, and the child reader: what are pictures in children's storybooks for? *Reading Horizons: A Journal of Literacy and Language Arts, 37*(2), 130 – 142.

Fenwick, M., & Jurcys, P. (2023). Originality and the future of copyright in an age of generative AI. *Computer Law & Security Report, 51*, C7–C105892. doi:10.1016/j.clsr.2023.105892

Flew, T. (2002). Beyond ad hocery: defining creative industries. *Cultural Sites, Cultural Theory, Cultural Policy, The Second International Conference on Cultural Policy Research.* Available at: http:// eprints.qut.edu.au/archive/00000256

Floridi, L., Cowls, J., Beltrametti, M., Chatila, R., Chazerand, P., Dignum, V., Luetge, C., Madelin, R., Pagallo, U., Rossi, F., Schafer, B., Valcke, P., & Vayena, E. (2018). AI4People - An ethical framework for a good AI society. *Minds and Machines, 28*(4), 689–707. doi:10.1007/s11023-018-9482-5 PMID:30930541

Fogelström, E. (2013). *Investigation of shapes and colours as elements of character design.* Degree project. Game Design. Uppsala Universitet.

Formosa, P. (2021). Robot autonomy vs human autonomy: Social robots, artificial intelligence (AI), and the nature of autonomy. *Minds and Machines, 31*(4), 595–616. doi:10.1007/s11023-021-09579-2

Fosso Wamba, S., Guthrie, C., Queiroz, M. M., & Minner, S. (2023). ChatGPT and generative artificial intelligence: An exploratory study of key benefits and challenges in operations and supply chain management. *International Journal of Production Research*, 1–21. Advance online publication. doi:10.1080/00207543.2023.2294116

Fosso Wamba, S., Queiroz, M. M., Chiappetta Jabbour, C. J., & Shi, C. V. (2023). Are both generative AI and ChatGPT game changers for 21st-Century operations and supply chain excellence? *International Journal of Production Economics*, *265*, C7–C109015. doi:10.1016/j.ijpe.2023.109015

Foster, D. (2019). *Generative deep learning: teaching machines to paint, write, compose, and play*. O'Reilly Media.

Franceschelli, G., & Musolesi, M. (2021). Creativity and machine learning. *Survey (London, England)*. Advance online publication. arXiv2104.02726. doi:10.48550/arXiv.2104.02726

Frey, C. B., & Osborne, M. A. (2013). The Future of Employment: How Susceptible are Jobs to Computerisation? *Technological Forecasting and Social Change*, *114*, 254–280. doi:10.1016/j.techfore.2016.08.019

Frich, J., Mose Biskjaer, M., & Dalsgaard, P. (2018). Twenty years of creativity research in human-computer interaction: Current state and future directions. *Proceedings of the 2018 Designing Interactive Systems Conference*, 1235-1257. 10.1145/3196709.3196732

Friess, P. (2021). Existence Beyond transhumanism–Context-based research-creation for critical art making. *Proceedings of Politics of the Machines-Rogue Research*, *2021*(3), 278–284. doi:10.14236/ewic/POM2021.36

Fry, C. (2018). Enchanting algorithms: How the reception of generative artworks is shaped by the audience's understanding of the experience. In *XXI Generative Art Conference Proceedings.* Available at: http://www. generativeart. com/GA2018_paper s/GA2018_Christopher% 20Fry. pdf

Fung, B. (2023, Nov. 18). *OpenAI. Why Sam Altman was fired and what's next after the shocking shakeup.* CNN. Retrieved Nov. 18, 2023, from https://www.cnn.com/2023/11/18/tech/openai-sam-altman-shakeup-what-happened/index.html

Gafni, O., Polyak, A., Ashual, O., Sheynin, S., Parikh, D., & Taigman, Y. (2022). Make-A-Scene: Scene-Based Text-to-Image Generation with Human Priors. *arXiv [cs.CV]*. arXiv. doi:10.1007/978-3-031-19784-0_6

Gannon, S. R. (1987). One more time: Approaches to repetition in children's literature. *Children's Literature Association Quarterly*, *12*(1), 2–5. doi:10.1353/chq.0.0202

Gaon, A. H. (2021). *The Future of Copyright in the Age of Artificial Intelligence*. Edward Elgar Publishing Ltd. doi:10.4337/9781839103155

García-Peñalvo, F., & Vázquez-Ingelmo, A. (2023). What do we mean by GenAI? a systematic mapping of the evolution, trends, and techniques involved in generative AI. *International Journal of Interactive Multimedia and Artificial Intelligence*, *8*(4), 7–16. doi:10.9781/ijimai.2023.07.006

Gardner, R. P. (2017). Discussing racial trauma using visual thinking strategies. *Language Arts*, *94*(5), 338–345. doi:10.58680/la201729058

Garg, D., & Bhambri, P. (2011). A novel approach for fusion of multimodality medical images. *CiiT International Journal of Digital Image Processing*, *3*(10), 576-580.

George, G. V. S., Arun, A. R. G., & Geetha, S. (2019). Generating Cross Domain Models using Generative Adversarial Networks. *International Journal of Innovative Technology and Exploring Engineering*, *8*(9), 1303–1306. doi:10.35940/ijitee.I8013.078919

Ghose, A. & Ali, A. S. M. (2023). Amplifying Music with Artificial Intelligence. *Economic and Political Weekly*, *58*(17), 4–6.

Ghosh, A., & Fossas, G. (2022). Can there be art without an artist? *arXiv preprint arXiv:*2209.07667. 1 - 8.

Ginsburg, J. C., & Budiardjo, L. A. (2019). Authors and machines. *Berkeley Technology Law Journal*, *34*(2), 343–448. https://www.jstor.org/stable/26954389

Glenza, J. (2020, Dec. 21). Coronavirus: Epidemiologist looks to the past to predict second post-pandemic 'roaring 20s'. *The Guardian.* Retrieved Nov. 8, 2023, from https://www.theguardian.com/world/2020/dec/21/epidemiologist-1918-flu-pandemic-roaring-20s-post-covid

Glück, J., Ernst, R., & Unger, F. (2002). How creatives define creativity: Definitions reflect different types of creativity. *Creativity Research Journal*, *14*(1), 55–67. doi:10.1207/S15326934CRJ1401_5

Golden, J. M. (1984). Children's concept of story in reading and writing. *The Reading Teacher*, *37*(7), 578–584.

Goodfellow, I. J., Pouget-Abadie, J., Mirza, M., Xu, B., Warde-Farley, D., Ozair, S., Courville, A., & Bengio, Y. (2014). Generative Adversarial Networks. *arXiv [stat.ML].* arXiv. http://arxiv.org/abs/1406.2661

Goodfellow, I., Pouget-Abadie, J., Mirza, M., Xu, B., Warde-Farley, D., Ozair, S., . . . Bengio, Y. (2014). Generative adversarial nets. *Advances in neural information processing systems (NeurIPS).*

Goodfellow, I., Bengio, Y., & Courville, A. (2016). *Deep Learning*. MIT Press.

Google. (2023). *Bard.* Available at: https://beta.google.com/bard

GPT-2. (n.d.). Accessed November 26, 2023. https://paperswithcode.com/method/gpt-2

Gregor, K., Danihelka, I., Graves, A., Rezende, D., & Wierstra, D. (2015). Draw: A recurrent neural network for image generation. In *International conference on machine learning* (pp. 1462–1471). PMLR.

Guadamuz, A. (2017). Artificial intelligence and copyright. *WIPO Magazine*. https://www.wipo.int/wipo_magazine/en/2017/05/article_0003.html

Guha, A., Grewal, D., & Atlas, S. (2023). Generative AI and Marketing Education: What the Future Holds. *Journal of Marketing Education.* Advance online publication. doi:10.1177/02734753231215436

Guilford, J. P. (1950). Creativity. *The American Psychologist*, *5*(9), 444–454. doi:10.1037/h0063487 PMID:14771441

Guljajeva, V., Sola, M. C., & Clarke, I. J. (2023). Artistic strategies to guide neural networks. *arXiv preprint arXiv:2307.07521.*

Gulz, A., Ahlner, F., & Haake, M. (2007). Visual femininity and masculinity in synthetic characters and patterns of affect. In *Affective Computing and Intelligent Interaction: Second International Conference, ACII 2007 Lisbon, Portugal, September 12-14, 2007 Proceedings 2* (pp. 654-665). Springer Berlin Heidelberg. 10.1007/978-3-540-74889-2_57

Guo, S., Jin, Z., Sun, F., Li, J., Li, Z., Shi, Y., & Cao, N. (2021). Vinci: An Intelligent Graphic Design System for Generating Advertising Posters. In *Conference on Human Factors in Computing Systems* (p. 17). Yokohama: ACM. 10.1145/3411764.3445117

Gupta, K., Damani, S., & Narahari, K. N. (2018). *Using AI to Design Stone Jewelry*. arXiv preprint arXiv:1811.08759.

Guzik, E. E., Byrge, C., & Gilde, C. (2023). The originality of machines: AI takes the Torrance Test. *Journal of Creativity*, *33*(3), 100065. doi:10.1016/j.yjoc.2023.100065

Guzik, T. J., & Sitek, A. (2023). Global accord on the integration of artificial intelligence in medical science publishing: Implications of the Bletchley Declaration. *Cardiovascular Research, 119*(17), 2681–2682. doi:10.1093/cvr/cvad170 PMID:37995330

Ha, D., & Schmidhuber, J. (2018). *World models.* arXiv preprint arXiv:1803.10122.

Hall, L., & Woods, S. (n.d.). *Empathic interaction with synthetic characters: The importance of similarity.* Academic Press.

Hall, L., Woods, S., Aylett, R., Newall, L., & Paiva, A. (2005). Achieving empathic engagement through affective interaction with synthetic characters. *Affective Computing and Intelligent Interaction: First International Conference, ACII 2005, Beijing, China, October 22-24, 2005 Proceedings, 1*, 731–738.

Halpin, H. R. (2003). *The plots of children and machines: The statistical and symbolic semantic analysis of narratives* [Unpublished master's thesis]. University of Edinburgh.

Haluza, D., & Jungwirth, D. (2023). Artificial intelligence and ten societal megatrends: An exploratory study using GPT-3. *Systems, 11*(3), 1 - 18.

Hanafy, N. O. (2023). Artificial Intelligence's Effects on Design Process Creativity: A Study on Used A.I. Text-to-Image in Architecture. *Journal of Building Engineering, 80*, 107999. doi:10.1016/j.jobe.2023.107999

Harrer, S. (2023). Attention is not all you need: The complicated case of ethically using large language models in healthcare and medicine. *EBioMedicine, 90*, 104512. doi:10.1016/j.ebiom.2023.104512 PMID:36924620

Hazan, S. (2023, July). The dance of the doppelgängers: AI and the cultural heritage community. *Proceedings of EVA London, 2023*, 77–84. doi:10.14236/ewic/EVA2023.13

Hencz, A. (2022, August 19). Digitized memories and machine hallucinations. *Artland Magazine.* https://magazine.artland.com/refik-anadol/

Hennessey, B. A., & Amabile, T. M. (2010). Creativity. *Annual Review of Psychology, 61*(1), 569–598. doi:10.1146/annurev.psych.093008.100416 PMID:19575609

Hertzmann, A. (2019). Aesthetics of neural network art. *arXiv preprint arXiv:1903.05696.*

Hessel, J., Holtzman, A., Forbes, M., Le Bras, R., & Choi, Y. (2021). CLIPScore: A Reference-free Evaluation Metric for Image Captioning. *Association for Computational Linguistics*, 7514-7528. doi:10.18653/v1/2021.emnlp-main.595

Heusel, M., Ramsauer, H., Unterthiner, T., Nessler, B., & Hochreiter, S. (2017). GANs Trained by a Two Time-Scale Update Rule Converge to a Local Nash Equilibrium. *arXiv [cs.LG].* arXiv. http://arxiv.org/abs/1706.08500

Higonnet, M. R. (1987). Narrative fractures and fragments. *Children's Literature, 15*(1), 37–54. doi:10.1353/chl.0.0617

Hinton, G., Deng, L., Yu, D., Dahl, G. E., Mohamed, A. R., Jaitly, N., Senior, A., Vanhoucke, V., Nguyen, P., Sainath, T., & Kingsbury, B. (2012). Deep neural networks for acoustic modeling in speech recognition: The shared views of four research groups. *IEEE Signal Processing Magazine, 29*(6), 82–97. doi:10.1109/MSP.2012.2205597

Hirsch, P. B. (2023a). At the crossroads: Generative AI and corporate risk management. *The Journal of Business Strategy, 44*(6), 426–429. doi:10.1108/JBS-09-2023-0196

Hirsch, P. B. (2023b). Cui bono: A conversation with ChatGPT. *The Journal of Business Strategy, 44*(4), 238–241. doi:10.1108/JBS-05-2023-0088

Hohenstein, J., Kizilcec, R. F., DiFranzo, D., Aghajari, Z., Mieczkowski, H., Levy, K., Naaman, M., Hancock, J., & Jung, M. F. (2023). Artificial intelligence in communication impacts language and social relationships. *Scientific Reports*, *13*(1), 5487. doi:10.1038/s41598-023-30938-9 PMID:37015964

Ho, J., Jain, A., & Abbeel, P. (2020). Denoising diffusion probabilistic models. *Advances in Neural Information Processing Systems*, *33*, 6840–6851.

Holmes, E. L. (2016). *Commercial Jewellery Techniques: Innovating Selected Contemporary Manufacturing Techniques* [Doctoral dissertation]. Central University of Technology, Free State.

Hoorn, J. F., Konijn, E. A., & Pontier, M. A. (2019). Dating a synthetic character is like dating a man. *International Journal of Social Robotics*, *11*(2), 235–253. doi:10.1007/s12369-018-0496-1

Hristov, K. (2017). Artificial Intelligence and the Copyright Dilemma. *IDEA: The Journal of the Franklin Pierce Center for Intellectual Property*, *57*(3), 431–454.

Huang, N., Tang, F., Dong, W., & Xu, C. (2022). Draw Your Art Dream: Diverse Digital Art Synthesis with Multimodal Guided Diffusion. *arXiv [cs.CV]*. arXiv. doi:10.1145/3503161.3548282

Huang, N., Zhang, Y., Tang, F., Ma, C., Huang, H., Zhang, Y., Dong, W., & Xu, C. (2022). DiffStyler: Controllable Dual Diffusion for Text-Driven Image Stylization. *arXiv [cs.CV]*. arXiv. http://arxiv.org/abs/2211.10682

Hudson, J., & Nelson, K. (1983). Effects of script structure on children's story recall. *Developmental Psychology*, *19*(4), 625–635. doi:10.1037/0012-1649.19.4.625

Huggingface. (2022). *Stable Diffusion with Diffusers*. Retrieved 02 12, 2024, from Stable Diffusion with Diffusers: https://huggingface.co/blog/stable_diffusion

Huggingface. (2023a). *DreamBooth training example*. Retrieved 02 12, 2024, from DreamBooth training example: https://github.com/huggingface/diffusers/tree/main/examples/dreambooth

Huggingface. (2023b). *BLIP-2*. Retrieved 02 12, 2024, from BLIP-2: https://huggingface.co/docs/transformers/model_doc/blip-2

Huggingface. (2024a). *Stable-diffusion-inpainting*. Retrieved from stable-diffusion-inpainting: https://huggingface.co/runwayml/stable-diffusion-inpainting

Huggingface. (2024b). *huggingface diffusers*. Retrieved from huggingface diffusers: https://github.com/huggingface/diffusers/tree/main/examples/research_projects/dreambooth_inpaint

Hughes, B., Bothe, S., Farooq, H., & Imran, A. (2019, February). Generative adversarial learning for machine learning empowered self-organizing 5G networks. In 2019 international conference on computing, networking and communications (ICNC) (pp. 282-286). IEEE.

Hughes, R., Zhu, L., & Bednar, T. (2021). Generative Adversarial Networks–Enabled Human–Artificial Intelligence Collaborative Applications for Creative and Design Industries: A Systematic Review of Current Approaches and Trends. *Frontiers in Artificial Intelligence*, *17*, 604234. Advance online publication. doi:10.3389/frai.2021.604234 PMID:33997773

Hunt, P. (1984). Narrative theory and children's literature. *Children's Literature Association Quarterly*, *9*(4), 191–194. doi:10.1353/chq.0.0415

Hutson, J., & Harper-Nichols, M. (2023). Generative AI and algorithmic art: Disrupting the framing of meaning and rethinking the subject-object dilemma. *Global Journal of Computer Science and Technology: D, 23*(1).

Hutson, J., & Robertson, B. (2023). Exploring the educational potential of AI generative art in 3D design fundamentals: A case study on prompt engineering and creative workflows. *Global Journal of Human-Social Science: A Arts & Humanities-Psychology, 23*(2), 1 - 11.

Hutson, J., & Cotroneo, P. (2023). Generative AI tools in art education: Exploring prompt engineering and iterative processes for enhanced creativity. *Metaverse, 4*(1), 1–13.

Hutson, J., & Lang, M. (2023). Content creation or interpolation: AI generative digital art in the classroom. *Metaverse, 4*(1), 1–14. doi:10.54517/m.v4i1.2158

Hu, Z. (2022). Analysis of the Impact of Artificial Intelligence Technology-Assisted Environmental Protection on the Integrity of Chinese Painting. *Journal of Environmental and Public Health, 8*, 1–8. Advance online publication. doi:10.1155/2022/3245947 PMID:36065168

Isbister, K., & Hayes-Roth, B. (1998, January). Social implications of using synthetic characters: An examination of a role-specific intelligent agent. In *Proc. of the IJCAI-97 Workshop on Animated Interface Agents: Making them Intelligent.* Stanford University.

Iskender, A. (2023). Holy or unholy? Interview with open AI's ChatGPT. *European Journal of Tourism Research, 34*(3414), 1–11. doi:10.54055/ejtr.v34i.3169

Isola, P., Zhu, J. Y., Zhou, T., & Efros, A. A. (2017). Image-to-image translation with conditional adversarial networks. *Proceedings of the Thirtieth IEEE Conference on Computer Vision and Pattern Recognition (CVPR 2017)*, 1125-1134. 10.48550/arXiv.1611.07004

Jackson, T. E. (2017). Imitative Identity, Imitative Art, and "AI: Artificial Intelligence." *Mosaic: An Interdisciplinary Critical Journal, 50*(2), 47–63. https://www.jstor.org/stable/45158927

Jackson, I., Jesus Saenz, M., & Ivanov, D. (2023). From natural language to simulations: Applying AI to automate simulation modelling of logistics systems. *International Journal of Production Research.* Advance online publication. doi:10.1080/00207543.2023.2276811

Jahanian, A., & Balakrishnan, G. (2018). *On the "steerability" of generative adversarial networks.* arXiv preprint arXiv:1812.00073.

Jang, K. M., Chen, J., Kang, Y., Kim, J., Lee, J., & Duarte, F. (2023). Understanding place identity with Generative AI. *arXiv preprint arXiv:2306.04662.*

Jansen, C., & Sklar, E. (2021). Exploring co-creative drawing workflows. *Frontiers in Robotics and AI, 8*(577770), 1–26. PMID:34055899

Jarrahi, M. H. (2018). Artificial intelligence and the future of work: Human-AI symbiosis in organizational decision making. *Business Horizons, 61*(4), 577–586. doi:10.1016/j.bushor.2018.03.007

John Amos Comenius. (2023, Dec. 19). In *Wikipedia.* Retrieved Jan. 3, 2024, from https://en.wikipedia.org/wiki/John_Amos_Comenius

Jordanous, A. (2012). A Standardised Procedure for Evaluating Creative Systems: Computational Creativity Evaluation Based on What it is to be Creative. *Cognitive Computation, 4*(3), 246–279. doi:10.1007/s12559-012-9156-1

Jordanous, A., & Keller, B. (2016). Modelling creativity: Identifying key components through a corpus-based approach. *PLoS One, 11*(10), e0162959. doi:10.1371/journal.pone.0162959 PMID:27706185

Jovanović, M., & Campbell, M. (2022). Generative Artificial Intelligence: Trends and Prospects. *Computer*, 107-112. https://doi.ieeecomputersociety.org/10.1109/MC.2022.3192720

Jovanović, M., & Campbell, M. (2022). Generative artificial intelligence: Trends and prospects. *Computer*, *55*(10), 107–112. doi:10.1109/MC.2022.3192720

Jung, G. (2020). Do androids dream of copyright?: Examining ai copyright ownership. *Berkeley Technology Law Journal*, *35*(4), 1151–1178. https://www.jstor.org/stable/27121773

Kadish, D., Risi, S., & Løvlie, A. S. (2021). Improving object detection in art images using only style transfer. In *2021 International Joint Conference on Neural Networks (IJCNN)* (pp. 1–8). 10.1109/IJCNN52387.2021.9534264

Kanbach, D. K., Heiduk, L., Blueher, G., Schreiter, M., & Lahmann, A. (2023). The GenAI is out of the bottle: Generative artificial intelligence from a business model innovation perspective. *Review of Managerial Science*. Advance online publication. doi:10.1007/s11846-023-00696-z

Kang, M., Zhu, J.-Y., Zhang, R., Park, J., Shechtman, E., Paris, S., & Park, T. (2023). Scaling up GANs for Text-to-Image Synthesis. *arXiv [cs.CV]*. arXiv. doi:10.1109/CVPR52729.2023.00976

Kang, Y., Gao, S., & Roth, R. E. (2019). Transferring multiscale map styles using generative adversarial networks. *International Journal of Cartography*, *5*(2–3), 115–141. doi:10.1080/23729333.2019.1615729

Kaplan, H. G. (2021). Border Tuner and Teeter-Totter Wall: Two works of participatory public pedagogy. *Visual Inquiry Learning & Teaching Art*, *10*(1), 31–48. doi:10.1386/vi_00024_1

Karakose, T., Demirkol, M., Yirci, R., Polat, H., Ozdemir, T. Y., & Tülübaş, T. (2023). A conversation with ChatGPT about digital leadership and technology integration: comparative analysis based on human–AI collaboration. *Administrative Sciences, 13*(7). doi:10.3390/admsci13070157

Karras, T., Aila, T., Laine, S., & Lehtinen, J. (2018*). Progressive growing of GANs for improved quality, stability, and variation.* arXiv preprint arXiv:1710.10196.

Karras, T., Laine, S., & Aila, T. (2018). A Style-Based Generator Architecture for Generative Adversarial Networks. *arXiv [cs.NE]*. arXiv. http://arxiv.org/abs/1812.04948

Kelley, L. (2018). Solution stories: A narrative study of how teachers support children's problem solving. *Early Childhood Education Journal*, *46*(3), 313–322. doi:10.1007/s10643-017-0866-6

Khalis, F. M., & Mustaffa, N. (2017). Cultural inspirations towards Malaysian animation character design. *Malaysian Journal of Communication*, *33*(1), 487–501.

Khan, K. S., Gugiu, M. R., Justice, L. M., Bowles, R. P., Skibbe, L. E., & Piasta, S. B. (2016). Age-related progressions in story structure in young children's narratives. *Journal of Speech, Language, and Hearing Research: JSLHR*, *59*(6), 1395–1408. doi:10.1044/2016_JSLHR-L-15-0275 PMID:27930767

Kim, G., & Chun, S. Y. (2022). DATID-3D: Diversity-Preserved Domain Adaptation Using Text-to-Image Diffusion for 3D Generative Model. *arXiv [cs.CV]*. arXiv. http://arxiv.org/abs/2211.16374

Kim, J. H., Kim, J., Kim, S. S., & Hailu, T. B. (2023). Effects of AI ChatGPT on travelers' travel decision-making. *Tourism Review*. Advance online publication. doi:10.1108/TR-07-2023-0489

Kim, J. H., Kim, J., Park, J., Kim, C., Jhang, J., & King, B. (2023). When ChatGPT gives incorrect answers: The impact of inaccurate information by Generative AI on tourism decision-making. *Journal of Travel Research*. Advance online publication. doi:10.1177/00472875231212996

Kim, T., Cha, M., Kim, H., Lee, J. K., & Kim, J. (2017). Learning to discover cross-domain relations with generative adversarial networks. *Proceedings of the International Conference on Machine Learning (ICML) 2017*, 1857-1865. 10.48550/arXiv.1703.05192

Kingma, D. P., & Ba, J. (2014). *Adam: A method for stochastic optimization*. arXiv preprint arXiv:1412.6980.

Kline, C., & Blumberg, B. (1999). The art and science of synthetic character design. *In Proceedings of the AISB 1999 Symposium on AI and Creativity in Entertainment and Visual Art* (pp. 1-6). Academic Press.

Köbis, N., & Mossink, L. D. (2021). Artificial intelligence versus Maya Angelou: Experimental evidence that people cannot differentiate AI-generated from human-written poetry. *Computers in Human Behavior*, *114*, 106553. doi:10.1016/j.chb.2020.106553

Ko, H. K., Park, G., Jeon, H., Jo, J., Kim, J., & Seo, J. (2023, March). Large-scale text-to-image generation models for visual artists' creative works. In *Proceedings of the 28th International Conference on Intelligent User Interfaces* (pp. 919-933). 10.1145/3581641.3584078

Korzynski, P., Mazurek, G., Altmann, A., Ejdys, J., Kazlauskaite, R., Paliszkiewicz, J., Wach, K., & Ziemba, E. (2023). Generative artificial intelligence as a new context for management theories: Analysis of ChatGPT. *Central European Management Journal*, *31*(1), 3–13. doi:10.1108/CEMJ-02-2023-0091

Kshetri, N., Dwivedi, Y. K., Davenport, T. H., & Panteli, N. (2023). Generative artificial intelligence in marketing: Applications, opportunities, challenges, and research agenda. *International Journal of Information Management*. doi:10.1016/j.ijinfomgt.2023.102716

Kulkarni, C., Druga, S., Chang, M., Fiannaca, A., Cai, C., & Terry, M. (2023). A word is worth a thousand pictures: Prompts as AI design material. *arXiv preprint arXiv:2303.12647*.

Kulkarni, R. M. (2016, December 16). *Of Artificial Intelligence and Authorship*. Spicy IP. https://spicyip.com/2016/12/of-artificial-intelligence-and-authorship.html

Kumar, A. H. (2023). Analysis of ChatGPT tool to assess the potential of its utility for academic writing in biomedical domain. *Biology, Engineering, Medicine and Science Reports*, *9*(1), 24–30. doi:10.5530/bems.9.1.5

Labatut, B. (2023). *The Maniac*. Pushkin Press.

LAION. (2022). *LAION-Aesthetics_Predictor V1*. Retrieved 02 12, 2024, from LAION-Aesthetics_Predictor V1: https://github.com/LAION-AI/aesthetic-predictor

LAION-AI. (2021). *Watermark-detection*. Retrieved 02 12, 2024, from watermark-detection: https://github.com/LAION-AI/watermark-detection

Laker, L. F., & Sena, M. (2023). Accuracy and detection of student use of ChatGPT in business analytics courses. *Issues in Information Systems*, *24*(2), 153–163. doi:10.48009/2_iis_2023_113

Lancia, P. J. (1997). Literary borrowing: The effects of literature on children's writing. *The Reading Teacher*, *50*(6), 470–475.

Lane, T. (2023). *What Does Artificial Intelligence Mean for Construction?* Building Magazine.

Lankoski, P. (2004). Character design fundamentals for role-playing games. *Beyond Role and Play,* 139-148.

Lath, A. (2022, October 10). *AI Art and Indian Copyright Registration.* Spicy IP. https://spicyip.com/2022/10/ai-art-and-indian-copyright-registration.html

Leach, N. (2019). Do robots dream of digital sheep? *Proceedings of ACADIA 19: Ubiquity and Autonomy.* 10.52842/conf.acadia.2019.298

LeCun, Y., Bengio, Y., & Hinton, G. (2015). Deep learning. *Nature, 521*(7553), 436–444. doi:10.1038/nature14539 PMID:26017442

Lee, Y. K., Park, Y. H., & Hahn, S. (2023). A portrait of emotion: Empowering self-expression through AI-generated art. *arXiv preprint arXiv:2304.13324.*

Lee, H. K. (2022). Rethinking creativity: Creative industries, AI and everyday creativity. *Media Culture & Society, 44*(3), 601–612. doi:10.1177/01634437221077009

Levantino, F. P. (2023). Generative and AI-powered oracles: "What will they say about you?" *Computer Law & Security Report, 51*, C7–C105898. doi:10.1016/j.clsr.2023.105898

Li, G., Zheng, H., Wang, C., Li, C., Zheng, C., & Tao, D. (2022). 3DDesigner: Towards Photorealistic 3D Object Generation and Editing with Text-guided Diffusion Models. *ArXiv.* /abs/2211.14108

Li, W., Zhang, P., Zhang, L., Huang, Q., He, X., Lyu, S., & Gao, J. (2019). Object-Driven Text-to-Image Synthesis via Adversarial Training. *arXiv [cs.CV].* arXiv. doi:10.1109/CVPR.2019.01245

Li, Y., Yu, A. W., Meng, T., Ben Caine, J. N., Peng, D., & Shen, J. (2022). DeepFusion: Lidar-Camera Deep Fusion for Multi-Modal 3D Object Detection. *arXiv [cs.CV].* arXiv. doi:10.1109/CVPR52688.2022.01667

Liang, M., & Wanli, Z. (2022). Emotional expression in jewellery design under the background of artificial intelligence. *Expert Systems: International Journal of Knowledge Engineering and Neural Networks*, 13134. doi:10.1111/exsy.13134

Li, J., Li, D., Savarese, S., & Hoi, S. (2023). *BLIP-2: Bootstrapping Language-Image Pre-training with Frozen Image Encoders and Large Language Models. In International Conference on Machine Learning.* ACM. https://dl.acm.org/doi/10.5555/3618408.3619222

Lim, W. M., Gunasekara, A., Pallant, J. L., Pallant, J. I., & Pechenkina, E. (2023). Generative AI and the future of education: Ragnarök or reformation? A paradoxical perspective from management educators. *International Journal of Management Education, 21*(2). doi:10.1016/j.ijme.2023.100790

Li, M., Lv, J., Wang, J., & Sang, Y. (2020). An Abstract Painting Generation Method Based on Deep Generative Model. *Neural Processing Letters, 52*(2), 949–960. doi:10.1007/s11063-019-10063-3

Lin, C.-H., Gao, J., Tang, L., Takikawa, T., Zeng, X., Huang, X., Kreis, K., Fidler, S., Liu, M.-Y., & Lin, T.-Y. (2022). Magic3D: High-Resolution Text-to-3D Content Creation. *arXiv [cs.CV].* arXiv. http://arxiv.org/abs/2211.10440

Lingua. (2022). *The most accurate natural language detection library.* Retrieved 02 12, 2024, from The most accurate natural language detection library: https://github.com/pemistahl/lingua

Lin, L., & Long, D. (2023, June). Generative AI futures: A speculative design exploration. In *Proceedings of the 15th Conference on Creativity and Cognition* (pp. 380-383). 10.1145/3591196.3596616

LinT.-Y.MaireM.BelongieS.BourdevL.GirshickR.HaysJ.PeronaP.RamananD.ZitnickC. L.DollárP. (2014). Microsoft COCO: Common Objects in Context. *arXiv [cs.CV].* doi:10.1007/978-3-319-10602-1_48

Lips-Wiersma, M., & Wright, S. (2012). Measuring the meaning of meaningful work: Development and validation of the comprehensive meaningful work scale. *Group & Organization Management, 37*(5), 655–685. doi:10.1177/1059601112461578

Liu, B. (2023, Apr.) Arguments for the rise of artificial intelligence art: Does AI art have creativity, motivation, self-awareness and emotion? *Arte,* 1 - 12.

Liu, V. (2023, April). Beyond text-to-image: Multimodal prompts to explore generative AI. In *Extended Abstracts of the 2023 CHI Conference on Human Factors in Computing Systems* (pp. 1-6). ACM.

Lively, J., Hutson, J., & Melick, E. (2023). Integrating AI-generative tools in web design Education: Enhancing student aesthetic and creative copy capabilities using image and text-based AI generators. *Journal of Artificial Intelligence and Robotics*, *1*(1), 23–33.

Li, Y. Q., & Xu, W. G. (2022). Using CycleGAN to Achieve the Sketch Recognition Process of Sketch-Based Modeling. *3rd International Conference on Computational Design and Robotic Fabrication*, 26-34. 10.1007/978-981-16-5983-6_3

Lozano-Hemmer, R. (2019). *Border Tuner / Sintonizador Fronterizo*. Retrieved from https://www.lozano-hemmer.com/border_tuner__sintonizador_fronterizo.php

Lozano-HemmerR. (2006). *Pulse Room*. Retrieved from https://www.lozano-hemmer.com/pulse_room.php

Lozano-Hemmer, R. (2019). *Atmospheric Memory*. Manchester International Festival.

Lubowitz, J. H. (2023). ChatGPT, an artificial intelligence chatbot, is impacting medical literature. *Arthroscopy*, *39*(5), 1121–1122. doi:10.1016/j.arthro.2023.01.015 PMID:36797148

Lucas, A., Chapin, M., Lin, M., & Jia, X. (2015). The Chinese Soul In Contemporary Jewelry Design. *Gems & Gemology*, *51*(1), 18–30. doi:10.5741/GEMS.51.1.18

Lucic, M., Kurach, K., Michalski, M., Gelly, S., & Bousquet, O. (2018). Are GANs created equal? A large-scale study. Advances in neural information processing systems (NeurIPS).

Lv, Z. (2022). Generative artificial intelligence in the metaverse era. *Cognitive Robotics*, *3*, 208–217. doi:10.1016/j.cogr.2023.06.001

Lysova, E. I., Allan, B. A., Dik, B. J., Duffy, R. D., & Steger, M. F. (2019). Fostering meaningful work in organizations: A multi-level review and integration. *Journal of Vocational Behavior*, *110*, 374–389. doi:10.1016/j.jvb.2018.07.004

Lyu, Y., Lin, C.-L., Lin, P.-H., & Lin, R. (2021). The cognition of audience to artistic style transfer. *Applied Sciences (Basel, Switzerland)*, *11*(7), 3290. doi:10.3390/app11073290

Lyu, Y., Shi, M., Zhang, Y., & Lin, R. (2023). From Image to Imagination: Exploring the Impact of Generative AI on Cultural Translation in Jewelry Design. *Sustainability (Basel)*, *16*(1), 65. doi:10.3390/su16010065

Ma, T., Ma, W., & Liu, W. (2024). The application of carving technique based on 3D printing digitalization technology in jewelry design. *International Journal on Interactive Design and Manufacturing*, 1-11.

Magni, F., Park, J., & Chao, M. M. (2023). Humans as Creativity Gatekeepers: Are We Biased Against AI Creativity? *Journal of Business and Psychology*, 1–14. doi:10.1007/s10869-023-09910-x

Magsamen, S., & Ivy, R. (2023). *Your Brain on Art: How the Arts Transform Us*. Canongate Books.

Ma, J., & Huang, K. (2023). ChatGPT in Real Estate. In A. I. Beyond (Ed.), *ChatGPT, Web3, and the Business Landscape of Tomorrow* (pp. 219–242). Springer Nature Switzerland. doi:10.1007/978-3-031-45282-6_8

Makhortykh, M., Zucker, E. M., Simon, D. J., Bultmann, D., & Ulloa, R. (2023). Shall androids dream of genocides? How generative AI can change the future of memorialization of mass atrocities. *Discover Artificial Intelligence*, *3*(1), 28. doi:10.1007/s44163-023-00072-6

Mäki-Reinikka, K. (2018). Cave paintings for the AI: Art in the age of singularity. *Politics of the Machines-Art and After*, *7*, 1–7. doi:10.14236/ewic/EVAC18.13

Maksymyuk, T., Gazda, J., Luntovskyy, A., & Klymash, M. (2018, September). Artificial intelligence based 5G coverage design and optimization using deep generative adversarial neural networks. In *2018 International Conference on Information and Telecommunication Technologies and Radio Electronics (UkrMiCo)* (pp. 1-4). IEEE. 10.1109/UkrMiCo43733.2018.9047611

Maldonado, H., & Hayes-Roth, B. (2004). Toward cross-cultural believability in character design. *Agent Culture: Human-Agent Interaction in a Multicultural World,* 143-175.

Malina, R. F. (1990). Digital image: Digital cinema: The work of art in the age of post-mechanical reproduction. *Leonardo*, 33-38.

Malo, E., & Bullard, J. (2000). *Storytelling and the emergent reader. International Reading Association World Congress on Reading*. Auckland, New Zealand.

Manavis, A., Nazlidou, I., Spahiu, T., & Kyratsis, P. (2020). Jewellery design and wearable applications: a design thinking approach. In *10th International Symposium on Graphic Engineering and Design 2020-Proceedings, GRID 2020, 12-14th November 2020, Novi Sad, Serbia* (pp. 591-596). 10.24867/GRID-2020-p67

Manovich, L. (2018). *Ai aesthetics*. Strelka Press.

Mansimov, E., Parisotto, E., Ba, J. L., & Salakhutdinov, R. (2015). Generating Images from Captions with Attention. *arXiv [cs.LG]*. arXiv. http://arxiv.org/abs/1511.02793

Marcus, G., Davis, E., & Aaronson, S. (2022). A Very Preliminary Analysis of DALL-E 2. *arXiv [cs.CV]*. arXiv. http://arxiv.org/abs/2204.13807

Marcus, M. (2019). *The Creativity Code: Art and Innovation in the Age of AI*. Academic Press.

Margetts, H. (2022). Rethinking AI for Good Governance. *Daedalus*, *151*(2), 360–371. https://www.jstor.org/stable/48662048. doi:10.1162/daed_a_01922

Mariani, M., & Dwivedi, Y. K. (2024). Generative artificial intelligence in innovation management: A preview of future research developments. *Journal of Business Research*, *175*, 114542. doi:10.1016/j.jbusres.2024.114542

Martela, F., & Riekki, T. J. J. (2018). Autonomy, competence, relatedness, and beneficence: A multicultural comparison of the four pathways to meaningful work. *Frontiers in Psychology*, *9*, 1157. doi:10.3389/fpsyg.2018.01157 PMID:30042710

Mascarenhas, S., Dias, J., Afonso, N., Enz, S., & Paiva, A. (2009, May). Using rituals to express cultural differences in synthetic characters. In *Proceedings of the 8th International Conference on Autonomous Agents and Multiagent Systems-Volume 1* (pp. 305-312). Academic Press.

Matoso, M. (2023). *Will Artificial Intelligence Replace Architects?* Archdaily.

Mazzone, M., & Elgammal, A. (2019). Art, Creativity, and the Potential of Artificial Intelligence. *Arts*, *8*(1), 26. doi:10.3390/arts8010026

McCormack, J., & d'Inverno, M. (2014). On the future of computers and creativity. *AISB 2014 Symposium on Computational Creativity*. Available at: https://doc.gold.ac.uk/aisb50/AISB50-S04/AISB50-S4-McCormack-paper.pdf

McCormack, J., Cruz Gambardella, C., Rajcic, N., Krol, S. J., Llano, M. T., & Yang, M. (2023, April). Is writing prompts really making art? In *International Conference on Computational Intelligence in Music, Sound, Art and Design (Part of EvoStar)* (pp. 196-211). Cham: Springer Nature Switzerland.

McCosker, A., Wilken, R., & Wilken, R. (2017). Rethinking 'ethics' in data science: Towards a speculative ethics for big data research. *Proceedings of the 2017 Data Science Conference*.

McGrath, J. (2005). *The jeweler's directory of decorative finishes: from enameling and engraving to inlay and granulation.* Academic Press.

McIntyre, N., & Lapata, M. (2010, July). Plot induction and evolutionary search for story generation. In *Proceedings of the 48th Annual Meeting of the Association for Computational Linguistics* (pp. 1562-1572). Academic Press.

McKinsey Global Publishing. (2023). *What is generative AI?* McKinsey Global Publishing. Retrieved from https://www.mckinsey.com/~/media/mckinsey/featured%20insights/mckinsey%20explainers/what%20is%20generative%20ai/what%20is%20generative%20ai.pdf

Meng, C., He, Y., Song, Y., Song, J., Wu, J., Zhu, J.-Y., & Ermon, S. (2021). SDEdit: Guided Image Synthesis and Editing with Stochastic Differential Equations. *arXiv [cs.CV].* arXiv. http://arxiv.org/abs/2108.01073

Menninghaus, W., Wagner, V., Wassiliwizky, E., Schindler, I., Hanich, J., Jacobsen, T., & Koelsch, S. (2019). What are aesthetic emotions? *Psychological Review, 126*(2), 171–195. doi:10.1037/rev0000135 PMID:30802122

Merchán, E. C. G., & Molina, M. (2020). A machine consciousness architecture based on deep learning and Gaussian processes. *Hybrid Artificial Intelligent Systems: 15th International Conference, HAIS 2020, Gijón, Spain, November 11-13, 2020 Proceedings, 15*, 350–361.

Merriam, P. (2020, Spring). Grappling with technology: The post digital printmaker. *IMPACT Printmaking Journal,* 1-10.

Meta. (2024). *Meta Horizon.* Retrieved from Meta Horizon Worlds: https://horizon.meta.com

Mezei, P. (2020). *From Leonardo to the Next Rembrandt--the need for AI-Pessimism in the age of algorithms.* Academic Press.

Michaelson, C., Pratt, M. G., Grant, A. M., & Dunn, C. P. (2014). Meaningful work: Connecting business ethics and organization studies. *Journal of Business Ethics, 121*(1), 77–90. doi:10.1007/s10551-013-1675-5

Microsoft. (2016). *The Next Rembrandt: Blurring The Lines Between Art, Technology And Emotion.* Microsoft News. Retrieved from https://news.microsoft.com/europe/features/next-rembrandt/

Midjourney. (2023). https://www.midjourney.com/

Miernicki, M., & Ng, I. (2021). Artificial intelligence and moral rights. *AI & Society, 36*(1), 319–329. doi:10.1007/s00146-020-01027-6

Mikalonytė, E., & Kneer, M. (2021). Can artificial intelligence make art? *arXiv Prepr. arXiv2104.07598.*

Mildenhall, Srinivasan, Tancik, Barron, Ramamoorthi, & Ng. (2020). NeRF: Representing Scenes as Neural Radiance Fields for View Synthesis. *arXiv [cs.CV].* arXiv. http://arxiv.org/abs/2003.08934

Ministerio de Justicia, Spain. (2012). *The Intellectual Property Act.* https://www.wipo.int/edocs/lexdocs/laws/en/es/es177en.pdf

Minsky, M. (1982). Why People Think Computers Can't. *AI Magazine, 3*(4), 3–15. doi:10.1609/aimag.v3i4.376

Mizumoto, A., & Eguchi, M. (2023). Exploring the potential of using an AI language model for automated essay scoring. *Research Methods in Applied Linguistics, 2*(2), 100050. doi:10.1016/j.rmal.2023.100050

Mondal, B. (2020). Artificial intelligence: state of the art. In *Recent Trends Adv* (pp. 389–425). Artif. Intell. Internet Things.

Monoyiou, E., & Symeonidou, S. (2016). The wonderful world of children's books? Negotiating diversity through children's literature. *International Journal of Inclusive Education, 20*(6), 588–603. doi:10.1080/13603116.2015.1102338

Moreira da Silva, A. (2021). Jewels Design Innovation—Van Cleef & Arpels as a Case Study. In *Advances in Design, Music and Arts: 7th Meeting of Research in Music, Arts and Design, EIMAD 2020, May 14–15, 2020* (pp. 373-384). Springer International Publishing.

Mori, M. (1970). The uncanny valley: The original essay by Masahiro Mori. *IEEE Spectrum*, 6.

Mori, M., MacDorman, K. F., & Kageki, N. (2012). The uncanny valley. *IEEE Robotics & Automation Magazine*, *19*(2), 98–100. doi:10.1109/MRA.2012.2192811

Morrow, L. M. (1985). Retelling stories: A strategy for improving young children's comprehension, concept of story structure, and oral language complexity. *The Elementary School Journal*, *85*(5), 647–661. doi:10.1086/461427

Mrosla, L., Koch, V., & von Both, P. (2019). Quo vadis AI in Architecture? Survey of the Current Possibilities of AI in the Architectural Practice. *37th Conference on Education and Research in Computer Aided Architectural Design in Europe*, 45-54.

Murphy, K. P. (2012). *Machine Learning: A Probabilistic Perspective*. MIT Press.

Murugesan, S., & Cherukuri, A. K. (2023). The Rise of Generative Artificial Intelligence and Its Impact on Education: The Promises and Perils. *Computer*, *56*(5), 116–121. doi:10.1109/MC.2023.3253292

Mustaqim, K., & Zahar, I. (2022, November). The presence of digital art: Towards the oblivion of aesthetics sense and beyond. In *IICACS: International and Interdisciplinary Conference on Arts Creation and Studies* (*Vol. 4*, pp. 106-114). Academic Press.

Na, H., & Kim, W. (2021). A Study on The Practical Use of Generative Design in the Product Design Process. *Archives of Design Research*, *34*(1), 85–99. doi:10.15187/adr.2021.02.34.1.85

Naruto et al v. David Slater (2018) WL 1902414.

Nast, C. (2022). *Sunspring | A Sci-Fi Short Film Starring Thomas Middleditch. Ars Technica.* Retrieved from https://arstechnica.com/video/watch/sunspring-sci-fi-short-film

Nguyen, D. (2023). The effects of AI on digital artist. Bachelor's thesis. Haaga-Helia University of Applied Sciences. *Business Information Technology,* 1 - 66.

Nguyen, A., Yosinski, J., & Clune, J. (2015). Deep neural networks are easily fooled: High confidence predictions for unrecognizable images. *Proceedings of the IEEE Conference on Computer Vision and Pattern Recognition (CVPR).* 10.1109/CVPR.2015.7298640

Nichol, A., Dhariwal, P., Ramesh, A., Shyam, P., Mishkin, P., McGrew, B., Sutskever, I., & Chen, M. (2021). Glide: Towards photorealistic image generation and editing with text-guided diffusion models. *arXiv preprint arXiv:2112.10741.*

Nicolopoulou, A. (2008). The elementary forms of narrative coherence in young children's storytelling. *Narrative Inquiry*, *18*(2), 299–325.

Nicolopoulou, A., & Richner, E. S. (2007). From actors to agents to persons: The development of character representation in young children's narratives. *Child Development*, *78*(2), 412–429. doi:10.1111/j.1467-8624.2007.01006.x PMID:17381781

Nieminen, M. (2017). *Psychology in character design: Creation of a character design tool* [Bachelor's thesis]. South-Eastern Finland University of Applied Sciences.

Nijstad, B. A., De Dreu, C. K., Rietzschel, E. F., & Baas, M. (2010). The dual pathway to creativity model: Creative ideation as a function of flexibility and persistence. *European Review of Social Psychology*, *21*(1), 34–77. doi:10.1080/10463281003765323

Nikolajeva, M. (1998). Exit children's literature? *The Lion and the Unicorn, 22*(2), 221–236. doi:10.1353/uni.1998.0028

Nikolajeva, M. (2001). The changing aesthetics of character in children's fiction. *Style (Fayetteville), 35*(3), 430–453.

Nikolajeva, M. (2003). Beyond the Grammar of Story, or How Can Children's Literature Criticism Benefit from Narrative Theory? *Children's Literature Association Quarterly, 28*(1), 5–16. doi:10.1353/chq.0.1702

Nilsson, N. J. (1998). *Artificial Intelligence: A New Synthesis*. Morgan Kaufmann.

Niszczota, P., & Conway, P. (2023). Judgements of research co-created by Generative AI: Experimental evidence. *Economics and Business Review, 9*(2), 101–114. doi:10.18559/ebr.2023.2.744

Nordström, P., Lundman, R., & Hautala, J. (2023). Evolving coagency between artists and AI in the spatial cocreative process of artmaking. *Annals of the Association of American Geographers*, 1–16.

Norton, D. E. (1992). Engaging children in literature: Understanding plot structures. *The Reading Teacher, 46*(3), 254–258.

Not, E., Balci, K., Pianesi, F., & Zancanaro, M. (2005, October). Synthetic characters as multichannel interfaces. In *Proceedings of the 7th International Conference on Multimodal Interfaces* (pp. 200-207). Academic Press.

Notaro, A. (2020). State-of-the-art: AI through the (artificial) artist's eye. *EVA London 2020: Electronic Visualisation and the Arts*, 322-328.

O'Leary, D. E. (2023). Enterprise large language models: Knowledge characteristics, risks, and organizational activities. *International Journal of Intelligent Systems in Accounting Finance & Management, 30*(3), 113–119. doi:10.1002/isaf.1541

Ojo, E., Mears, H., & Stylianou, N. (2022). Fashioning Africa. *Creating African Fashion Histories: Politics, Museums, and Sartorial Practices*, 280.

Ollandezou, E. (2022). *New Media Art & Legal Aspects* [Master Thesis in Art, Law and Arts Management]. International Hellenic University, Thessaloniki, Greece.

Olver, E. (2002). *The Art of Jewelry Design: From Idea to Reality*. Northlight.

O'Neil, C. (2016). *Weapons of Math Destruction: How Big Data Increases Inequality and Threatens Democracy*. Academic Press.

O'Neil, M. (2018). *Artificial Unintelligence: How Computers Misunderstand the World*. Academic Press.

Onformative. (n.d.). *Meandering river*. https://onformative.com/work/meandering-river

Open, A. I. (2019). *GPT-2: Language Models are Few-Shot Learners*. Retrieved from https://openai.com/research/gpt-2

OpenA. I. (2023). *Dall-e-2*. https://openai.com/product/dall-e-2

OpenAI (2022a). *ChatGPT*. Available at: https://beta.openai.com/docs/models/gpt

OpenAI (2022b). *DALL-E*. Available at: https://openai.com/dall-e/

Oxford English Dictionary. (2023). *Creativity*. Available at: https://www.oed.com/search/dictionary/?scope=Entries&q=creativity

Pagan, S. (2014). Crafting new spatial and sensorial relationships in contemporary jewellery. *Craft+ Design Enquiry, 6*, 117.

Paiva, A., Dias, J., Sobral, D., Aylett, R., Woods, S., Hall, L., & Zoll, C. (2005). Learning by feeling: Evoking empathy with synthetic characters. *Applied Artificial Intelligence, 19*(3-4), 235–266. doi:10.1080/08839510590910165

Pantaleo, S. (2005). "Reading" young children's visual texts. *Early Childhood Research & Practice*, *7*(1), n1.

Papers With Code. (n.d.). https://paperswithcode.com/sota/text-to-image-generation-on-coco?tag_filter=246

Passmore, J., & Tee, D. (2023). The library of Babel: Assessing the powers of artificial intelligence in knowledge synthesis, learning and development and coaching. *Journal of Work-Applied Management*. Advance online publication. doi:10.1108/JWAM-06-2023-0057

Paul, C. (2020). Digital art now: Histories of (im) materialities. *International Journal for Digital Art History*, (5), 2–2.

Peirce, K., & Edwards, E. D. (1988). Children's construction of fantasy stories: Gender differences in conflict resolution strategies. *Sex Roles*, *18*(7-8), 393–404. doi:10.1007/BF00288391

Pelletier, J., & Wilde Astington, J. (2004). Action, consciousness and theory of mind: Children's ability to coordinate story characters' actions and thoughts. *Early Education and Development*, *15*(1), 5–22. doi:10.1207/s15566935eed1501_1

Peres, R., Schreier, M., Schweidel, D., & Sorescu, A. (2023). Editorial: On ChatGPT and beyond: How generative artificial intelligence may affect research, teaching, and practice. *International Journal of Research in Marketing*, *40*(2), 269–275. doi:10.1016/j.ijresmar.2023.03.001

Pfeiffer Consulting. (2018). *Creativity and technology in the age of AI.* Pfeiffer Consulting. Retrieved from https://www.pfeifferreport.com/wp-content/uploads/2018/11/Creativity_and_AI_Report_INT.pdf

Piotrovsky, K. D. M., Kondrashova, V., & Ozerkov, D. (2019). *Artificial Intelligence and Intercultural Dialogue: Playing With Shadow*. The Hermitage Museum XXI Century Foundation.

Piskopani, A. M., Chamberlain, A., & Ten Holter, C. (2023, July). Responsible AI and the arts: The ethical and legal implications of AI in the arts and creative industries. In *Proceedings of the First International Symposium on Trustworthy Autonomous Systems* (pp. 1-5). 10.1145/3597512.3597528

Pitt, C. S., Bal, A. S., & Plangger, K. (2020). New approaches to psychographic consumer segmentation: Exploring fine art collectors using artificial intelligence, automated text analysis and correspondence analysis. *European Journal of Marketing*. Advance online publication. doi:10.1108/EJM-01-2019-0083

Plucker, J. A., Beghetto, R. A., & Dow, G. T. (2004). Why isn't creativity more important to educational psychologists? Potentials, pitfalls, and future directions in creativity research. *Educational Psychologist*, *39*(2), 83–96. doi:10.1207/s15326985ep3902_1

Pointon, M. R. (2009). *Brilliant effects: a cultural history of gem stones and jewellery*. Paul Mellon Centre.

Pokhariyal, P., Kashyap, A. K., & Prasad, A. B. (2020). *Artificial Intelligence: Law And Policy Implications*. Eastern Book Company.

Pokrivcakova, S. (2017). The digital age in literary education. *Teaching Literature for the 21st Century*, 11.

Poole, D. L., & Mackworth, A. K. (2017). *Artificial Intelligence: Foundations of Computational Agents*. Academic Press.

Prada, R., & Paiva, A. (2005, July). Believable groups of synthetic characters. In *Proceedings of the Fourth International Joint Conference on Autonomous Agents and Multiagent Systems* (pp. 37-43). 10.1145/1082473.1082479

Pritchett, G. (2021). *Pulse Topology: A Conversation with Artist Rafael Lozano-Hemmer*. MIKCexplore. Retrieved from https://mikcexplore.com/home/2021/11/8/pulse-topology-a-conversation-with-artist-rafael-lozano-hemmer

Qian, W. L., Yang, F., Mei, H. Y., & Li, H. (2023). Artificial Intelligence-designer for high-rise Building Sketches with User Preferences. *Engineering Structures*, *275*, 115171. doi:10.1016/j.engstruct.2022.115171

Radford, A., Kim, J. W., Hallacy, C., Ramesh, A., Goh, G., Agarwal, S., & Sastry, G. (2021). Learning Transferable Visual Models From Natural Language Supervision. *arXiv [cs.CV]*. arXiv. http://arxiv.org/abs/2103.00020

Radford, A., Metz, L., & Chintala, S. (2015). *Unsupervised representation learning with deep convolutional generative adversarial networks*. arXiv preprint arXiv:1511.06434.

Rafner, J., Beaty, R. E., Kaufman, J. C., Lubart, T., & Sherson, J. (2023). Creativity in the age of generative AI. *Nature Human Behaviour*, *7*(11), 1836–1838. doi:10.1038/s41562-023-01751-1 PMID:37985916

Raimundo, R., & Rosário, A. T. (2022). Cybersecurity in the Internet of Things in Industrial Management. *Applied Sciences (Basel, Switzerland)*, *12*(3), 1598. doi:10.3390/app12031598

Ramalho, A. (2022). *Intellectual Property Protection for AI-generated Creations Europe, United States, Australia and Japan*. Routledge, Taylor & Francis Group.

Ramesh, A., Pavlov, M., Goh, G., Gray, S., Voss, C., Radford, A., Chen, M., & Sutskever, I. (2021). Zero-shot text-to-image generation. In *The International Conference on Machine Learning* (pp. 8821–8831). PMLR.

Raneri, S., Lecron, F., Hermans, J., & Fouss, F. (2023). Predictions through Lean startup? Harnessing AI-based predictions under uncertainty. *International Journal of Entrepreneurial Behaviour & Research*, *29*(4), 886–912. doi:10.1108/IJEBR-07-2021-0566

Rathmann, C., Mann, W., & Morgan, G. (2007). Narrative structure and narrative development in deaf children. *Deafness & Education International*, *9*(4), 187–196. doi:10.1179/146431507790559932

Rauniyar, A., Raj, A., Kumar, A., Kandu, A. K., Singh, A., & Gupta, A. (2023). Text to Image Generator with Latent Diffusion Models. *2023 International Conference on Computational Intelligence, Communication Technology and Networking (CICTN)*, 144-148, 10.1109/CICTN57981.2023.10140348

Raza, S., Venaik, A., & Khalil, S. N. (2023). Unveiling the Impact of AI and ChatGPT on Architectural and Interior Design Studies: A Comprehensive Exploration. *Tuijin Jishu/Journal of Propulsion Technology*, *44*(3), 580-591.

Reed, S., Akata, Z., Yan, X., Logeswaran, L., Schiele, B., & Lee, H. (2016). Generative adversarial text to image synthesis. In *The International conference on machine learning* (pp. 1060–1069). PMLR.

Reed, S. E., Akata, Z., Yan, X., Logeswaran, L., Schiele, B., & Lee, H. (2016). Generative adversarial text-to-image synthesis. *Proceedings of the 33rd International Conference on Machine Learning (ICML)*.

Reeves, B., Sarsa, S., Prather, J., Denny, P., Becker, B. A., Hellas, A., ... Leinonen, J. (2023). Evaluating the performance of code generation models for solving parsons problems with small prompt variations. *Annual Conference on Innovation and Technology in Computer Science Education, ITiCSE*. 10.1145/3587102.3588805

Rehan. (n.d.). *Who owns computer generated works*. Learn and Digest. https://learndigest.blogspot.com/2014/06/who-owns-computer-generated-works.html

Reid, S. F., & Serafini, F. (2018). More than words: An investigation of the middle-grade multimodal novel. *Journal of Children's Literature*, *44*(2), 32–44.

Rhodes, M. (1961). An analysis of creativity. *Phi Delta Kappan*, *42*(7), 305–310.

Richey, R. G. Jr, Chowdhury, S., Davis-Sramek, B., Giannakis, M., & Dwivedi, Y. K. (2023). Artificial intelligence in logistics and supply chain management: A primer and roadmap for research. *Journal of Business Logistics*, *44*(4), 532–549. doi:10.1111/jbl.12364

Ritala, P., Ruokonen, M., & Ramaul, L. (2023). Transforming boundaries: How does ChatGPT change knowledge work? *The Journal of Business Strategy*. Advance online publication. doi:10.1108/JBS-05-2023-0094

Ritchie, G. (2001). Assessing creativity. *Proceedings of AISB Symposium on AI and Creativity in Art and Science*. Available at: https://citeseerx.ist.psu.edu/document?repid=rep1&type=pdf&doi=bc6d0d0a04de633978fa924b097c50eb1d6db467

Robertson, J., & Good, J. (2004, June). Children's narrative development through computer game authoring. In *Proceedings of the 2004 Conference on Interaction Design and Children: Building a Community* (pp. 57-64). 10.1145/1017833.1017841

Rodrigues, S. H., Mascarenhas, S. F., Dias, J., & Paiva, A. (2009, September). "I can feel it too!": Emergent empathic reactions between synthetic characters. In *2009 3rd International Conference on Affective Computing and Intelligent Interaction and Workshops* (pp. 1-7). IEEE.

Rombach, R., Blattmann, A., Lorenz, D., Esser, P., & Ommer, B. (2021). High-Resolution Image Synthesis with Latent Diffusion Models. *arXiv [cs.CV]*. arXiv. http://arxiv.org/abs/2112.10752

Rombach, R., Blattmann, A., Lorenz, D., Esser, P., & Ommer, B. (2022). High-resolution image synthesis with latent diffusion models. *Proceedings of the IEEE/CVF Conference on Computer Vision and Pattern Recognition*, 10684–10695. 10.1109/CVPR52688.2022.01042

Rosário, A. T., & Dias, J. C. (2023). How Industry 4.0 and Sensors Can Leverage Product Design: Opportunities and Challenges. *Sensors (Basel)*, *23*(3), 1165. doi:10.3390/s23031165 PMID:36772206

Rosário, A. T., Lopes, P. R., & Rosário, F. S. (2023). Metaverse in Marketing: Challenges and Opportunities. In A. Khang, V. Shah, & S. Rani (Eds.), *Handbook of Research on AI-Based Technologies and Applications in the Era of the Metaverse* (pp. 204–227). IGI Global. doi:10.4018/978-1-6684-8851-5.ch010

Rose, K., Massey, V., Marshall, B., & Cardon, P. (2023). IS professors' perspectives on AI-assisted programming. *Issues in Information Systems*, *24*(2), 178–190. doi:10.48009/2_iis_2023_115

Rubegni, E., Landoni, M., Malinverni, L., & Jaccheri, L. (2022). Raising awareness of stereotyping through collaborative digital storytelling: Design for change with and for children. *International Journal of Human-Computer Studies*, *157*, 102727. doi:10.1016/j.ijhcs.2021.102727

Rubinstein, R. Z. (2021). *Machine Learning and Human Values*. Academic Press.

Runco, M. A., & Jaeger, G. J. (2012). The standard definition of creativity. *Creativity Research Journal*, *24*(1), 92–96. doi:10.1080/10400419.2012.650092

Russell, S. J., & Norvig, P. (2010). Artificial intelligence a modern approach. Academic Press.

Russell, S. J., & Norvig, P. (1995). *Artificial Intelligence a Modern Approach*. Pearson Education, Inc.

Russell, S., & Norvig, P. (2010). *Artificial Intelligence: A Modern Approach* (3rd ed.). Prentice Hall.

Sachan, S., Almaghrabi, F., Yang, J. B., & Xu, D. L. (2021). Evidential reasoning for preprocessing uncertain categorical data for trustworthy decisions: An application on healthcare and finance. *Expert Systems with Applications*, *185*, 115597. doi:10.1016/j.eswa.2021.115597

Sætra, H. S. (2023). Generative AI: Here to stay, but for good? *Technology in Society*, *75*, 102372. doi:10.1016/j.techsoc.2023.102372

Saharia, C., Chan, W., Saxena, S., Li, L., Whang, J., Denton, E., & Seyed, K. S. G. (2022). Photorealistic Text-to-Image Diffusion Models with Deep Language Understanding. *arXiv [cs.CV]*. arXiv. http://arxiv.org/abs/2205.11487

Salah, A. A. A. (2021). AI bugs and failures: How and why to render AI-algorithms more human? In P. Verdegem (Ed.), *AI for Everyone?* (pp. 161–180). University of Westminster Press. https://www.jstor.org/stable/j.ctv26qjjhj.12

Salah, M., Abdelfattah, F., & Al Halbusi, H. (2023). Generative Artificial Intelligence (ChatGPT & Bard) in public administration research: A double-edged sword for street-level bureaucracy studies. *International Journal of Public Administration*, 1–7. Advance online publication. doi:10.1080/01900692.2023.2274801

Salehi, H., & Burgueño, R. (2018). Emerging artificial intelligence methods in structural engineering. *Engineering Structures*, *171*, 170–189. doi:10.1016/j.engstruct.2018.05.084

Salimans, T., Goodfellow, I., Zaremba, W., Cheung, V., Radford, A., & Chen, X. (2016). Improved techniques for training GANs. Advances in neural information processing systems (NeurIPS).

Sarkar, S. (2021, August 5). *India recognises AI as co-author of copyrighted artwork.* Managing IP, https://www.managingip.com/article/2a5czmpwixyj23wyqct1c/exclusive-india-recognises-ai-as-co-author-of-copyrighted-artwork

Sarmiento, S. M. (2014, August 22). *Us copyright office says animal authors aren't protected by copyright.* Hyperallergic. https://hyperallergic.com/145217/us-copyright-office-says-animals-authors-arent-protected-by-copyright/

Satpathy, C. (2017). *Jewelry: A Medium of Symbolic Communication.* Morehead State University.

Sawyer, R. K. (2014). *Explaining Creativity: The Science of Human Innovation.* Oxford University Press.

Scalise Sugiyama, M. (2009). The plot thickens: What children's stories tell us about mindreading. *Journal of Consciousness Studies*, *16*(6-7), 94–117.

Scarpitti, C. (2021). Post Digital Jewellery. The future scenarios of contemporary jewelry design. In *Spirit of Luxury and Design. A perspective from Contemporary Fashion and Jewellery* (pp. 274–285). ORO Editions.

Schank, R. C., & Childers, P. (1984). *The Cognitive Computer: on Language, Learning, and Artificial Intelligence.* Addison-Wesley.

Schick, N. (2023). Faking It: Navigating the new era of generative AI may be the most critical challenge to democracy yet. *RSA Journal, 169*(2), 40–43. https://www.jstor.org/stable/48737215

Schneider, M., & Fischer, M. (2019). A survey of digital art history. arXiv preprint arXiv:1906.02102.

Schulte, C. M. (2019). Plot holes in children's drawing. *Art Education*, *72*(3), 15–19. doi:10.1080/00043125.2019.1577942

Schumann, E. (2021). Artificial Intelligence in the Arts: An Overview of AI-Generated Art and Its Ethical Implications. *Frontiers in Robotics and AI.*

Schwind, V., Wolf, K., & Henze, N. (2018). Avoiding the uncanny valley in virtual character design. *Interactions (New York, N.Y.)*, *25*(5), 45–49. doi:10.1145/3236673

Selvaraju, R. R., Cogswell, M., Das, A., Vedantam, R., Parikh, D., & Batra, D. (2017). Grad-CAM: Visual explanations from deep networks via gradient-based localization. *Proceedings of the IEEE International Conference on Computer Vision (ICCV).* 10.1109/ICCV.2017.74

Serafini, F., Kachorsky, D., & Reid, S. (2018). Revisiting the multimodal nature of children's literature. *Language Arts*, *95*(5), 311–321. doi:10.58680/la201829586

Shaarani, A. S., & Romano, D. M. (2007). Perception of emotions from static postures. In *Affective Computing and Intelligent Interaction: Second International Conference, ACII 2007 Lisbon, Portugal, September 12-14, 2007 Proceedings 2* (pp. 761-762). Springer Berlin Heidelberg.

Shah, N., Engineer, S., Bhagat, N., Chauhan, H., & Shah, M. (2020). Research Trends on the Usage of Machine Learning and Artificial Intelligence in Advertising. *Augmented Human Research*, *5*(1), 19. doi:10.1007/s41133-020-00038-8

Shakked, N., & Whitney, Z. (2023). Experimental Evidence on the Productivity Effects of Generative Artificial Intelligence. *SSRN*, *15*. Advance online publication. doi:10.2139/ssrn.4375283

Shapiro, L. R., & Hudson, J. A. (1991). Tell me a make-believe story: Coherence and cohesion in young children's picture-elicited narratives. *Developmental Psychology*, *27*(6), 960–974. doi:10.1037/0012-1649.27.6.960

Shoshan, A., Bhonker, N., Kviatkovsky, I., & Medioni, G. (2021). GAN-Control: Explicitly Controllable GANs. *arXiv [cs.CV]*. arXiv. doi:10.1109/ICCV48922.2021.01382

Siamptani, M. (2023). Investigating the use of digital technology in Jewellery Design: A thematic analysis. In *Fashion Heritage: Narrative and Knowledge Creation* (pp. 241–261). Springer International Publishing.

Silva, A., Vala, M., Paiva, A., & Redol, R. A. (2001, May). The Storyteller: Building a synthetic character that tells stories. In *Proc. Workshop Multimodal Communication and Context in Embodied Agents* (pp. 53-58). Autonomous Agents 2001.

Simon, C., Faraki, M., Tsai, Y. H., Yu, X., Schulter, S., Suh, Y., ... Chandraker, M. (2022). On generalizing beyond domains in cross-domain continual learning. In *Proceedings of the IEEE/CVF Conference on Computer Vision and Pattern Recognition* (pp. 9265-9274). 10.1109/CVPR52688.2022.00905

Sinan, A. T., Demir, S., & Dogan, F. D. (2017). Teacher's views regarding the place of children's literature in first language education. *Journal of Education and Training Studies*, *5*(12), 133–145. doi:10.11114/jets.v5i12.2691

Singer, U., Polyak, A., Hayes, T., Yin, X., An, J., Zhang, S., & Hu, Q. (2022). Make-A-Video: Text-to-Video Generation without Text-Video Data. *arXiv [cs.CV]*. arXiv. http://arxiv.org/abs/2209.14792

Singh, P., & Bhambri, P. (2007). Alternate Organizational Models for Ports. *Apeejay Journal of Management and Technology*, *2*(2), 9–17.

Sipe, L. R. (2002). Talking back and taking over: Young children's expressive engagement during storybook read-alouds. *The Reading Teacher*, *55*(5), 476–483.

Slonim, N., Bilu, Y., Alzate, C., Bar-Haim, R., Bogin, B., Bonin, F., Choshen, L., Cohen-Karlik, E., Dankin, L., Edelstein, L., Ein-Dor, L., Friedman-Melamed, R., Gavron, A., Gera, A., Gleize, M., Gretz, S., Gutfreund, D., Halfon, A., Hershcovich, D., ... Aharonov, R. (2021). An autonomous debating system. *Nature*, *591*(7850), 379–384. doi:10.1038/s41586-021-03215-w PMID:33731946

Sohl-Dickstein, J., Weiss, E., Maheswaranathan, N., & Ganguli, S. (2015). Deep unsupervised learning using nonequilibrium thermodynamics. In *The International Conference on Machine Learning* (pp. 2256–2265). PMLR.

Soikun, T. M., & Ibrahim, A. A. A. (2018). Kansei engineering approach in designing appealing computer animation character. In *Proceedings of the 7th International Conference on Kansei Engineering and Emotion Research 2018: KEER 2018, 19-22 March 2018, Kuching, Sarawak, Malaysia* (pp. 470-478). Springer Singapore. 10.1007/978-981-10-8612-0_49

Somaya, D., & Varshney, L. R. (2020). Ownership Dilemmas in an Age of Creative Machines. *Issues in Science and Technology*, *36*(2), 79–85. https://www.jstor.org/stable/26949112

Song, Y., & Ermon, S. (2019). Generative Modeling by Estimating Gradients of the Data Distribution. *ArXiv*. /abs/1907.05600

Sovhyra, T. (2021). Artificial Intelligence and Issue of Authorship and Uniqueness for Works of Art (Technological Research of the Next Rembrandt). *Kult. i mystetstvo u suchasnomu sviti, 22*, 156–163. . doi:10.31866/2410-1915.22.2021.235903

Spennemann, D. H. R. (2023). Children of AI: A protocol for managing the born-digital ephemera spawned by Generative AI language models. *Publications, 11*(3). doi:10.3390/publications11030045

Stahl, B. C., & Eke, D. (2024). The ethics of ChatGPT – Exploring the ethical issues of an emerging technology. *International Journal of Information Management, 74*, C7–C102700. doi:10.1016/j.ijinfomgt.2023.102700

Stanford University Human-Centered Artificial Intelligence. (2023). *Generative AI: Perspectives from Stanford HAI*. Stanford University. Retrieved from https://hai.stanford.edu/sites/default/files/2023-03/Generative_AI_HAI_Perspectives.pdf

STEAM. (2024). *Traveler - The AI Story*. Retrieved from Traveler - The AI Story: https://store.steampowered.com/app/2216270/Traveler__The_AI_Story/

Steinfeld, K. (2023). Clever little tricks: A socio-technical history of text-to-image generative models. *International Journal of Architectural Computing, 21*(2), 211–241. doi:10.1177/14780771231168230

Stein, M. I. (1963). A transactional approach to creativity. In C. W. Taylor & F. Barron (Eds.), *Scientific Creativity: Its Recognition and Development* (pp. 217–227). John Wiles & Sons.

Sternberg, R. J., & Lubart, T. I. (1999). The concept of creativity: Prospects and paradigms. In R. J. Sternberg (Ed.), *Handbook of creativity* (pp. 3–15). Cambridge University Press.

Still, A., & d'Inverno, M. (2019). Can machines be artists? A Deweyan response in theory and practice. *Arts, 8*(1), 36. doi:10.3390/arts8010036

Suryna, K., & Serrano, R.G. (2019). Agents without agency: Artificial Intelligence as artistic medium. *Taboo Transgression Transcendence,* 200 - .209.

Tai, L. (2023). The Application and Impact of Digital Technology in Jewelry Art. *MA Theses*. 145.

Takagi, Y., & Nishimoto, S. (2023). High-Resolution Image Reconstruction With Latent Diffusion Models From Human Brain Activity. In *Conference on Computer Vision and Pattern Recognition* (pp. 14453-14463). IEEE. 10.1109/CVPR52729.2023.01389

Takeuchi, Y., & Katagiri, Y. (1999, September). Social character design for animated agents. In *8th IEEE International Workshop on Robot and Human Interaction. RO-MAN'99 (Cat. No. 99TH8483)* (pp. 53-58). IEEE. 10.1109/ROMAN.1999.900313

Tan, H., Chan, C., Aggarwal, V., & Gupta, D. (2019). Deep neural network models for computational microscopy. *Proceedings of the IEEE Conference on Computer Vision and Pattern Recognition (CVPR).*

Tao, F., Zou, X., & Ren, D. (2018). The art of human intelligence and the technology of artificial intelligence: artificial intelligence visual art research. In *Intelligence Science II: Third IFIP TC 12 International Conference, ICIS 2018, Beijing, China, November 2-5, 2018, Proceedings 2* (pp. 146-155). Springer International Publishing.

Tao, M., Bao, B.-K., Tang, H., & Xu, C. (2023). GALIP: Generative Adversarial CLIPs for Text-to-Image Synthesis. *arXiv [cs.CV]*. arXiv. doi:10.1109/CVPR52729.2023.01366

Tao, F. (2022). A new harmonisation of art and technology: Philosophic interpretations of artificial intelligence art. *Critical Arts, 36*(1-2), 110–125. doi:10.1080/02560046.2022.2112725

Tasioulas, J. (2022). Artificial intelligence, humanistic ethics. *Daedalus, 151*(2), 232–243. doi:10.1162/daed_a_01912

Tavares, T., & Magalhães, C. F. (2020). *New Technologies Shift in Jewelry Design: From Traditional Optimization to Contemporary Speculation. Global Fashion Conference.*

Taylor, J. (2022, July 28). No Quick Fix: How OpenAI's DALL-E 2 illustrated the challenges of bias in AI. *NBC News*. https://www.nbcnews.com/tech/tech-news/no-quick-fix-openais-dalle-2-illustrated-challenges-bias-ai-rcna39918

Tharib, S. (2013). *An investigation into the uncanny: Character design, behaviour and context* [Doctoral dissertation]. Bournemouth University.

The Copyright Act, 1957 (Act 14 of 1957), India. s. 2(d). https://copyright.gov.in/documents/copyrightrules1957.pdf

Thomas, E. E. (2016). Stories still matter: Rethinking the role of diverse children's literature today. *Language Arts*, *94*(2), 112–119. doi:10.58680/la201628803

Thrun, S., Burgard, W., & Fox, D. (2005). *Probabilistic Robotics*. MIT Press.

Tigre Moura, F. (2023). Artificial intelligence, creativity, and intentionality: The need for a paradigm shift. *The Journal of Creative Behavior*, *57*(3), 336–338. doi:10.1002/jocb.585

Tigre Moura, F., Castrucci, C., & Hindley, C. (2023). Artificial intelligence creates art? An experimental investigation of value and creativity perceptions. *The Journal of Creative Behavior*, *57*(4), 534–549. doi:10.1002/jocb.600

Tovar, E. (2023). *Prompting Creativity: The Role of AI in Visualization and Design Tools for Architects*. ArchDaily. Accessed 20 Dec 2023. https://www.archdaily.com/1010426/prompting-creativity-the-role-of-ai-in-visualization-and-design-tools-for-architects

Triantoro, T., Przegalinska, A., & Kovbasiuk, A. (2023). Human-AI collaboration in the contemporary workplace: the job demands-resources model perspective. *36th Bled eConference: Digital Economy and Society: The Balancing Act for Digital Innovation in Times of Instability, BLED 2023 – Proceedings*.

Tschida, C. M., Ryan, C. L., & Ticknor, A. S. (2014). Building on windows and mirrors: Encouraging the disruption of "single stories" through children's literature. *Journal of Children's Literature*, *40*(1), 28–39.

Tubaro, P., Casilli, A. A., & Coville, M. (2020). The trainer, the verifier, the imitator: Three ways in which human platform workers support artificial intelligence. *Big Data & Society*, *7*(1). Advance online publication. doi:10.1177/2053951720919776

Turchi, T., Carta, S., Ambrosini, L., & Malizia, A. (2023). Human-AI Co-creation: Evaluating the Impact of Large-Scale Text-to-Image Generative Models on the Creative Process. In *International Symposium on End User Development* (pp. 35–51). Springer. 10.1007/978-3-031-34433-6_3

Turing, A. M. (2009). Computing Machinery and Intelligence. In R. Epstein, G. Roberts, & G. Beber (Eds.), *Parsing the Turing Test*. Springer., doi:10.1007/978-1-4020-6710-5_3

Ulberg, E., Llach, D. C., & Byrne, D. (2020). Hand-crafting neural networks for art-making. In ICCC (pp. 508-511). Academic Press.

UN WIPO. (1886, September 9). *Berne Convention for the Protection of Literary and Artistic Works,* No. 11850.

Untracht, O. (2011). *Jewelry concepts & technology*. Doubleday.

Vakratsas, D., & Wang, X. (2021). Artificial Intelligence in Advertising Creativity. *Journal of Advertising*, *50*(1), 39–51. doi:10.1080/00913367.2020.1843090

Vaswani, A., Shazeer, N., Parmar, N., Uszkoreit, J., Jones, L., Gomez, A. N., . . . Polosukhin, I. (2017). Attention is all you need. Advances in neural information processing systems (NeurIPS).

Vaswani, A., Shazeer, N., Parmar, N., Uszkoreit, J., Jones, L., Gomez, A. N., ... Polosukhin, I. (2017). Attention is all you need. *Proceedings of 31st Conference on Neural Information Processing Systems (NIPS 2017)*, 1-11. 10.48550/arXiv.1706.03762

Veit, A., Alldrin, N., Chechik, G., Krasin, I., Gupta, A., & Belongie, S. (2016). COCO-Text: Dataset and benchmark for text detection and recognition in natural images. *Proceedings of the IEEE Conference on Computer Vision and Pattern Recognition*, 1200-1209. 10.48550/arXiv.1601.07140

Verhallen, M. J., Bus, A. G., & de Jong, M. T. (2006). The promise of multimedia stories for kindergarten children at risk. *Journal of Educational Psychology*, *98*(2), 410–419. doi:10.1037/0022-0663.98.2.410

Verma, P., Adam, V., & Solin, A. (2023). Variational Gaussian Process Diffusion Processes. *arXiv [cs.LG]*. arXiv. http://arxiv.org/abs/2306.02066

Vezina, B., & Moran, B. (n.d.). *Artificial Intelligence and Creativity: Why We're Against Copyright Protection for AI-Generated Output*. Creative Commons. https://creativecommons.org/2020/08/10/no-copyright-protection-for-ai-generated-output/

Vigliensoni, G., Perry, P., & Fiebrink, R. (2022). A small-data mindset for generative AI creative work. Association for Computing Machinery.

Vinchon, F., Lubart, T., Bartolotta, S., Gironnay, V., Botella, M., Bourgeois-Bougrine, S., Burkhardt, J.-M., Bonnardel, N., Corazza, G. E., Glăveanu, V., Hanchett Hanson, M., Ivcevic, Z., Karwowski, M., Kaufman, J. C., Okada, T., Reiter-Palmon, R., & Gaggioli, A. (2023). Artificial Intelligence & Creativity: A manifesto for collaboration. *The Journal of Creative Behavior*, *57*(4), 472–484. Advance online publication. doi:10.1002/jocb.597

Voynov, Abernan, & Cohen-Or. (2022). *Sketchguided text-to-image diffusion models*. Academic Press.

Walczak, K., & Cellary, W. (2023). Challenges for higher education in the era of widespread access to Generative AI. *Economics and Business Review*, *9*(2), 71–100. doi:10.18559/ebr.2023.2.743

Wallace, B., Gokul, A., & Naik, N. (2022). *EDICT: Exact diffusion inversion via coupled transformations*. arXiv:2211.12446v2 [cs.CV]

Wallach, W. (Ed.). (2011). Artificial Intelligence and Ethics: An Open Letter. Academic Press.

Walsh, K. R., Mahesh, S., & Trumbach, C. C. (2021). Autonomy in ai systems: Rationalizing the fears. *The Journal of Technology Studies*, *47*(1), 38–47. https://www.jstor.org/stable/48657934

Wang, W., Bao, J., Zhou, W., Chen, D., Chen, D., Yuan, L., & Li, H. (2022). SinDiffusion: Learning a Diffusion Model from a Single Natural Image. *arXiv [cs.CV]*. arXiv. http://arxiv.org/abs/2211.12445

Wang, Y. C., Xue, J., Wei, C., & Kuo, C. C. J. (2023). *An Overview on Generative AI at Scale with Edge-Cloud Computing*. https://arxiv.org/pdf/2306.17170.pdf

Wang, Zhang, Zhang, Hao, Chen, Chen, & Wen. (2022). *Pretraining is all you need for image-to-image translation*. Academic Press.

Wang, J., Duan, H., Liu, J., Chen, S., Min, X., & Zhai, G. (2023). *AIGCIQA2023: A Large-scale Image Quality Assessment Database for AI Generated Images: from the Perspectives of Quality*. Authenticity and Correspondence.

Wang, L., Chen, W., Yang, W., Bi, F., & Yu, F. R. (2020). A state-of-the-art review on image synthesis with generative adversarial networks. *IEEE Access : Practical Innovations, Open Solutions*, *8*, 63514–63537. doi:10.1109/ACCESS.2020.2982224

Wang, X., Yu, K., Wu, S., Gu, J., Liu, Y., Dong, C., & Loy, C. (2019). *ESRGAN: Enhanced Super-Resolution Generative Adversarial Networks. In Computer Vision – ECCV Workshops*. ACM. doi:10.1007/978-3-030-11021-5_5

Wannarumon, S. (2011). Reviews of computer-aided technologies for jewelry design and casting. *Naresuan University Engineering Journal*, *6*(1), 45–56.

Wannarumon, S., & Bohez, E. L. (2006). A new aesthetic evolutionary approach for jewelry design. *Computer-Aided Design and Applications*, *3*(1-4), 385–394. doi:10.1080/16864360.2006.10738477

Wan, S., & Kaneko, T. (2017). Imitation Learning for Playing Shogi Based on Generative Adversarial Networks. *Proceedings of 2017 Conference on Technologies and Applications of Artificial Intelligence (TAAI)*, 92-95. 10.1109/TAAI.2017.17

Wardropper, I. (2000). Between art and nature: Jewelry in the Renaissance. *Art Institute of Chicago Museum Studies*, *25*(2), 7–104. doi:10.2307/4113057

Wasielewski, A. (2023). "Midjourney can't count": Questions of representation and meaning for text-to-image generators. *The Interdisciplinary Journal of Image Sciences*, *37*(1), 71–82.

Watiktinnakorn, C., Seesai, J., & Kerdvibulvech, C. (2023). Blurring the lines: How AI is redefining artistic ownership and copyright. *Discover Artificial Intelligence*, *3*(1), 37. doi:10.1007/s44163-023-00088-y

Weisz, J. D., Muller, M., He, J., & Houde, S. (2023). Toward general design principles for generative AI applications. *arXiv preprint arXiv:2301.05578.*

Willey, L., White, B. J., & Deale, C. S. (2023). Teaching AI in the college course: Introducing the AI prompt development life cycle (PDLC). *Issues in Information Systems*, *24*(2), 123–138. doi:10.48009/2_iis_2023_111

Wiltse, L. (2015). Mirrors and windows: Teaching and research reflections on Canadian Aboriginal children's literature. *Language and Literature*, *17*(2), 22–40.

Winkler, C., Hammoda, B., Noyes, E., & Van Gelderen, M. (2023). Entrepreneurship education at the dawn of generative artificial intelligence. *Entrepreneurship Education and Pedagogy*, *6*(4), 579–589. doi:10.1177/25151274231198799

Winner, S. S. G. (2010). *The Ethics of Invention: Technology and the Human Future*. Academic Press.

WIPO. (2020, May 21). *Conversation on Intellectual Property (IP) and Artificial Intelligence (AI)*, Second Session, Revised Issues Paper on Intellectual Property Policy and Artificial Intelligence, WIPO. https://www.wipo.int/edocs/mdocs/mdocs/en/wipo_ip_ai_2_ge_20/wipo_ip_ai_2_ge_20_1_rev.pdf

WIPO. France. Intellectual Property Code, 2022. https://www.wipo.int/wipolex/en/legislation/details/19865

WIPO. Germany. Copyright Act, 2017. https://www.wipo.int/wipolex/en/legislation/details/17676

Wisnioski, T. P., & Hendler, J. A. (2020). Ethical Considerations for AI in the Creative Industries. *AI Magazine*.

Wong, I. A., Lian, Q. L., & Sun, D. (2023). Autonomous travel decision-making: An early glimpse into ChatGPT and generative AI. *Journal of Hospitality and Tourism Management*, *56*, 253–263. doi:10.1016/j.jhtm.2023.06.022

World Economic Forum. (2023). *Top 10 Emerging Technologies of 2023*. World Economic Forum. Retrieved from https://www3.weforum.org/docs/WEF_Top_10_Emerging_Technologies_of_2023.pdf

Wright, S. (2007). Graphic-narrative play: Young children's authoring through drawing and telling. *International Journal of Education & the Arts*, *8*(8), 1–28.

Wu, C. H. (2022). Unifying Diffusion Models' Latent Space, with Applications to CycleDiffusion and Guidance. *ArXiv*. /abs/2210.05559

Wu, Z., Ji, D., Yu, K., Zeng, X., Wu, D., & Shidujaman, M. (2021). AI creativity and the human-AI co-creation model. In Human-Computer Interaction. Theory, Methods and Tools: Thematic Area, HCI 2021 (pp. 171-190). Springer International Publishing. doi:10.1007/978-3-030-78462-1_13

Xu, T., Zhang, P., Huang, Q., Zhang, H., Gan, Z., Huang, X., & He, X. (2017). AttnGAN: Fine-Grained Text to Image Generation with Attentional Generative Adversarial Networks. *arXiv [cs.CV]*. arXiv. http://arxiv.org/abs/1711.10485

Xu, M., Du, H., Niyato, D., Kang, J., Xiong, Z., Mao, S., Han, Z., Jamalipour, A., Kim, D. I., Shen, X., Leung, V. C. M., & Poor, H. V. (2024). Unleashing the power of edge-cloud generative ai in mobile networks: A survey of aigc services. *IEEE Communications Surveys and Tutorials*, 1. Advance online publication. doi:10.1109/COMST.2024.3353265

Yampolskiy, R. V. (2018). *Artificial intelligence in art*. arXiv preprint arXiv:1803.09518.

Yang, L., Zhang, Z., Song, Y., Hong, S., Xu, R., Zhao, Y., Zhang, W., Cui, B., & Yang, M.-H. (2022). Diffusion Models: A Comprehensive Survey of Methods and Applications. *arXiv [cs.LG]*. arXiv. http://arxiv.org/abs/2209.00796v11

Yang, W. (2022). Artificial Intelligence education for young children: Why, what, and how in curriculum design and implementation. *Computers and Education: Artificial Intelligence*, *3*, 100061. doi:10.1016/j.caeai.2022.100061

Yin, H., Molchanov, P., Alvarez, J. M., Li, Z., Mallya, A., Hoiem, D., ... Kautz, J. (2020). Dreaming to distill: Data-free knowledge transfer via deepinversion. In *Proceedings of the IEEE/CVF Conference on Computer Vision and Pattern Recognition* (pp. 8715-8724). 10.1109/CVPR42600.2020.00874

Yoon, S. Y., Burke, R. C., Blumberg, B., & Schneider, G. E. (2000). Interactive training for synthetic characters. *AAAI/IAAI, 2000*, 249-254.

Yoon, B. (2022). How does children's literature portray global perspectives? *Journal of Global Education and Research*, *6*(2), 206–222. doi:10.5038/2577-509X.6.2.1090

Yoon, S. Y., Blumberg, B. M., & Schneider, G. E. (2000, June). Motivation driven learning for interactive synthetic characters. In *Proceedings of the Fourth International Conference on Autonomous Agents* (pp. 365-372). 10.1145/336595.337537

Yousif, S., & Vermisso, E. (2022). *Towards AI-assisted design workflows for an expanded design space. In International Conference of the Association for Computer-Aided Architectural Design Research in Asia*. CAADRIA. Retrieved from https://papers.cumincad.org/data/works/att/caadria2022_503.pdf

Yusa, I. M. M., & Putra, I. N. A. S. (2016). *Literasi visual tokoh Hanoman Bali dengan pendekatan augmented reality*. An1mage.

Yusa, I. M. M., Putra, P. S. U., & Putra, I. N. A. S. (2017). Sinergy of art and animation technology in multimedia performance art creation entitled sad ripu. In *2017 4th International Conference on New Media Studies (CONMEDIA)* (pp. 174–181). 10.1109/CONMEDIA.2017.8266052

Yusa, I. M. M., & Aditama, P. W. (2020). Expression of spirituality concept through augmented reality technique in digital painting works entitled Sarvaprani Hitankara. *Proceedings of the 4th International Symposium of Arts, Crafts & Design in South East Asia (ARCADESA)*. 10.2139/ssrn.3807700

Yusa, I. M. M., Pandawana, I., Putra, I., & Herawan, T. (2021). Manik angkeran storytelling based on android mobile tap gameplay. *Journal of Physics: Conference Series*, *1810*(1), 12034. doi:10.1088/1742-6596/1810/1/012034

Yu, T., Lin, C., Zhang, S., Wang, C., An, H., Liu, X., ... Zhang, J. (2022). Artificial Intelligence for Dunhuang Cultural Heritage Protection: The Project and the Dataset. *International Journal of Computer Vision*, *130*(11), 2646–2673. doi:10.1007/s11263-022-01665-x

Yu, Y. (2016). Research on digital art creation based on artificial intelligence. Rev. Ibérica Sist. e Tecnol. *Informação,* (18B), 116.

Yu, Y., Binghong, Z., Fei, G., & Jiaxin, T. (2020). Research on artificial intelligence in the field of art design under the background of convergence media. *IOP Conference Series. Materials Science and Engineering*, *825*(1), 12027. doi:10.1088/1757-899X/825/1/012027

Zapata, A., Fugit, M., & Moss, D. (2017). Awakening socially just mindsets through visual thinking strategies and diverse picturebooks. *Journal of Children's Literature*, *43*(2), 62–69.

Zeilinger, M. (2021). Generative adversarial copy machines. *Culture Machine*, *20*, 1–23.

Zeilinger, M. (2021). *Tactical entanglements: AI art, creative agency, and the limits of intellectual property*. Meson Press.

Zeng, Z., Sun, X., & Liao, X. (2019). Artificial Intelligence Augments Design Creativity: A Typeface Family Design Experiment. In *International Conference on Human-Computer Interaction* (pp. 400–411). Springer. 10.1007/978-3-030-23541-3_29

Zhang, H., Xu, T., Li, H., Zhang, S., Wang, X., Huang, X., & Metaxas, D. (2016). StackGAN: Text to Photo-Realistic Image Synthesis with Stacked Generative Adversarial Networks. *arXiv [cs.CV]*. arXiv. http://arxiv.org/abs/1612.03242

Zhang, H., Xu, T., Li, H., Zhang, S., Wang, X., Huang, X., & Metaxas, D. (2017). StackGAN++: Realistic Image Synthesis with Stacked Generative Adversarial Networks. *arXiv [cs.CV]*. arXiv. doi:10.1109/ICCV.2017.629

Zhang, H., Xu, T., Li, H., Zhang, S., Wang, X., Huang, X., & Metaxas, D. (2018). StackGAN++: Realistic image synthesis with stacked generative adversarial networks. *IEEE Transactions on Pattern Analysis and Machine Intelligence.*

ZhangL.RaoA.AgrawalaM. (2023). Adding Conditional Control to Text-to-Image Diffusion Models. *arXiv [cs.CV]*. doi:10.1109/ICCV51070.2023.00355

Zhang, Z. H., Fort, J. M., & Mateu, L. G. (2023). Exploring the Potential of Artificial Intelligence as a Tool for Architectural Design: A Perception Study Using Gaudi's Work. *Buildings*, *13*(7), 1–18. doi:10.3390/buildings13071863

Zhao, S., Chen, D., Chen, Y.-C., Bao, J., Hao, S., Yuan, L., & Wong, K.-Y. K. (2023). Uni-ControlNet: All-in-One Control to Text-to-Image Diffusion Models. *arXiv [cs.CV]*. arXiv. http://arxiv.org/abs/2305.16322

Zhao, J., & Wang, X. (2023). Unleashing efficiency and insights: Exploring the potential applications and challenges of ChatGPT in accounting. *Journal of Corporate Accounting & Finance*. Advance online publication. doi:10.1002/jcaf.22663

Zhou, E., & Lee, D. (2023). Generative AI, Human Creativity, and Art. *SSRN*, *50*. Advance online publication. doi:10.2139/ssrn.4594824

Zhou, L., Wang, Q., Huang, K., & Lo, C. (2019). An Interactive and Generative Approach for Chinese Shanshui Painting Document. In *International Conference on Document Analysis and Recognition* (pp. 819-824). IEEE. 10.1109/ICDAR.2019.00136

Zhou, W., Zhang, C., Wu, L., & Shashidhar, M. (2023). ChatGPT and marketing: Analyzing public discourse in early Twitter posts. *Journal of Marketing Analytics*, *11*(4), 693–706. doi:10.1057/s41270-023-00250-6

Zhu, J. Y., Park, T., Isola, P., & Efros, A. A. (2017). Unpaired image-to-image translation using cycle-consistent adversarial networks. *Proceedings - IEEE International Conference on Computer Vision*, *2017*, 2223–2232. doi:10.1109/ICCV.2017.244

Zibrek, K., Cabral, J., & McDonnell, R. (2021, November). Does synthetic voice alter social response to a photorealistic character in virtual reality? In *Proceedings of the 14th ACM SIGGRAPH Conference on Motion, Interaction and Games* (pp. 1-6). 10.1145/3487983.3488296

Zittrain, J. L. (2006). The Generative Internet. *Harvard Law Review, 119*(7), 1974–2040. https://www.jstor.org/stable/4093608

Zuboff, S. (2019). *The Age of Surveillance Capitalism: The Fight for a Human Future at the New Frontier of Power.* Academic Press.

Zylinska, J. (2020). *AI art: machine visions and warped dreams.* Open Humanities Press.

About the Contributors

Shalin Hai-Jew works as a grant writer at Hutchinson Community College (HutchCC) in Hutchinson, Kansas. Just prior, she worked as an instructional designer at Kansas State University (K-State), where she worked for 17.5 years. She has taught at the university and college levels for many years (including four years in the People's Republic of China) and was tenured at Shoreline Community College but left tenure to pursue instructional design work. She has Bachelor's degrees in English and psychology, a Master's degree in Creative Writing from the University of Washington (Hugh Paradise Scholar), and an Ed.D in Educational Leadership with a focus on public administration from Seattle University (where she was a Morford Scholar). She tested into the University of Washington at 14. She reviews for several publishers and publications. She has worked on a number of instructional design projects, including public health, biosecurity, one health, mental health, PTSD, grain science, turfgrass management, social justice, and others. She has authored and edited a number of books. Hai-Jew was born in Huntsville, Alabama, in the U.S. Currently, she is working on multiple projects.

* * *

S. M. Aamir Ali is presently Assistant Professor at Symbiosis Law School Pune, Symbiosis International (Deemed University), Pune. He is currently pursuing his PhD from West Bengal National University of Juridical Sciences (WBNUJS), Kolkata, and has completed his LL.M from National Law School of India University (NLSIU), Bengaluru, with a specialization in Human Rights Law. Mr Ali has been teaching across specializations in Constitutional Law, Human Rights and Criminal Law at UG and PG levels since 2019.

Marcellus Amadeus is a scientist specializing in Natural Language Processing, Machine Learning, and Software Engineering. I already worked extensively with most of the available Machine Learning and Data Science frameworks, libraries, and AWS and Oracle Cloud platforms. I am fluent in Python, SQL, and JavaScript. I am very comfortable with working under pressure and on complex projects. I have years of experience managing remote multi-cultural technical teams, and I taught myself many things, from human languages to advanced mathematics.

Nishat Afshan Ansari has received her B.E. in 2002 from Amravati University, M.Tech. and Ph.D. in 2009 and 2018 respectively from Visvesvaraya National Institute of Technology Nagpur, India, all in Computer Science and Engineering. She is actively involved in the field of teaching at premier institutes and has 18+ years of experience in this field. She is currently working as Assistant professor at Indian

Institute of Information Technology Nagpur, India. She has published several research papers in various journals and International conferences. Her research interests include Artificial Intelligence, Machine Learning and Wireless Sensor Networks.

Pankaj Bhambri is affiliated with the Department of Information Technology at Guru Nanak Dev Engineering College in Ludhiana. Additionally, he fulfills the role of the Institute's Coordinator for the Skill Enhancement Cell and acts as the Convener for his Departmental Board of Studies. He possesses nearly two decades of teaching experience. Dr. Bhambri acquired a Master of Technology degree in Computer Science and Engineering and a Bachelor of Engineering degree in Information Technology with Honours from I.K.G. Punjab Technical University in Jalandhar, India, and Dr. B.R. Ambedkar University in Agra, India, respectively. Dr. Bhambri obtained a Doctorate in Computer Science and Engineering from I.K.G. Punjab Technical University, located in Jalandhar, India. Over an extended period, he fulfilled many responsibilities including those of an Assistant Registrar (Academics), Member (Academic Council/ BoS/DAB/RAC), Hostel Warden, APIO, and NSS Coordinator within his institution. His research work has been published in esteemed worldwide and national journals, as well as conference proceedings. Dr. Bhambri has made significant contributions to the academic field through his role as both an editor and author of various textbooks. Additionally, he has demonstrated his innovative thinking by filing several patents. Dr. Bhambri has received numerous prestigious awards from esteemed organizations in recognition of his exceptional achievements in both social and academic/research domains. These accolades include the ISTE Best Teacher Award in 2022 and 2023, the I2OR National Award in 2020, the Green ThinkerZ Top 100 International Distinguished Educators award in 2020, the I2OR Outstanding Educator Award in 2019, the SAA Distinguished Alumni Award in 2012, the CIPS Rashtriya Rattan Award in 2008, the LCHC Best Teacher Award in 2007, and several other commendations from various government and non-profit entities. He has provided guidance and oversight for numerous research projects and dissertations at the undergraduate, postgraduate, and Ph.D. levels. He successfully organized a diverse range of educational programmes, securing financial backing from esteemed institutions such as the All India Council for Technical Education (AICTE), the Technical Education Quality Improvement Programme (TEQIP), among others. Dr. Bhambri's areas of interest encompass machine learning, bioinformatics, wireless sensor networks, and network security. Dr. Bhambri possesses a wide array of professional responsibilities, encompassing the duties of an educator, editor, author, reviewer, expert speaker, motivator, and technical committee member for esteemed national and worldwide organizations.

Ankit A. Bhurane has received his B.E. in Electronics and Communication, M.Tech. in Electronics, and Ph.D. in 2008, 2011, and 2016 respectively from SGBAU Amravati University, SGGSIET Nanded, and Indian Institute of Technology Bombay (IITB). He has 9+ years of experience teaching undergraduate and postgraduate courses at various institutes of national importances like Indian Institute of Information Technology, National Institute of Technology etc. He has published several papers in various International conferences and journals. He has been an active reviewer for reputed IEEE and Elsevier conferences and journals. Furthermore, he has on his name two Indian Patents Granted, and three filed with IPR office, India. His research interests include embedded systems, biomedical signal processing, scalable video coding and green Communication.

Metin Coskun graduated from Mersin University, Department of Jewelry Design Technologies. Education. He received his M.S. degree from Gazi University, Department of Fine Arts Education, and his Ph.D. degree from Hacı Bayram University, Department of Handicrafts. He is still working as a Dr. Instructor at Kastamonu University, Faculty of Fine Arts.

William Alberto Cruz Castañeda is an Artificial Intelligence Researcher. Bachelor's degree in Computer Science from Benemérita Universidad Autónoma de Puebla, México. Computer Engineer from the Federal University of Rio Grande do Sul. Master's and PhD in Electrical Engineering with an emphasis on Biomedical Engineering from the Federal University of Santa Catarina. PostDoc in Artificial Intelligence and Biomedical Engineering by the State University of Santa Catarina with a focus on synthetic health data generation. Research topics include ubiquitous computing, the Internet of Things, wearable devices, healthcare 4.0/5.0, machine learning, generative AI, multi-criteria decision-analysis, healthcare technology management, home care, chronic disease management, and digital assistive technologies. It includes the design, development, and implementation of large-scale computational solutions that empower the acquisition, processing, transmission, and management of heterogeneous data.

Orkan Zeynel Güzelci received B.Arch. (2010) degree in Architecture from Istanbul Kultur University (IKU), M.Sc. (2012) degree in Architectural Design Program, Ph.D. (2018) degree in Architectural Design Computing Program from Istanbul Technical University (ITU), and Post Doctoral certificate (2021) from University of Porto. Currently, he is an associate professor at ITU and a researcher at FAUP+DFL/CEAU.

Ilker Karadag, after receiving his bachelor's degree in architecture (2010), started his master's degree in the building sciences program of the METU architecture department in the same year. He continued his graduate education as a research assistant in the same program since 2011. In 2013, he was entitled to graduate with the the thesis he wrote on Natural Ventilation in Higher Buildings. In 2014, he started his doctoral education in the structural sciences program of the ITU faculty of architecture and worked as a research assistant in the Building Physics and Environmental Control Chair. He developed the software called ArchPLUS, which allows wind analysis in an augmented reality environment within the scope of his doctoral thesis he completed in 2019. He produced numerous articles and papers in the field of sustainable architecture and artificial intelligence. After the doctorate, he developed ArchiDynamics software, which reached widespread use at the international level. He received a national patent with the experimental setup he developed in 2023. In the same year, he received the title of Associate Professor in the field of Architecture. Working areas include energy-efficient design, building aerodynamics, fire safety in buildings, the use of microprocessors in architecture, architectural production technologies and machine learning in architecture.

Felipe Mahlow's passion for science has shaped his life's journey. After completing high school, he earned a degree in Physics Education and a Bachelor's in Materials Physics, delving into the profound mysteries of the universe. However, his trajectory took a new turn with the discovery of a new passion: Artificial Intelligence (AI). Currently, in the final year of a Ph.D. in Computer Science, his work revolves around the intersection of AI and quantum computing. Research interests span image generation through advanced AI techniques to applying machine learning in quantum phenomena.

Albérico Travassos Rosário is a Ph.D. Marketing and Strategy of the Universities of Aveiro (UA), Minho (UM) and Beira Interior (UBI). With affiliation to the GOVCOPP research center of the University of Aveiro. Master in Marketing and Degree in Marketing, Advertising and Public Relations, degree from ISLA Campus Lisbon-European University I Laureate International Universities. Has the title of Marketing Specialist and teaches with the category of Assistant Professor at IADE-Faculty of Design, Technology and Communication of the European University and as a visiting Associate Professor at the Santarém Higher School of Management and Technology (ESGTS) of the Polytechnic Institute of Santarém. He taught at IPAM-School of Marketing I Laureate International Universities, ISLA- Higher Institute of Management and Administration of Santarém (ISLA-Santarém), was Director of the Commercial Management Course, Director of the Professional Technical Course (TeSP) of Sales and Commercial Management, Chairman of the Pedagogical Council and Member of the Technical Council and ISLA-Santarém Scientific Researcher. He is also a marketing and strategy consultant for SMEs.

Shrishti Shah is an undergraduate student at Indian Institute of Information Technology Nagpur, India. Her research interests include Generative AI, Deep Learning and Machine Learning.

Shubhasri Tadepalli is a fourth-year undergraduate student at Indian Institute of Information Technology Nagpur India. Her research interests include Artificial Intelligence, Machine Learning and full stack development. Her curiosity and passion for these fields have led her to engage in different real time projects which includes integration of Machine Learning and Full-Stack development.

Lalitha Tanmai Vaddiparthi is a fourth-year undergraduate student from Computer Science engineering at Indian Institute of Information Technology Nagpur, India. She is curious and passionate in Machine learning and she is engaged in a couple of real-time projects. One of them is an integration of machine learning and full-stack development. Her research interests include Artificial Intelligence and Machine Learning.

André Felipe Zanella holds a degree in Mathematics and an MSc in Computer Science from the State University of Maringá. His primary interests involve machine learning, computational systems, and combinatorial optimization problems. However, with the rise of generative AI, his new research interests include generative deep learning models, particularly text-to-image systems focusing on low-resource languages, such as Brazilian Portuguese.

Index

www.ingramcontent.com/pod-product-compliance
Lightning Source LLC
LaVergne TN
LVHW060305011026
849161LV00011B/2774